The Architect's Portable Handbook

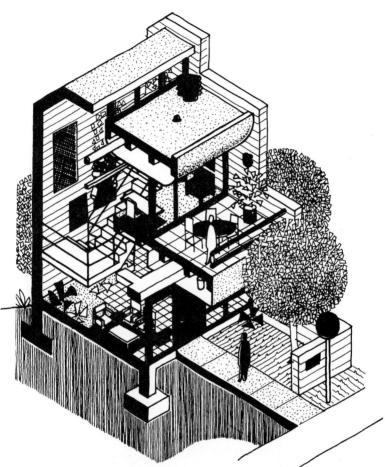

THE ARCHITECT'S
PORTABLE HANDBOOK
FIRST STEP RULES OF THUMB FOR BUILDING DESIGN

BY PAT GUTHRIE
ARCHITECT

McGraw-Hill, Inc.

New York   San Francisco   Washington, D.C.   Auckland   Bogotá
Caracas   Lisbon   London   Madrid   Mexico City   Milan
Montreal   New Delhi   San Juan   Singapore
Sydney   Tokyo   Toronto

Library of Congress Cataloging-in-Publication Data

Guthrie, Pat.
    The architect's portable handbook / Pat Guthrie.
        p.   cm.
    Includes bibliographical references (p.   –   ) and index.
    ISBN 0-07-025302-1
    1. Architectural design—Handbooks, manuals, etc.   I. Title.
NA2750.G87   1995
721—dc20   94-33398
                                                               CIP

    4 5 6 7 8 9 0   DOC/DOC   9 0 9 8 7 6

ISBN 0-07-025302-1

The sponsoring editor for this book was Joel Stein, and the production supervisor was Pamela A. Pelton. It was set in Times Ten by North Market Street Graphics.

This book is printed on acid-free paper.

Dedicated to Eric, Jan, and Erin

Contents

How to Use
This Book

The concept of this book is that of a *personal tool* that compacts 20% of the data that is needed 80% of the time by *design professionals* in the preliminary design of *buildings* of all types and sizes.

This tool is meant to always be at one's *fingertips* (open on a drawing board or desk, carried in a briefcase, or kept in one's pocket). It is never meant to sit on a bookshelf. It is meant to be *used everyday!*

Because design professionals are individualistic and their practices are so varied, the user is encouraged to *individualize this book* over time, by adding notes or changing data as experience dictates.

The addition of rough construction **costs,** throughout the book (making this type of handbook truly unique) will "date" the data. But building laws, new technologies, and materials are changing just as fast. Therefore, this book should be looked on as a *starter of simple data collection* that must be updated over time. New editions *may* be published in the future. See p. 25, for more information on **costs.**

Because this book is so broad in scope, yet so compact, information can be presented only at one place, and not repeated. There is little room for examples of how to use the information provided. Information is presented by simple ratios or coefficients that leave the need for *commonsense judgment.*

The whole book is laid out in checklist format, to be quickly read and checked against the design problem at hand.

Where ◯ is shown, refer to p. 459 for further explanation of references.

This book is *not a substitute* for professional expertise or other books of a more detailed and specialized nature, but will be a continuing everyday aid that takes the more useful "cream" off the top of other sources.

The Architect's
Portable Handbook

NOTES

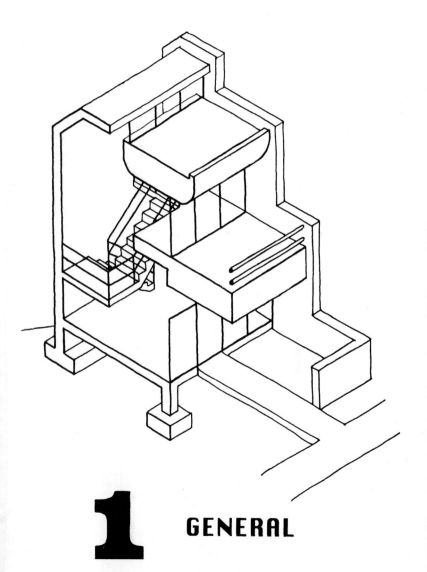

1

GENERAL

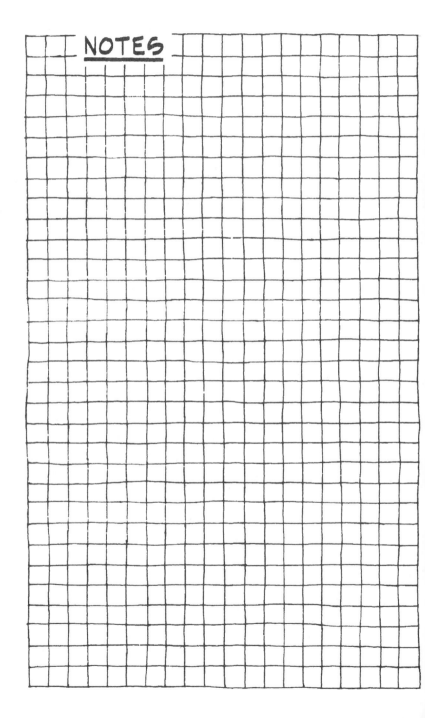

NOTES

___ A. PRACTICE (5) (21) (42)

___ 1. Services: Use "Schedule of Designated Services" on p. 6 to plan the services for building design.

___ 2. Compensation (A/E Fees)

    ___ *a.* See App. A, item E for A/E fees as a percentage of construction cost by building type.

    ___ *b.* Total fees can be broken down as follows:

___ Schematic design phase	15%	or
___ Design develop-ment	20%	25% Preliminary design
___ Construction documents	40%	50% Const. doc.
___ Bid/negotiation	5%	25% Const. adm.
___ Construction administration	20%	
	100%	100%

    ___ *c.* Of the total A/E fees, standard *consultants' fees* can be broken out as follows:

        ___ (1) Civil Engineering and Landscape Architect   2.5 to 6%

        ___ (2) Structural Engineering   1 to 2.5%

        ___ (3) Mechanical Engineering   4 to 10%

        ___ (4) Electrical Engineering   4 to 10%

        ___ (5) Other

___ 3. Rules of Thumb for Business Practice

    ___ *a.* Watch *cash flow:* For a small firm: balance check-book. For a medium or large firm: cash statements; balance and income statements. Estimate future cash flow based on past with 15% "fudge factor," plus desired profit.

    ___ *b.* Have *financial reserves:* Six months' worth.

    ___ *c.* Monitor *time* by these *ratios:*

        ___ (1) $\text{Chargeable ratio} = \dfrac{\text{direct job labor cost}}{\text{total labor cost}}$

This tells what percent of total labor cost is being spent on paying work. The higher the percent the better. Typical range is 55 to 85%, but lower than 65% is poor. However, principals often have a 50% ratio.

        ___ (2) $\text{Multiplier ratio} = \dfrac{\text{dollars of revenue}}{\text{dollars of direct labor}}$

This ratio is multiplied times wages for billing rates. Usually *2.5 to 3.0.* Will vary with firm and time.

___ (3) Overhead rate: looks at total indirect expenses as they relate to total direct labor. An overhead rate of 180 means $1.80 spent for ea. $1.00 working on revenue-producing projects.

___ (4) Profit: measured as total revenue minus expenses. Expressed as percent percent of total revenue.

___ d. Monitor *accounting reports:* A financial statement consists of:

___ (1) Balance Sheet: Tells where you are on a given date by Assets and Liabilities.

___ (2) Earnings Statement (Profit and Loss): Tells you how you got there by Income less Direct (job) costs, and Indirect (overhead) costs = Profit, or Loss.

___ e. *Mark up* for Reimbursable Expenses (travel, printing, etc.): Usually 10%.

___ f. Negotiating *contracts*

___ (1) Estimate scope of services.

___ (2) Estimate time, costs, and profit.

___ (3) Determine method of compensation:

___ (*a*) Percent of construction cost

___ (*b*) Lump sum

___ (*c*) Hourly rates

___ (*d*) Hourly rates with maximum "upset"

___ g. Contract checklist

___ (1) Detailed scope of work, no interpretation necessary.

___ (2) Responsibilities of both parties.

___ (3) Monthly progress payments.

___ (4) Interest penalty on overdue payments.

___ (5) Limit length of construction administration phase.

___ (6) Construction cost estimating responsibilities.

___ (7) For cost-reimbursable contracts, specify a provisional overhead rate (changes year to year).

___ (8) Retainer, applied to fee but not costs.

___ (9) Date of agreement, and time limit on contract.

___ (10) Approval of work—who, when, where.

___ (11) Ways to terminate contract, by both parties.

___ (12) For changes in scope, bilateral agreement, and an equitable adjustment in fee.

___ (13) Court or arbitration remedies and who pays legal fees.

___ (14) Signature and date by both parties.

(5)

ARTICLE 1.1: SCHEDULE OF DESIGNATED SERVICES

PROJECT:

PROJECT #:

DATE:

Phases (columns 1–8):
- Pre-Design Phase
- Site Analysis Phase
- Schematic Design Phase
- Design Development Phase
- Contract Documents Phase
- Bidding or Negotiations Phase
- Contract Administration Phase
- Post-Contract Phase

*R: RESPONSIBILITY   **M: METHOD OF COMPENSATION

	Service	1 R M	2 R M	3 R M	4 R M	5 R M	6 R M	7 R M	8 R M	Remarks and Exceptions
Project Admin. & Mgmt. Services	.01 Project Administration									
	.02 Disciplines Coordination/Document Checking									
	.03 Agency Consulting/Review/Approval									
	.04 Owner-Supplied Data Coordination									
	.05 Schedule Development/Monitoring									
	.06 Preliminary Estimate of Cost of the Work									
	.07 Presentation									
Pre-Design Services	.08 Programming									
	.09 Space Schematics/Flow Diagrams									
	.10 Existing Facilities Surveys									
	.11 Marketing Studies									
	.12 Economic Feasibility Studies									
	.13 Project Financing									
Site Development Services	.14 Site Analysis and Selection									
	.15 Site Development Planning									
	.16 Detailed Site Utilization Studies									
	.17 On-Site Utility Studies									
	.18 Off-Site Utility Studies									
	.19 Environmental Studies and Reports									
	.20 Zoning Processing Assistance									
	.21 Geotechnical Engineering									
	.22 Site Surveying									
Design Services	.23 Architectural Design/Documentation									
	.24 Structural Design/Documentation									
	.25 Mechanical Design/Documentation									
	.26 Electrical Design/Documentation									
	.27 Civil Design/Documentation									
	.28 Landscape Design/Documentation									
	.29 Interior Design/Documentation									
	.30 Special Design/Documentation									
	.31 Materials Research/Specifications									
Bidding or Negotiation Services	.32 Bidding Materials									
	.33 Addenda									
	.34 Bidding/Negotiation									
	.35 Analysis of Alternates/Substitutions									
	.36 Special Bidding									
	.37 Bid Evaluation									
	.38 Contract Award									
Contract Administration Services	.39 Submittal Services									
	.40 Observation Services									
	.41 Project Representation									
	.42 Testing and Inspection Administration									
	.43 Supplemental Documentation									
	.44 Quotation Requests/Change Orders									
	.45 Contract Cost Accounting									
	.46 FF&E Installation Administration									
	.47 Interpretations and Decisions									
	.48 Project Closeout									
Post-Contract Services	.49 Maintenance and Operational Programming									
	.50 Start-Up Assistance									
	.51 Record Drawing									
	.52 Warranty Review									
	.53 Post-Contract Evaluation									

ARTICLE 1.1: SCHEDULE OF DESIGNATED SERVICES (continued)

PROJECT:

Supplemental Services

PROJECT #:

DATE:

9

*R RESPONSIBILITY	**M: METHOD OF COMPENSATION	R	M	Remarks and Exceptions
	.54 Special Studies			
	.55 Tenant-Related Services			
	.56 Special Furnishings Design			
	.57 FF&E Services			
	.58 Special Disciplines Consultation			
	.59 Special Building Type Consultation			
	.60 Fine Arts and Crafts			
	.61 Graphic Design			
	.62 Renderings			
	.63 Model Construction			
	.64 Still Photography			
	.65 Motion Picture and Videotape			
	.66 Life Cycle Cost Analysis			
Supplemental Services	.67 Value Analysis			
	.68 Energy Studies			
	.69 Quantity Surveys			
	.70 Detailed Cost Estimating			
	.71 Environmental Monitoring			
	.72 Expert Witness			
	.73 Materials and Systems Testing			
	.74 Demolition Services			
	.75 Mock-Up Services			
	.76 Coordination of Designated Services			
	.77 FF&E Purchasing/Installation			
	.78 Computer Applications			
	.79 Project Promotion/Public Relations			
	.80 Leasing Brochures			
	.81 Pre-Contract Administration/Management			
	.82 Extended Bidding			
	.83 Extended Contract Administration/Management			
Other Services				

*R: RESPONSIBILITY	**M: METHOD OF COMPENSATION	
A Architect	1. Multiple of Direct Personnel Expense	In conjunction with the descriptions of terms and conditions of this Agreement, the Designated Services, where identified above by appropriate initial, shall be provided by the Owner or the Architect or not at all. In conjunction with the compensation and payment terms of this Agreement, the Owner shall compensate the Architect for such designated services performed by the Architect on the basis of the Method of Compensation identified above by an appropriately keyed number.
O Owner	2. Professional Fee Plus Expenses	
N Not Provided	3. Percentage of Construction Cost	
	4. Stipulated Sum	
	5. Hourly Billing Rates	
	6. Multiple of Amounts Billed to Architect	
	7. Other: _____	

KEY

☐ All services performed in normal chronological order.

■ Services performed out of normal sequence, or not typically provided during these phases, as in FAST-TRACK construction. Such services may warrant special requirements as to responsibility and/or compensation.

OWNER _____
(Signature)

ARCHITECT _____
(Signature)

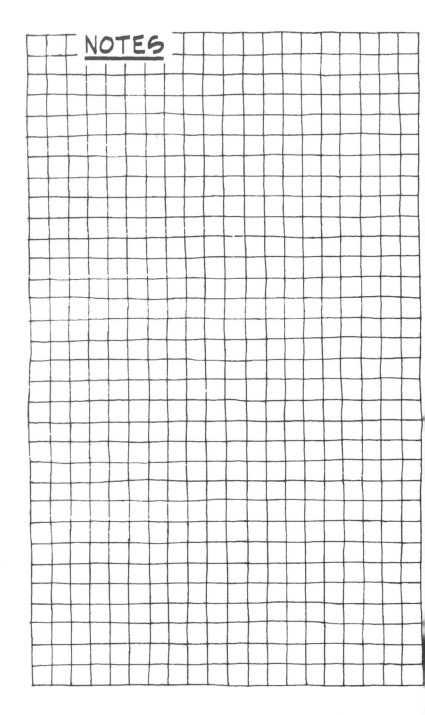

NOTES

___ B. "SYSTEMS" THINKING

In the planning and design of buildings, a helpful, all-inclusive tool is to think in terms of overall "systems" or "flows." For each of the following checklist items, follow from the beginning or "upper end" through to the "lower end" or "outfall":

___ 1. People Functions
    ___ *a.* Follow flow of occupants from one space to another. This includes sources of vertical transportation (stairs, elevators, etc.) including pathways to service equipment.
    ___ *b.* Follow flow of occupants to enter building from off site.
    ___ *c.* Follow flow of occupants to exit building as required by code.
    ___ *d.* Follow flow of accessible route as required by law.
    ___ *e.* Follow flow of materials to supply building, (including furniture and off site).
    ___ *f.* Follow flow of trash to leave building (including to off site).
    ___ *g.* Way finding: do graphics or other visual clues aid flow of the above six items?

___ 2. Structural Functions
    ___ *a.* Follow flow of gravity loads from roof down columns, through floors, to foundations and soils.
    ___ *b.* Follow flow of lateral loads:
        ___ (1) Earthquake from ground up through foundations, columns, walls, floors, and roof.
        ___ (2) Wind from side walls to roof and floors, through columns, to foundations and the earth.
        ___ (3) Follow flow of uplift loads from wind and earthquake by imagining the roof being pulled up and that there are positive connections from roof to columns and walls (through floors) down to foundations and the earth.

___ 3. Water, Moisture, and Drainage
    ___ *a.* Follow rainwater from highest point on roof to drain, through the piping system to outfall (storm sewer or site) off site.
    ___ *b.* Follow rainwater from highest points of site, around building, to outfall off site.
    ___ *c.* Follow rain or moisture at exterior walls and windows down building sides or "weeped" through assemblies to outfall.

___ *d.* Follow vapor from either inside or outside the building, through the "skin" (roof and walls) to outfall.

___ *e.* Follow supply of water from source to farthest point of use.

___ *f.* Follow contaminated water from farthest point of use to outfall (sewer main or end of septic tank).

___ *g.* Follow vapor flow into materials over year and allow for blockage, swelling, or shrinkage.

___ 4. Heat

___ *a.* Follow sun paths to and into building to plan for access or blocking.

___ *b.* Follow excessive external (or internal) heat through building skin and block if necessary.

___ *c.* Follow source of internal heat loads (lights, people, equipment, etc.) to their "outfall" (natural ventilation or AC, etc.).

___ *d.* Follow heat flow into materials over a year, a day, etc. and allow for expansion and contraction.

___ 5. Air

___ *a.* Follow wind patterns through site to encourage or block natural ventilation through building, as required.

___ *b.* Follow air patterns through building. When natural ventilation is used, follow flow from inlets to outlets. When air is still, hot air rises and cold air descends.

___ *c.* Follow forced air ventilation patterns through building to address heat (add or dissipate) and odors.

___ 6. Light

___ *a.* Follow paths of natural light (direct or indirect sun) to and into building. Encourage or block as needed.

___ *b.* Follow paths of circulation and at spaces to provide artificial illumination where necessary. This includes both site and building.

___ 7. Energy and Communications

___ *a.* Follow electric supply from off site to transformer, to breakers or panels to each outlet or point of connection.

___ *b.* Follow telephone lines from off site to TMB to each phone location.

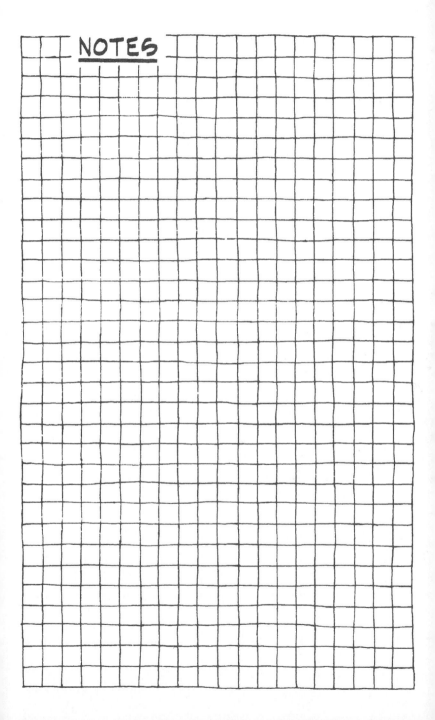

NOTES

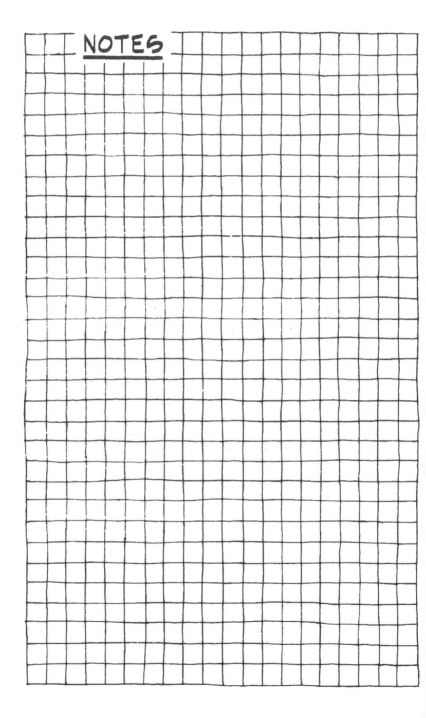

NOTES

___ C. SPECIFICATIONS (CSI FORMAT)

Use this section as a checklist of everything that makes or goes into buildings, to be all-inclusive in the planning and design of buildings, their contents, and their surroundings:

Bidding Requirements, Contract Forms, and Conditions of the Contract
  ___ 00010 Pre-bid information
  ___ 00100 Instructions to bidders
  ___ 00200 Information available to bidders
  ___ 00300 Bid forms
  ___ 00400 Supplements to bid forms
  ___ 00500 Agreement forms
  ___ 00600 Bonds and certificates
  ___ 00700 General conditions
  ___ 00800 Supplementary conditions
  ___ 00900 Addenda

Specifications—By Division

Division 1—General Requirements
  ___ 01010 Summary of work
  ___ 01020 Allowances
  ___ 01025 Measurement and payment
  ___ 01030 Alternates/alternatives
  ___ 01035 Modification procedures
  ___ 01040 Coordination
  ___ 01050 Field engineering
  ___ 01060 Regulatory requirements
  ___ 01070 Identification systems
  ___ 01090 References
  ___ 01100 Special project procedures
  ___ 01200 Project meetings
  ___ 01300 Submittals
  ___ 01400 Quality controls
  ___ 01500 Construction facilities and temporary controls
  ___ 01600 Material and equipment
  ___ 01650 Starting of systems/commissioning
  ___ 01700 Contract closeout
  ___ 01800 Maintenance

Division 2—Sitework
  ___ 02010 Subsurface investigation
  ___ 02050 Demolition
  ___ 02100 Site preparation
  ___ 02140 Dewatering
  ___ 02150 Shoring and underpinning

___ 02160 Excavation support systems
___ 02170 Cofferdams
___ 02200 Earthwork
___ 02300 Tunneling
___ 02350 Piles and caissons
___ 02450 Railroad work
___ 02480 Marine work
___ 02500 Paving and surfacing
___ 02600 Utility piping materials
___ 02660 Water distribution
___ 02680 Fuel and steam distribution
___ 02700 Sewerage and drainage
___ 02760 Restoration of underground pipelines
___ 02770 Ponds and reservoirs
___ 02780 Power and communications
___ 02800 Site improvements
___ 02900 Landscaping

Division 3—Concrete
___ 03100 Concrete formwork
___ 03200 Concrete reinforcement
___ 03250 Concrete accessories
___ 03300 Cast-in-place concrete
___ 03370 Concrete curing
___ 03400 Precast concrete
___ 03500 Cementitious decks and toppings
___ 03600 Grout
___ 03700 Concrete restoration and cleaning
___ 03800 Mass concrete

Division 4—Masonry
___ 04100 Mortar and masonry grout
___ 04150 Masonry accessories
___ 04200 Unit masonry
___ 04400 Stone
___ 04500 Masonry restoration and cleaning
___ 04550 Refactories
___ 04600 Corrosion-resistant masonry
___ 04700 Simulated masonry

Division 5—Metals
___ 05010 Metal materials
___ 05030 Metal finishes
___ 05050 Metal fastenings
___ 05100 Structural metal framing
___ 05200 Metal joists
___ 05300 Metal decking

___ 05400 Cold-formed metal framing
___ 05500 Metal fabrications
___ 05580 Sheet metal fabrications
___ 05700 Ornamental metal
___ 05800 Expansion control
___ 05900 Hydraulic structures

Division 6—Wood and Plastic
___ 06050 Fasteners and adhesives
___ 06100 Rough carpentry
___ 06130 Heavy timber construction
___ 06150 Wood-metal systems
___ 06170 Prefabricated structural wood
___ 06200 Finish carpentry
___ 06300 Wood treatment
___ 06400 Architectural woodwork
___ 06500 Structural plastics
___ 06600 Plastic fabrications
___ 06650 Solid polymer fabrications

Division 7—Thermal and Moisture Protection
___ 07100 Waterproofing
___ 07150 Dampproofing
___ 07180 Water repellents
___ 07190 Vapor retarders
___ 07195 Air barriers
___ 07200 Insulation
___ 07240 Exterior and finish systems
___ 07250 Fireproofing
___ 07270 Fire-stopping
___ 07300 Shingles and roofing tiles
___ 07400 Manufactured roofing and siding
___ 07480 Exterior wall assemblies
___ 07500 Membrane roofing
___ 07570 Traffic coatings
___ 07600 Flashing and sheet metal
___ 07700 Roof specialties and accessories
___ 07800 Skylights
___ 07900 Joint sealers

Division 8—Doors and Windows
___ 08100 Metal doors and frames
___ 08200 Wood and plastic doors
___ 08250 Door-opening assemblies
___ 08300 Special doors
___ 08400 Entrances and storefronts
___ 08500 Metal windows

___ 08600 Wood and plastic windows
___ 08650 Special windows
___ 08700 Hardware
___ 08800 Glazing
___ 08900 Glazed curtain walls

Division 9—Finishes
___ 09100 Metal support systems
___ 09200 Lath and plaster
___ 09250 Gypsum board
___ 09300 Tile
___ 09400 Terrazzo
___ 09450 Stone facing
___ 09500 Acoustical treatment
___ 09540 Special wall surfaces
___ 09545 Special ceiling surfaces
___ 09550 Wood flooring
___ 09600 Stone flooring
___ 09630 Unit masonry flooring
___ 09650 Resilient flooring
___ 09680 Carpet
___ 09700 Special flooring
___ 09780 Floor treatment
___ 09800 Special coatings
___ 09900 Painting
___ 09950 Wall covering

Division 10—Specialties
___ 10100 Visual display boards
___ 10150 Compartments and cubicles
___ 10200 Louvers and vents
___ 10240 Grilles and screens
___ 10250 Service wall systems
___ 10260 Wall and corner guards
___ 10270 Access flooring
___ 10290 Pest control
___ 10300 Fireplaces and stoves
___ 10340 Manufactured exterior specialties
___ 10350 Flagpoles
___ 10400 Identifying devices
___ 10450 Pedestrian control devices
___ 10500 Lockers
___ 10520 Fire protection specialties
___ 10530 Protective covers
___ 10550 Postal specialties
___ 10600 Partitions
___ 10650 Operable partitions

___ 10670 Storage shelving
___ 10700 Exterior protection devices for openings
___ 10750 Telephone specialties
___ 10800 Toilet and bath accessories
___ 10880 Scales
___ 10900 Wardrobe and closet specialties

Division 11—Equipment
___ 11010 Maintenance equipment
___ 11020 Security and vault equipment
___ 11030 Teller and service equipment
___ 11040 Ecclesiastical equipment
___ 11050 Library equipment
___ 11060 Theater and stage equipment
___ 11070 Instrumental equipment
___ 11080 Registration equipment
___ 11090 Checkroom equipment
___ 11100 Mercantile equipment
___ 11110 Commercial laundry and dry-cleaning equipment
___ 11120 Vending equipment
___ 11130 Audiovisual equipment
___ 11140 Vehicle service equipment
___ 11150 Parking control equipment
___ 11160 Loading dock equipment
___ 11170 Solid-waste-handling equipment
___ 11190 Detention equipment
___ 11200 Water supply and treatment equipment
___ 11280 Hydraulic gates and valves
___ 11300 Fluid waste treatment and disposal equipment
___ 11400 Food service equipment
___ 11450 Residential equipment
___ 11460 Unit kitchens
___ 11470 Darkroom equipment
___ 11480 Athletic, recreational, and therapeutic equipment
___ 11500 Industrial and process equipment
___ 11600 Laboratory equipment
___ 11650 Planetarium equipment
___ 11660 Observatory equipment
___ 11680 Office equipment
___ 11700 Medical equipment
___ 11780 Mortuary equipment
___ 11850 Navigational equipment
___ 11870 Agricultural equipment

Division 12—Furnishings
___ 12050 Fabrics
___ 12100 Artwork

___ 12300 Manufactured casework
___ 12500 Window treatment
___ 12600 Furniture and accessories
___ 12670 Rugs and mats
___ 12700 Multiple seating
___ 12800 Interior plants and planters

Division 13—Special Construction
___ 13010 Air-supported structures
___ 13020 Integrated assemblies
___ 13030 Special purpose rooms
___ 13080 Sound, vibration, and seismic control
___ 13090 Radiation protection
___ 13100 Nuclear reactors
___ 13120 Preengineered structures
___ 13150 Aquatic facilities
___ 13175 Ice rinks
___ 13180 Site-constructed incinerators
___ 13185 Kennels and animal shelters
___ 13200 Liquid and gas storage tanks
___ 13220 Filter underdrains and media
___ 13230 Digester covers and appurtenances
___ 13240 Oxygenation systems
___ 13260 Sludge-conditioning systems
___ 13300 Utility control systems
___ 13400 Industrial and process control systems
___ 13500 Recording instrumentation
___ 13550 Transportation control instrumentation
___ 13600 Solar energy systems
___ 13700 Wind energy systems
___ 13750 Cogeneration systems
___ 13800 Building automation systems
___ 13900 Fire suppression and supervisory systems
___ 13950 Special security construction

Division 14—Conveying Systems
___ 14100 Dumbwaiters
___ 14200 Elevators
___ 14300 Escalators and moving walks
___ 14400 Lifts
___ 14500 Material-handling systems
___ 14600 Hoists and cranes
___ 14700 Turntables
___ 14800 Scaffolding
___ 14900 Transportation systems

Division 15—Mechanical
___ 15050 Basic mechanical materials and methods
___ 15250 Mechanical insulation
___ 15300 Fire protection
___ 15400 Plumbing
___ 15500 HVAC
___ 15550 Heat generation
___ 15650 Refrigeration
___ 15750 Heat transfer
___ 15850 Air handling
___ 15880 Air distribution
___ 15950 Controls
___ 15990 Testing, adjusting, and balancing

Division 16—Electrical
___ 16050 Basic electrical materials and methods
___ 16200 Power generation—built-up systems
___ 16300 Medium voltage distribution
___ 16400 Service and distribution
___ 16500 Lighting
___ 16600 Special systems
___ 16700 Communications
___ 16850 Electrical resistance heating
___ 16900 Controls
___ 16950 Testing

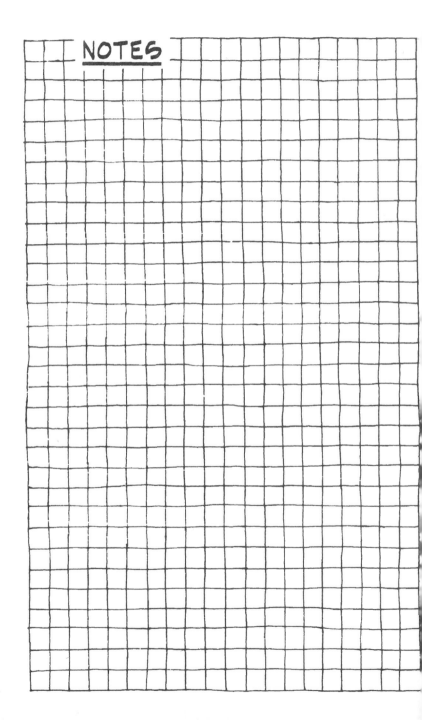

___ 1. *Programming* is a process leading to the statement of an architectural problem and the requirements to be met in offering a solution. It is the search for sufficient information to clarify, to understand, to state the problem. Programming is problem seeking and design is problem solving.

___ 2. Use the Information Index, shown on p. 22 as a guide for creating a program, for more complex projects.

___ 3. Efficiency Ratios: Use the following numbers to aid in planning the size of buildings in regard to the ratio of net area to gross area:

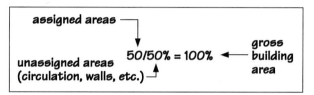

Common Range		
Automobile analogy	For buildings	Ratios
Super Luxury	Superb	50/50
Luxury	Grand	55/45
Full	Excellent	60/40
Intermediate	Moderate	65/35
Compact	Economical	67/33
Subcompact	Austere	70/30
Uncommon Range		
	Meager	75/25
	Spare	80/20
	Minimal	85/15
	Skeletal	90/10

See p. 423 for common ratios by building type.

The following table gives common breakdowns of unassigned areas:

Circulation	16.0	20.0	22.0	24.0	25.0
Mechanical	5.0	5.5	7.5	8.0	10.0
Structure & walls	7.0	7.0	8.0	9.5	10.0
Public toilets	1.5	1.5	1.5	2.0	2.5
Janitor closets	0.2	0.5	0.5	0.5	1.0
Unassigned storage	0.3	0.5	0.5	1.0	1.5
	30.0%	35.0%	40.0%	45.0%	50.0%

INFORMATION INDEX

	GOALS What does the client want to achieve & why?	FACTS What is it all about?

FUNCTION What's going to happen in the building?
  People
  Activities
  Relationships
	Mission
	Maximum number
	Individual identity
	Interaction/privacy
	Hierarchy of values
	Security
	Progression
	Segregation
	Encounters
	Efficiency
		Statistical data
		Area parameters
		Manpower/workloads
		User characteristics
		Community characteristics
		Value of loss
		Time-motion study
		Traffic analysis
		Behavioral patterns
		Space adequacy

FORM What is there now & what is to be there?
  Site
  Environment
  Quality
	Site elements
	(Trees, water, open space,
	  existing facilities,
	  utilities)
	Efficient land use
	Neighbors
	Individuality
	Direction
	Entry
	Projected image
	Level of quality
		Site analysis
		Climate analysis
		Cope survey
		Soils analysis
		F.A.R. and G.A.C.
		Surroundings
		Psychological implications
		Cost/SF
		Building efficiency
		Functional support

ECONOMY Concerns the initial budget & quality of construction.
  Initial budget
  Operating costs
  Lifecycle costs
	Extent of funds
	Cost effectiveness
	Maximum return
	Return on investment
	Minimize oper. costs
	Maint. & oper. costs
	Reduce life cycle costs
		Cost parameters
		Maximum budget
		Time-use factors
		Market analysis
		Energy source-costs
		Activities & climate
		  factors
		Economic data

TIME Deals with the influences of history, the inevitability of change from the present, & projections into the future.
  Past
  Present
  Future
	Historic preservation
	Static/dynamic
	Change
	Growth
	Occupancy date
		Significance
		Space parameters
		Activities
		Projections
		Linear schedule

CONCEPTS How does the client want to achieve the goals?	NEEDS How much money, space, & quality (as opposed to wants)?	PROBLEM What are the significant conditions & the general directions the design of the building should take?
Service grouping People grouping Activity grouping Priority Security controls Sequential flow Separated flow Mixed flow Relationships	Space requirements Parking requirements Outdoor space req'mts. Building efficiency Functional alternatives	Unique and important performance requirements which will shape building design.

Enhancement
Climate control
Safety
Special
  foundations
Density
Interdependence
Home base
Orientation
Accessibility
Character
Quality control
	Quality (cost/SF)
	Environmental & site
	  influences on costs
		Major form considerations which will affect building design.

Cost control Efficient allocation Multifunction Merchandising Energy conservation Cost control	Cost estimate analysis Entry budget (FRAS) Operating costs Life cycle costs	Attitude toward the initial budget and its influence on the fabric and geometry of the building.
Adaptability Tailored/loose fit Convertibility Expansibility Concurrent scheduling	Phasing Escalation	Implications of change/growth on long-range performance.

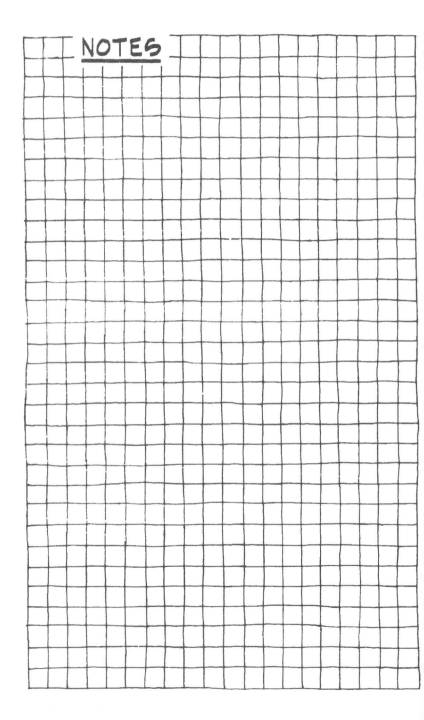

NOTES

__ E. CONSTRUCTION COSTS

$\textcircled{11}$ $\textcircled{16}$ $\textcircled{17}$ $\textcircled{33}$ $\textcircled{34}$ $\textcircled{40}$

___ 1. This book has rough cost data throughout. Rough costs are **boldface.** Subcontractor's overhead and profit are included. Both material (M) and labor (L) are included, usually with a general idea of percentage of each to the total (100%). Since there is room for only one cost per "element," often an idea of possible variation (higher or lower) of cost is given. Sometimes, two numbers are given—the first being for residential and the second for commercial. One must use judgment in this regard to come up with a reasonable but rough cost estimate. As costs change, the user will have to revise costs in this book. The easiest way to do this will be to add historical modifiers, published each year, by various sources. The costs in this book are approx. those at mid 1993. Over the last few years costs have increased about 2% to 3%/yr.

___ 2. Cost Control and Estimating

Cost estimating can be time-consuming. It can also be dangerous in that wrong estimates may require time-consuming and expensive redesign. In doing estimates, the architect should consider the following points:

___ a. Variables: The $/SF figures for various building types shown in App. A, item D are for average simple buildings. They (as all other costs in this book) may need to be modified by the following variables:

___ (1) *Location.* Modify costs for actual location. Use modifiers often published or see App. B, item V.

___ (2) *Historical Index.* If cost data is old, modify to current or future time by often-published modifiers.

___ (3) *Building Size.* The $/SF costs may need to be modified due to size of the project (see App. A, item C). Median sizes may be modified roughly as follows:

As size goes down, cost goes up by ratio of *5 to 1.*

As size goes up, cost goes down by ratio of *25 to 1.*

___ (4) *Shape and Perimeter.* Increases in perimeter and more complicated shapes will cause costs to go up. Where single elements are articulated (e.g., rounded corners or different types of coursing and materials in a masonry wall), add 30% to the costs involved.

___ (5) *Quality of Materials, Construction, and Design.* Use the following rough guidelines to increase or decrease as needed:

Automobile analogy	For buildings	%
Super Luxury	Superb	+120
Luxury	Grand	+60
Full	Excellent	+20
Intermediate	Moderate	100
Compact	Economical	−10
Subcompact	Austere	−20

___ *b.* Costs (and construction scheduling) can be affected by weather, season, materials shortages, labor practices.

___ *c.* Beyond a 20-mile radius of cities, extra transportation charges increase material costs slightly. This may be offset by lower wage rates.

___ *d.* In doing a total estimate, an allowance for general conditions should be added. This usually ranges from 5 to 15%, with *10%* a typical average.

___ *e.* At the end of a total estimate, an allowance for the general contractor's overhead and profit should be added. This usually ranges from *10 to 20%*. Market conditions at the time of bidding will often affect this percentage as well as all items. The market can swing 10 to 20% from active to inactive times.

___ *f.* Contingencies should always be included in estimates as listed below. On alterations or repair projects, *20%* is not an unreasonable allowance to make.

___ *g.* Use rounding of numbers in all estimating items.

___ *h.* Consider using "add alternates" to projects where the demand is high but the budget tight. These alternates should be things the client would like but does not have to have and should be clearly denoted in the drawings.

___ *i.* It is often wise for the architect to give estimates in a range.

___ *j.* Because clients often change their minds or things go wrong that cannot be foreseen in the beginning, it may pay to advise the client to withhold from his budget a confidential *5 to 10%* contingency. On the other hand, clients often do this anyway, without telling the architect.

___ *k.* Costs can further be affected by other things:
Government overhead   ≈+100%
Award winning designs are often   ≈+200 to 300%

___ 3. Cost Control Procedure

    ___ *a.* At the *predesign phase* or beginning of a project, determine the client's *budget* and what it includes, as well as anticipated size of the building. Back out all non construction costs such as cost of land, furniture and fixtures, design fees, etc. Verify, in a simple format (such as $/SF, $/room, etc.) that this is reasonable. See App. A, item D for average $/SF costs as a comparison and guideline.

    ___ *b.* At the *schematic design phase,* establish a reasonable $/SF target. Include a *20% contingency.*

    ___ *c.* At the *design development phase,* as the design becomes more specific, do a "systems" estimate. See Part 13 as an aid. For small projects a "unit" estimate might be appropriate, especially if basic plans (i.e., framing plans, etc.) not normally done at this time, can be quickly sketched up for a "take off." Include a *10% contingency.*

    ___ *d.* At the *construction documents phase,* do a full unit "take off." For smaller projects, the estimate in the last phase may be enough, provided nothing has changed or been added to the project. Add a *5% contingency.*

___ 4. Typical Single Family Residential Costs
The following guidelines may be of use to establish $/SF budgets (site work not included):

    ___ *a.* Production Homes:

        ___ (1) For a 4-corner, 1600-SF tract house, wood frame, 1 story, with a 450-SF garage, no basement, and of average quality, use ***$60.50/SF*** (conditioned area only) as a 1993 national average. Break down as follows:

Item	*% of total*
1 General (including O & P)	18
2 Sitework (excavation only)	1
3 Concrete	6
4 Masonry (brick hearth & veneer)	.5
5 Metals	

6	Wood	
	Rough carpentry	16
	Finish carpentry & cabinetry	7
7	Thermal & moisture protection (insulation & roofing)	8
8	Doors, windows, & hardware	4
9	Finishes (stucco, wallboard, resilient flooring, carpet, paint)	19
10	Specialties (bath accessories & prefab fireplace)	1.5
11	Equipment (built-in appliances)	1.5
12–14		
15	Mechanical	
	Plumbing	8
	HVAC (heating only)	5
16	Electrical (lighting & wiring)	4.5
		100%

___ (2) Modify as follows:

     ___ (a) For perimeter per the following percentages:
For 6 corners, add 2½%. For 8 corners add 5½%. For 10 corners add 7½%.

     ___ (b) Quality of construction:

Low	Average	Good	Best
–15%	100%	+20%	+50%

     ___ (c) Deduct for rural areas: 5%

     ___ (d) Add for 1800-SF house (better quality) 4%

     ___ (e) Add for 2000-SF house (better quality) 3%

     ___ (f) Deduct for over 2400 SF house (same quality) 3%

     ___ (g) Add for split-level house 3%

     ___ (h) Add for 3-story house 10%

     ___ (i) Add for masonry construction 9%

     ___ (j) Add for finished basement 40%

     ___ (k) Adjust for garage (larger or smaller): use 50% of house area.

     ___ (l) *No site work is included!*

___ b. Custom-Designed Homes:
The result of the above can be easily increased by ⅓ to ¾ or more.

___ 5. Typical Commercial Building Cost Percentages

Division	New const.	Remodeling
1. General requirements	6 to 8%	about ⅓
2. Sitework	4 to 6%	for general
3. Concrete	15 to 20%	
4. Masonry	8 to 12%	
5. Metals	5 to 7%	
6. Wood	1 to 5%	
7. Thermal and moisture protection	4 to 6%	
8. Doors, windows, and glass	5 to 7%	
9. Finishes	8 to 12%	about ⅓
10. Specialties*		for divisions
11. Equipment*		8–12
12. Furnishings*	6 to 10%	
13. Special construction*		
14. Conveying systems*		about ⅓
15. Mechanical	15 to 25%	for mech.
16. Electrical	8 to 12%	and elect.
Total	100%	

Note: F.F.&E. (furniture, fixtures, and equipment) are often excluded from building cost budget.

___ 6. Guidelines for Demolition
    ___ a. Total buildings: *$2 to $4/SF*
    ___ b. Separate elements: *10 to 50%* of in-place const. cost of element.

___ 7. Project Budgeting
    ___ a. At the programming phase a total project budget may be worked using the following guidelines:

A. Building cost (net area/efficiency ratio = Gross area, gross area × unit cost = building cost)	$_____
B. Fixed equipment costs (lockers, kit. equip., etc.), percent of line A*	$_____
C. Site development cost, percent of line A*	$_____
D. Total construction cost (A + B + C)	$_____
E. Site acquisition and/or demolition (varies widely)	$_____

F. Movable equipment (such as furnishings) percent of line A* (also see App. A, item F) $_____

G. Professional fees (vary from 5 to 10%), percent of line D $_____

H. Contingencies* $_____

J. Administrative costs (varies from 1 to 2%), percent of line D† $_____

K. Total budget required (D, E–J) $_____

---

*Percentages: low: 5%; medium: 10–15%; high: 20%; very high: 30%.
†For those projects which require financing costs, the following can be added to line J:
  1. Permanent financing (percent of line K):
     Investment banker fee varies, 2.5 to 6%.
     Construction loan fee varies, 1 to 2%.
  2. Interim financing (percent of line D):
     Approximately varies 1.5 to 2% above prime rate per year of construction time.

___ *b.* How to work back from total budget to building cost

The following formula can be used to reduce line K, total budget required, to line A, building cost:

$$\text{Building cost} = \frac{\text{total budget} - \text{site acquisition}}{X + Y + Z}$$

$X = 1 + (\underline{\quad}\% \text{ fixed equip.}) + (\underline{\quad}\% \text{ site dev.})$
$Y = (X) [(\underline{\quad}\% \text{ contingency}) + (\underline{\quad}\% \text{ prof. fee}) + (\underline{\quad}\% \text{ adm. cost})]$
$Z = \underline{\quad}\% \text{ movable equipment}$

Where necessary, interim financing percentage is added to admin. cost. Permanent financing percentage becomes T in $X + Y + Z + T$.

___ 8. Use Architectural Areas of Buildings as an aid in cost-estimating. See Architectural Area Diagram.

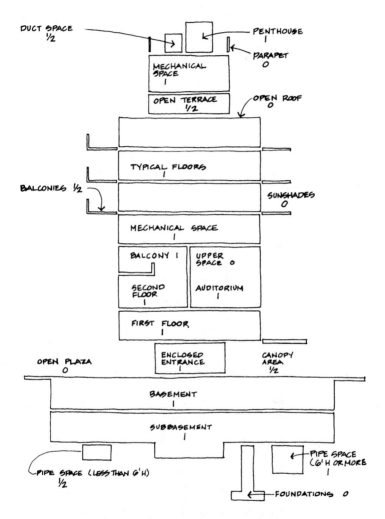

ARCHITECTURAL AREA DIAGRAM

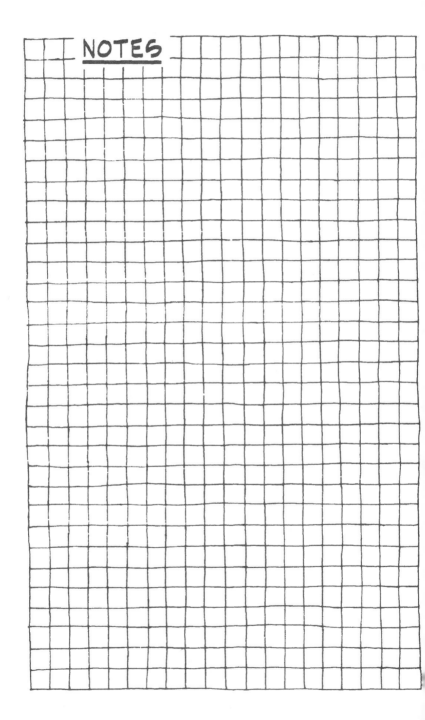

NOTES

__ 1. Estimate *Scheduling*

Project value	*Const. time*
Under $1,400,000	10 months
Up to $3,800,000	15 months
Up to $19,000,000	21 months
Over $19,000,000	28 months

    __ *a.* Design time runs 25 to 40% of construction time (up to 100% for small projects, including government review).

    __ *b.* Construction time can be affected by building type. Using commercial buildings as a base, modify other building types: industrial: −20%; research and development: +20%; institutional buildings: +30%.

__ 2. Site Observation Visits

    __ *a.* Take:

        __ (1) Plans
        __ (2) Specifications
        __ (3) Project files
        __ (4) Tape
        __ (5) Chalk
        __ (6) Camera
        __ (7) Paper
        __ (8) Pencil
        __ (9) Calculator
        __ (10) Checklist
        __ (11) Field report forms
        __ (12) Flashlight
        __ (13) String line and level

    __ *b.* List of site visits for small projects:

        __ (1) After building stake out is complete
        __ (2) After excavation is complete
        __ (3) When foundation is being placed
        __ (4) When under slab utilities and stem walls under way
        __ (5) During placement of concrete slab on grade
        __ (6) During masonry and/or frame walls and columns
        __ (7) During floor and/or roof framing, wall and roof sheathing (prior to roofing)
        __ (8) During roofing
        __ (9) During drywall, plaster, plumbing, electrical, and HVAC
        __ (10) At end of project (punch list)

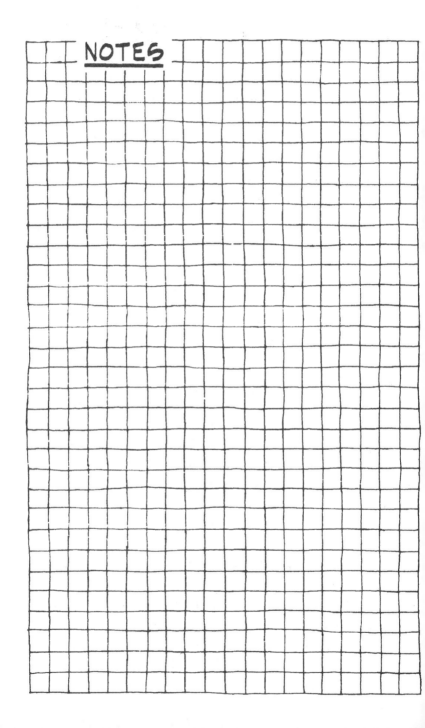

NOTES

__ G. PRACTICAL MATH AND TABLES

(13) (29) (45)

___ 1. Decimals of a Foot

1″ = .08″	7″ = .58′
2″ = .17′	8″ = .67′
3″ = .25′	9″ = .75′
4″ = .33′	10″ = .83′
5″ = .42′	11″ = .92′
6″ = .50′	12″ = 1.0′

___ 2. Decimals of an Inch

⅛″ = 0.125″	⅝″ = 0.625″
¼″ = 0.250″	¾″ = 0.750″
⅜″ = 0.375″	⅞″ = 0.875″
½″ = 0.50″	1″ = 1.0″

___ 3. Simple Algebra
One unknown and
two knowns

$A = B/C$
$B = A \times C$
$C = B/A$

Example: $3 = 15/5$
$15 = 3 \times 5$
$5 = 15/3$

___ 4. Ratios and Proportions
One unknown and three knowns (cross multiplication)

$$\frac{A}{B} = \frac{C}{D}$$

Example: $\dfrac{X}{5} \bowtie \dfrac{10}{20}$ $20 X = 5 \times 10$

$A \times C = B \times D$ $X = \dfrac{5 \times 10}{20} = 2.5$

___ 5. Exponents and Powers
$10^6 = 10 \times 10 \times 10 \times 10 \times 10 \times 10 = 1,000,000$ [1 + 6 zeros]
$10^0 = 1.0$
$10^{-6} = 0.000001$ [6 places to left or 5 zeros in front of 1]

___ 6. Percent Increases or Decreases
50% increase = ½ increase, use × 1.5
100% increase = double, use × 2.0
200% increase = triple, use × 3.0
Example: 20 increases to 25
To find percent increase: 25−20 = 5 [amount of increase]
5/20 = 0.25 or 25% increase

___ 7. Slopes, Gradients, and Angles
(see p. 37)

___ *a.* Slope = "rise over run" or

% slope = $\dfrac{\text{rise}}{\text{run}} \times 100$

___ *b.* Gradient:
as ratios of rise to run
Example: expressed as 1 in 12
for a ramp or as 4″ in 12″ for a
roof

___ *c.* Angle
Degree angle based on rise and
run (see properties of right
angles)

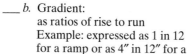

35

___ 8. Properties of Right Angles

45° angle: $a^2 + b^2 = c^2$

or $c = \sqrt{a^2 + b^2}$

For other right angles use simple *trigonometry*:

Sin angle = opp/hyp
Cos angle = adj/hyp
Tan angle = opp/adj

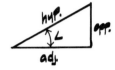

Use calculators with trig. functions or table on p. 38.

___ 9. Properties of Nonright Angles
Use law of sines:

$a/\sin A = b/\sin B = c/\sin C$
$a/b = \sin A/\sin B$, etc.

___ 10. Properties of Circles
A circle is divided into 360 equal parts, called *degrees* (°). One degree is an angle at the center of a circle which cuts off an arc that is $\frac{1}{360}$ of the circumference. Degrees are subdivided into 60 min. ('). Minutes are subdivided into 60 seconds ("). See p. 40.

___ 11. Equivalents of Measure
Use the three bar graphs, shown on p. 40, for quick metric conversions.

___ 12. Geometric Figures
Use the formulas shown, starting on p. 41, to calculate areas and volumes.

___ 13. Units and Conversions
Use the formulas shown, starting on p. 43, to convert units.

Table of Slopes, Grades, Angles

% Slope	Inch/ft	Ratio	Deg. from horiz.
1	⅛	1 in 100	
2	¼	1 in 50	
3	⅜		
4	½	1 in 25	
5	⅝	1 in 20	3
6	¾		
7	⅞		
8	approx. 1	approx. 1 in 12	
9	1⅛		
10	1¼	1 in 10	6
11	1⅜	approx. 1 in 9	
12	1½		
13	1⅝		
14	1¾		
15			8.5
16	1⅞		
17	2	approx. 2 in 12	
18	2⅛		
19	2¼		
20	2⅜	1 in 5	11.5
25	3	3 in 12	14
30	3.6	1 in 3.3	17
35	4.2	approx. 4 in 12	19.25
40	4.8	approx. 5 in 12	21.5
45	5.4	1 in 2.2	24
50	6	6 in 12	26.5
55	6⅝	1 in 1.8	28.5
60	7¼	approx. 7 in 12	31
65	7¾	1 in 1½	33
70	8⅜	1 in 1.4	35
75	9	1 in 1.3	36.75
100	12	1 in 1	45

Trigonometry Tables

Deg	Sin	Cos	Tan	Deg	Sin	Cos	Tan	Deg	Sin	Cos	Tan
1	.0175	.9998	.0175	31	.5150	.8572	.6009	61	.8746	.4848	1.8040
2	.0349	.9994	.0349	32	.5299	.8480	.6249	62	.8829	.4695	1.8807
3	.0523	.9986	.0524	33	.5446	.8387	.6494	63	.8910	.4540	1.9626
4	.0698	.9976	.0699	34	.5592	.8290	.6745	64	.8988	.4384	2.0503
5	.0872	.9962	.0875	35	.5736	.8192	.7002	65	.9063	.4226	2.1445
6	.1045	.9945	.1051	36	.5878	.8090	.7265	66	.9135	.4067	2.2460
7	.1219	.9925	.1228	37	.6018	.7986	.7536	67	.9205	.3907	2.3559
8	.1392	.9903	.1405	38	.6157	.7880	.7813	68	.9272	.3746	2.4751
9	.1564	.9877	.1584	39	.6293	.7771	.8098	69	.9336	.3584	2.6051
10	.1736	.9848	.1763	40	.6428	.7660	.8391	70	.9397	.3420	2.7475
11	.1908	.9816	.1944	41	.6561	.7547	.8693	71	.9455	.3256	2.9042
12	.2079	.9781	.2126	42	.6691	.7431	.9004	72	.9511	.3090	3.0777
13	.2250	.9744	.2309	43	.6820	.7314	.9325	73	.9563	.2924	3.2709
14	.2419	.9703	.2493	44	.6947	.7193	.9657	74	.9613	.2756	3.4874
15	.2588	.9659	.2679	45	.7071	.7071	1.0000	75	.9659	.2588	3.7321
16	.2756	.9613	.2867	46	.7193	.6947	1.0355	76	.9703	.2419	4.0108
17	.2924	.9563	.3057	47	.7314	.6820	1.0724	77	.9744	.2250	4.3315
18	.3090	.9511	.3249	48	.7431	.6691	1.1106	78	.9781	.2079	4.7046
19	.3256	.9455	.3443	49	.7547	.6561	1.1504	79	.9816	.1908	5.1446
20	.3420	.9397	.3640	50	.7660	.6428	1.1918	80	.9848	.1736	5.6713
21	.3584	.9336	.3839	51	.7771	.6293	1.2349	81	.9877	.1564	6.3138
22	.3746	.9272	.4040	52	.7880	.6157	1.2799	82	.9903	.1392	7.1154
23	.3907	.9205	.4245	53	.7986	.6018	1.3270	83	.9925	.1219	8.1443
24	.4067	.9135	.4452	54	.8090	.5878	1.3764	84	.9945	.1045	9.5144
25	.4226	.9063	.4663	55	.8192	.5736	1.4281	85	.9962	.0872	11.4301
26	.4384	.8988	.4877	56	.8290	.5592	1.4826	86	.9976	.0698	14.3007
27	.4540	.8910	.5095	57	.8387	.5446	1.5399	87	.9986	.0523	19.0811
28	.4695	.8829	.5317	58	.8480	.5299	1.6003	88	.9994	.0349	28.6363
29	.4848	.8746	.5543	59	.8572	.5150	1.6643	89	.9998	.0175	57.2900
30	.5000	.8660	.5774	60	.8660	.5000	1.7321	90	1.000	.0000	∞

Note: Deg = degrees of angle; Sin = sine; Cos = cosine; Tan = tangent.

___ 14. Perspective Sketching

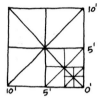

Use the following simple techniques of using 10′ cubes and lines at 5′ with diagonals for quick perspective sketching:

___ *a.* The sketches shown on p. 46 show two techniques:

The *first* establishes Diagonal Vanishing Points (DVP) on the Horizon Line (HL) at certain distances from the Vanishing Points (VP), also on the HL. 10′ cubes are established by projecting diagonals to the DVPs. The *second* technique has 10′ cubes and lines at the 5′ half points. Diagonals through the half points continue the 5′ and 10′ module to the VPs. The vertical 5′ roughly equals eye level, and establishes the HL. Half of 5′ or 2.5′ is a module for furniture height and width.

___ *b.* The sketch shown on p. 47 shows the most common way people view buildings. That is, close up, at almost a one-point perspective. To produce small sketches, set right vertical measure at ½″ apart. Then, about 10½″ to left, set vertical measure at ⅜″ apart. This will produce a small sketch to fit on 8½ × 11 paper. Larger sketches can be done using these proportions.

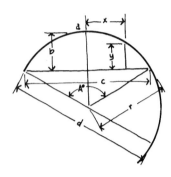

$$\text{Circumference} = 6.28318\,r = 3.14159\,d$$
$$\text{Diameter} = 0.31831\ \text{circumference}$$
$$\text{Area} = 3.14159\,r^2 = \pi r^2$$

$$\text{Arc} \quad a = \frac{\pi r A^\circ}{180^\circ} = 0.017453\,r A^\circ$$

$$\text{Angle} \quad A^\circ = \frac{180^\circ d}{\pi r} = 57.29578\,\frac{d}{r}$$

$$\text{Radius} \ r = \frac{4b^2 + c^2}{8b}$$

$$\text{Chord} \ c = 2\sqrt{2br - b^2} = 2r\sin\frac{A}{2}$$

$$\text{Rise} \quad b = r - \tfrac{1}{2}\sqrt{4r^2 - c^2} = \frac{c}{2}\tan\frac{A}{4}$$

$$= 2r\sin^2\frac{A}{4} = r + y - \sqrt{r^2 - x^2}$$

$$y = b - r + \sqrt{r^2 - x^2}$$

$$x = \sqrt{r^2 - (r + y - b)^2}$$

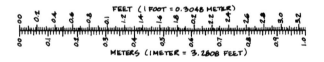

FEET (1 FOOT = 0.3048 METER)

METERS (1 METER = 3.2808 FEET)

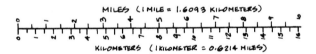

MILES (1 MILE = 1.6093 KILOMETERS)

KILOMETERS (1 KILOMETER = 0.6214 MILES)

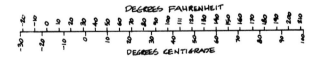

DEGREES FAHRENHEIT

DEGREES CENTIGRADE

GEOMETRIC FIGURES

PLANE SHAPES (TWO - DIMENSIONAL)

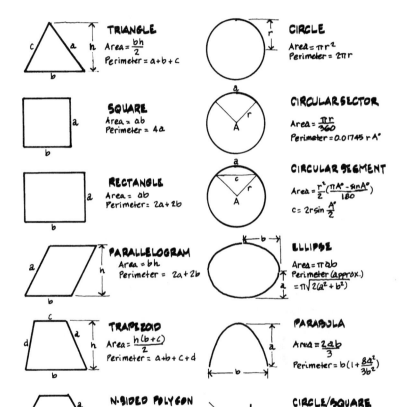

TRIANGLE
Area $= \dfrac{bh}{2}$
Perimeter $= a+b+c$

CIRCLE
Area $= \pi r^2$
Perimeter $= 2\pi r$

SQUARE
Area $= ab$
Perimeter $= 4a$

CIRCULAR SECTOR
Area $= \dfrac{\pi r}{360}$
Perimeter $= 0.01745\, r\, A°$

RECTANGLE
Area $= ab$
Perimeter $= 2a + 2b$

CIRCULAR SEGMENT
Area $= \dfrac{r^2}{2}\left(\dfrac{\pi A° - \sin A°}{180}\right)$
$c = 2r \sin \dfrac{A°}{2}$

PARALLELOGRAM
Area $= bh$
Perimeter $= 2a + 2b$

ELLIPSE
Area $= \pi ab$
Perimeter (approx.)
$= \pi \sqrt{2(a^2 + b^2)}$

TRAPEZOID
Area $= \dfrac{h(b+c)}{2}$
Perimeter $= a+b+c+d$

PARABOLA
Area $= \dfrac{2ab}{3}$
Perimeter $= b\left(1 + \dfrac{8a^2}{3b^2}\right)$

N-SIDED POLYGON
Area $= \dfrac{N(ra)}{2}$
Perimeter $= Na$

CIRCLE/SQUARE
Area $= 0.2146 a^2$
Perimeter $= 2a + \dfrac{\pi a}{2}$

GEOMETRIC FIGURES

SOLID BODIES (THREE-DIMENSIONAL)

CUBE

$Area = 6a^2$
$Volume = a^3$

CYLINDER

$Area = 2\pi r^2 + 2\pi rh$
$Volume = \pi r^2 h$

RECTANGULAR PRISM

$Area = 2ab + 2ac + 2bc$
$Volume = abc$

CONE

$Area = \pi r \sqrt{r^2 + h^2} + \pi r^2$
$Volume = \dfrac{\pi r^2 h}{3}$

SPHERE

$Area = 4\pi r^2$
$Volume = \dfrac{4\pi r^3}{3}$

SPHERICAL SEGMENT

$Area = 2\pi ra$
$Volume = \dfrac{\pi a^2 (3r - a)}{3}$

ELLIPSOID

$Volume = \dfrac{\pi abc}{3}$

PARABOLOID

$Volume = \dfrac{\pi r^2 h}{2}$

Unit Conversions

Multiply	By	To Get	Multiply	By	To Get
Length			Mile	1,760	Yards
Centimeter	0.3937	Inches	Mile	1,609	Meters
Centimeter	10	Millimeters	Mile	1.609	Kilometers
Centimeter	0.01	Meters			
Inch	2.54	Centimeters	**Area**		
Inch	0.0833	Feet	Square centimeter	0.1550	Square inches
Inch	0.0278	Yards	Square centimeter	100	Square millimeters
Foot	30.48	Centimeters	Square centimeter	0.0001	Square meters
Foot	0.3048	Meters	Square inch	6.4516	Square centimeters
Foot	12	Inches	Square inch	0.0069	Square feet
Foot	0.3333	Yards	Square inch	7.72×10^{-4}	Square yards
Yard	91.44	Centimeters	Square foot	929	Square centimeters
Yard	0.9144	Meters	Square foot	0.0929	Square meters
Yard	36	Inches	Square foot	144	Square inches
Yard	3	Feet	Square foot	0.1111	Square yards
Meter	39.37	Inches	Square yard	8,361	Square centimeters
Meter	3.281	Feet	Square yard	0.8361	Square meters
Meter	1.094	Yards	Square yard	1,296	Square inches
Meter	100	Centimeters	Square yard	9	Square feet
Meter	0.001	Kilometers	Square meter	1,550	Square inches
Kilometer	3,281	Feet	Square meter	10.765	Square feet
Kilometer	1,094	Yards	Square meter	1.1968	Square yards
Kilometer	0.6214	Miles	Square meter	10,000	Square centimeters
Kilometer	1,000	Meters	Square meter	1.0×10^{-6}	Square kilometers
Mile	5,280	Feet	Square kilometer	1.076×10^{7}	Square feet

Unit Conversions—*Continued*

Multiply	By	To Get	Multiply	By	To Get
Square kilometer	1.197×10^6	Square yards	Cubic yard	4.667×10^4	Cubic inches
Square kilometer	0.3861	Square miles	Cubic yard	27	Cubic feet
Square kilometer	1.0×10^6	Square meters	Cubic meter	6.102×10^4	Cubic inches
Square mile	2.788×10^7	Square feet	Cubic meter	35.320	Cubic feet
Square mile	3.098×10^6	Square yards	Cubic meter	1.3093	Cubic yards
Square mile	640	Acres	Cubic meter	1.0×10^6	Cubic centimeters
Square mile	2.590	Square kilometers	Cubic meter	1,000	Liters

Volume			**Mass**		
Cubic centimeter	0.0610	Cubic inches	Pound	4.448	Newtons
Cubic centimeter	1,000	Cubic millimeters	Pound	32.17	Poundals
Cubic centimeter	1.0×10^{-6}	Cubic meters	Ton, US short	2,000	Pounds
Cubic inch	16.387	Cubic centimeters	Ton, US long	2,240	Pounds
Cubic inch	5.787×10^{-4}	Cubic feet	Ton, metric	2,205	Pounds
Liter	0.2642	Gallons, US	Ton, metric	1,000	Kilograms
Liter	1.0568	Quarts	Gram	0.0353	Ounces
Liter	1,000	Cubic centimeters	Gram	2.205×10^{-3}	Pounds
Gallon, US	0.0238	Barrels (42 gallons)	Gram	0.001	Kilograms
Gallon, US	4	Quarts	Gram	15.432	Grains
Gallon, US	231	Cubic inches	Ounce	28.35	Grams
Gallon, US	3,785	Cubic centimeters	Ounce	0.0284	Kilograms
Cubic foot	2.832×10^4	Cubic centimeters	Ounce	0.0625	Pounds
Cubic foot	0.0283	Cubic meters	Pound	453.6	Grams
Cubic foot	1,728	Cubic inches	Pound	0.4536	Kilograms
Cubic foot	0.0370	Cubic yards	Pound	16	Ounces
Cubic yard	7.646×10^5	Cubic centimeters	Kilogram	35.28	Ounces
Cubic yard	0.7646	Cubic meters	Kilogram	2.205	Pounds

Units and Conversions

Multiply	By	To Get
Kilogram	1,000	Grams
Ton, US	0.9070	Tons metric
Ton, US	907	Kilograms
Ton, US	2,000	Pounds
Ton, metric	1.102	Tons, US
Ton, metric	2,205	Pounds
Ton, metric	1,000	Kilograms

Energy

Multiply	By	To Get
Erg	1.0×10^{-7}	Joules
Joule	1	Newton-meters
Joule	1.0×10^{7}	Ergs
Joule	0.2389	Calories
Joule	9.48×10^{-4}	British thermal units
Joule	0.7376	Foot-pounds
Calorie	3.97×10^{-3}	British thermal units
Btu/hour	0.293	Joules/second
Btu/hour	252	Calories/hour
Btu	3412	Kwh

Light

Multiply	By	To Get
Lux	1	Lumens/square meter
Lux	0.0929	Lumens/square foot
Lux	0.0929	Footcandles
Footcandle	10.76	Lux
Lumen/square foot	10.76	Lux

Multiply	By	To Get
Temperature		
Degree C	1.8	Degrees F
Degree F	0.5556	Degrees C
Degree K	1	Degrees C
Degree C	1.8 (°C+32)	Degrees F
Degree F	0.556 (°F-32)	Degrees C
Degree K	(°K-273)	Degrees C

Surveyor's Measure

Multiply	By	To Get
Link	7.92	Inches
Rod	16.5	Feet
Chain	4	Rods
Rood	40	Square rods
Acre	160	Square rods
Acre	43,560	Square feet
Square mile	640	Acres
Township	36	Square miles

PERSPECTIVE SKETCHING

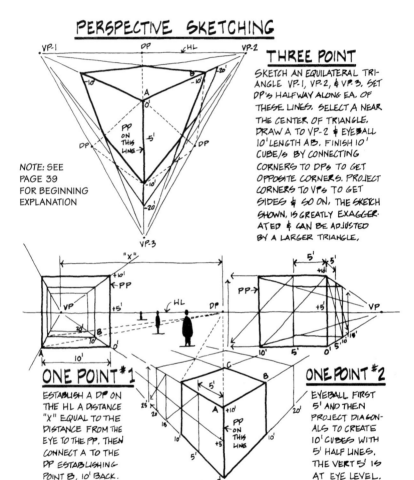

THREE POINT

SKETCH AN EQUILATERAL TRI-
ANGLE VP-1, VP-2, & VP-3. SET
DP's HALFWAY ALONG EA. OF
THESE LINES. SELECT A NEAR
THE CENTER OF TRIANGLE.
DRAW A TO VP-2 & EYEBALL
10' LENGTH AB. FINISH 10'
CUBE/s BY CONNECTING
CORNERS TO DP's TO GET
OPPOSITE CORNERS. PROJECT
CORNERS TO VP's TO GET
SIDES & SO ON. THE SKETCH
SHOWN, IS GREATLY EXAGGER-
ATED & CAN BE ADJUSTED
BY A LARGER TRIANGLE.

NOTE: SEE
PAGE 39
FOR BEGINNING
EXPLANATION

ONE POINT #1

ESTABLISH A DP ON
THE HL A DISTANCE
"X" EQUAL TO THE
DISTANCE FROM THE
EYE TO THE PP. THEN
CONNECT A TO THE
DP ESTABLISHING
POINT B, 10' BACK.
THE FACE OF THE
CUBE AT THE PP
IS EYEBALLED.

ONE POINT #2

EYEBALL FIRST
5' AND THEN
PROJECT DIAGON-
ALS TO CREATE
10' CUBES WITH
5' HALF LINES.
THE VERT 5' IS
AT EYE LEVEL.

TWO POINT

#1 EYEBALL LVP & RVP AND THEN DP, ALL ON THE HL.
CONNECT A TO DP. EYEBALL FIRST 10' ON LINE AB.
CONNECT B TO LVP. THE INTERSECTION ESTABLISH-
ES POINT C, 10' BACK, & SO ON.

#2 5' DIAGONALS CAN ALSO BE USED BY EYEBALLING
THE FIRST 5'.

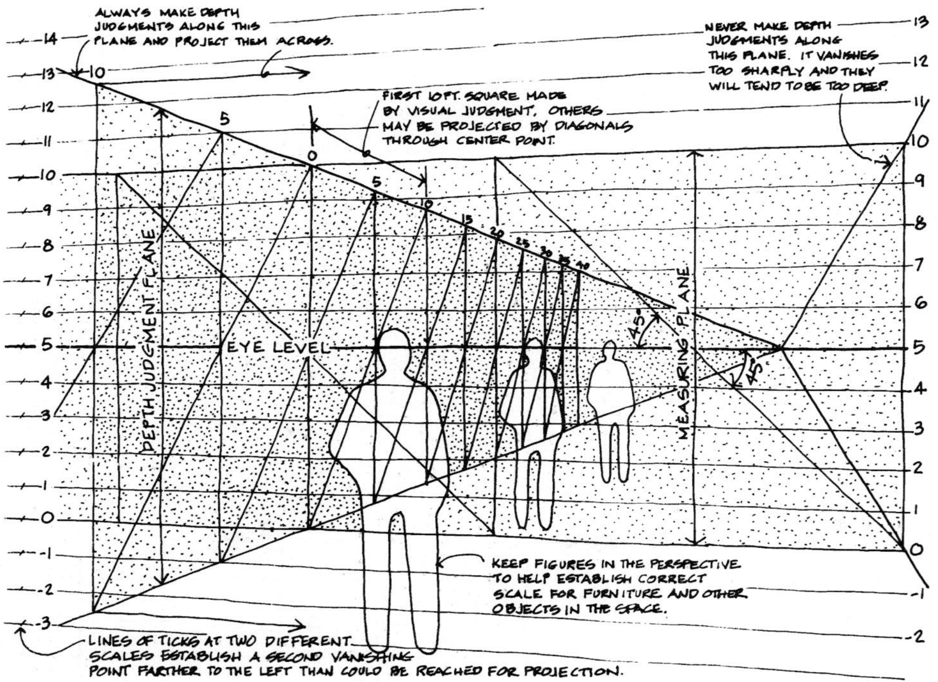

PERSPECTIVE

NEVER MAKE DEPTH JUDGEMENTS ALONG THIS PLANE. IT VANISHES TOO SHARPLY AND THEY WILL TEND TO BE TOO DEEP

ALWAYS MAKE DEPTH JUDGEMENTS ALONG THIS PLANE AND PROJECT THEM ACROSS.

FIRST LOFT SQUARE MADE BY VISUAL JUDGMENT, OTHERS MAY BE PROJECTED BY DIAGONALS THROUGH CENTER POINT.

KEEP FIGURES IN THE PERSPECTIVE TO HELP ESTABLISH CORRECT SCALE FOR FURNITURE AND OTHER OBJECTS IN THE SPACE.

LINES OF TICKS AT TWO DIFFERENT SCALES ESTABLISH A SECOND VANISHING POINT FURTHER TO THE LEFT THAN COULD BE REACHED FOR PROJECTION.

MEASURING PLANE

DEPTH JUDGEMENT PLANE

EYE LEVEL

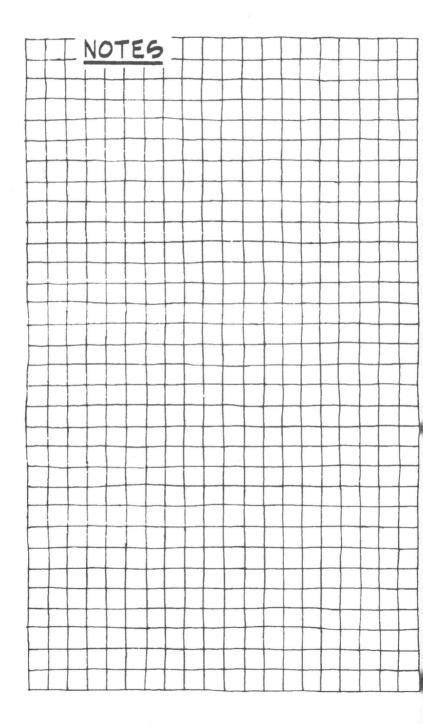

NOTES

__ H. BUILDING LAWS

__ 1. *Zoning* (42)

Zoning laws vary from city to city. The following checklist is typical of items in a zoning ordinance:

___ *a.* Zone
___ *b.* Allowable use
___ *c.* Prohibited uses or special-use permit
___ *d.* Restrictions on operation of facility
___ *e.* Minimum lot size
___ *f.* Maximum building coverage
___ *g.* Floor area ratio
___ *h.* Setbacks for landscaping
___ *i.* Building setbacks: front, side, street, rear
___ *j.* Required open space
___ *k.* Maximum allowable height
___ *l.* Restrictions due to adjacent zone(s)
___ *m.* Required parking
___ *n.* Required loading zone
___ *o.* Parking layout restrictions
___ *p.* Landscape requirements
___ *q.* Environmental impact statements
___ *r.* Signage
___ *s.* Site plan review
___ *t.* "Design review"
___ *u.* Special submittals required for approval and/or hearings:
    ___ (1) Fees
    ___ (2) Applications
    ___ (3) Drawings
    ___ (4) Color presentations
    ___ (5) Sample boards
    ___ (6) List of adjacent land owners
    ___ (7) Other
___ *v.* Although not part of the zoning ordinance, private "Covenants, Conditions, and Restrictions (CC&Rs) that "run" with the land should be checked.
___ *w.* Other

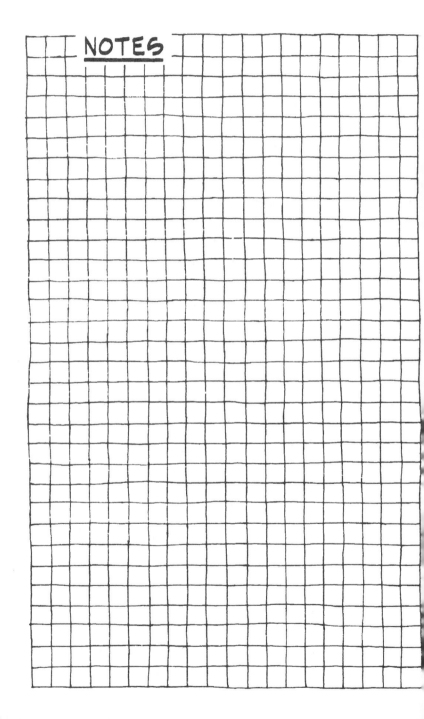

NOTES

___ 2. *Code Requirements for Residential*   (26)
Construction (1991 UBC)
Use the following checklist for single-family residences:
___ *a.* Location on lot
    ___ (1) Openings must be 3′ from property line.
    ___ (2) Walls less than 3′ must be 1-hour construction.
___ *b.* Separation between dwelling units must be a min. of 1-hour construction.
___ *c.* Windows and ventilation
    ___ (1) Habitable rooms must have natural light by exterior windows with area of at least $\frac{1}{10}$ floor area, but min. of 10 SF.
    ___ (2) Bath and laundry-type rooms must have ventilation by operable exterior windows with area of not less than $\frac{1}{20}$ floor area. Min. of 1.5 SF.
    ___ (3) Habitable rooms must have natural ventilation by operable exterior windows with area of not less than $\frac{1}{20}$ floor area. Min. of 5 SF.
    ___ (4) In lieu of natural ventilation, mechanical ventilation may be used:
        ___ (*a*) In habitable rooms, two air changes per hour. $\frac{1}{5}$ of air supply taken from outside.
        ___ (*b*) In bath and laundry-type rooms, five air changes per hour.
        ___ (*c*) The point of discharge must be at least 3 ft from any building opening.
        ___ (*d*) Both rooms with lav. and WC only may have circulating fan.
    ___ (5) Any room may be considered as a portion of an adjoining room when $\frac{1}{2}$ of area of the common wall is open and provides an opening of at least $\frac{1}{10}$ of floor area of interior room, or 25 SF, whichever is greater.
    ___ (6) Eaves over windows shall not be less than 30″ from side and rear property lines.
___ *d.* Ceiling heights
    ___ (1) Habitable rooms, 7′6″ min.
    ___ (2) Other rooms, 7′0″ min.
    ___ (3) Where exposed beams are used, height is to bottom when spacing less than 48″; otherwise, it is measured to the top.
    ___ (4) At sloped ceilings, the min. ceiling height is required at only $\frac{1}{2}$ the area, but never less than 5′ height.

___ (5) At furred ceilings, the min. ceiling ht. is required at only ⅔ the area, but furred ceiling to be at 7'0" min.

___ *e.* Sanitation

___ (1) Room with WC shall be separated from food prep. or storage area by a tight-fitting door.

___ (2) Every DU shall have a kitchen with a sink.

___ (3) Every DU shall have a bath with a WC, lav., bathtub, or shower.

___ (4) Every sink, lav., bathtub, or shower shall have hot and cold running water.

___ *f.* Room dimensions

___ (1) At least one room shall have at least 120 SF.

___ (2) Other habitable rooms, except kitchens, shall have at least 70 SF and shall be not less than 7' in any dimension.

___ (3) Each WC shall be located in a clear space of 30" wide and have 24" clearance in front.

___ *g.* Fire warning system

___ (1) Each dwelling must have smoke detectors in each sleeping room and the corridor to sleeping rooms, at each story (close proximity to stairways) and basement.

___ (2) In new construction, smoke detectors to be powered by building wiring but equipped with backup battery.

___ (3) If additions or alterations (exceeding $1000) or sleeping rooms are being added, the entire building shall have smoke detectors.

___ (4) In existing buildings, smoke detectors may be solely battery-operated.

___ *h.* Exits

___ (1) Doors

___ (*a*) At least one entry door shall be 3' wide by 6'8" high.

___ (*b*) There must be a floor or landing at each side of each door, not more than 1" below door and sloped not greater than 2%.

___ (*c*) At interior stairs, doors may open at the top step; if door swings away from step and step or landing is now lower than 8", the landing must be the width of stair or door and 36" deep.

___ (2) Emergency exits

    ___ (*a*) Sleeping rooms below 4th floor, and basements shall have at least one operable window.

    ___ (*b*) The windows shall be operable from the inside and have a min. clear opening of 5.7 SF (24″ high min., 20″ wide min.) and sill shall not be higher than 44″ above floor.

    ___ (*c*) Bars, grilles, or grates may be installed provided they are operable from inside, and the building has smoke detectors.

___ *i.* Stairs

    ___ (1) Rise: 4″ min., 7″ max., except stairs serving occ. load of less than 10, rise = 8″ max, tread = 9″ min.

    ___ (2) Run: 11″ min.

    ___ (3) Variation in treads and risers = ⅜″ max.

    ___ (4) Winders: require tread at 12″ out from narrow side, but always no less than 6″ at any point.

    ___ (5) Spiral stairs limited to 400 SF of area served with 26″ min. clear width. Tread at 12″ from center to be 7½″. Max. riser = 9½″.

    ___ (6) Handrails

        ___ (*a*) At least one, at open side, continuous with terminations to posts or walls

        ___ (*b*) Height: 34″ to 38″ above tread nosing

        ___ (*c*) Clearance from walls: 1½″

        ___ (*d*) Width of grip: 1½″ to 2″

    ___ (7) Headroom: 6′8″ min.

    ___ (8) Guardrails at floor or roof openings, more than 30″ above grade. Height = 36″ min. If open, submembers must be spaced so a 4″ dia. sphere cannot pass through.

___ *j.* Garages and carports

    ___ (1) Garage of 1000 SF max. may be attached to dwelling provided ceiling has ½″ type X gyp. board and separation wall is 1 hr (20 min. door).

    ___ (2) Open carport does not have the above requirements.

___ *k.* Fireplaces: see p. 302.

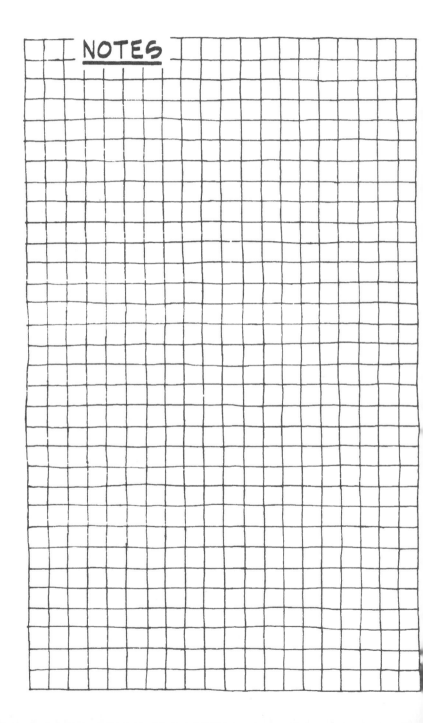

NOTES

___ 3. *Building Code (Based on 1991 UBC)* (10) (24)

Configuring a building that meets the code's fire safety requirements is one of the architect's primary responsibilities. This handbook uses only the Uniform Building Code (UBC) as a guide. However, all other model codes in the U.S. are similar in approach.

Steps in preliminary code check are:

___ *a.* Establish occupant load (see UBC Table 33-A, p. 66).

___ *b.* Determine occupancy classification (see UBC Table 5-A, p. 68). Also, see App. A, item A.

___ *c.* Determine allowable area (see UBC Table 5-C, p. 72).

___ *d.* Determine allowable height (see UBC Table 5-D, p. 73).

___ *e.* Determine construction type (see UBC Tables 5-C and 5-D, pp. 72–73).

___ *f.* Determine hourly ratings of construction components for construction type (see UBC Table 17-A, p. 74).

___ *g.* Determine required occupancy separations (see UBC Table 5-B, p. 71).

___ *h.* Determine sprinkler requirements.

___ *i.* Determine if area separation walls are needed.

___ *j.* Determine if exterior walls and windows have adequate fire protection (see UBC Table 5-A, pp. 68 and 75).

___ *k.* Check exiting.

___ *l.* Other.

___ *a.* *Occupant Load:* Determining the occupant load from UBC Table 33-A (in some cases) will help determine the occupancy classification. When starting a project, a listing of architectural program areas by name, along with their floor area, occupant classification, and occupant load should be compiled. Total the occupant load to help determine the final overall occupancy classification and for design of the exiting.

___ *b.* *Occupancy Classification:* The building code classifies buildings by occupancy in order to group similar life-safety problems together. Table 5-A of the UBC provides a concise definition of all occupancy classifications.

___ c. *Allowable Floor Area:* UBC Table 5-C coordinates the level of hazard (occupancy classification) to the required fire resistance (allowable construction type) by defining the allowable area for a one-story building. High-hazard occupancies (like large assembly) can be built only out of the most fire resistant construction types. A lower-hazard occupancy (like a small office or a residence), can be built using any of the construction types. The allowable construction types are listed from right to left in approximately decreasing order of fire safety and construction cost. Thus choosing a construction type as far to the right as possible will provide the least expensive construction for the type of occupancy in question.

Allowable areas can be further increased by keeping the building away from property lines, from other buildings (a property line is "assumed" halfway between two buildings for the purposes of "yard separation"), or facing on a wide street. When separations are different widths, must use smallest of the two.

___ *Separation on two sides,* where public ways or yards exceed 20′ in width on two sides, the floor area can be increased by 1.25% for each foot of excess yard width. The increase cannot exceed 50%.

___ *Separation on three sides,* where public ways or yards exceed 20′ in width on three sides, the floor area can be increased by 2.5% for each foot of excess yard width. The increase cannot exceed 100%.

___ *Separation on all sides,* where public ways or yards exceed 20′ in width on all sides, the floor area can be increased by 5% for each foot of excess yard width. The increase cannot exceed 100%.

___ Allowable areas can still be further increased for credit for having *FIRE SPRINKLERS.* The allowable floor area for a 1-story building can be tripled and for a multistory building, doubled. The floor area increase can be taken even if the code requires sprinklers for the occupancy (but cannot be used for H-1, -2, or -3 occupancies or atria, increase in stories, or substitution for 1-hr construction).

___ These area modifications can be compounded on top of the area increases for separation of side yards.

___ *d.* *Allowable building height:* UBC Table 5-D specifies the maximum number of stories that can be built in a particular construction type. A building that is not otherwise required to be sprinklered can have on additional story if sprinklered. You cannot take both a height increase and an area increase for sprinklers. You have to choose one or the other.

___ *e.* *Construction type:* Based on the above, you can now select the construction type. Construction types are based on whether or not the building construction materials are combustible or noncombustible, and the hours that a wall, column, beam, floor, or other structural element can resist fire. Steel and concrete are examples of noncombustible materials. Steel, however, will lose structural strength as it begins to soften in the heat of a fire. Wood is an example of a material that is combustible.

There are two ways that construction can be resistant to fire. First it can be *fire-resistive*-built of a monolithic, noncombustible material like concrete or masonry. Second, it can be *protected*—encased in a noncombustible material such as steel columns or wood studs covered with gypsum plaster.

The following are the construction types per the UBC:

___ *Type I and Type II (Fire resistive)* construction is noncombustible, built from concrete, masonry, and/or steel and requires substantial hourly ratings (4 to 2 hours).

___ *Type II, 1-hour and unprotected (N)* construction is also of the same materials as above, but the hourly ratings are less. Light steel framing would fit into this category.

___ *Type III, 1-hour and unprotected (N)* has noncombustible exterior walls of masonry or concrete, and interior construction of any allowable material including wood.

___ *Type IV* construction is combustible *heavy timber* framing. It achieves its rating from the large size of the timber (2″ thickness, min., actual). The outer surface chars creating a fire-resistant layer protecting the remaining wood. Exterior walls must be of noncombustible materials.

___ *Type V, 1-hour and unprotected (N)* is of light wood framing.

___ *f. Hourly ratings:* See UBC Table 17-A for specific requirements of each construction type. See p. 305, on how to achieve these ratings.

___ *g. Required occupancy separations:* For hourly ratings, these are determined from UBC Table 5-B. Most buildings will have some mix of occupancies. If one of the occupancies is a minor area and subservient to the major one, the whole building can often be classified as the major occupancy. It will then have to meet the requirements of the more restrictive occupancy, but no separating walls will be necessary.

Some buildings will have different occupancies, none of which is the dominant one. UBC Table 5-B gives the required fire resistance of the walls and/or floors that separate the occupancies. Openings through separation walls must meet the following criteria:

___ For *4-hour walls,* no opening allowed.

___ For *3-hour walls,* openings must be less than 25% of the length of the wall and no one opening larger than 120 SF.

___ For *2-hour and 1-hour walls,* protection of the opening is the only criteria.

___ *h. Sprinkler requirements:* A sprinkler system can be used to *substitute for 1-hour const.,* if it is not required by the code and is not used for area or height increases. However, exit access corridors, exit stairs, shafts, area separation walls and similar structures must maintain their required fire protection.

A sprinkler system is the most effective way to provide fire safety in a building. The UBC requires fire sprinklers in the following situations:

___ *A occupancies* that are: drinking establishments greater than 5000 SF; multitheater complexes; amusement buildings (unless small and temporary); and theaters with/legitimate stages.

___ *H occupancies,* Division 1, 2, 3, 6, and 7 or Division 4 less than 3000 SF.

___ *I occupancies*

___ *R-1 occupancies* that are:

Apartments, three or more stories with 16 or more DUs.

Congregate residences, three or more stories with 50 or more occupants.

Hotels, three or more stories or with 20 or more DUs.

___ *Basements* for Group A or E occupancies, greater than 1500 SF.

___ *Exhibition, display, or retail sales areas:*

Group A or B-2, greater than 12,000 SF.

Group B-2, greater than 24,000 SF on all floors or more than three stories in height.

___ *Stairs,* at enclosed usable space above and below for Group A-2, 2.1, 3,4, and E occupancies.

___ *All occupancies without sufficient fire department access through outside wall* (Group R-1 and Group M excluded). Sufficient access is 20 SF of openings with a minimum dimension of 30″ per 50 LF of wall. If these openings are only on one side, the floor dimension cannot exceed 75′ from the opening. Highrise, Group B office buildings, and R-1 apartment buildings, where floors are located 75′ above lowest level of fire truck access.

See p. 364 for sprinkler installations.

___ *i.* *Area separation walls:* One building can be divided into what the code considers separate buildings through the use of area separation walls. The allowable floor area criteria is then applied individually to each of the separate areas. The following criteria apply to area separation walls:

___ Type I and Type II require 4 hours.

___ Type II—1 hour and N require 2 hours.

___ Type III—1 hour and N require 4 hours

___ Type IV—Require 4 hours

___ Type V—1 hour and N require 2 hours.

The total width of openings cannot exceed 25% of the length of the wall and must be protected by a fire assembly with a 3-hour rating for a 4-hour wall or a 1½-hour rating for a 2-hour wall. Area separation walls must extend from the foundation to a point 30″ above the roof, unless the roof has a 2-hour rating. See p. 256 for fire doors.

___ *j.* *Fire protection of exterior walls and windows:* This is a function of location of the building on the property and the occupancy type. For Types IIN, II-1, or V, see UBC Table 5-A for requirements. For other types, see p. 75. As buildings get closer together, the requirements become more restrictive.

___ *k.* *Exiting and stairs:* At the conceptual stage of architectural design, the most important aspect of the building code requirements is the number and distribution of exits.

A *means of egress* is a continuous path of travel from any point in a building or structure to the open air outside at ground level. It consists of three separate and distinct parts:

___ 1. Exit access
___ 2. The exit
___ 3. The exit discharge

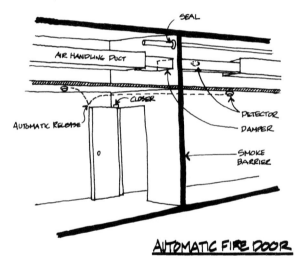

AUTOMATIC FIRE DOOR

The *Exit Access* leads to an exit. A minimum of two exits is almost always required (See UBC Table 33-A). Other general requirements:

___ 1. Corridor width is to be no less than 44″ for an occupancy load of 10 or more people. It can be 36″ for fewer than 10 people.
___ 2. Dead-end corridors limited to 20 ft long.
___ 3. When more than one exit is required, the occupant should be able to go toward either exit from any point in the corridor system.

___ 4. Corridors used for exit access require 1-hour construction.

___ 5. Maximum travel distance from any point to an exit is *150 ft* for a nonsprinklered building or *200 ft* for a sprinklered building. This distance can be *increased by 100 ft* if the corridor meets all the requirements of this section. Some occupancies require less travel distance.

___ 6. Handrails or fully open doors cannot extend more than 7 inches into the corridor.

___ 7. Doors at their worst extension into the corridor cannot obstruct the required width by more than half.

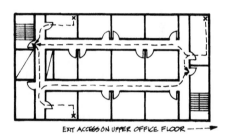

EXIT ACCESS ON UPPER OFFICE FLOOR — — —▶

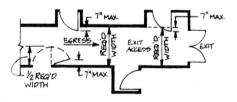

The exit is that portion of a means of egress that is separated from the area of the building from which escape is made, by walls, floors, doors, or other means that provide the protected path necessary for the occupants to proceed with safety to a public space. The most common form the exit takes is an enclosed stairway. In a single-story building the exit is the door opening to the outside.

After determining occupant load (Table 33-A, UBC) for spaces, rooms, floors, etc., use the following guidelines:

___ 1.   Almost all buildings need 2 exits (see UBC Table 33-A). In more than one story, stairs become part of an exit. Elevators are not exits.

___ 2.   An occupant load of 501 to 1000 requires 3 exits.

___ 3.   An occupant load of 1001 or more requires 4 exits.

___ 4.   In buildings 4 stories and higher and in Types 1 and 2 FR construction, the exit stairs are required to have 2-hour enclosure; otherwise, 1 hour is acceptable.

___ 5.   When 2 exits are required, they have to be separated by a distance equal to half the diagonal dimension of the floor and/or room the exits are serving (measured in straight lines). See sketch on p. 64.

___ 6.   Where more than two exits are required, two of them need to be separated by half the diagonal dimension. The others are spaced to provide good access from any direction.

___ 7.   The total exit width required is determined by multiplying the occupant load by *0.3* for *stairs* and *0.4* for *other exits*. This width should be divided equally among the required number of exits.

___ 8.   Total occupant load for calculating exit stair width is defined as the sum of the occupant load on the floor in question, plus 50% of the occupant load of the first adjacent floor. The adjacent floors are usually above the floor in question, but they could be below if the exiting was from a basement level. The maximum exit stair width calculated is maintained for the entire exit. See sketch on p. 63.

___ 9.   Minimum exit door width is 36″ with 32″ clear opening. Maximum door width is 48″.

___ 10. The width of exit stairs, and the width of landings between flights of stairs, must all be the same and must meet the minimum exit stair width requirements as calculated or:

44″ minimum width for an occupant load of 50 or more

36″ minimum width for 49 or less, whichever is greater

___ 11. Doors must swing in the direction of travel when serving a hazardous area or when serving an occupant load of 50 or more.

___ A *Horizontal exit* is a way of passage through a 2-hour fire wall into another area of the same building or into a different building that will provide refuge from smoke and fire. Horizontal exits cannot provide more than half of the required exit capacity, and any such exit must discharge into an area capable of holding the occupant capacity of the exit. The area is calculated at 3 SF/occupant. In institutional occupancies the area needed is 15 SF/ambulatory person, and 30 SF/nonambulatory person.

___ *Exit discharge* is that portion of a means of egress between the termination of an exit and a public way. The most common form this takes is the door out of an exit stairway opening onto a public street. Exits can discharge through an enclosed 2-hour passageway that connects the exit with a public way. In type B-2 occupancy office buildings, 50% of the exits can discharge through a street floor lobby area

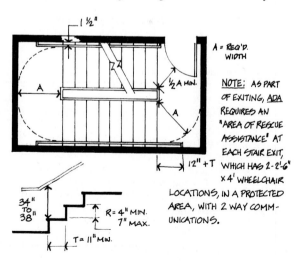

1 ½″

A = REQ'D. WIDTH

½ A MIN.

NOTE: AS PART OF EXITING, ADA REQUIRES AN "AREA OF RESCUE ASSISTANCE" AT EACH STAIR EXIT, WHICH HAS 2-2'-6" X 4' WHEELCHAIR LOCATIONS, IN A PROTECTED AREA, WITH 2 WAY COMMUNICATIONS.

12″ + T

34″ TO 38″

R = 4″ MIN.
7″ MAX.

T = 11″ MIN.

if the entire street floor is sprinklered and the path through the lobby is unobstructed and obvious.

___ *Smokeproof enclosures* for exits are required in any tall building with floors 75′ above the lowest ground level where fire trucks have access. A smokeproof enclosure is an exit stair that is entered through a vestibule that is ventilated by either natural or mechanical means such that products of combustion from a fire will be limited in their penetration of the exit-stair enclosure. Smokeproof enclosures are required to be 2-hour construction. They must discharge directly to the outside, or directly through a 2-hour exit passageway to the outside. In a *sprinklered* building, mechanically pressurized and vented stairways can be substituted for smokeproof enclosures.

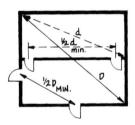

Code Requirements for Stairs

		Riser	
UBC requirements	Tread min.	Min.	Max.
General (including HC)	11″	4″	7″
Private Stairways (occ. <10)	9″		8″
Winding—Min. required T at 12″			
from narrow side*	6″ at any pt.		
Spiral—at 12″ from column*	7½″		
Only permitted in R-3 dwellings and R-1 private apartments*			
Rules of thumb for stairs:			
Interior	2R + T = 25		
Exterior	2R + T = 26		

*Requires handrails for ramps >1:15.

Code Requirements for Ramp Slopes

Type	Max. slope	Max. rise	Max. run
UBC, required for accessible access	1:12*	5'	
UBC others	1:8*	5'	
Assembly with fixed seats	1:5		
HC, new facilities	1:12*	2.5'	30'
HC, existing facilities	1:10*	6″	5'
	1:8*	3″	2'
HC, curb ramps	1:10	6″	5'

*Requires handrails for ramps >1:15.

1991 UNIFORM BUILDING CODE   33-A

TABLE NO. 33-A—MINIMUM EGRESS REQUIREMENTS[1]

USE[2]	MINIMUM OF TWO EXITS OTHER THAN ELEVATORS ARE REQUIRED WHERE NUMBER OF OCCUPANTS IS AT LEAST	OCCUPANT LOAD FACTOR[3] (sq. ft.)
1. Aircraft hangars (no repair)	10	500
2. Auction rooms	30	7
3. Assembly areas, concentrated use (without fixed seats) Auditoriums Churches and chapels Dance floors Lobby accessory to assembly occupancy Lodge rooms Reviewing stands Stadiums	50	7
Waiting Area	50	3
4. Assembly areas, less-concentrated use Conference rooms Dining rooms Drinking establishments Exhibit rooms Gymnasiums Lounges Stages	50	15
5. Bowling alley (assume no occupant load for bowling lanes)	50	4
6. Children's homes and homes for the aged	6	80
7. Classrooms	50	20
8. Congregate residences (accommodating 10 or less persons and having an area of 3,000 square feet or less) Congregate residences (accommodating more than 10 persons or having an area of more than 3,000 square feet)	10 10	300 200
9. Courtrooms	50	40
10. Dormitories	10	50
11. Dwellings	10	300
12. Exercising rooms	50	50

(Continued)

TABLE NO. 33-A—MINIMUM EGRESS REQUIREMENTS[1]—(Continued)

USE[2]	MINIMUM OF TWO EXITS OTHER THAN ELEVATORS ARE REQUIRED WHERE NUMBER OF OCCUPANTS IS AT LEAST	OCCUPANT LOAD FACTOR[3] (sq. ft.)
13. Garage, parking	30	200
14. Hospitals and sanitariums— Nursing homes		
Sleeping rooms	6	80
Treatment rooms	10	80
Health-care center	10	80
15. Hotels and apartments	10	200
16. Kitchen—commercial	30	200
17. Library reading room	50	50
18. Locker rooms	30	50
19. Malls (see Chapter 56)	—	—
20. Manufacturing areas	30	200
21. Mechanical equipment room	30	300
22. Nurseries for children (day care)	7	35
23. Offices	30	100
24. School shops and vocational rooms	50	50
25. Skating rinks	50	50 on the skating area; 15 on the deck
26. Storage and stock rooms	30	300
27. Stores—retail sales rooms	50	30
28. Swimming pools	50	50 for the pool area; 15 on the deck
29. Warehouses	30	500
30. All others	50	100

[1]Access to, and egress from, buildings for persons with disabilities shall be provided as specified in Chapter 31.

[2]For additional provisions on number of exits from Groups H and I Occupancies and from rooms containing fuel-fired equipment or cellulose nitrate, see Sections 3319, 3320 and 3321, respectively.

[3]This table shall not be used to determine working space requirements per person.

[4]Occupant load based on five persons for each alley, including 15 feet of runway.

1991 UNIFORM BUILDING CODE (24)   5-A

TABLE NO. 5-A—WALL AND OPENING PROTECTION OF OCCUPANCIES BASED ON LOCATION ON PROPERTY
TYPES II ONE-HOUR, II-N AND V CONSTRUCTION: For exterior wall and opening protection of Types II One-hour, II-N and V buildings, see table below and Sections 504, 709, 1903 and 2203.
This table does not apply to Types I, II-F.R., III and IV construction, see Sections 1803, 1903, 2003 and 2103.

GROUP	DESCRIPTION OF OCCUPANCY	FIRE RESISTANCE OF EXTERIOR WALLS	OPENINGS IN EXTERIOR WALLS[1]
A See also Section 602	1—Any assembly building or portion of a building with a legitimate stage and an occupant load of 1,000 or more	Not applicable (See Sections 602 and 603)	
	2—Any building or portion of a building having an assembly room with an occupant load of less than 1,000 and a legitimate stage	2 hours less than 10 feet, 1 hour less than 40 feet	Not permitted less than 5 feet Protected less than 10 feet
	2.1—Any building or portion of a building having an assembly room with an occupant load of 300 or more without a legitimate stage, including such buildings used for educational purposes and not classed as a Group E or Group B, Division 2 Occupancy		
	3—Any building or portion of a building having an assembly room with an occupant load of less than 300 without a stage, including such buildings used for educational purposes and not classed as a Group B, Division 2 Occupancy	2 hours less than 5 feet, 1 hour less than 20 feet	Not permitted less than 5 feet Protected less than 10 feet
	4—Stadiums, reviewing stands and amusement park structures not included within other Group A Occupancies	1 hour less than 10 feet	Protected less than 10 feet
B See also Section 702	1—Repair garages where work is limited to exchange of parts and maintenance requiring no open flame. welding, or use of Class I, II or III-A liquids		
	2—Drinking and dining establishments having an occupant load of less than 50, wholesale and retail stores, office buildings, printing plants, police and fire stations, factories and workshops using material not highly flammable or combustible, storage and sales rooms for combustible goods, paint stores without bulk handling Buildings or portions of buildings having rooms used for educational purposes, beyond the 12th grade, with less than 50 occupants in any room	1 hour less than 20 feet	Not permitted less than 5 feet Protected less than 10 feet

(Continued)

TABLE NO. 5-A—Continued
TYPES II ONE-HOUR, II-N AND V ONLY

GROUP	DESCRIPTION OF OCCUPANCY	FIRE RESISTANCE OF EXTERIOR WALLS	OPENINGS IN EXTERIOR WALLS
B (Cont.)	3¹—Aircraft hangars where no repair work is done except exchange of parts and maintenance requiring no open flame, welding, or the use of Class I or II liquids Open parking garages (For requirements, see Section 709) Helistops	1 hour less than 20 feet	Not permitted less than 5 feet Protected less than 20 feet
	4—Ice plants, power plants, pumping plants, cold storage and creameries Factories and workshops using noncombustible and nonexplosive material Storage and sales rooms of noncombustible and nonexplosive materials that are not packaged or crated in or supported by combustible material	1 hour less than 5 feet	Not permitted less than 5 feet
E See also Section 802	1—Any building used for educational purposes through the 12 grade by 50 or more persons for more than 12 hours per week or four hours in any one day	2 hours less than 5 feet, 1 hour less than 10 feet²	Not permitted less than 5 feet Protected less than 10 feet²
	2—Any building used for educational purposes through the 12th grade by less than 50 persons for more than 12 hours per week or four hours in any one day		
	3—Any building or portion thereof used for day-care purposes for more than six persons		
H	See Table No. 9-C		
I See also Section 1002	1.1—Nurseries for the full-time care of children under the age of six (each accommodating more than five persons) Hospitals, sanitariums, nursing homes with nonambulatory patients and similar buildings (each accommodating more than five persons)	2 hours less than 5 feet, 1 hour elsewhere	Not permitted less than 5 feet Protected less than 10 feet
	1.2—Health-care centers for ambulatory patients receiving outpatient medical care which may render the patient incapable of unassisted self-preservation (each tenant space accommodating more than five such patients)		

M³ See also Section 1102	2—Nursing homes for ambulatory patients, homes for children six years of age or over (each accommodating more than five persons)	1 hour	
	3—Mental hospitals, mental sanitariums, jails, prisons, reformatories and buildings where personal liberties of inmates are similarly restrained	2 hours less than 5 feet, 1 hour elsewhere	Not permitted less than 3 feet
	1—Private garages, carports, sheds and agricultural buildings	1 hour less than 3 feet (or may be protected on the exterior with materials approved for 1-hour fire-resistive construction)	Not permitted less than 3 feet
	2—Fences over 6 feet high, tanks and towers	Not regulated for fire resistance	
R See also Section 1202	1—Hotels and apartment houses Congregate residences (each accommodating more than 10 persons)	1 hour less than 5 feet	Not permitted less than 5 feet
	3—Dwellings and lodging houses, congregate residences (each accommodating 10 persons or less)	1 hour less than 3 feet	Not permitted less than 3 feet

[1]Openings shall be protected by a fire assembly having at least a three-fourths-hour fire-protection rating.

[2]Group E, Divisions 2 and 3 Occupancies having an occupant load of not more than 20 may have exterior wall and opening protection as required for Group R, Division 3 Occupancies.

[3]For agricultural buildings, see Appendix Chapter 11.

NOTES: (1) See Section 504 for types of walls affected and requirements covering percentage of openings permitted in exterior walls.

(2) For additional restrictions, see chapters under Occupancy and Types of Construction

(3) For walls facing yards and public ways, see Part IV.

TABLE NO. 5-B—REQUIRED SEPARATION IN BUILDINGS OF MIXED OCCUPANCY[1]
(In Hours)

	A-1	A-2	A-2.1	A-3	A-4	B-1	B-2	B-3[2]	B-4	E	H-1	H-2	H-3	H-4-5	H-6-7[3]	I	M[4]	R-1	R-3
A-1		N	N	N	N	4	3	3	3	N		4	4	4	4	3	1	1	1
A-2	N		N	N	N	3	1	1	1	N		4	4	4	4	3	1	1	1
A-2.1	N	N		N	N	3	1	1	1	N		4	4	4	4	3	1	1	1
A-3	N	N	N		N	3	N	1	1	N		4	4	4	3	2	1	1	1
A-4	N	N	N	N		3	1	1	1	N		4	4	4	4	3	1	1	1
B-1	4	3	3	3	3		1	1	1	3		2	1	1	1	4	1	3	1
B-2	3	1	1	N	1	1		1		1		2			1	2	1	1	1
B-3[4]	3	1	1	1	1	1	1					2				3			
B-4	3	1	1	1	1	1						2			1	4	N	1	1
E	N	N	N	N	N	3	1					4	4	4	3				
H-1	Not Permitted in Mixed Occupancies. See Chapter 9.																		
H-2	4	4	4	4	4	2	2	2	2	4			1	1	2	4		4	4
H-3	4	4	4	4	4	1				4		1		1		4		3	3
H-4-5	4	4	4	4	4	1				4		1	1		1	4		3	3
H-6-7[2]	4	4	4	3	4	1	1		1	3		2		1		4	3	4	4
M[3]	3	3	2	2	3	4	3	3	4			4	4	4	4			1	1
R-1	1	1	1	1	1	3	1	1	1			4	3	3	4		1		N
R-3	1	1	1	1	1	1	1	1	1			4	3	3	4	1	1	N	

[1] For detailed requirements and exceptions, see Section 503.
[2] Open parking garages are excluded, except as provided in Section 702 (a).
[3] For special provisions on highly toxic materials, see Fire Code.
[4] For agricultural buildings, see also Appendix Chapter 11.

Not Permitted in Mixed Occupancies. See Chapter 9.

TABLE NO. 5-C—BASIC ALLOWABLE FLOOR AREA FOR BUILDINGS ONE STORY IN HEIGHT[1]
(In Square Feet)

OCCUPANCY	I F.R.	II F.R.	II ONE-HOUR	II N	III ONE-HOUR	III N	IV H.T.	V ONE-HOUR	V N
A-1	Unlimited	29,900	Not Permitted	Not Permitted	Not Permitted	Not Permitted	Not Permitted	Not Permitted	Not Permitted
A-2-2.1[2]	Unlimited	29,900	13,500	Not Permitted	13,500	Not Permitted	13,500	10,500	Not Permitted
A-3-4[2]	Unlimited	29,900	13,500	9,100	13,500	9,100	13,500	10,500	6,000
B-1-2-3[3]	Unlimited	39,900	18,000	12,000	18,000	12,000	18,000	14,000	8,000
B-4	Unlimited	59,900	27,000	18,000	27,000	18,000	27,000	21,000	12,000
E-1-2-3	Unlimited	45,200	20,200	13,500	20,200	13,500	20,200	15,700	9,100
H-1	15,000	12,400	5,600	3,700	5,600	3,700	Not Permitted	4,400	2,500
H-2[4]	15,000	12,400	5,600	3,700	5,600	3,700	5,600	8,800	5,100
H-3-4-5[4]	Unlimited	24,800	11,200	7,500	11,200	7,500	11,200	8,800	5,100
H-6-7	Unlimited	39,900	18,000	12,000	18,000	12,000	18,000	14,000	8,000
I-1.1-1.2-2	Unlimited	15,100	6,800	Not Permitted[8]	6,800	Not Permitted	6,800	5,200	Not Permitted
I-3	Unlimited	15,100	Not Permitted[5]						
M[6]	See Chapter 11								
R-1	Unlimited	29,900	13,500	9,100[7]	13,500	9,100[7]	13,500	10,500	6,000[7]
R-3	Unlimited	Unlimited							

[1] For multistory buildings, see Section 505 (b).   [5] See Section 1002 (b).
[2] For limitations and exceptions, see Section 602.   [6] For agricultural buildings, see also Appendix Chapter 11.
[3] For open parking garages, see Section 709.   [7] For limitations and exceptions, see Section 1202 (b).
[4] See Section 903.   [8] In hospitals and nursing homes, see Section 1002 (a) for exception.

N—No requirements for fire resistance   F.R.—Fire resistive   H.T.—Heavy timber

TABLE NO. 5-D—MAXIMUM HEIGHT OF BUILDINGS

OCCUPANCY	I	II			III		IV	V	
	F.R.	F.R.	ONE-HOUR	N	ONE-HOUR	N	H.T.	ONE-HOUR	N
MAXIMUM HEIGHT IN FEET									
	Unlimited	160	65	55	65	55	65	50	40
MAXIMUM HEIGHT IN STORIES									
A-1	Unlimited	Not Permitted	Not Permitted	Not Permitted	Not Permitted	Not Permitted	Not Permitted	Not Permitted	Not Permitted
A-2-2.1	Unlimited	4	2	Not Permitted	2	Not Permitted	2	2	Not Permitted
A-3-4[1]	Unlimited	12	2	1	2	1	2	2	1
B-1-2-3[2]	Unlimited	12	4	2	4	2	4	3	2
B-4	Unlimited	12	4	2	4	2	4	3	2
E[3]	Unlimited	4	2	1	2	1	2	2	1
H-1[4]	1	1	1	1	1	1	Not Permitted	1	1
H-2[4]	Unlimited	2	1	1	2	1	Not Permitted	2	1
H-3-4-5[4]	Unlimited	5	2	1	3	2	Not Permitted	3	1
H-6-7	3	3	3	2	3	2	1	1	2
I-1.1[5]-1.2	Unlimited	3	1	Not Permitted	1	Not Permitted	1	1	Not Permitted
I-2	Unlimited	3	2	Not Permitted	2	Not Permitted	2	2	Not Permitted
I-3	Unlimited	2	Not Permitted[6]	Not Permitted[6]	Not Permitted[6]	Not Permitted[6]	Not Permitted[6]	Not Permitted[6]	Not Permitted[6]
M[7]	See Chapter 11								
R-1	Unlimited	12	4	2[8]	4	2[8]	4	3	2[8]
R-3	Unlimited	3	3	3	3	3	3	3	3

TABLE NO. 17-A—TYPES OF CONSTRUCTION—FIRE-RESISTIVE REQUIREMENTS (In Hours)
For details see chapters under Occupancy and Types of Construction and for exceptions see Section 1705.

BUILDING ELEMENT	TYPE I NONCOMBUSTIBLE Fire-resistive	TYPE II Fire-resistive	TYPE II 1-Hr.	TYPE II N	TYPE III 1-Hr.	TYPE III N	TYPE IV COMBUSTIBLE H.T.	TYPE V 1-Hr.	TYPE V N
1. Exterior Bearing Walls	4 Sec. 1803 (a)	4 1903 (a)			4 2003 (a)	4 2003 (a)	4 2103 (a)		
2. Interior Bearing Walls	3	2	1	N	1	N	1	1	N
3. Exterior Nonbearing Walls	4 Sec. 1803 (a)	4 1903 (a)	1 1903 (a)	N	4 2003 (a)	4 2003 (a)	4 2103 (a)	1 2103 (a)	N
4. Structural Frame[1]	3	2	1[2]	N	1	N	1 or H.T.	1	N
5. Partitions—Permanent	1[2]	1[2]	1	N	1	N	1 or H.T.	1	N
6. Shaft Enclosures[3]	2	2	1	—	1	—	1 or H.T.	1	—
7. Floors-Ceilings/Floors	2	2	1	N	1	N	H.T.	1	N
8. Roofs-Ceilings/Roofs	2 Sec. 1806	1 1906	1 1906	N	1	N	H.T.	1	N
9. Exterior Doors and Windows	Sec. 1803 (b)	1903 (b)	1903 (b)	1903 (b)	2003 (b)	2003 (b)	2103 (b)	2203	2203
10. Stairway Construction	Sec. 1805	1905	1905	1905	2004	2004	2104	2204	2204

N—No general requirements for fire resistance.   H.T.—Heavy Timber.

[1] Structural frame elements in an exterior wall that is located where openings are not permitted or where protection of openings is required, shall be protected against external fire exposure as required for exterior bearing walls or the structural frame, whichever is greater.

[2] Fire-retardant-treated wood (see Section 407) may be used in the assembly, provided fire-resistance requirements are maintained. See Sections 1801 and 1901, respectively.

[3] For special provisions, see Sections 1706, 706 and 906.

FIRE PROTECTION OF EXTERIOR WALLS

OCC. CLASS.	CONSTRUCTION TYPES			
	I ①⑤	II FR ①④⑤⑧⑨	III ①⑧⑨	IV ①⑧
A	④⑥	⑥	④⑤⑥	④⑤⑥
B 1	②④⑥	③⑥	②④⑤⑥	②④⑤⑥
2	②④⑥	③⑥	②④⑤⑥	②④⑤⑥
3	②④⑥	③⑥	②④⑤⑥	②④⑤⑥
4	②④⑦	③⑦	②④⑤⑦	②④⑤⑦
E	④⑥	⑥	④⑤⑥	④⑤⑥
I	⑥	⑥	⑥	⑥
M	④⑦	⑦	④⑤⑦	④⑤⑦
R 1	②④⑦	③⑦	②④⑤⑦	②④⑤⑦
2	④⑦	⑦	④⑤⑦	④⑤⑦

NOTES:

① EXTERIOR NON BEARING WALLS MAY BE NON RATED, NON-COMB. CONST. WHEN DISTANCE TO P.L. OR STREET WIDTH IS 40' OR MORE.

② WHERE OPENINGS ARE PERMITTED, A 2 HR. WALL IS REQUIRED.

③ AT BEARING WALLS, WHERE OPENINGS PERMITTED, A 2 HR. WALL IS REQ'D.

④ AT NON-BEARING WALLS, WHERE UNPROTECTED OPENINGS PERMITTED, A 1 HR. WALL IS REQUIRED.

⑤ AT NON-BEARING WALLS, WHERE PROTECTED OPENING ARE REQUIRED, A 2 HR. WALL IS REQUIRED.

⑥ WHERE EXTERIOR WALL IS LESS THAN 5' FROM P.L., NO OPENING ALLOWED.

⑦ WHERE EXTERIOR WALL IS LESS THAN 3' FROM P.L., NO OPENING ALLOWED.

⑧ WHERE EXTERIOR WALL IS LESS THAN 20' FROM P.L., ¾ HR. OPENING REQ'D.

⑨ WHERE TABLE 5A REQUIRES PROTECTED OPENINGS, PROVIDE ¾ HR.

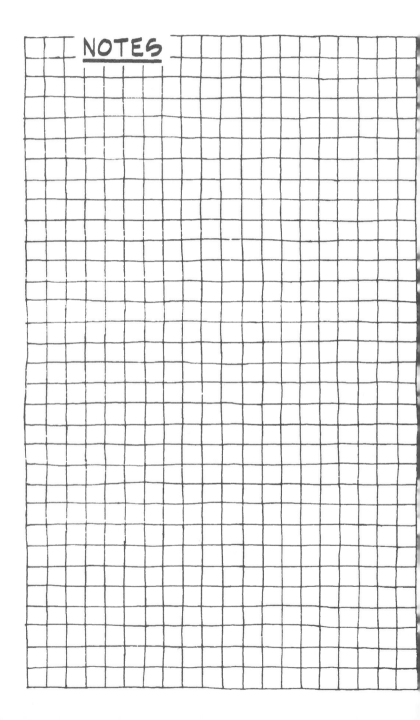
NOTES

___ 4. *Accessibility (ADA requirements)*   (20)

    ___ *a.* *General:* This section concerns accessibility for the disabled as required by *ADA* (Title 3, the national civil rights law) in nongovernment buildings (Title 2 applies to government buildings). Local or state laws may (in part) be more restrictive regarding alterations and new buildings. For each item under consideration, *the more restrictive law applies.*

    ___ *b.* *ADA* applies to:

        ___ (1) *Places of public accommodation* (excluding private homes, and clubs, as well as churches). Often buildings will have space for both the general public and space for employees only.

        ___ (2) *Commercial facilities* (employees only) requirements are less restrictive requiring only an accessible entry, exit, and route through each type of facility function. Only when a disabled employee is hired (under Title 1) do more restrictive standards apply.

    ___ *c.* *Existing buildings* are to comply by removing "architectural barriers," as much as possible, when this is "readily achievable" (not requiring undue expense, hardship, or loss of space). This effort, in theory, is to be ever on-going until all barriers are removed. When barriers can't be readily removed, "equivalent facilitation" is allowed. Priorities of removal are:

        ___ (1) Entry to places of public accommodation

        ___ (2) Access to areas where goods and services are made available to the public

        ___ (3) Access to restroom facilities

        ___ (4) Removal of all other barriers

    ___ *d.* *Alterations* to existing buildings require a higher standard. To the maximum extent possible, the altered portions are to be made accessible. If the altered area is a "primary function" of the building, then an accessible "path of travel" must be provided from the entry to the area (including public restrooms, telephones, and drinking fountains) with exemption only possible when cost of the path exceeds 20% of the cost to alter the primary function.

    ___ *e.* *New buildings or facilities* must totally comply, with only exceptions being situations of "structural impracticability."

    ___ *f.* See *Index,* p. 467, for a complete list of *ADA* requirements.

ACCESSIBLE ROUTE PER A.D.A.
(INTERIOR AND EXTERIOR)

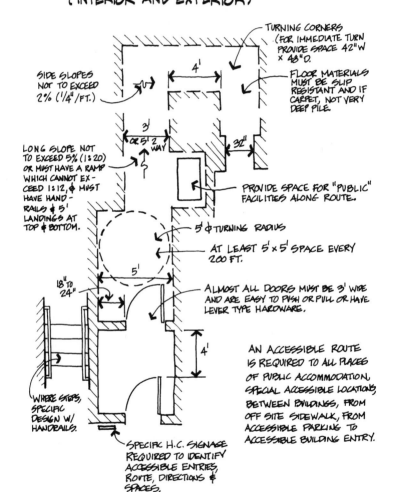

TURNING CORNERS
(FOR IMMEDIATE TURN
PROVIDE SPACE 42"W
X 48"D.

FLOOR MATERIALS
MUST BE SLIP
RESISTANT AND IF
CARPET, NOT VERY
DEEP PILE.

SIDE SLOPES
NOT TO EXCEED
2% (¼"/FT.)

4'

3'
OR 5'2
WAY

32"

LONG SLOPE NOT
TO EXCEED 5% (1:20)
OR MUST HAVE A RAMP
WHICH CANNOT EX-
CEED 1:12, & MUST
HAVE HAND-
RAILS & 5'
LANDINGS AT
TOP & BOTTOM.

PROVIDE SPACE FOR "PUBLIC"
FACILITIES ALONG ROUTE.

5' ø TURNING RADIUS

AT LEAST 5' x 5' SPACE EVERY
200 FT.

18" TO
24"

5'

ALMOST ALL DOORS MUST BE 3' WIDE
AND ARE EASY TO PUSH OR PULL OR HAVE
LEVER TYPE HARDWARE.

4'

AN ACCESSIBLE ROUTE
IS REQUIRED TO ALL PLACES
OF PUBLIC ACCOMMODATION,
SPECIAL ACCESSIBLE LOCATIONS,
BETWEEN BUILDINGS, FROM
OFF SITE SIDEWALK, FROM
ACCESSIBLE PARKING TO
ACCESSIBLE BUILDING ENTRY.

WHERE STEPS,
SPECIFIC
DESIGN W/
HANDRAILS.

SPECIFIC H.C. SIGNAGE
REQUIRED TO IDENTIFY
ACCESSIBLE ENTRIES,
ROUTE, DIRECTIONS &
SPACES.

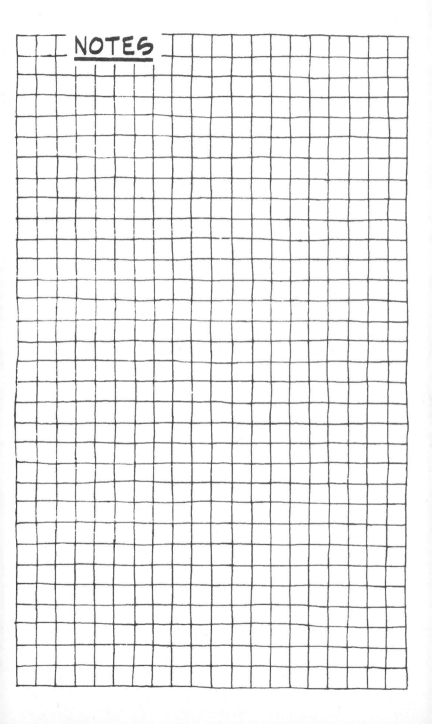

NOTES

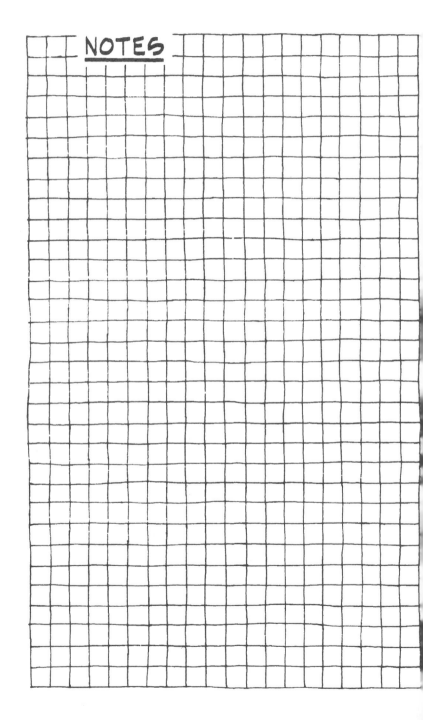

NOTES

__ I. STRUCTURAL SYSTEMS

(1) (2) (7) (10) (19) (24) (38)

Deciding which structural system to use is one of the most prominent choices the architect will have to make. Factors affecting the choice:

- ___ 1. Construction type by code
- ___ 2. Long vs. short spans
- ___ 3. Live loads
- ___ 4. Low vs. high rise
- ___ 5. Lateral and uplift
- ___ 6. Rules of thumb for estimating structural sizes

___ 1. Construction Type by Code

    ___ a. *Type I and Type II FR Construction*—require noncombustible materials (concrete, masonry, and steel) and substantial fire-resistive ratings (2, 3, and 4 hours). Both these construction types can be used to build large, tall buildings. The difference is that Type I has no height or area limits for most occupancies. Type I construction requires 3- and 4-hour fire resistance for structural members. Type II has a maximum height limit of 160′ as well as floor area and maximum story limitations as a function of occupancy. Type II requires 3- and 2-hour ratings and thus is less expensive. Typical systems are:

Concrete solid slabs	10′–25′ spans
Concrete slabs win drop panels	20′–35′
Concrete 2-way slab on beam	20′–35′
Concrete waffle slabs	30′–40′
Concrete joists	25′–45′
Concrete beams	15′–40′
Concrete girders	20′–60′
Concrete tees	20′–120′
Concrete arches	60′–150′
Concrete thin shell roofs	50′–70′
Steel decking	5′–15′
Steel beams	15′–60′
Steel plate girders	40′–100′

    ___ b. *Type II 1-Hour and NR Construction*—uses structural members of noncombustible construction materials for exterior walls, interior bearing walls, columns, floors, and roof. This is usually steel framing combined with concrete or masonry walls. Typical systems are:

Steel decking	5′–15′ spans
Steel beams	15′–60′

Steel joists	15'–60'
Steel plate girders	40'–100'
Steel trusses	40'–80'

___ *c.   Type III 1-Hour and NR Construction*—has exterior walls of noncombustible construction material, usually masonry or concrete; interior columns, beams, floors, and roofs can be constructed of any material, including wood. Typical systems are:

Wood joists	10'–25' spans
Wood beams	15'–30'
Wood girders	20'–35'
Glu-lam beams	15'–120'
Wood trusses	30'–100'

___ *d.   Type IV Heavy Timber Construction*—achieves its fire resistance from the large size of the timber members used to frame it (2″ actual +). Exterior walls must be noncombustible. Typical systems are:

Wood planks, T and G, 3″	2'–6' spans
Wood beams, 6 × 10, min.	15'–30'
Wood girders, 6 × 10, min.	20'–35'
Wood trusses supporting floors 8″ oc. min. and roofs 6″ × 8″	30'–100'
Wood arches supporting floors 8' oc. min. and roofs 6″ × 8″ min.	30'–120'
Wood glu-lam beams	15'–120'

___ *e.   Type V 1-Hour and N Construction*—is essentially light wood-frame construction. Typical systems are:

Plywood	2'–4' spans
Wood planks	2'–6'
Wood joists	10'–25'
Wood beams	15'–30'
Wood girders	20'–35'
Glu-lam beams	15'–150'
Wood trusses	30'–100'

Note: When tentative structural system selected, see Part 13 for details and **costs.**

___ 2. Long vs. Short Spans

Select shortest span for required functional use of the space. *Short spans* (10, 20, or 30') suggest beams, girders, and slabs in bending. This method encloses the space economically with a minimum of structural depth.

Long spans (50 to 100′ and beyond) suggest the use of shape to aid the structural material. Arches, shells, domes, space frames trusses, and similar structures use their shape to help the structural material span the long distance.

Extra-long spans (such as stadiums) involve roofs spanning great distances. The economics suggest tension and inflatable membrane structures.

___ 3. Loads

   ___ *a.* *Live loads* are determined by occupancy use. See p. 84.

   ___ *b.* *Snow loads* should be considered when required (especially when loads are 20/SF or more). See App. B, item T. Take into account:

      ___ (1) Heavier loads at drift locations

      ___ (2) Pitch of roof

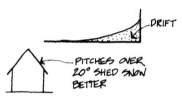

___ 4. Low vs. High Rise

Low-rise structural design is dominated by the collection of dead and live loads through slabs, beams, and girders onto the walls and columns where the load is taken down to the foundation and onto the earth below.

High-Rise design is dominated by the need to withstand the lateral loading of wind and earthquake on the building. This domination of lateral loading forces a building to become more symmetrical as it gets taller. There is substantial additional cost involved in a high-rise solution because of this increased need to resist lateral loads.

___ 5. Lateral and Uplift: Beyond vertical loads, consideration should always be given to horizontal and uplift forces. For these, the UBC factors in the *importance* of the occupancies ("Essential occupancy with higher safety factor") such as hospitals, police and fire stations, emergency structures, hazardous facilities, etc.

(24)   **TABLE NO. 23-A—UNIFORM AND CONCENTRATED LOADS**

USE OR OCCUPANCY		UNIFORM LOAD[1]	CONCENTRATED LOAD
Category	Description		
1. Access floor systems	Office use	50	2,000[2]
	Computer use	100	2,000[2]
2. Armories		150	0
3. Assembly areas[3] and auditoriums and balconies therewith	Fixed seating areas	50	0
	Movable seating and other areas	100	0
	Stage areas and enclosed platforms	125	0
4. Cornices, marquees and residential balconies		60	0
5. Exit facilities[4]		100	0[5]
6. Garages	General storage and/or repair	100	[6]
	Private or pleasure-type motor vehicle storage	50	[6]
7. Hospitals	Wards and rooms	40	1,000[2]
8. Libraries	Reading rooms	60	1,000[2]
	Stack rooms	125	1,500[2]
9. Manufacturing	Light	75	2,000[2]
	Heavy	125	3,000[2]
10. Offices		50	2,000[2]
11. Printing plants	Press rooms	150	2,500[2]
	Composing and linotype rooms	100	2,000[2]
12. Residential[7]		40	0[5]
13. Restrooms[8]			
14. Reviewing stands, grandstands, bleachers, and folding and telescoping seating		100	0
15. Roof decks	Same as area served or for the type of occupancy accommodated		
16. Schools	Classrooms	40	1,000[2]
17. Sidewalks and driveways	Public access	250	[6]
18. Storage	Light	125	
	Heavy	250	
19. Stores	Retail	75	2,000[2]
	Wholesale	100	3,000[2]

(Continued)

___ *a.* *Wind forces* are based on known *wind speeds.* Minimum is usually 70 mph (13 lbs/SF) up to 130 mph (44 lbs/SF) for hurricanes (with the range between being 4 lbs to 7 lbs/SF added for each added 10 mph). See App. B, item S. Added to this are *factors for height* of the building. Also, see p. 240 for shingles.

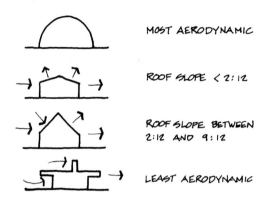

MOST AERODYNAMIC

ROOF SLOPE < 2:12

ROOF SLOPE BETWEEN 2:12 AND 9:12

LEAST AERODYNAMIC

___ *b.* *Seismic forces* are caused by ground waves due to earthquake shock, causing vertical and horizontal movement.

The weight of the building usually absorbs the vertical element, leaving the horizontal force transmitted through the building foundations to the structure, above. The weight of the building resists side movement. Present engineering procedure is to design the building for a side force, like wind.

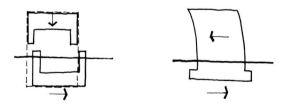

The total seismic force the building must withstand is a percent of its total weight. This force is usually 10 to 50% of the total weight of the building. In determining the required force, the UBC considers:

___ (1) *Risk:* based on location. Zones 4 and 3 most hazardous. Zones 0 and 1 are the least hazardous. See App. B, item E.

___ (2) Importance of *occupancy:* See p. 83.

___ (3) *Soils* and site geology: Rock-like materials best. Soft clays are poor.

___ (4) *Resistance* of the structure:

   ___ (*a*) The least weight the better

   ___ (*b*) The more flexible the better, or

   ___ (*c*) The stiffer the better

_____ *c.* Lateral design and overall building shape

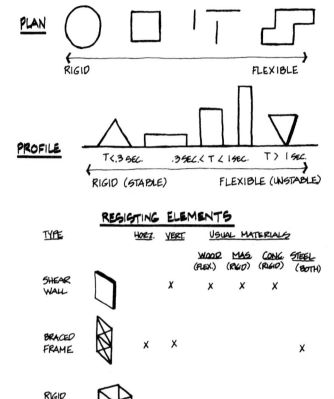

PLAN

RIGID ←————————————————→ FLEXIBLE

PROFILE

T < .3 SEC.   .3 SEC. < T < 1 SEC.   T > 1 SEC.

RIGID (STABLE) ←————————————→ FLEXIBLE (UNSTABLE)

RESISTING ELEMENTS

TYPE		HORZ.	VERT.	USUAL MATERIALS			
				WOOD (FLEX.)	MAS. (RIGID)	CONC. (RIGID)	STEEL (BOTH)
SHEAR WALL			X	X	X	X	
BRACED FRAME		X	X				X
RIGID FRAME *		X	X				X
DIAPHRAM		X		X		X	X

*ALSO TERMED "MOMENT RESISTING FRAME" IS ACTUALLY VERY FLEXIBLE W/ POSSIBLE SWAY AND NON-STRUCTURAL DAMAGE.

DESIGNS CAN MIX VARIOUS ELEMENTS. THE AMOUNT NEEDED IS BASED ON THE AMOUNT OF FORCE TO BE RESISTED. THESE ELEMENTS MUST BE FACED BOTH WAYS, IDEALLY IN EQUAL AMOUNTS OR THE BUILDING WILL BE SUBJECT TO TORSION.

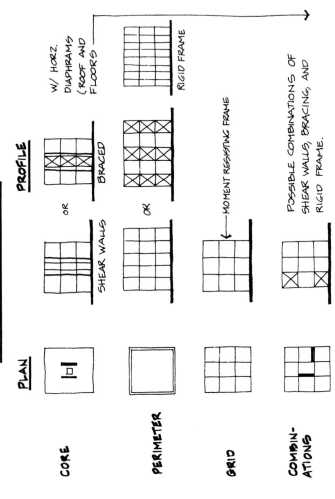

LATERAL DESIGN STRATEGIES

PLAN

PROFILE

CORE

SHEAR WALLS   or   BRACED

PERIMETER

or

GRID

← MOMENT RESISTING FRAME

COMBIN-
ATIONS

POSSIBLE COMBINATIONS OF
SHEAR WALLS, BRACING, AND
RIGID FRAME.

W/ HORZ.
DIAPHRAMS
(ROOF AND
FLOORS

RIGID FRAME

DESIGN FOR IRREGULARITIES

UNSYMMETRICAL SHAPE — ADD SEISMIC JOINTS — OR — OR — STIFFEN

OPENINGS IN FLOORS/ROOF — ADD SEISMIC JOINTS

"SOFT" STORIES — INFILL — OR — STIFFEN

SHEAR WALLS ONE DIRECTION — ADD WALLS — OR — STIFFEN FRAME

DIFFERENT MASSES — ADD SEISMIC JOINTS

89

___ *d.* Nonstructural seismic considerations
In seismic zones 3 and 4, the following things should be considered:

___ (1) Overhead utility lines, antennae, poles, and large signs pose a hazard.

___ (2) Secure and brace roof-mounted and floor-mounted equipment for lateral load and up-lift. This would include AC equip., hot water heaters, and electrical service sections.

___ (3) Brace structure supported piping and ducts for side sway. Avoid long, straight runs.

___ (4) Brace structure supported suspended ceilings for side sway. Allow for movement where wall occurs.

___ (5) Sleeve piping through foundation walls.

___ (6) Locate building exits to avoid falling elements such as power poles or signs.

___ (7) Anchor veneers to allow for movement.

___ (8) Partitions should be constructed to assume the added seismic lateral load caused by the furniture or equipment.

___ (9) Seismic joints should include partition construction details to provide a continuous separation through the roof, floor, walls, and ceiling.

___ (10) Interior partitions and fire-rated walls that are floor-to-floor need to be designed for lateral movement. Also, consider corners, tee-junctions of walls, and junctions of walls and columns.

___ (11) Brace-suspended light fixtures. Consider plastic rather than glass lenses.

___ (12) Battery-powered emergency lighting needs positive attachment.

___ (13) Use tempered, laminated, or plastic at large glass areas that could cause damage. Do resilient mountings.

___ (14) Laterally secure tall furniture and shelving.

___ 6. *Structural Components (A Primer):* Many of today's engineering courses have become so cluttered with theory and mathematics that even graduate engineers sometimes lose sight of the simple basic principles. Use this section to remind you of basic structural principles.

___ *a.* Types of forces
    ___ (1) Tension
    ___ (2) Compression
    ___ (3) Bending

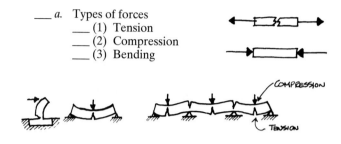

___ (4) Shear

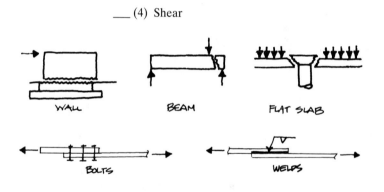

___ (5) Torsion

___ (6) Buckling

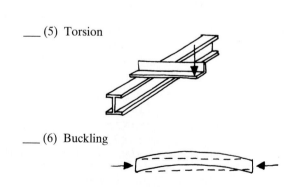

___ *b.* Beams

    ___ (1) Simple beams have tension at the bottom and compression at the top.

    ___ (2) If the beam is made deeper, "d" (the moment arm) is increased and the compressive and tensile forces decreased. The deeper the beam, the stronger.

    ___ (3) Within limits, small holes can often be cut through the beams at center, middepth, without harm. But notches or holes at top or bottom will reduce strength.

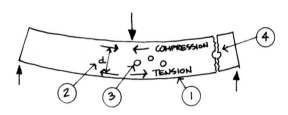

    ___ (4) Since shear is usually greatest close to the supports, judgment must be used regarding cutting holes or notches in the web close to the support. Also, see p. 217.

    ___ (5) Continuous beams can often carry more load than simple span beams.

    ___ (6) A point to watch for in cantilever and continuous beams is possible uplift at a rear support.

    ___ (7) Beams may be fixed or restrained. The bending stress at midspan is less (so beam depth is less) but connections become more involved.

___ *c.* Slabs

    ___ (1) Are nothing more than wide, flat beams.

    ___ (2) Generally, by far, the greatest stress in flat slabs occurs where the columns try to punch through the slab. Slab openings next to columns can trigger failures!

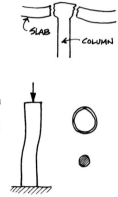

___ *d.* Columns Because of the tendency for columns to buckle, fatter ones carry more load than thinner ones (with same cross-sectional area and length).

___ *e.* Walls

    ___ (1) Bearing walls act as wide, flat columns, carrying their loads in compression.

    ___ (2) Walls must be tied to the floor and roof.

    ___ (3) Bond beams tie the wall together, so more of it will act to resist any specific load.

    ___ (4) Shear walls fail by:

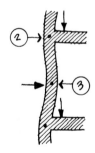

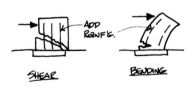

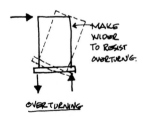

___ *f.* Trusses

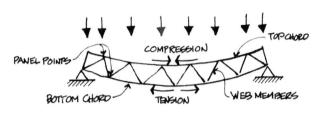

___ (1) Are usually lighter and more efficient than solid beams carrying the same load, but take more vertical space.

___ (2) Are made by a series of triangles supporting load at panel points. Patterns other than triangles can change shape easily and must be avoided or specially treated.

___ (3) Connections of web and chords become very important. The center of gravity of intersecting web members should meet at or very close to the center of gravity of the chord.

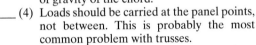

___ (4) Loads should be carried at the panel points, not between. This is probably the most common problem with trusses.

___ (5) Field shifting or removal of web members to allow passage of ducts or other items may be dangerous.

___ (6) If trusses cantilever over a support or are continuous over a support, the bottom chords must often be

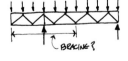

braced against sideways buckling where they are in compression.

___ *g.* Arches (or sloped roofs) Need resistance to lateral thrust by either of the following:

    ___ (1) Strengthening or thickening the supports

    ___ (2) Tension members added

___ *h.* Connections

    ___ (1) Connections are usually the most critical of any structure. Failures statistically are much more apt to occur at a connection than anywhere else. When connections fail, they often fail suddenly, not giving the warnings of deflection and cracking inherent in, say, a bending failure of a beam. Thus a connection failure is apt to be more hazardous to life and limb than are some other types of failures.

    ___ (2) Connections are often more sensitive to construction tolerances or errors than are the structural members themselves.

    ___ (3) In cases where a strong material (such as steel or prestressed concrete), must be connected to a weaker material (such as CMU), the stronger material may carry a load that is not easily carried by the weaker. The connection must spread the load over a large area of the weaker material and must also not cause undue bending.

    ___ (4) Don't pare connection designs to the bone! Estimate the maximum amount of probable field error and design the connection for it. If possible, provide a second line of defense. Try to make connections as fool-proof as possible. Allow as much room as possible for field tolerances.

___ (5) Where possible, locate construction joints at a point of low beam shear and locate connections where loads transmitted through the connection are a minimum.

___ (6) Consider the prying, levering, or twisting action in connections. Consider the effects of connection eccentricities on the members themselves.

___ (7) Consider the effects of shrinkage or other lateral movement.

___ (8) Use care in stacking beams and girders on top of columns, particularly deep beams and girders that want to overturn. Provide bracing.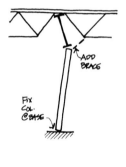

___ (9) Consider using shop over field connections, when possible, because they are done under more favorable conditions.

___ 7. *Rules of Thumb for Estimating Structural Sizes (Span-to-Depth Ratios):* Most rules of thumb for structural estimating are based on *span-to-depth ratios*. First select likely spans from structural systems (page 81). Then, the span in feet or inches is divided by the ratio to get the depth in either feet or inches.

Example: If ratio is 8 and span is 8 ft, then depth is 1 ft.

Ratios for Typical Elements:

Beams and joists of all kinds range from 10 to 24. Lower ratios for heavy or concentrated loads. The ratio of *20* is a good all-purpose average for steel, wood, and concrete.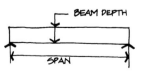

Cantilevered beams: In general, the optimal length of a cantilever is *one-third* the supported span.

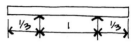

Columns: The ratios of unbraced length to least thickness of most column types range from 10 to 30, with *20* being a good average.

Slabs: Reinforced concrete slabs of various types have ratios ranging from 20 to 35, with *24* being a good average.

SEE BEAM, ABOVE.

Trusses of various types and materials have ratios ranging from 4 to 12. The lower ratio is appropriate for trusses carrying heavy floor loads or concentrated loads. The ratio *8* is a good average for estimating roof trusses.

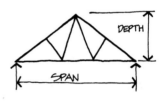

For more specific ratios based on materials and specific types of structural elements, see pp. 163, 183, 203, and 223.

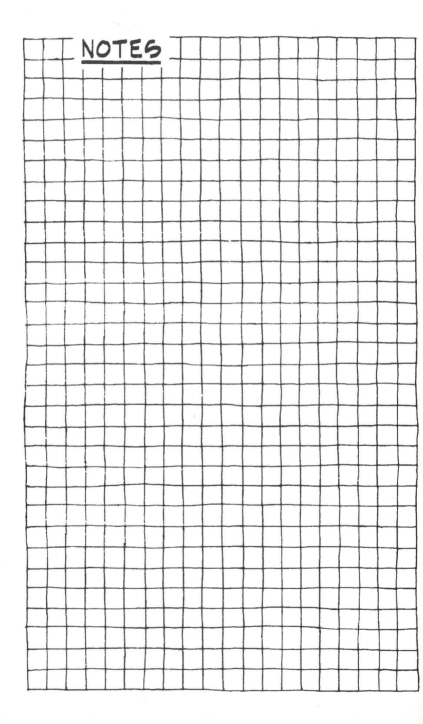

NOTES

___ J. ENERGY   "Passive" and "Active" approaches to conservation: (30) (44)

___ 1. Building Type

All buildings produce internal heat. All buildings are affected by external loads (heating or cooling) based on the climate and internal loads (heat from equipment, lights, people, etc.). Large commercial buildings tend to be internally dominated. Residences or small commercial buildings tend to be the exact opposite.

___ 2. Human Comfort

The comfort zone may be roughly defined as follows: Most people in the temperate zone, sitting indoors in the shade in light clothing, will feel tolerably comfortable at temperatures ranging from *70 to 80°F* as long as the relative humidity lies between *20 and 50%*. As humidity increases, they will begin to become uncomfortable at lower and lower temperatures until the relative humidity reaches *75 to 80%*, when discomfort at any temperature sets in. But if they are sitting in a draft, the range of tolerable temperature shifts upward, so that temperatures of *85°F* may be quite comfortable in the *20 to 50%* relative humidity range, if local air is moving at *200 ft/min.* Indoor air moving more slowly than *50 ft/min* is generally unnoticed, while flows of *50 to 100 ft/min* are pleasant and hardly noticed. Breezes from *100 to 200 ft/min* are pleasant but one is constantly aware of them, while those from *200 to 300 ft/min* are first slightly unpleasant, then annoying and drafty. See psychrometric chart for "passive" strategies on p. 107.

___ 3. Climate

In response to a climate, if a building is to be designed for "passive" (natural) strategies, it is important to determine the demands of the climate. Is the climate severe (for either heating or cooling, as well as humidity) or temperate? Which predominates, heating or cooling? Is the climate wet or dry? Once the climatic demands are determined, what climatic elements are available to offer comfort relief? Is sun available for winter heating? Are breezes available for summer cooling?

In determining passive and energy conservation strategies for a building in an unfamiliar climate consult App. B to make the following determinations:

___ *a.* If two-thirds of the heating degree days exceed the cooling degree days, *winter heating* will need to be the predominant strategy or a major consideration.

___ *b.* If cooling degree days are greater than two-thirds of the heating degree days, *summer cooling* should be the major strategy or consideration.

___ *c.* If two-thirds of the heating degree days roughly equals the cooling degree days, both winter heating and summer cooling will be needed strategies though these will be likely *temperate* climates.

___ *d.* When heating degree days exceed 6000, a *severely cold climate* will have to be designed for.

___ *e.* When cooling degree days exceed 2000, a *severely hot climate* will have to be designed for.

___ *f.* When annual average evening relative humidity exceeds 80% and rainfall averages 40″/yr, or more, an *extremely humid climate* will have to be designed for.

___ *g.* When annual average evening relative humidity is less than 65% and rainfall averages 15″/yr, or less, an *extremely dry climate* will have to be designed for.

___ *h.* When annual winter sunshine exceeds 50%, *passive winter heating* may be a good strategy, if needed. Summer shading will be an important factor in a hot climate.

___ *i.* Most locations in the United States have annual average daily wind exceeding 5 mph, so *natural ventilation* as a means of cooling may be a good strategy, if needed. But this may also be a problem if in a cold climate.

___ *j.* *Microclimates* at specific sites can vary from the overall climate due to:

  ___ (1) Large bodies of water (10°F milder).

  ___ (2) Built-up area (5°F warmer).

  ___ (3) Elevation (5°F cooler for each 1000 ft rise).

  ___ (4) Land forms: Tops of hills receive wind. Valleys get cool in evenings. Breezes rise up slopes in day and descend in evenings: South slopes receive most year-around sun; north, the least, with east and west slopes the most summer morning and afternoon sun.

___ 4. Checklist for Passive Building Design (Strategies for Energy Conservation)

Note: Many of the following items conflict, so it is impossible to choose all.

_X_   Cold climate or winter
  _X_   Hot climate or summer

Windbreaks

___   ___ (1) Use neighboring land forms, structures, or vegetation for winter wind protection.

___   ___ (2) Shape and orient building shell to minimize wind turbulence.

Plants and water

___   ___ (3) Use ground cover and planting for site cooling.

___   ___ (4) Maximize on-site evaporative cooling; ocean or water zones, such as fountains, modify climate 10°F.

___   ___ (5) Use planting next to building skin.

___   ___ (6) Use roof spray or roof ponds for evaporative cooling.

Indoor/outdoor rooms

___   ___   ___ (7) Provide outdoor semiprotected areas for year-round climate moderation.

___   ___ (8) Provide solar-oriented interior zone for maximizing heat.

___   ___   ___ (9) Plan specific rooms or functions to coincide with solar orientation (i.e., storage on "bad" orient such as west, living on "good" such as south).

Earth sheltering

___   ___   ___ (10) Recess structure below grade or raise existing grade for earth-sheltering effort.

___   ___   ___ (11) Use slab-on-grade construction for ground temperature heat exchange. See p. 236 for perimeter insulation.

___   ___   ___ (12) Use sod roofs (12″ of earth will give about a 9-hour time lag).

___   ___ (13) Use high-capacitance materials at interiors to store "coolth." Works best with night ventilation.

Solar walls and windows

___   ___ (14) Maximize reflectivity of ground and building surfaces outside windows facing winter sun.

Cold   Hot

___   ___ (15) Shape and orient building shell to maximize exposure to winter sun. Glass needs to face to within 15 degrees of facing south.

___   ___ (16) Use high-capacitance materials to store solar heat gain. Best results are by distributing "mass" locations throughout interior. On average, provide 1 to 1¼ CF of concrete or masonry per each SF of south-facing glass. For an equivalent effect, 4 times more mass is needed when not exposed to sun.

___ ___ (17) This same "mass effect" (see 16) can be used in reverse in hot, dry (clear sky) climates. "Flush" building during cool night to precool for next day.

___ ___ ___ (18) Use solar wall and/or roof collectors on south orient surfaces (also hot-water heating). Optimum tilt angle for roof solar collectors is equal to latitude of site (+/– 15°). See page 439.

___   ___ (19) Maximize south-facing glazing (with overhangs as needed). On average, south-facing glass should be 10 to 25% of floor area. For north latitude/cold climates this can go up to 50%. For south latitude/hot climates this strategy may not be appropriate.

___   ___ (20) Provide reflective panels outside of glazing to increase winter irradiation.

___   ___ (21) Use skylights for winter solar gain and natural illumination. See p. 393.

Thermal envelope

___ ___ ___ (22) Minimize the outside wall and roof areas (ratio of exterior surface to enclosed volume). Best ratios:
2-story dome—12% 2-story cylinder—14%
2-story square—15% 3-story square—16%
1-story square—17%

___ ___ ___ (23) Use attic space as buffer zone between interior and outside climate. Vent above ceiling insulation. See p. 231 & 236.

Cold   Hot

___   ___ (24) Use basement or crawl space as buffer zone between interior and grounds. See p. 236 for insulation.

___   ___   ___ (25) Provide air shafts for natural or mechanically assisted house-heat recovery. This can be recirculated warm at high ceilings or recovered heat from chimneys.

___   ___ (26) Centralize heat sources within building interior. (Fireplaces, furnaces, hot water heater, cooking, laundry, etc.) Lower level for these most desirable.

___   ___ (27) Put heat sources (HW, laundry, etc.) outside building.

___   ___   ___ (28) Use vestibule or exterior "wind shield" at entryways. Orient away from undesirable winds.

___   ___   ___ (29) Locate low-use spaces, storage, utility, and garage areas to provide buffers. Locate at "bad" orientations (i.e., north side of cold climate or west side of hot climate).

___   ___   ___ (30) Subdivide interior to create separate heating and cooling zones. One example is separate living and sleeping zones.

___   ___   ___ (31) Select insulating materials for resistance to heat flow through building envelope. For minimum insulation recommendations, see p. 236 and/or guidelines by *ASHRAE* 90A-80.

___   ___   ___ (32) Apply vapor barriers to control moisture migration. See p. 233.

___   ___ (33) Use of radiant barriers. See p. 235.

___   ___   ___ (34) Develop construction details to minimize air infiltration and exfiltration. See p. 251.

___   ___   ___ (35) Provide insulating controls at glazing. See p. 273.

___   ___   ___ (36) Minimize window and door openings (usually N, E, and W).

___   ___   ___ (37) Detail window and door construction to prevent undesired air infiltration. See p. 257 for doors and 261 for windows.

Cold Hot

___ ___ ___ (38) Provide ventilation openings for air flow to and from specific spaces and appliances. See p. 302 for fireplaces.

Sun shading

___ ___ (39) Minimize reflectivity of ground and building faces outside windows facing summer sun.

___ ___ (40) Use neighboring land forms, structures, or vegetation for summer shading.

___ ___ (41) Shape and orient building shell to minimize solar exposure. Best rectangular proportions are 1 (east and west) to between 1.5 and 2 (north and south).

___ ___ (42) Provide shading for walls exposed to summer sun.

___ ___ (43) Use heat reflective materials on solar oriented surfaces. White or light colors, best.

___ ___ (44) Provide shading for glazing exposed to sun. See p. 309.

Natural ventilation

___ ___ (45) Use neighboring land forms, structures, or vegetation to increase exposure to breezes.

___ ___ (46) Shape and orient building shell to maximize exposure to breezes. Long side should face prevailing breeze within 20 to 30 degrees.

___ ___ (47) Use "open plan" interior to promote air flow.

___ ___ (48) Provide vertical air shafts to promote interior air flow.

___ ___ (49) Use double roof and wall construction for ventilation within the building shell.

___ ___ (50) Orient door and window openings to facilitate natural ventilation from prevailing breezes. For best results:
Windows on opposite sides of rooms.
Inlets and outlets of equal size giving maximum air change.
A smaller inlet increases air speed.

Cold Hot

___   ___ (51) Use wing walls, overhangs, and louvers to direct summer wind flow into
interior.

___   ___ (52) Use louvered wall for maximum ventilation control.

___ (53) Use roof monitors for "stack effect
ventilation."

___ 5. Checklist for Active Building Design (Strategies for Energy
Conservation)

___ *a.* Whenever possible, use fans in lieu of compressors.

___ *b.* Design for natural lighting in lieu of artificial lighting. In hot climates or summers, avoid direct sun.

___ *c.* Use high-efficiency lighting (50–100 lumens per
watt). See Part 16A. Provide switches or controls to
light only areas needed and to take advantage of
daylighting. See Part 16B.

___ *d.* Use gas rather than electric, when possible.

___ *e.* Use efficient equipment and appliances

___ (1) Microwave rather than convection ovens.

___ (2) Refrigerators rated 5–10 kBtu/day or 535–
1070 kwh/yr.

___ *f.* If fireplaces, use high-efficiency type with tight-fitting, high-temperature glass, insulated and radiant-
inducing boxed with outside combustion air.

___ *g.* Use night setback and load control devices.

___ *h.* Use multizone HVAC.

___ *i.* Locate ducts in conditioned space or tightly seal and
insulate.

___ *j.* Insulate hot and cold water pipes. (R = 1 to 3).

___ *k.* Locate air handlers in conditioned space.

___ *l.* Install thermostats away from direct sun and supply
grilles.

___ *m.* Use heating equipment with efficiencies of 70% for
gas and 175% for electric, or higher.

___ *n.* Use cooling equipment with efficiencies of SEER =
10, COP = 2.5 or higher.

___ *o.* Use "economizers" on commercial HVAC to take
advantage of good outside temperatures.

___ *p.* At dry, hot climates, use evaporative cooling.

___ *q.* Use gas or solar in lieu of electric hot water heating.
Insulate hot water heaters. For solar hot water, see
p. 366.

___ *r.* For solar electric (photovoltaic), see p. 419.

_____ *s.*   For some building types and at some locations, utilities have peak load rates, such as on summer afternoons. These peak rates should be identified and designed for. Therefore, designing for peak loads may be more important than yearly energy savings. In some cases saving energy and saving energy cost may not be the same.

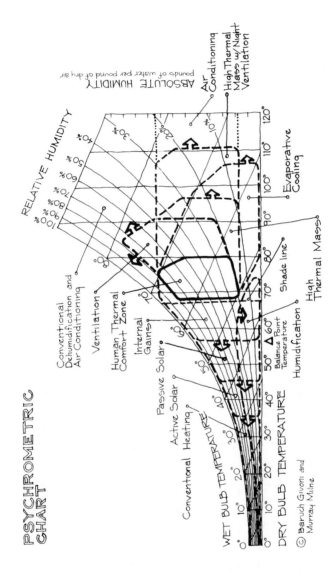

PSYCHROMETRIC CHART

RELATIVE HUMIDITY

ABSOLUTE HUMIDITY
pounds of water per pound of dry air

Air Conditioning

High Thermal Mass w/ Night Ventilation

Evaporative Cooling

High Thermal Mass

Shade line

Humidification

Balance Point Temperature

Internal Gains

Human Thermal Comfort Zone

Ventilation

Conventional Dehumidification and Air Conditioning

Passive Solar

Active Solar

Conventional Heating

WET BULB TEMPERATURE

DRY BULB TEMPERATURE

© Baruch Givoni and Murray Milne

Psychrometric Chart—Design Strategies

107

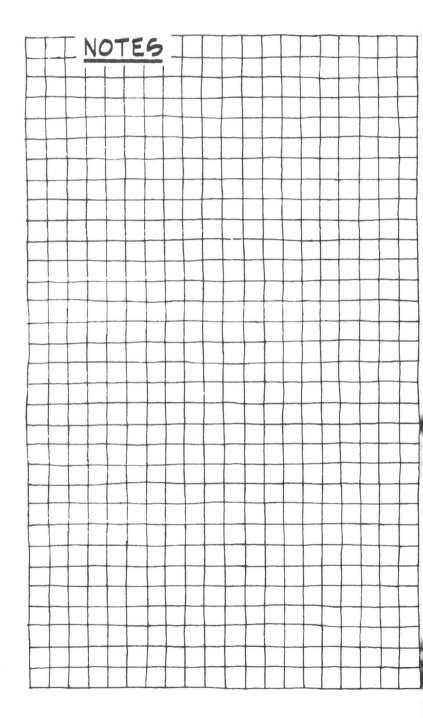

NOTES

__ K. ACOUSTICS ③ ④ ⑩

There is a negative and a positive function to consider in acoustic design.

The positive function is to ensure that the reverberation characteristics of a building are appropriate to their function. See 1.

On the negative side, the task is to make certain that unwanted outside noises are kept out of quiet areas of the building. See 2.

__ 1. *Room Acoustics*
Sound can be likened to light. *Sound control* uses reflection and diffusion for spaces such as auditoriums and sound studios.

__ *a.* Reflection: The geometry of the room is important (large concave surfaces should be avoided as they concentrate sound while convex surfaces disperse sound).

__ *b.* Diffusion promotes uniform distribution of continuous sound and improves "liveness" (very important in performing arts). Is increased by objects and surface irregularities. Ideal diffusing surfaces neither absorb nor reflect sound but scatter it.

__ *c.* Absorption: Noise control for more typical spaces, such as offices; absorption is the most effective. Sound pressure waves travel at the speed of sound (1100 fps), which is a slow enough speed so that reflections of the original sound-wave form can interfere with perception of the original, intended signal. *Reverberation time* is the measure of this problem.

Sound of any kind emitted in a room will be absorbed or reflected off the room surfaces. Soft materials absorb sound energy. Hard materials reflect sound energy back into the space. The reflected sound can reinforce the direct sound and enhance communication if the room size and room surfaces are configured appropriately. Annoying reverberation (echoes) occur in rooms more than *30 ft.* long. Echoes are stronger when the reflection surface is highly reflective and is concave toward the listener.

The room volume and surface characteristics will determine the reverberation time for the room. Reverberation time is the time in seconds that it takes for a sound to decay through 60 decibels. It is calculated as follows:

$$RT = \frac{0.05 \times \text{Room Volume (cf)}}{\text{Average Absorption of Room}}$$

Desirable room reverberation times are:

Office and commercial space	0.5 seconds
Rooms for speech	1.0 seconds
Rooms for music	1.5 seconds

The *absorption* of a surface is the product of the acoustic coefficient for the surface multiplied by the area of the surface. The sound absorption of the room is the sum of the sound absorptions of all the surfaces in the room. The higher the coefficient, the more sound absorbed, with *1.0* the highest possible. Generally, a material with a coefficient below *0.2* is considered to be reflective and above to be absorbing. Some common acoustic coefficients are:

Carpet and pad	0.6
Acoustic tile (no paint)	0.8
Cloth-upholstered seats	0.6
An audience	0.8
Concrete	0.02
Gypsum board	0.05
Glass	0.09
Tile	0.01
Fabric	0.30

The average absorption coefficient of a room should be at least *0.2*. Average absorption above *0.5* is usually not desirable, nor is it economically justified. A lower value is suitable for large rooms; larger values for small or noisy rooms. Although absorptive materials can be placed anywhere, ceiling treatment is more effective in large rooms, while wall treatment is more effective in small rooms. If additional absorptive material is being added to a room to improve it, the total absorption should be increased at least *3 times* to bring absorption to between *0.2 and 0.5.* An increase of *10 times* is about the practical limit. Each doubling of the absorption in a room reduces RT by ½.

EXAMPLE:
WHAT IS THE ABSORPTION COEFFICIENT AND REV. TIME FOR A 20' x 10' x 9' H OFFICE WITH CARPET FLOOR, A.T.C., & GYP B'D. WALL (BUT ⅓ OF WHICH HAS SOUND ABSORPTION MATERIAL)?

ABSORPTION COEFFICIENT:

FLOOR	0.6 x 200 =	120
2/3 WALL	0.05 x 356 =	18
1/3 WALL	0.8 x 178 =	142
CEILING	0.8 x 200 =	160
		440

$$\text{AVER. COEF. OF ABSORPTION} = \frac{\text{TOTAL ABSORP.}}{\text{TOTAL RM. SURF.}} = \frac{440}{20 \times 9 \times 2 + 10 \times 9 \times 2 + 10 \times 20 \times 2}$$

$$= \frac{440}{940 \text{ SF}} = .47 \text{ o.k.}$$

$$\text{REVERBERATION TIME} = \frac{0.05 \times (10 \times 20 \times 9)}{440} = 0.2 < 0.5, \text{ so o.k.}$$

___ *d.* Other

___ If a corridor is appreciably higher than its width, some absorption material should be placed on the walls as well as the ceiling, especially if the floor is hard. If the corridor is wider than its height, ceiling treatment is usually enough.

___ Acoustically critical rooms require an appropriate volume of space. Rooms for speech require 120 CF per audience seat. Rooms for music require 270 CF per audience seat.

___ "Ray diagramming," as with light beams, can be useful as the incident angle equals the reflected angle of the sound wave. As with light, concave shapes will focus sound and convex shapes will disperse sound.

___ 2. *Sound Isolation*
Sound travels through walls and floors by causing building materials to vibrate and then broadcast the noise into the quiet space.

There are two methods of setting up the vibration:
Structure-borne sound
Air-borne sound

Structure-borne sound is the vibration of building materials by vibrating pieces of equipment, or caused by walking on hard floors.

Air-borne sound is a pressure vibration in the air. When it hits a wall, the wall materials are forced to vibrate. The vibration passes through the materials of the wall. The far side of the wall then passes the vibration back into the air.

Noise Reduction and Sound Isolation Guidelines

___ *a.* Choose quiet, protected site. Orient building with doors and windows away from noise.

___ *b.* Use site barriers such as walls or landscape (dense tree lines or hedges).

___ *c.* Avoid placing noisy areas near quiet areas. Areas with similar noise characteristics should be placed next to each other. Place bedrooms next to bedrooms and living rooms next to living rooms.

LOUD SPACES   QUIET SPACES

___ *d.* Orient spaces to minimize transmission problems. Space windows of adjoining apartments max. distance apart. Place noisy areas back to back. Place closets between noisy and quiet areas.

___ *e.* Massive materials (concrete or masonry) are the best noise-isolation materials.

___ *f.* Choose quiet mechanical equipment. Use vibration isolation, sound-absorbing duct lining, resilient pipe connections. Design for low flow velocities in pipes and ducts.

___ *g.* Reducing structure-borne sound from walking on floors is achieved by carpet (with padding, improves greatly).

___ *h.* Avoid flanking of sound over ceilings.

___ *i.* Avoid flanking of sound at wall and floor intersections.

___ *j.* Wall and floor penetrations (such as elect. boxes) can be a source of sound leakage. A 1-sq.-inch wall opening in a 100-SF gyp'bd. partition can transmit as much sound as the entire partition.

___ *k.* Walls and floors are classified by sound transmission class (*STC*) which is the amount of reduction of loudness. The higher the number, the better. In determining the required STC rating of a barrier, the following rough guidelines may be used:

STC Effect on Hearing

25	Normal speech clearly heard through barrier.
30	Loud speech can be heard and understood fairly well. Normal speech can be heard but barely understood.
35	Loud speech is not unintelligible but can be heard.
42–45	Loud speech can be heard only faintly. Normal speech cannot be heard.
46–50	Loud speech not audible. Loud sounds other than speech can be heard only faintly, if at all.

See p. 116 for recommended STC room barriers.

Rough Estimating of STC Ratings

When the wall or floor assembly is less than that desired, the following modifications can be made. Select the appropriate wall or floor assembly. To improve the rating, select modifications (largest number, + ½ next largest, + ½ next largest, etc):

a. Light frame walls

Base design	*STC Rating*
Wood studs W/ ½″ gyp'bd.	32
Metal studs W/ ⅝″ gyp'bd.	39

Modification	*Added STC*
Staggered Studs	+9
Double surface skin	+3 to +5
Absorption insulation	+5

b. Heavy walls
The greater the density, the higher the rating. Density goes up in the following order: CMU, brick, concrete.

Base Design	*STC Rating*
4-inch CMU, brick, concrete	37–41, 42
6-inch	42, 46
8-inch	47, 49, 51
12-inch	52, 54, 56

Modification	*Added STC*
Furred-out surface	+7 to +10
Add plaster, ½″	+2 to +4
Sand-filled cores	+3

c. Wood floors

Base Design	STC Rating
½-in plyw'd, subfloor with oak floor, no ceiling	25

Modification	Added STC
Add carpet	+10
⅝-inch gyp'bd. ceiling	+10
Add resilient damping board	+7
Add absorbtion insul.	+3

d. Concrete floors

Base Design	STC Rating
4-, 6-, 8-inch thick concrete	41, 46, 51

Modification	Added STC
Resil. Susp. Ceiling	+12
Add sleepers	+7
Add absorption insul.	+3

EXAMPLE:

ROUGHLY ESTIMATE HOW TO GET S.T.C. = 45 FOR AN OFFICE WALL PARTITION MADE OF WOOD STUDS AND GYP'BD.

FROM ABOVE, A WOOD STUD PARTITION W/ ½" GYP'BD. IS ...... S.T.C.= 32

ADD STAGGERED STUDS FOR FULL CREDIT	+9
ADD DOUBLE GYP'BD. FOR ½ CREDIT, BOTH SIDES: ½ × 5 =	+2.5
ADD ABSORPTION BATTS BETWEEN STUDS: 1/2 × 5 =	+2.5
TOTAL =	46.0

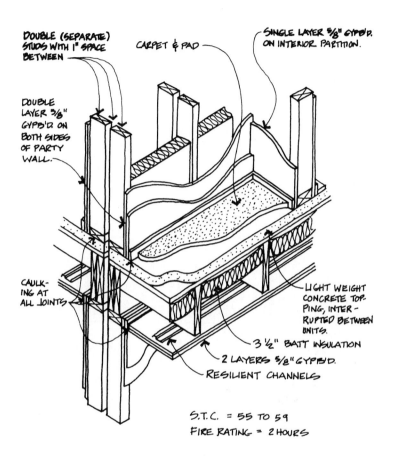

DOUBLE (SEPARATE) STUDS WITH 1" SPACE BETWEEN

CARPET & PAD

SINGLE LAYER 5/8" GYPB'D. ON INTERIOR PARTITION.

DOUBLE LAYER 5/8" GYPB'D. ON BOTH SIDES OF PARTY WALL.

CAULKING AT ALL JOINTS

LIGHT WEIGHT CONCRETE TOPPING, INTERRUPTED BETWEEN UNITS.

3 1/2" BATT INSULATION

2 LAYERS 5/8" GYPB'D.

RESILIENT CHANNELS

S.T.C. = 55 TO 59
FIRE RATING = 2 HOURS

PARTY WALL DETAIL

SOUND ISOLATION CRITERIA   (4)

SOURCE ROOM OCCUPANCY	RECEIVER ROOM ADJACENT	SOUND ISOLATION REQUIREMENT (MINIMUM) FOR ALL PATHS BETWEEN SOURCE AND RECEIVER.
EXECUTIVE AREAS, DOCTOR'S SUITES, PERSONNEL OFFICES, LARGE CONFERENCE ROOMS, CONFIDENTIAL PRIVACY REQUIREMENTS	ADJACENT OFFICES AND RELATED SPACES	STC 50-55
NORMAL OFFICES, REGULAR CONFERENCE ROOMS FOR GROUP MEETINGS, NORMAL PRIVACY REQM'TS.	ADJACENT OFFICES & SIMILAR ACTIVITIES	STC 45-50
LARGE GENERAL BUSINESS OFFICES, DRAFTING AREAS, BANKING FLOORS	CORRIDORS, LOBBIES, DATA PROCESSING, SIMILAR ACTIVITIES	STC 40-45
SHOP AND LABORATORY OFFICES IN MANUFACT'G USING LABORATORY OR TEST AREAS, NORM. PRIV.	ADJACENT OFFICES, TEST AREAS, CORRIP.	STC 40-45
MECHANICAL EQUIPMENT ROOMS	ANY SPACE	STC 50-60+
MULTIFAMILY DWELLINGS		
(a) BEDROOMS	NEIGHBORS (SEPARATE OCCUPANCY) BEDROOMS BATHROOMS KITCHENS LIVING ROOMS CORRIDORS	STC 48-55 STC 52-58 STC 52-58 STC 50-57 STC 52-58
(b) LIVING ROOMS	LIVING ROOMS BATHROOMS KITCHENS	STC 48-55 STC 50-57 STC 48-50
SCHOOL BUILDINGS (a) CLASSROOMS	ADJACENT CLASS ROOMS LABORATORIES CORRIDORS	STC 50 STC 50 STC 45
(b) LARGE MUSIC OR DRAMA AREA	ADJACENT MUSIC OR DRAMA AREA	STC 60
(c) MUSIC PRACTICE ROOMS	MUSIC PRACTICE RMS.	STC 55
INTERIOR OCCUPIED SPACES	EXTERIOR OF BLDG.	STC 35-60
THEATERS, CONCERT HALLS, LECTURE HALLS, RADIO AND T.V. STUDIOS	ANY AND ALL ADJACENT	USE QUALIFIED ACOUSTICAL CONSULTANT.

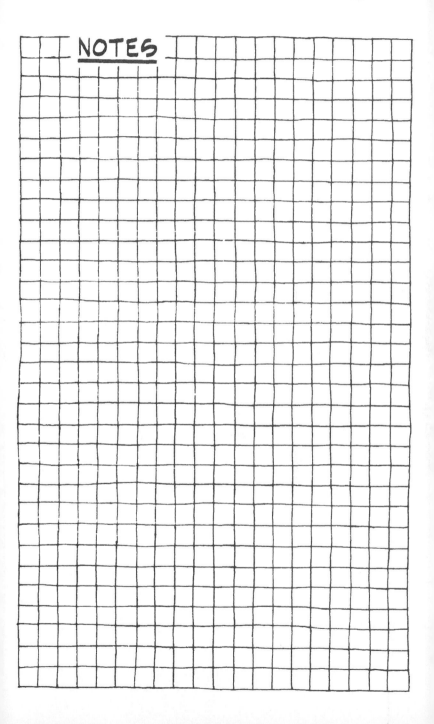

NOTES

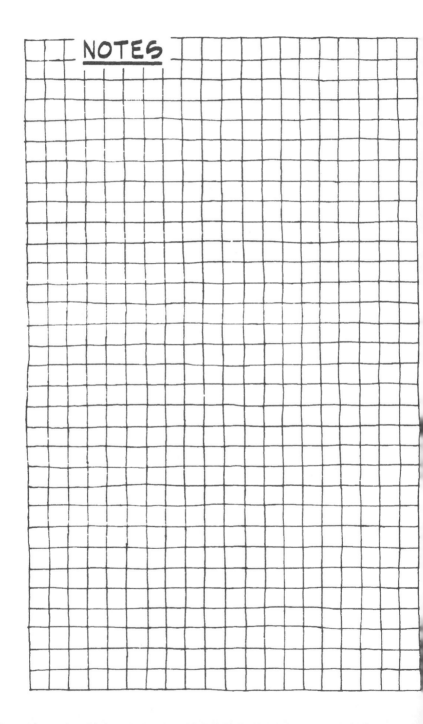

NOTES

2 SITE

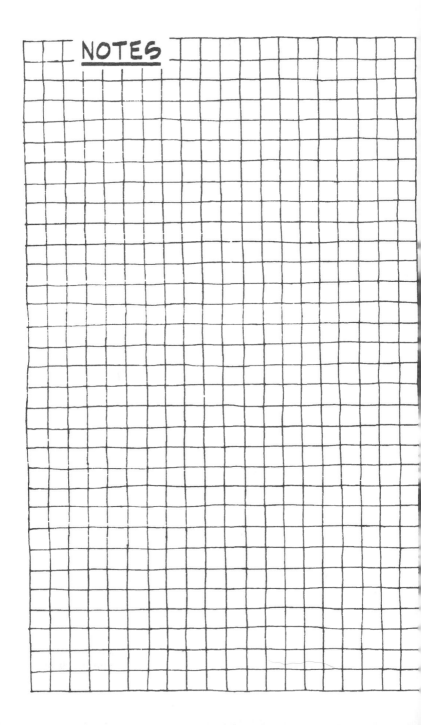

NOTES

__ A. LAND PLANNING ⑦ ㉚

__ 1. *Slopes:* Use the following guidelines for land selection:
  __ *a.* Slopes under 1% do not drain well.
  __ *b.* Slopes under 4% seem flat and are usable for all kinds of activity.
  __ *c.* Slopes of 4 to 10% are easy grades.
  __ *d.* Slopes over 10% are steep.
  __ *e.* Slopes at 15% approach limit of an ordinary loaded vehicle.
  __ *f.* Slopes at 25% are the limit of mowed surfaces.
  __ *g.* Slopes over 50% may have erosion problems.

__ 2. *Site Selection* (For Temperate Climates)
  Avoid or make special provision for steep north slopes; west slopes facing water; hilltops; frost pockets or positions at the foot of long, open slopes; bare, dry ground; nearby sources of noise or air pollution. Best sites are middle slopes facing south, near water, that are well-planted ones.

__ 3. *Streets* (Typical Widths)

Type	Width	R.O.W.
One-way	18′	25′
Minor road	20′	35′
Minor residential street	26′	
Major street	52′	80′
Highway	12′/lane + 8′ shoulder	up to 400′

__ 4. *Parking*
  __ *a.* In general, estimate *400 SF/car* for parking, drives, and walks.
  __ *b.* For very efficient double-bay aisle parking, estimate *300 SF/car* for parking and drives only.
  __ *c.* Typical parking stall: 9′ × 19′.
  __ *d.* Parking structure stall: 8.5′ × 19′.
  __ *e.* Compact parking stall: 7.5′ × 15′.
  __ *f.* *ADA* req'd. HC parking: As close to the accessible entry as possible. One HC stall for ea. 25 up to 100, then 1 per 50 up to 200, then 1 per 100 up to 500. From 501 to 1000: 2%. Over 1001: 20 + 1 for ea. 100 over 1000. First, plus 1 in every 8 HC stalls shall have 8-ft side aisle (for van parking). All other HC spaces shall have 5-ft side aisle (but may be shared). Stalls to be at least 8 feet wide. Grade at these locations cannot exceed 2%.

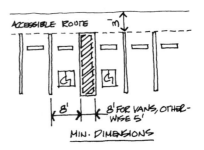

ACCESSIBLE ROUTE   m

8'   8' FOR VANS, OTHER-
WISE 5'

MIN. DIMENSIONS

___ *g.* Loading dock parking: $10' \times 35' \times 14'$ high.
___ *h.* One-way drive, no parking: 12' wide.
___ *i.* Two-way drive, no parking: 18' to 24' wide.
___ *j.* Recommended pavement slope: 1 to 5%.
___ *k.* Primary walks: 6' to 10' wide.
___ *l.* Secondary walks: 3' to 6' wide.
___ *m.* Walks adjacent to parking areas with overhanging car bumpers: 6' minimum.
___ *n.* Above are for rough estimating; always verify local zoning ordinance.
___ *o.* See following diagram and table for typical sizes:

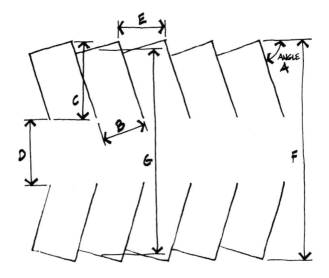

A	B	C	D	E	F	G
					Center-to-center width of two parking rows with access btw'n.	
Parking angle	Stall width	Stall to curb	Aisle width	Curb length	Curb to curb	Overlap center line to center line
0°	7'6"	7.5*	11.0	19.0	26.0	26.0
	8'0"	8.0	12.0	23.0	28.0	—
	8'6"	8.5	12.0	23.0	29.0	—
	9'0"	9.0	12.0	23.0	30.0	—
	9'6"	9.5	12.0	23.0	31.0	—
30°	7'6"	14.0*	11.0	15.0	39.0	32.5
	8'0"	16.5	11.0	16.0	44.0	37.1
	8'6"	16.9	11.0	17.0	44.8	37.4
	9'0"	17.3	11.0	18.0	45.6	37.8
	9'6"	17.8	11.0	19.0	46.6	38.4
40°	8'0"	18.3	13.0	12.4	49.6	43.5
	8'6"	18.7	12.0	13.2	49.4	42.9
	9'0"	19.1	12.0	14.0	50.2	43.3
	9'6"	19.5	12.0	14.8	51.0	43.7
45°	7'6"	15.9*	11.0	10.6	42.8	37.9
	8'0"	19.1	14.0	11.3	52.2	46.5
	8'6"	19.4	13.5	12.0	52.3	46.3
	9'0"	20.1	13.0	13.4	53.2	46.2
	9'6"	20.1	13.0	13.4	53.2	46.5
50°	8'0"	19.7	14.0	10.5	53.4	48.3
	8'6"	20.0	12.5	11.1	52.5	47.0
	9'0"	20.4	12.0	11.7	52.8	47.0
	9'6"	20.7	12.0	12.4	53.4	47.3
60°	7'6"	16.7*	14.0	8.7	47.5	40.4
	8'0"	20.4	19.0	9.2	59.8	55.8
	8'6"	20.7	18.5	9.8	59.9	55.6
	9'0"	21.0	18.0	10.4	60.0	55.5
	9'6"	21.2	18.0	11.0	60.4	55.6
90°	7'6"	15.0*	18.0	7.5	48.0	48.0
	8'0"	19.0	26.0†	8.0	64.0	—
	8'6"	19.0	25.0†	8.5	63.0	—
	9'0"	19.0	24.0†	9.0	62.0	—
	9'6"	19.0	24.0†	9.5	62.0	—

* Based on 15'0" stall length for compact cars; all others based on 19'0" stall length.
† Two-way circulation.

___ 5. *Open-Space Proportions*

AN OBJECT (BUILDING) WHOSE MAJOR DIMENSION (VERTICAL OR HORIZONTAL EQUALS IT'S DISTANCE FROM THE EYE IS DIFFICULT TO SEE AS A WHOLE BUT TENDS TO BE ANALYSED IN DETAIL.

WHEN IT IS TWICE AS FAR, IT APPEARS CLEARLY AS A WHOLE.

WHEN IT IS 3 TIMES AS FAR, IT STILL DOMINATES, BUT IS ALSO SEEN IN RELATION TO OTHER OBJECTS.

WHEN IT IS 4 TIMES, OR MORE, IT BECOMES PART OF THE GENERAL SCENE.

AN EXTERNAL ENCLOSURE IS MOST COMFORTABLE WHEN IT'S WALLS ARE 1/2 TO 1/3 AS HIGH AS THE WIDTH OF THE SPACE ENCLOSED.

IF THE RATIO FALLS BELOW 1/4, THE SPACE CEASES TO SEEM ENCLOSED.

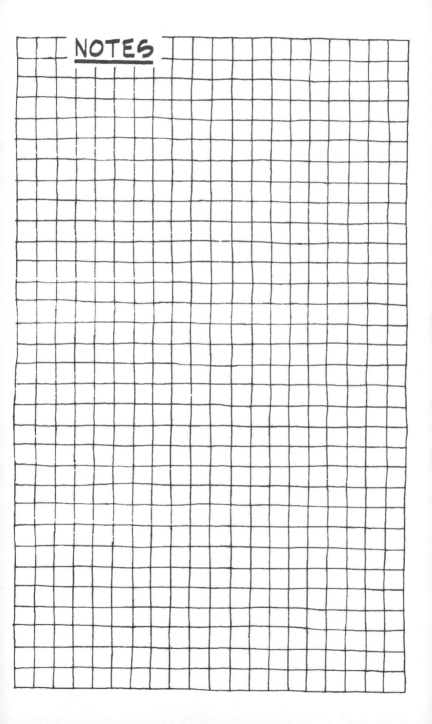

NOTES

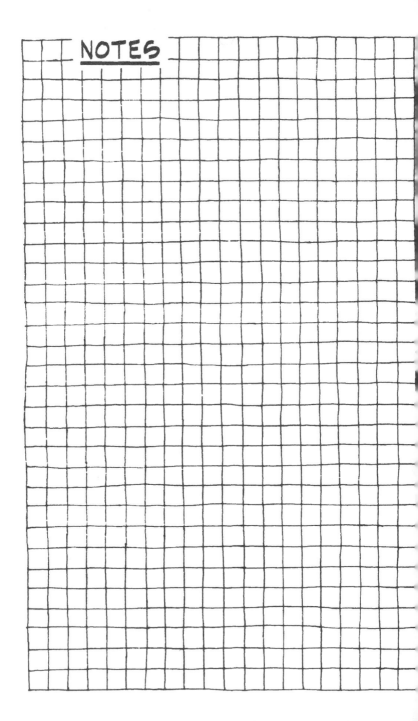

NOTES

__ B. GRADING AND DRAINAGE

$\textcircled{4}$ $\textcircled{14}$ $\textcircled{18}$ $\textcircled{24}$ $\textcircled{39}$

___ 1. *Grading for Economy*
     ___ a. Keep finished grades as close to the natural as possible.
     ___ b. Amounts of cut and fill should balance over the site.

___ 2. *Maximum Slopes*
     ___ a. Solid rock   ¼:1
     ___ b. Loose rock   ½:1 (1:1 for round rock)
     ___ c. Loose gravel   1½:1
     ___ d. Firm earth   1½:1
     ___ e. Soft earth   2:1
     ___ f. Mowing grass   4:1

___ 3. *Desirable Grades*

		% of slopes	
Situation		Max.	Min.
___ a. Paved areas			
	___ (1) AC	5	1
	___ (2) Concrete	5	0.5
___ b. Streets			
	___ (1) Length	6–10	0.5
	___ (2) Cross	4	2
___ c. Walks			
	___ (1) Cross slope	2	2
	___ (2) Long slope		
	___ (3) (Subj. to freeze and accessible)	5	
	___ (4) (Not subj. to above)	14	
___ d. Ramps			
	___ (1) Accessible (*ADA*)	8.33	
	___ (2) Nonaccessible	12.5	
___ e. At buildings			
	___ (1) Grade away 10′		2
	___ (2) Impervious materials	21	
___ f. Outdoor areas			
	___ (1) Impervious surface	5	0.5
	___ (2) Pervious		
	___ (*a*) Ground frost	5	2
	___ (*b*) No ground frost	5	1
___ g. Swales and gutters (concrete)			.3
___ h. Stairs			
	___ (1) Landings and treads	2	1

___ 4. *Grades at Buildings*

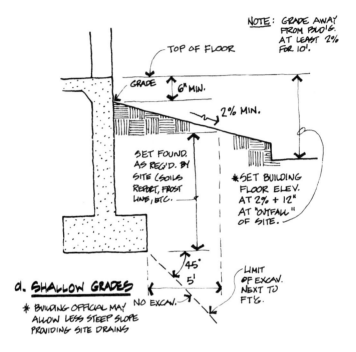

NOTE: GRADE AWAY FROM BLD'G. AT LEAST 2% FOR 10'.

TOP OF FLOOR

GRADE — 6" MIN.

2% MIN.

SET FOUND. AS REQ'D. BY SITE (SOILS REPORT, FROST LINE, ETC.

*SET BUILDING FLOOR ELEV. AT 2% + 12" AT "OUTFALL" OF SITE.

45°

5'

LIMIT OF EXCAV. NEXT TO FT'G.

a. **SHALLOW GRADES**   NO EXCAV.

* BUILDING OFFICIAL MAY ALLOW LESS STEEP SLOPE PROVIDING SITE DRAINS

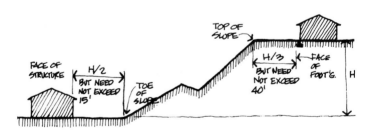

TOP OF SLOPE

FACE OF STRUCTURE

H/2 BUT NEED NOT EXCEED 15'

TOE OF SLOPE

H/3 BUT NEED NOT EXCEED 40'

FACE OF FOOT'G.

H

b. **STEEP GRADES** FOR SLOPES STEEPER THAN 3 TO 1.
* BUILDING OFFICIAL MAY APPROVE ALTERNATE SETBACKS & CLEARANCES.

___ 5. *Retaining Walls*

    ___ **COSTS ≈ $250/CY, all sizes, not including cut, backfill, or compaction.**

H	B	d	b	c
3'	2.08 (2.67)	.67 (.75)	1.0 (1.5)	.58 (.5)
6'	3.75 (5.33)	.67 (.83)	2.47 (2.93)	.67 (1.58)
9'	5.17 (7.5)	1.0 (1.0)	3.17 (4.17)	1.0 (2.33)
12'	7.25 (12)	1.17 (1.17)	4.58 (7.83)	1.5 (3)
15'	9 (15)	1.33 (1.5)	5.75 (9.75)	1.93 (3.75)
18'	10.83 (18)	1.5 (1.83)	7.08 (11.67)	2.25 (4.5)
21'	12.58 (21)	1.75 (2.17)	8.17 (13.58)	2.67 (5.25)

SURCHARGE   LEVEL

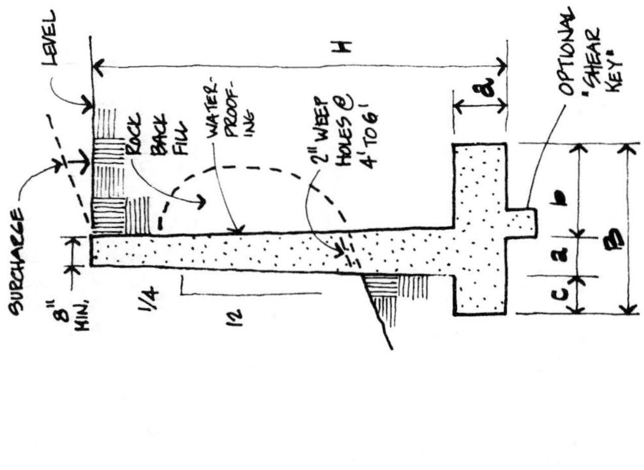

CANTILEVER RETAINING WALL

1. REINFORCING NOT SHOWN.
2. CONTROL JOINTS @ 25' & EXPAN. JOINTS @ 100'.

LEVEL

ROCK BACK FILL

WATER-PROOF-ING

2" WEEP HOLES @ 4' TO 6'

SURCHARGE

8" MIN.

1/4

12

OPTIONAL "SHEAR KEY"

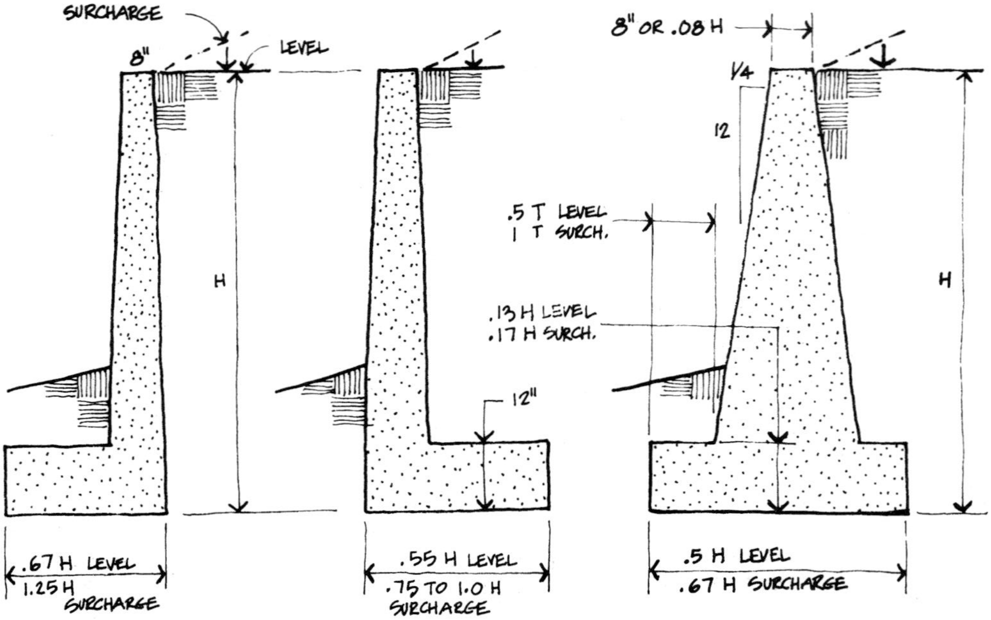

GRAVITY TYPE

CANTILEVER "L" TYPES

.5 H LEVEL
.67 H SURCHARGE

.55 H LEVEL
.75 TO 1.0 H
SURCHARGE

.67 H LEVEL
1.25 H
SURCHARGE

8" OR .08 H

1/4

12

.5 T LEVEL
1 T SURCH.

.13 H LEVEL
.17 H SURCH.

12"

SURCHARGE

LEVEL

8"

H

___ 6. *Earthwork Conversion Factors*

Native, in-place soils can be compacted for greater density. When dug up the density decreases and the volume increases. Use the following to estimate earthwork volumes:

Soil	In place	Loose	Compacted
Sand	1.00	1.10	.95
Earth	1.00	1.25	.80
Clay	1.00	1.40	.90
Rock (blasted)	1.00	1.5	1.30

___ **7. Earthwork Costs**

The costs given below are based on machinery-moved and compacted earthwork, normal soils, suburban sites, of medium size (2000–15,000 CY):

___ **On site**
   ___ **Cut**   **$1.50/CY**
   ___ **Fill and compaction**   **$1.50/CY**
   (Compaction 20% of total)
___ **Off site**
   ___ **Import**   **$5/CY (5 miles or less) to $10/CY**
   ___ **Export**   **$2/CY (5 miles or less) to $5/CY**

Modifiers:
___ **Difficult soils (soft clays or hard,**
   cementitious soils)   **+100%**
___ **Hand-compacted**   **+400 to 500%**
___ **Volume**
   ___ **Smaller**   **+50 to 200%**
   ___ **Larger**   **−0 to 35%**
___ **Location**
   ___ **Urban sites**   **+100 to 300%**
   ___ **Rural sites**   **−0 to 25%**
   ___ **Situations of severe weather**
   (rain or freezing)   **+5 to 10%**

Other materials:
___ **Sand**   **$4 to $5/CY**
___ **Gravel**   **$10 to $20/CY**
___ **Rock (blasting only)**
   ___ **Rural sites**   **$6 to $8/CY**
   ___ **Urban sites**   **$105/CY**
___ **Jackhammering**   **$1350/CY**

___ 8. *Drainage*

     ___ *a.* General: Rainwater that falls on the surface of a property either evaporates, percolates into the soil (see p. 141), flows off the site, or drains to some point or points on the site. That portion that does not enter the soil is called the *runoff* and provision must be made for this excess water. The grading must be so designed that surface water will flow away from the building. This may sheet-flow across the property line or out driveways to the street. Or, this may necessitate drainage channels with catch basins and storm drains (see p. 145). Each community should be checked for its requirements by contacting the city (or county) engineering or public works department.

     ___ *b.* Rainfall: For small drainage systems, the maximum rainfall in any *2-year* period is generally used. For a more conservative design, the *5- to 10-year* period may be employed. For establishing floor elevations, *100-year* floods, are often used. Lacking more specific data, see App. B, item J, and divide the quantity by half. One inch of rain per hour is equal to approximately one CF of water falling on one acre of ground per second.

     ___ *c.* Runoff: Volume may be estimated by:

$Q = C\ I\ A$, where:

     Q = Quantity of runoff in CF/sec
     C = Coefficient of runoff:

Roofs	0.95
Conc. or asphalt	0.95
Gravel areas	
Loose	0.30
Compact	0.70
Vacant land, unpaved streets	
Light plant growth	0.60
No plants	0.75
Lawns	0.35
Wooded areas	0.20

     I = Intensity of rainfall in inches per hour
     A = Area to be drained, in acres

___ *d.*   Storm drains

The following nomograph can be used to estimate storm drain sizes. It is for rough concrete. Materials of smoother surfaces will have smaller sizes. Also, see pp. 145 and 363.

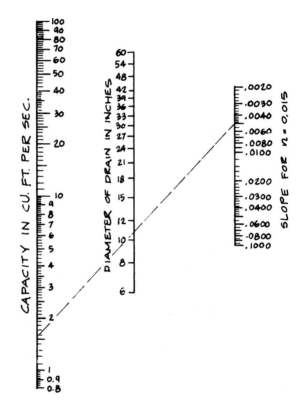

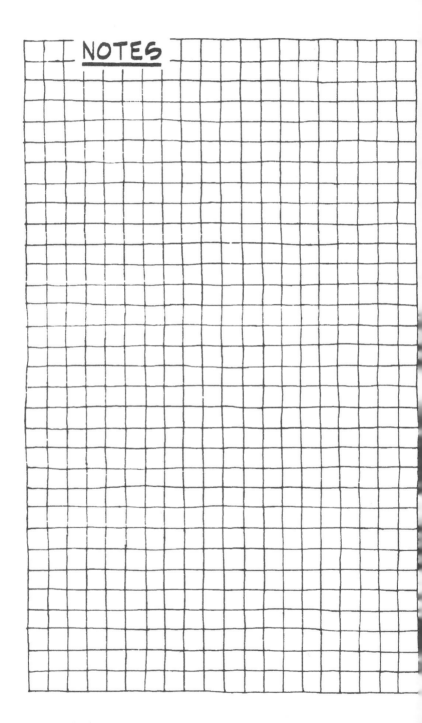

NOTES

__ C. SOILS ② ④ ⑱ ㉚ ㊴ ㊺

___ 1. Danger "Flags"
    ___ *a.* High-water table.
    ___ *b.* Presence of trouble soils: Peat, other organic materials, or soft clay, loose silt, or fine water bearing sand.
    ___ *c.* Rock close to surf.
    ___ *d.* Dumps or fills.
    ___ *e.* Evidence of slides or subsidence.
___ 2. Ranking of Soil for Foundations
    ___ *a.* *Best:* Sand and gravel
    ___ *b.* *Good:* Medium to hard clays
    ___ *c.* *Poor:* Silts and soft clays
    ___ *d.* *Undesirable:* Organic silts and clays
    ___ *e.* *Unsuitable:* Peat
___ 3. Basic Soil Types (Identification)
    ___ *a.* *Inorganic* (for foundations)
        ___ (1) Rock: good bearing but hard to excavate
        ___ (2) Course grain
            ___ (*a*) Gravel: 3″ to 2 mm. Well-drained, stable mat'l.
            ___ (*b*) Sand: 0.05 to 2 mm. Gritty to touch and taste. Good, well-drained material if confined, but "quick" if saturated.
        ___ (3) Fine grain
            ___ (*a*) Silt: 0.005 to 0.05 mm. Feels smooth to touch. Grains barely visible. Stable when dry but may creep under load. Unstable when wet. Frost heave problems.
            ___ (*b*) Clays: Under 0.005 mm. Cannot see grains. Sticks to teeth. Wide variety in clays, some suitable and some not. Can become expansive when wet.
    ___ *b.* *Organic* (not suitable for foundations). Have fibrous texture with dark brown or black color.
___ 4. Most soils have *combinations:*
    ___ *a.* Consisting of air, water, and solids
    ___ *b.* Size variation of solids a factor

WELL GRADED

UNIFORMLY GRADED (POORLY GRADED)

___ 5. Amounts of types of solids vary, giving different characteristics per following table:

Unified Soil Classification

Soil type	Description	Allow. bearing (lb/SF) (1)	Drain-age (2)	Frost heave potent	Expan. potent (3)
___ BR	Bedrock	30,000	Poor	Low	Low
Gravels					
Clean gravels					
___ GW	Well-graded gravel-sand mixtures, little or no sands	8000	Good	Low	Low
___ GP	Poorly graded gravels or gravel-sand mixtures, little or no fine	8000	Good	Low	Low
Gravels with fines					
___ GM	Silty gravels, gravel-sand-silt mixtures	4000	Good	Med.	Low
___ GC	Clayey gravels, gravel-clay-sand mixtures	4000	Med.	Med.	Low
Sand					
Clean sands					
___ SW	Well-graded sands, gravelly sands, little or no fines	6000	Good	Low	Low
___ SP	Poorly graded sands or gravelly sands, little or no fines	5000	Good	Low	Low
Sands with fines					
___ SM	Silty sand, sand-silt mixtures	4000	Good	Med.	Low
___ SC	Clayey sands, sand-clay mixture	4000	Med.	Med.	Low
Fine grained					
Silts					
___ ML	Inorganic silts and very fine sands, rock flour, silty or clayey fine sands w/slight plasticity	2000	Med.	High	Low
___ MH	Inorganic silts, micaceous or diatomaceous fine sandy or silty soils, elastic silts	2000	Poor	High	High

Clays					
___ CL	Inorganic clays of low to med. plasticity, gravelly, sandy, silty, or lean clays	2000	Med.	Med.	Med.
___ CH	Inorganic clays of high plasticity, fat clays	2000	Poor	Med.	High
Organic					
___ OL	Organic silts and organic silty clays	400	Poor	Med.	Med.
___ OH	Organic clays of medium to high plasticity	0	Unsat.	Med.	High
___ PT	Peat and other highly organic soils	0	Unsat.	Med.	High

Notes:

1. Allowable bearing value may be increased 25% for very compact, coarse-grained, gravelly or sandy soils, or for very stiff, fine-grained, clayey or silty soils. Allowable bearing value should be decreased 25% for loose, coarse-grained, gravelly or sandy soils or soft, fine-grained, clayey or silty soils.
2. Percolation rate for good drainage is over 4″/hr; medium drainage is 2–4″/hr; poor is less than 2″/hr. Also, see page 141.
3. Dangerous expansion might occur if these soil types are dry but subject to future wetting.

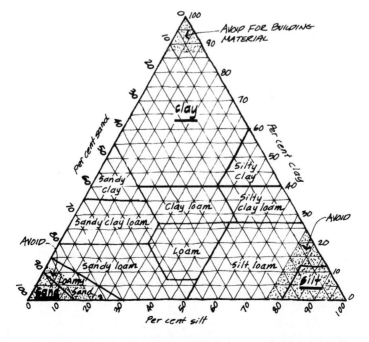

___ 6. *Clays* usually give greatest problems for foundations.
    ___ *a.* Measure expansiveness:

The greater the PI (Plasticity Index), the greater the potential for shrinkage and swelling. Some clays swell up to 20-fold with pressures of several tons/SF. Problems of upheaval vs. settlement usually are 2 to 1.

    ___ *b.* Strength of clays

Consistency	Shear (ton/SF)	Compression (ton/SF)	Rule of thumb
___ Soft	0.25–0.5	<0.5	¼" pencil makes 1" penetration with med. effort.
___ Medium stiff	0.5–1.0	0.5–1.0 1.0–2.0	¼" pencil makes ½" penetration with med. effort.
___ Very stiff	1.0–3.0	2.0–4.0	¼" pencil makes ¼" penetration with much effort.
___ Hard	3.0>	4.0>	¼" steel rod can penetrate less than ⅛". Can hardly scratch.

    ___ 7. Testing
        ___ *a.* Simple field tests
            ___ (1) Separation of gravel
                ___ (*a*) Remove from sample all particles larger than ⅛" diameter.
                ___ (*b*) Estimate percent gravel.
            ___ (2) Sedimentation test
                ___ (*a*) Place sample (less gravel) in canteen cup and fill with water.
                ___ (*b*) Shake mixture rigorously.
                ___ (*c*) Allow mixture to stand for 30 seconds to settle out.

___ (d) Pour off water after 30 seconds of settlement and save.

___ (e) Repeat (b) through (d) above until water poured off is clear.

___ (f) Evaporate water from (d) above.

___ (g) Estimate percent fines.

___ (3) Comparison of gravel and sand

   ___ (a) Gravels have been removed in test (1).

   ___ (b) Fines have been removed in test (2).

   ___ (c) Dry soil remaining in cup.

   ___ (d) Soil remaining in cup will be sand.

   ___ (e) Compare dry sand in cup with gravel.

___ (4) Dry strength

   ___ (a) Form moist pat 2″ in diameter by ½″ thick.

   ___ (b) Allow to dry with low heat.

   ___ (c) Place dry pat between thumb and index finger only and attempt to break.

   ___ (d) Breakage easy—silt.
   Breakage difficult—CL.
   Breakage impossible—CH.
   (see p. 136, Typical)

___ (5) Powder test

   ___ (a) Rub portion of broken pat with thumb and attempt to flake particles off.

   ___ (b) Pat powders—silt (M).
   Pat does not powder—clay (C).

___ (6) Thread test (toughness test)

   ___ (a) Form ball of moist soil (marble size).

   ___ (b) Attempt to roll ball into ⅛″-diameter thread (wooden match size).

   ___ (c) Thread easily obtained—clay (C).
   Thread cannot be obtained—silt (M).

___ (7) Ribbon test

   ___ (a) Form cylinder of soil approximately cigar-shaped in size.

   ___ (b) Flatten cylinder over index finger with thumb; attempting to form ribbon 8″ to 9″ long, ⅛″ to ¼″ thick, and 1″ wide.

___ (c) 8″ to 9″ ribbon obtained—CH.
        Less than 8″ ribbon—CL.

___ (8) Wet shaking test
    ___ (a) Place pat of moist (not sticky) soil in palm of hand (vol. about ½ cu. in.).
    ___ (b) Shake hand vigorously and strike against other hand.
    ___ (c) Observe rapidity of water rising to the surface.
    ___ (d) If fast, sample is silty (M).
             If no reaction, sample is clayey (C).

___ (9) Grit, or bite test
    ___ (a) Place pinch of sample between teeth and bite.
    ___ (b) If sample feels gritty, sample is silt (M).
    ___ (c) If sample feels floury, sample is clay (C).

___ (10) Feel test
    ___ (a) Rub portion of dry soil over a sensitive portion of skin, such as inside of wrist.
    ___ (b) If feel is harsh and irritating, sample is silt (M).
    ___ (c) If feel is smooth and floury, sample is clay (C).

___ (11) Shine test
    ___ (a) Draw smooth surface, such as knife blade or thumb nail, over pat of slightly moist soil.
    ___ (b) If surface becomes shiny and lighter in texture, sample is a high compressible clay (CH).
    ___ (c) If surface remains dull, sample is a low compressible clay (CL).

___ (12) Odor test
    ___ (a) Heat sample with match or open flame.
    ___ (b) If odor becomes musty or foul smelling, there is a strong indication that organic material is present.

___ (13) Cast test
    ___ (a) Compress a handful of moist soil into a ball.

___ (b) Crumbles with handling—GW, SW, GP or SP.

___ (c) Withstands careful handling—SM or SC.

___ (d) Handled freely—ML or MH.

___ (e) Withstands rough handling—CL or CH.

___ (14) Slaking test

___ (a) Place soil or rock in sun to dry.

___ (b) Soak in water for 24 hours.

___ (c) Repeat (a) and (b) above several times.

___ (d) If soil or rock disintegrates, it is poor material.

___ (15) Amounts of soil

		Sieve	Jar of water
___	Gravel	Remains on #10	Settles immediately
___	Sand	Remains on #200	Settles in 30 sec
___	Silt	Goes to bottom	Settles in 15–60 min
___	Clay	Goes to bottom	Settles in several hrs

Measure each amount to get approximate percent of each soil type.

___ (16) Testing for percolation: Absorption capacity of soil for sanitary septic systems (see p. 363) may be checked by digging a test pit at the drain field site in the wet season to the depth that the field will lie. Fill the pit with 2′ of water, let fall to a 6″ depth, and time the drop from 6″ to 5″. Repeat until it takes same time to make the 1″ drop in two tests running. The allowable absorption rate of soil, in gal per SF of drain field per day, is:

Time for 1″ fall, minutes	Absorption rate, gals per SF per day
___ 5 or less	2.5
___ 8	2.0
___ 10	1.7
___ 12	1.5
___ 15	1.3
___ 22	1.0

Total sewage flow = 100 gal per person per day.

___ *b.* Soils reports and data
___ (1) Geotechnical or *soils report recommendations* are based on lab tests of materials obtained from on-site borings. Request the following info:
___ (*a*) Bearing capacity of soil
___ (*b*) Foundation design recommendations
___ (*c*) Paving design recommendations
___ (*d*) Compaction recommendations
___ (*e*) Lateral strength (active and passive pressure, and coef. of friction)
___ (*f*) Permeability
___ (*g*) Frost depth
___ (2) Typical investigations require *borings* at the center and each corner of the "foot print" of the building, or one per 3000 to 5000 SF.
___ (3) **Costs: $2000 to $3500 per report.**
___ (4) Typical soils report strength characteristics

___ Noncohesive (granular) soils

Relative density	Blows per foot (N)
___ Very loose	0–4
___ Loose	5–10
___ Firm	11–30
___ Dense	31–50
___ Very dense	51+

___ Cohesive (claylike) soils

Comparative consistency	Blows per foot	Unconfined compressed strength (T/SF)
___ Very soft	0–2	0–0.25
___ Soft	3–4	0.25–0.50
___ Med. stiff	5–8	0.50–1.00
___ Stiff	9–15	1.00–2.00
___ Very stiff	16–30	2.00–4.00
___ Hard	31+	4.00+

Degree of plasticity	PI	Degree of expan. pot.	PI
___ None to slight	0–4	Low	0–15
___ Slight	5–10	Medium	15–25
___ Medium	11–30	High	25+
___ High	31+		

___ (5) For small projects, especially in rural areas, *soils surveys* by USDA Soils Conservation Service are available (free of charge) through the local soil and water conservation district office.

___ 8. Foundations

   ___ *a.* Differential Settlement of Foundations: ¼″ to ½″, maximum.

   ___ *b.* For more on foundations, see pp. 162 and 163.

___ 9. Radon

   ___ *a.* See App. B for likely radon locations.

   ___ *b.* A colorless, odorless, radioactive gas found in soils and underground water.

   ___ *c.* Is drawn from the soil through the foundation when the indoor pressure is less than the pressure outside, in the soil. This usually occurs in winter.

   ___ *d.* Reduction Approaches:

      ___ (1) For slab-on-grade construction, a normal uniform rock base course, vapor barrier, and concrete slab may be satisfactory.

      ___ (2) Basements

         ___ (*a*) Barrier approach, by complete waterproofing.

         ___ (*b*) Suction approach collects the gas outside the foundation and under the slab, and vents it to the outside. Consists of a collection system of underground pipes (or individual suction pipes at 1/500 SF), and discharge system.

NOTES

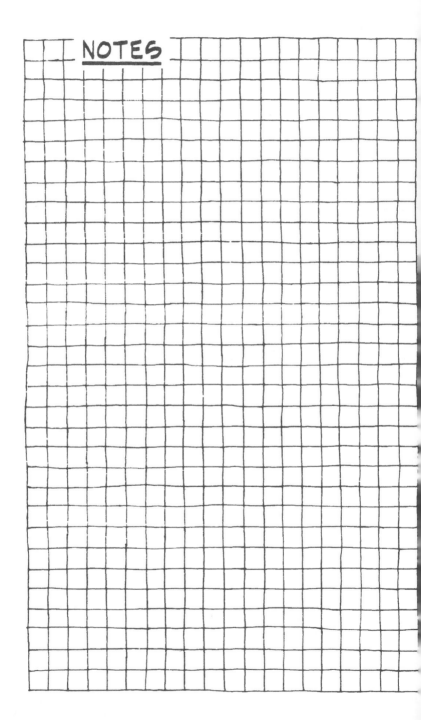

___ D. UTILITIES

The five main utilities are water, sewer, power, gas, and tele-phone—with storm drains and cable TV as added options.

UTILITY TRENCHES

Typical Costs for Trench, Excavation, and Compacted Backfill:
___ **For 2′ × 2′ trench with 0 to 1 side slope: $0.45/SF sect./LF trench**
___ **Double cost for 2 to 1 side slope. Add 1% for each additional ft depth past 2′.**
___ **Add to above for pipe bedding: in 0 to 1 side slope: 6″ to 84″ dia. pipe = $0.12 to $0.245/inch diameter. In 2 to 1 side slope: revise above to $0.54 to $0.80/inch diameter.**
___ **Add to above cost of pipe or conduit listed below.**

___ 1. Storm Drains
     ___ *a.* Most expensive, avoid where possible.
     ___ *b.* Separate from sanitary sewer.
     ___ *c.* MHs at ends, each change of horizontal or vertical dimension, and each 300′ to 500′.
     ___ *d.* Surface drain no more than 800′ to 1000′ to catch basins, or 500′ if coming from two directions.
     ___ *e.* 4′ deep in cold climates.
     ___ *f.* Minimum slope of 0.3% for a minimum velocity of 2′/sec (never exceed 10′/sec)
     ___ *g.* 12″ minimum diameter in 3″ increments up to 36″.
     ___ *h.* See p. 133 for sizing.

See below for Costs.

___ 2. Sanitary Sewer
     ___ *a.* CO at ends, branchings, turns (less than 90°).
     ___ *b.* Typically, 4″ for house branch up to 8″ diameter for mains and laterals. 6″ for most commercial.
     ___ *c.* Street mains often at −6′, or greater.
     ___ *d.* Slopes of from 1/16″ to 1/4″/ft.
     ___ *e.* Place below water lines or 10′ away.
     ___ *f.* Also, see p. 362.

Typical Drainage and Sewage Piping Costs: (per LF)
___ **Reinforced concrete: 12″ to 84″ diameter = $0.95 to $3.50/inch dia.**
___ **Corrig. metal: 12″ to 72″ diameter = $0.95 to $2.00**
___ **Plain metal: 12″ to 72″ diameter = $0.75 to $2.80**

___ **PVC: 4″ to 15″ diameter = $0.65 to $0.95**
___ **Clay: 4″ to 36″ diameter = $0.95 to $3.10**

Typical Costs of MH and Catch basins:
___ **For 4′ × 4′ deep, c.m.u. = $1380**
___ **Adjust: –8% for p.c. concrete, +20% to 50% for brick, and +50% for CIP conc.**
___ **Add: $250 to $385 each ft down to 14′.**

    ___ 3. Water
        ___ *a.* Flexible in layout.
        ___ *b.* Best located in ROW for mains.
        ___ *c.* Layouts: branch or loop (best).
        ___ *d.* Effected by frost. Must be at –5′ in cold climates.
        ___ *e.* Valves at each branch and at each 1000′ max.
        ___ *f.* FHs layed out to reach 300′ to buildings but no closer than 25′ to 50′. Sometimes high pressure fire lines installed.
        ___ *g.* Typical size: 8″ dia., min., mains
                                 6″ dia., min., branch
        ___ *h.* Typical city pressure 60 psi
        ___ *i.* Where city water not available, wells can be put in (keep 100′ from newest sewer, drain field, or stream bed).
        ___ *j.* Also, see p. 361.

Typical Piping Costs (per LF):
___ **Iron: 4″ dia. to 8″ dia. = $3 to $30/inch dia.**
___ **Copper: ¾″ dia. to 6″ dia. = $4.80 to $17.50/inch dia.**
___ **PVC: 1½″ dia. to 8″ dia. = $2 to $12.00/inch dia.**

    ___ 4. Power
        ___ *a.* Brought in on primary high-voltage lines, either overhead or underground.
        ___ *b.* Stepped down at transformers to secondary (lower voltage) lines. Secondary lines should be kept down to 400′ or less to building service-entrance sections.
        ___ *c.* Underground distribution may be 2 to 5 times more expensive but is more reliable, does not interfere with trees, and eliminates pole clutter. Always place in conduit.
        ___ *d.* If over head, transformers are hung on poles with secondary overhead to building. Gayed poles typically 125′ (max.) apart. Where not in R.O.W., 8′

easement required. For footings, provide 1′ of
inbedment per every 10′ of height plus 1 extra foot.

___ *e.* See p. 413.

Typical Costs: 3″ to 4″ conduit: $4 to $6/LF
PC conc. transformer pad, 5′ sq.: $50/ea.

___ 5. Gas

    ___ *a.* Underground, similar to water.

    ___ *b.* Main problem is danger of leakage or explosion, so
lines should be kept away from buildings, except at
entry.

    ___ *c.* Lines should not be in same trench as electric cable.

    ___ *d.* Also, see p. 366.

Typical Piping Costs:
___ Steel: $6.85/LF for 5″ dia. to $22.00/LF for 8″ dia.
___ Plastic: $2 for 1″ dia. to $8/LF for 4″ dia.

___ 6. Fire Protection: Generally, fire departments want:

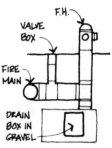

    ___ *a.* Fire hydrants at streets
or drives that are located
about 300 ft apart and
located so that a 300-ft
hose can extend around
building.

    ___ *b.* Min. of at least 16-ft-
wide drives around
building with 30′ to 60′
turning radius for fire
truck access.

    ___ *c.* Also, see p. 364.

Typical Costs:
Piping costs, same as water (iron or PVC)
Hydrants: $1500/ea.
Siamese: $200 to $300/ea.

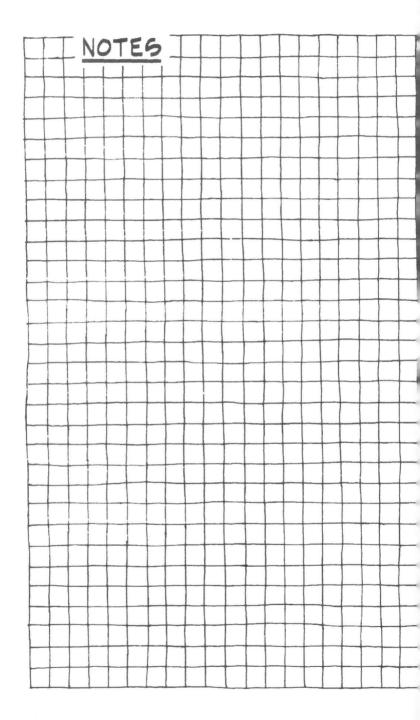

NOTES

__ E. SITE IMPROVEMENTS

Item	Costs
__ 1. Paving	
__ *a.* Asphalt:	
2″ AC	**$.40 to .90/SF (70%M and 40%L)**
For each added inch:	**Increase 25 to 45%**
4″ base:	**$.35 to .55/SF (60%M and 40%L)**
For each added inch:	**Increase 25%**
__ *b.* Concrete drives, walks, patios:	
½″ score joints at 5′ and expan. joints at 20′ to 30′	
4″ concrete slab:	**$1.50 to 2/SF (60%M and 40%L)**
Add:	
For base	**See AC, above**
For each inch more	**Add 15%**
For reinforcing	**5 to 10%**
For special finishes	**Add 100%**
For vapor barriers	**See p. 233.**
__ 2. Miscellaneous Concrete	
__ *a.* Curb	**$7.35/LF (30%M and 70%)**
__ *b.* Curb and gutter	**$12/LF**
Add for "rolled"	**+25%**
__ *c.* Conc. parking bumpers	**$40/ea. (65%M and 35%L)**
__ *d.* Paint stripes	**$.25/LF (20%M and 80%L)**
__ 3. Fences and Walls	
__ *a.* Chain link	
4′ high	**$4.85 to $5.80/LF (50% and 50%L)**
6′ high	**$8.60 to $9.30/LF**
__ *b.* Wrought iron, 3′ to 4′	**$20/LF (70% and 30%)**
__ *c.* Wood fending	**$1.30 to $6.30/SF (60% and 40%L) depending on material, type, and height**
__ *d.* Walls	**See Parts 3 and 4.**

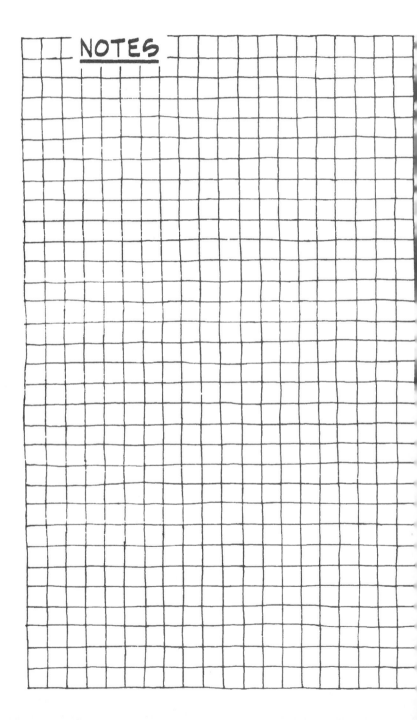

NOTES

__ F. LANDSCAPE AND IRRIGATION

__ 1. General
   __ a. Landscaping can be one of the greatest aesthetic enhancements for the design of buildings.
   __ b. Landscaping can be used for energy conservation. See p. 101.
   __ c. Landscaping can be used for noise reduction. See p. 112.
   __ d. At locations with expansive soils, be careful about plants and irrigation next to buildings.
   __ e. Existing: Mature trees will not survive a violent change of habitat. The ground may not be cut away near their roots, nor may more than a few inches be added to grade; although a large well with radial drains and 6″ of crushed stone out to the drip may work. As a rule, though, up to 50% of the root system can be lost without killing a plant, providing the other 50% is completely undisturbed. Trees which grew in a wood must be preserved in a clump, since they have shallow roots, while trees that were originally isolated or in open fence lines should be kept so.
   __ f. As a general rule, trees should be located no closer to buildings than the extent of the mature "drip line." When closer, deeper foundations may be needed, especially in expansive soils.
   __ g. For interior plants and pots, see p. 319.
   __ h. Trees are often selected by profile for aesthetics and function:

CANOPY   TALL   ROUND   FOCAL

__ 2. Materials
   __ a. Select material based on USDA Plant Zones, shown below. See App. B, item H, for various zones.

Zone	Approx. range of ave. annual min. temp.
2	−50 to −40°F
3	−40 to −30°F
4	−30 to −20°F
5	−20 to −10°F
6	−10 to 10°F
7	0 to −30°F
8	10 to 20°F
9	20 to 30°F
10	30 to 40°F

___ *b.* Next, select plants for microclimate of site (see p. 100) and location around building, as follows:
    ___ (1) Shaded locations and north sides
    ___ (2) Semi shaded locations and east sides
    ___ (3) Sunny locations and south and west sides

___ *c.* Select material by the following types:
    ___ (1) Large trees (over 20′, often up to 50′ high)
    ___ (2) Small trees (under 20′ high)
    ___ (3) High shrubs (over 8′ high)
    ___ (4) Moderate shrubs (4′ to 8′ high)
    ___ (5) Low shrubs (under 4′ high)
    ___ (6) Ground covers (spreading plants under 24″ high)

___ *d.* Select material based on growing season, including:
    ___ (1) Evergreen versus deciduous
    ___ (2) Annuals (put in seasonally, not returning) versus perennials (die in winter but return in spring)

___ *e.* Selection based on aesthetics:
    ___ (1) Shape (see item 1-*h*, above) and texture
    ___ (2) Color, often dependent on blooming season

Costs: Shown below, (50%M and 50%L), variation of +/−25%, depending on soil, and growing season. For *commercial jobs, add 20%* due to warranties and maintenance.

Trees	15 gal $95/ea.		**Shrubs** 1 gal $8/ea.	
	24″ box $300/ea.		5 gal $32/ea.	
	specimens $500 to $2500/ea.		specimens $60/ea.	
Vines	1 gal $8.50/ea.		**Ground covers**	
	5 gal $36/ea.		plants 1 gal	$8/ea.
			lawn sod	$.55/SF
			seed	$.25/SF

Other

Brick border	**$5.50/LF**
Rock	**$6/SF**
Preemergent	**$.06/SF**
Pots, 14″ ceramic with saucer	**$100/ea.**

___ 3. Irrigation

    ___ *a.* Can be in the following forms:

Type	Material	Costs
Bubbler	Plants and trees	**$3/SF**
Spray	Lawn	**$3–$5/SF**
Drip	Plants and trees	**$3/SF**

    ___ *b.* System should "tee" off water line before entering building. The tee size usually ranges between ¾″ and 2″.

    ___ *c.* Controls usually require a 110V outlet.

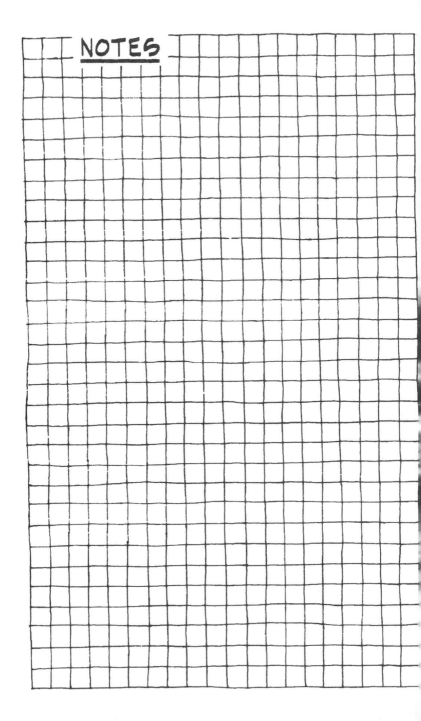
NOTES

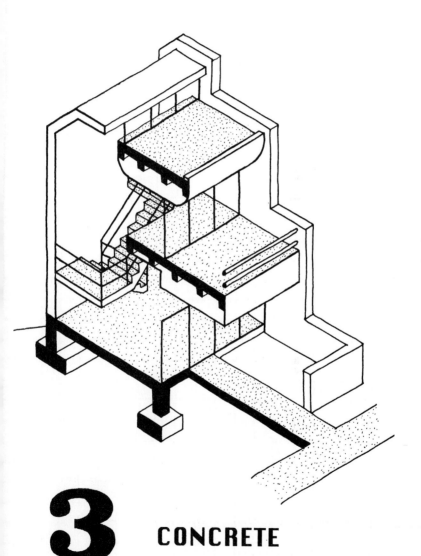

3 CONCRETE

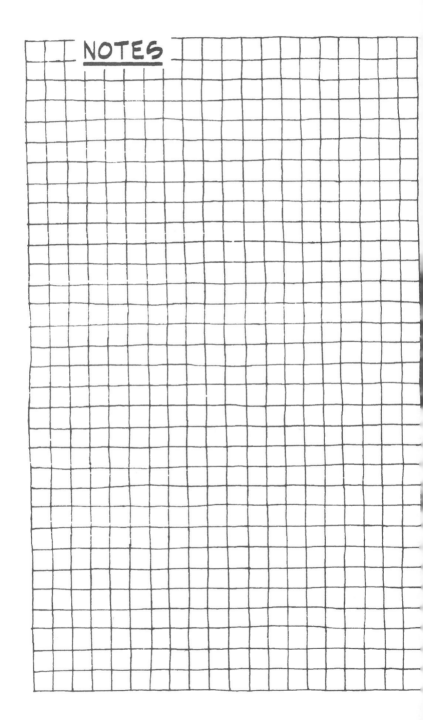

NOTES

___ A. CONCRETE MATERIALS

④ ⑲ ㊳ ㊸ ㊺

___ **1. General Cast-in-Place Costs**
   ___ *a.* **Substructure: $210/CY (40%M and 60%L)**
   ___ *b.* **Superstructure: $390/CY (30%M and 70%L)**
___ 2. Concrete: Consists of (using the general 1-2-3 mix, 1 part cement, 2 parts sand, and 3 parts rock, plus water):
   ___ *a.* Portland cement
      ___ (1) Type I: Normal for general construction.
      ___ (2) Type II: Modified for a lower heat of hydration, for large structures or warm weather.
      ___ (3) Type III: Modified for high, early strength, where forms must be removed as soon as possible, such as high-rise construction or cold weather.
      ___ (4) Type IV: Modified for low heat for very large structures.
      ___ (5) Type V: Modified for sulfate resistance.
      ___ (6) Types IA, IIA, or IIIA: Air entrained to resist frost.
   ___ *b.* Fine aggregate (sand): ¼″ or smaller.
   ___ *c.* Course aggregate (rock and gravel): ¼″ to 2″.
   ___ *d.* Clean water: Just enough to permit ready working of mix into forms. Mix should not slide or run off a shovel. Major factor effecting strength and durability is the *water-cement ratio,* expressed as gallons of water per sack of cement (usually ranging from 5 to 8). Slump is a measure of this:

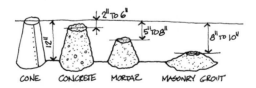

CONE   CONCRETE   MORTAR   MASONRY GROUT

___ 3. Structural Characteristics (Primer)
   ___ *a.* Strength

AVERAGE PHYSICAL PROPERTIES

MATERIAL	ELASTIC LIMIT (PSI)		ULTIMATE STRENGTH (PSI)			ALLOWABE WORKING UNIT STRESS (PSI)				MODULUS OF ELASTICITY (PSI)	WT. (#/CF.)
	TEN-SION	COM-PRESSION	TEN-SION	COM-PRESSION	SHEAR	TEN-SION	COM-PRESSION	SHEAR	EXTREME FIBER BENDING		
CONCRETE				2500			1125	75		3,000,000	150

157

___ *b.* Bending

___ (1) Concrete is strong in compression, but has little dependable tensile strength. Steel is strong in tension. When they are combined in a reinforced concrete bending member, such as a beam or slab, the concrete resists compression and the steel resists the tension. Thus, the reinforcing must be located at the tension face of the member.

Reinforcing splices in continuous top reinforcing are usually located at midspan. Splices at bottom reinforcing are usually located over supports.

___ (2) Reinforcing: Steel bars start at #2s, which are ¼″ dia. Sizes go up to #11s, with each size an added ⅛″. All bars are deformed except #2s. A common problem is trying to cram too many bars into too small a section.

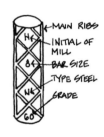

___ (3) Shear

___ (*a*) When concrete fails in shear it is generally due to a tension

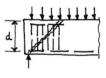

failure along a diagonal line. Vertical steel "stirrups" or diagonal bars are often used to tie the top and bottom parts together across the potential crack and prevent failure. This steel must be placed accurately in the field.

____ (b) The weakness of concrete in diagonal tension leads to problems with keys and construction joints.

SPALLED KEY

BETTER

SPALLED KEY

BETTER

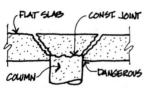

CONSTRUCTION JOINT IN COLUMN POURED TOO HIGH.

BETTER

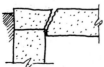

WALL POURED HIGHER THAN SLAB

SOLUTION

___ (4) Bond: Reinforcing lap splices need to be long enough to bond with the concrete. These splices close to the surface are weak, so reinforcing needs to be centered or kept clear of surfaces. In general, bars should not be lap-spliced at points of maximum stress.

___ (5) Columns

   ___ (*a*) In columns, both the concrete and the steel can work in compression.

   ___ (*b*) Bars need steel ties to keep them from buckling outward. Also, closely spaced ties help confine the concrete against breaking apart.

   ___ (*c*) 90° hooks are often used, but should *not* be used in seismic areas. The best anchor for the end of a tie is a 135° hook around the rebar and back into the concrete.

   ___ (*d*) The ultimate in tying bars against outward buckling and confining concrete against breaking apart is the spirally reinforced column.

   ___ (*e*) Reinforcing is often lap-spliced at floor levels.

___ (6) Concrete shrinks: Details must allow for this. Try to avoid locking fresh concrete between two immovable objects. Pouring sequences should consider this problem.

___ (7) Prestressed Concrete:

   ___ (*a*) Differs from ordinary, reinforced concrete in that prestressing steel is under a very high tension, compressing the concrete together, before any load is placed on the member. This strengthens the concrete in shear as well as bending. This requires very high strength steel which is impractical in ordinary reinforced concrete but results in large steel savings.

   ___ (*b*) *Postensioning* involves tightening the rods or cables *after* the concrete is poured and cured. This concentrates a large stress at each end of the cables and requires special care

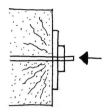

(bearing plates, special hardware, reinforcing, etc.) to prevent failure at these points. If an end connection fails in unbonded postensioning, there's no reinforcing strength left!

___ (c) *Pretensioning* has none of these "all the eggs in one basket" problems. Pretensioning lends itself to precast, plant-produced members, while posttensioning lends itself to work at the job site.

___ (d) Problems

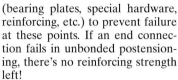

___ 1. Continuing shrinkage is the most common problem with prestressed concrete. All details must consider long-term shrinkage.

___ 2. Notches in precast tees at bearing may cause problems.

___ 4. Testing: Typical design compressive strengths are f′c = 2500 to 3000 psi. To be sure of actual constructed strengths, compressive cylinder tests are made:

7-Day Break	28-Day Break
60 to 70% of final strength	Final strength

The UBC requires average of three tests to meet or exceed f′c. No test must fall below f′c by 500 psi.

___ 5. FINISHES: Different wall finishes can be achieved by:

Type	Cost
___ a. Cast shapes and textures	**$1.60 to 6.00/SF**
___ b. Abrasive treatment (bush hammering, etc.)	**$1.00 to 3.20/SF**
___ c. Chemical retardation (exposed aggregate, etc.)	**$0.50/SF**

CAST

BUSH HAMMERED

EXP, AGG.

__ B. FOUNDATIONS

___ 1. Functions
     ___ *a.* Transfers building loads to ground
     ___ *b.* Anchors the building against wind and seismic loads
     ___ *c.* Isolates the building from frost heaving
     ___ *d.* Isolates building from expansive soils
     ___ *e.* Holds building above or from ground moisture
     ___ *f.* Retards heat flow to or from conditioned space
     ___ *g.* Provides storage space (basements)
     ___ *h.* Provides living space (basements)
     ___ *i.* Houses mechanical systems (basements)
___ 2. Types
     ___ *a.* Slab-on-grade   ___ *b.* Crawl space   ___ *c.* Basement

__ C. CONCRETE MEMBERS (SIZES AND COSTS)

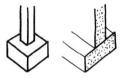

See p. 96 for span-to-depth ratios.

___ 1. *Concrete Substructure*
  ___ *a. Spread footings*

Spread footings located under walls and columns are appropriate for low-rise buildings (one to four stories) where soil conditions are firm enough to support the weight of the building on the area of the spread footings. When needed, footings at columns can be connected together with grade beams to provide more lateral stability in earthquakes. If the bearing capacity of the soil is four times greater than the overall weight of the building divided by the area of its footprint, spread footings are called for. These are the most widely used type of footing, especially in mild climates, because they are the most economical. Depth of footing should be below topsoil and frost line, on compacted fill (or firm native soil) but should be above water table.

Concrete spread footings are normally 1′ thick, but at least as thick as the width of stem wall. Width is normally twice that of stem wall. Typical column footings are 3′ to 4′ square for one- or two-story buildings.

Approximate cost for a column-spread footing (M and L) with excavation, backfill, and reinforcing with 3000 psi concrete, 3′ × 3′, 12″: $95.50/ea.

Approximate cost for a wall-spread (strip) footing (stem wall not included) is $28.50/LF.

Approximate cost of concrete stem walls: $33.00/LF.

  ___ *b. Other foundation systems:* As the weight of the building increases in relation to the bearing capacity (or depth of good bearing) soil, the footings need to expand in size or different systems need to be used.

___ (1) For expansive soils with low to medium loads (or high loads with rock not too far down) *Drilled piers (caissons) and grade beams* can be used. The pier may be straight like a column or

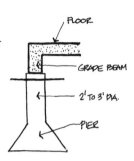

"belled" out to spread the load at the bearing level of soil. The grade beam is designed to resist expansion or compression of the soil as if it were in the air.

Approximate cost of a 28″ deep × 1′ wide, 8-KLF load *GRADE BEAM* spanning 15′ is $46.25/LF (M and L).

Approximate cost of a 2′ × 50′ concrete caisson (3000 psi concrete) is $1740/each (M and L).

___ (2) *Piles:*   Piles are long columns that are driven into the ground. Piles transfer the loads to a lower, stronger stratum or can transfer the load by friction along the length of the pile (skin friction). Piles are usually grouped together under a footing (pile cap) of reinforced concrete.

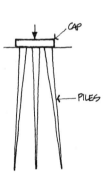

Approximate cost of reinforced concrete (3000 psi) *PILE CAP* for two piles with a dimension of 6.5′ × 3.5′ by 1′–8′ deep for 45K load is $300/ea. (M & L).

Different types of piles, their loads, and approximate costs (M and L):

___ **CIP concrete, end-bearing, 50k, with 12″ to 14″ steel shell, 25′ long, $630/ea.**
___ **Precast concrete, end-bearing, 50k, 10″ sq., 50′ long, $780/ea.**

___ Steel pipe, end-bearing, 50k, 12″ dia., 50′ long, $1560/ea.

___ Steel H Piles, end-bearing, 100k, 50′ long, $1160/ea.

___ Steel-step tapered, end-bearing, 50k, 50′ long, $630/ea.

___ Treated wood pile, 3 ea. in cluster, end-bearing, 50k, 25′ long, $1230/ea. group.

___ Pressure-injected footings, end-bearing, 50k, 50′ long, $1300/ea.

H

O

o o
o

O

    ___ (3) *Mat foundations:* For poor soil conditions and tall buildings (10 to 20 stories) with their overturning moments, a mat foundation is required. A mat foundation is a large mass of concrete laid under the entire building. Mat foundations range from 4′ to 8′ thick.

Approximate cost: See p. 157.

___ 2. *Concrete Superstructure*
   ___ *a. Concrete slabs*
      ___ (1) *Slab-on-grade:* General rule on paving slabs is that depth should be ½ to ⅓ of average annual frost penetration. Typical thickness:

Floors	4″
Garage Floors	5″
Terraces	5″
Driveways	6″ to 8″
Sidewalks	4″ to 6″

Approximate cost of 4″ reinforced slab is $2 to $2.50/SF.
For rock base see p. 149.
For vapor barrier see p. 233.
For compacted subgrade see p. 131.

      ___ (2) *Reinforced concrete slabs in the air:* For general span-to-depth ratios, see p. 96.
        ___ (*a*) *Two-way flat plate slabs*
        ___ Flat plate
          ___ Usual spans of 10′ to 30′.
          ___ Usual thickness: 6″ to 10″

___ Usual maximum ratio of long to short side of bay: 1.33.
___ Typical ratio of span to depth: *30*.
___ Another common rule is to allow 1″ thickness for each 3′ of span.

Approx. costs of $6.50/SF (15′ bays, 40 psf) to $8.30/SF (25′b bays, 125 psf). 25%M & 75%L.

___ Flat slab with drop panels
___ Usual spans: 16′ to 36′
___ Usual thickness: 6″ to 12″
___ Usual maximum ratio of long to short side of bay: 1.33
___ Side of drop panels: +/– ⅓ span
___ Typical ratios of span to depth 30 to 40 with *36* a good average

Approx. costs of $7/SF (15′ bays, 40 psf) to $10.50/SF (35′ bays, 125 psf). 35%M & 65%L.

___ (*b*) Two-way waffle slabs
___ Usual spans: 25′ to 40′.
___ Standard pan sizes: 20″ to 30″ square with other sizes available. Standard pan depths 8″ to 20″ in 2″ increments.
___ Usual maximum ratio of long to short side of bay is 1.33.
___ Typical ratio of span to depth: 25.

Approximate cost of $9.10/SF (20′ bays, 40 psf) to $11.35/SF (40′ bays, 125 psf). 40%M and 60%L.

___ (*c*) Precast concrete planks
___ Thickness of 6″ to 12″ in 2″ increments.
___ Spans of 8′ to 36′ (long, prestressed spans up to 50′).
___ Span-to-depth ratio of approximately *35*.
___ 1½″ to 2″ conc. topping often used.

Approximate cost of $7.20/SF (M 85% and L 15%) with 35% variation higher or lower.

___ *b. Concrete beams and joists*
___ (1) Precast concrete I beams (prestressed)
___ (*a*) Typical beam thickness of 12″ to 16″.
___ (*b*) Spans range from 20′ to 100′.
___ (*c*) Approximate ratios of span to depth of *20 to 25.*

Approximate cost of $65/LF (M 90% and L 10%) with variations of 20% higher or lower.

___ (2) Prestressed T beams (single and double tees)
___ (*a*) Typical flange widths of ½ to ⅓ the effective depth (8′ to 10′)
___ (*b*) Usual spans of 20′ to 120′
___ (*c*) Approximate ratio of span-to-depth ratio: 30
___ (*d*) Usually has 1½″ to 2″ concrete topping

Approximate cost of double tee 2′ deep with 35′ to 100′ span is $4.80/SF (M 90% and L 10%) with variation of 10% higher or lower.

___ (3) Concrete beams and joists. See p. 96 for typical span-to-depth ratios, or 1″ to 1¼″ for every foot of span. Width should be ½ to ¾ the effective depth. The clear distance between lateral supports should never exceed 32 times the least width of compression flange.

For costs see page 157.

___ *c. Concrete columns*
___ (1) See p. 96, for general span-to-depth ratio.
___ (2) Round columns usually 12″ minimum.
___ (3) Rectangular: 12 in sq. minimum.
___ (4) Usual minimum rectangular tied columns 10″ × 12″.
___ (5) Square or round spiral columns: 14″; add 2″ for each story.
___ (6) Most columns are "short": maximum height *10* times least cross-section dimension.

___ (7) Maximum unbraced height for "engineered" long columns: *20* times least cross-section dimension.

Approximate cost of $100/CY (M 65% and L 35%) with variation of 5% higher or lower.

___ *d. Concrete walls*
   ___ (1) Wall Thickness
      ___ (*a*) Multistory: 6″ top 15′, add 1″ for each successive 25′ down.
      ___ (*b*) Basements: 8″ minimum.
      ___ (*c*) Nonbearing: Minimum thickness 2″. Maximum ratio of unsupported height, H/25.
      ___ (*d*) Precast wall panels:
           Minimum thickness: 4″
           Maximum ratio of unbraced length to thickness: 50

Approximate cost of $11/SF for 6″, reinf. wall (M ⅔ and L ⅓) with variation of 25% higher or lower.

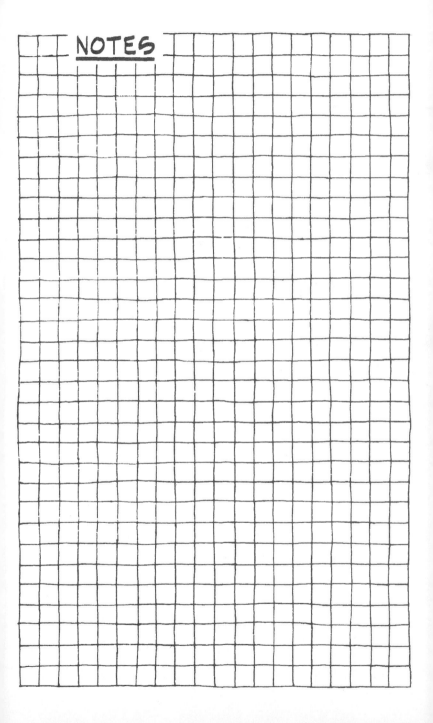

NOTES

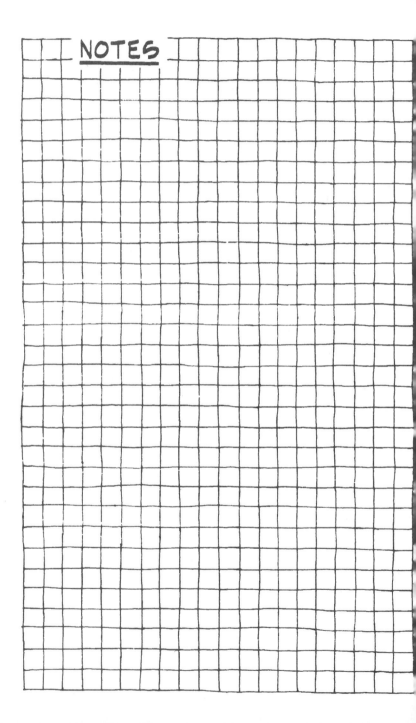

NOTES

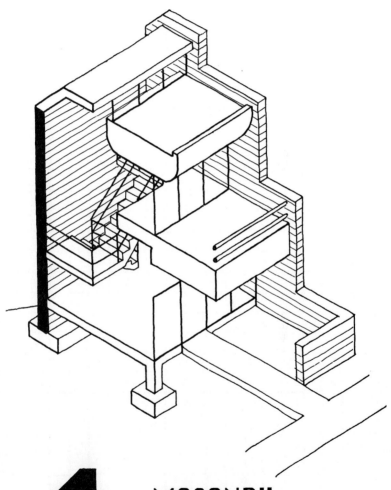

4 MASONRY

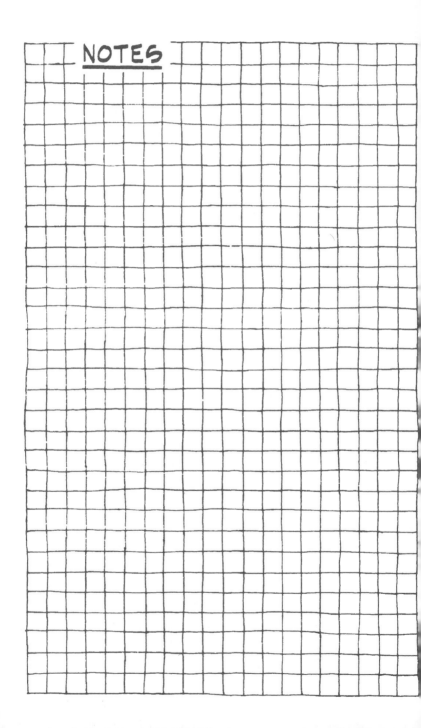

NOTES

__ A. MASONRY MATERIALS

(4) (19) (38) (43) (45)

___ 1. General: Masonry consists of:
 ___ *a.* Brick
  ___ (1) Fired
  ___ (2) Unfired ("adobe")
 ___ *b.* Concrete block (concrete masonry units)
 ___ *c.* Stone
___ 2. Structural Characteristics
 ___ *a.* Strength

AVERAGE PHYSICAL PROPERTIES

	ELASTIC LIMIT (PSI)		ULTIMATE STRENGTH (PSI)			ALLOWABLE WORKING UNIT STRESS (PSI)				MODULUS OF ELASTICITY (PSI)	WT. (#/CF)
	TEN-SION	COM-PRESSION	TEN-SION	f'm COM-PRESSION	SHEAR	TEN-SION	COM-PRESSION	SHEAR	EXTREME FIBER BENDING		
ADOBE				300-500			30	8			110
BRICK				2800		800	100-250	50		2,500,000	120
CMU				1500		500	300	38		1,900,000	145
STONE				2500			200-400	8			145

 ___ *b.* Reinforcing: Like concrete, masonry is strong in compression, but weak in tension. Therefore, steel reinforcement must usually be added to walls to simulate columns and beams.
  ___ (1) Like *columns:* Vertical bars @ 2' to 4' oc.
  ___ (2) Like *beams:* "Bond Beams" @ 4' to 8' oc.
  ___ (3) Also, added *Horizontal Wire Reinforcement* (ladder or truss type) @ 16" oc. vertically, to help resist lateral forces and cracking.
___ 3. Bonds
 ___ *a.* Structural (method of laying units together):
  ___ (1) Overlapping units.
  ___ (2) *Metal ties* (should be galvanized with zinc coating of 2 oz/SF, or stainless steel). Wire ties usually @ every 3 SF, or . . .
   Metal anchors, usually at 16" oc, vertical and 24" oc, horizontal.
  ___ (3) Grout and mortar:
   ___ (*a*) *Grout* encases reinforcing bars (a "soup" of sand, cement, water, and often with pea gravel). Usually 2000 psi comp. strength. Always poured

in cavities and high slump. See p. 157.

___ (*b*) *Mortar:* Stiffer mix of sand, cement, lime, and water, to bond units together by trowel work. Types:

    ___ N General purpose, medium strength, for above grade.

    ___ M High strength for high compression, for above grade.

    ___ S High strength for compression and tension.

    ___ O High lime, low strength, easily workable for veneers, not subject to freezing.

    ___ K Low strength, for interiors.

___ (4) Bond joints

___ (5) Bond pattern

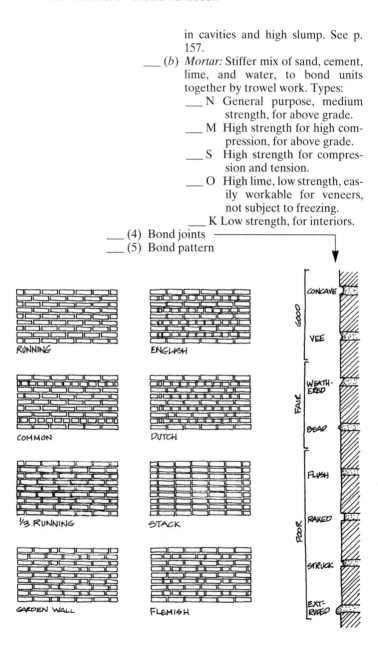

RUNNING

COMMON

⅓ RUNNING

GARDEN WALL

ENGLISH

DUTCH

STACK

FLEMISH

GOOD
  CONCAVE
  VEE

FAIR
  WEATH-ERED
  BEAD

POOR
  FLUSH
  RAKED
  STRUCK
  EXT-RUDED

___ 4. Control and Expansion Joints

    ___ *a.* Width

        ___ (1) Thermal movement. See p. 248.   = ___
Plus,

        ___ (2) Movement due to moisture: = ___

            ___ (*a*) Bricks expand; should be laid wet.

            ___ (*b*) CMU shrinks like conc.; should be laid dry. Plus,

        ___ (3) Construction tolerance.   = ___

                        Total width   = ___

    ___ *b.* Locations

        ___ (1) Corners

        ___ (2) Length of walls: 20′ to 25′ oc (double at parapets and bond beams.

        ___ (3) Offsets, returns, and intersections.

        ___ (4) Openings:

            ___ (*a*) One side of opening, less than 6′ wide.

            ___ (*b*) Two sides of opening, greater than 6′ wide.

        ___ (5) Against other materials.

___ 5. Coatings: Must be

        ___ (1) "Bridgeable" (seal cracks)

        ___ (2) Breathable (do not trap vapor)

___ 6. Brick

    ___ *a.* Types

        ___ (1) Common (building)

        ___ (2) Face

            ___ (*a*) FBX Select

            ___ (*b*) FBS Standard

            ___ (*c*) FBA Architectural

        ___ (3) Clinker

        ___ (4) Glazed

        ___ (5) Fire

        ___ (6) Cored

        ___ (7) Sand-lime (white, yellow)

        ___ (8) Pavers

    ___ *b.* Weatherability

        ___ (1) NW Negligible weathering; for indoor or sheltered locations.

        ___ (2) MW Moderate weather locations.

        ___ (3) SW Severe weather locations and/or earth contact.

_____ *c.* Positions

_____ *d.* Sizes:
(modular brick based on 4″ module with ⅜″ jt.)

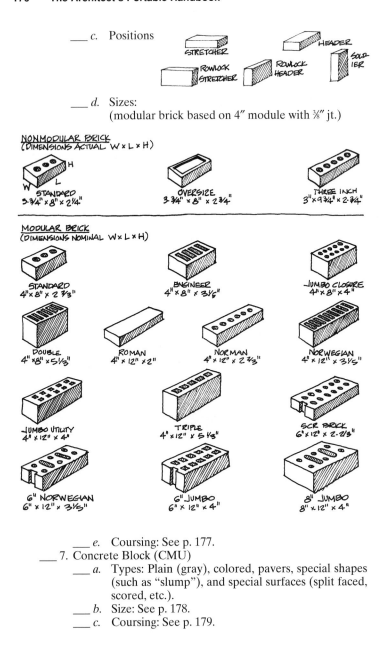

_____ *e.* Coursing: See p. 177.
_____ 7. Concrete Block (CMU)
    _____ *a.* Types: Plain (gray), colored, pavers, special shapes (such as "slump"), and special surfaces (split faced, scored, etc.).
    _____ *b.* Size: See p. 178.
    _____ *c.* Coursing: See p. 179.

BRICK COURSING

COURSE	NONMODULAR						MODULAR				
	2 1/4" THICK BRICKS		2 5/8" THICK BRICKS		2 3/4" THICK BRICKS		NOMINAL THICKNESS (HEIGHT) OF BRICK				
	3/8" JOINT	1/2" JOINTS	3/8" JOINT	1/2" JOINT	3/8" JOINT	1/2" JOINT	2"	2 2/3"	3 1/5"	4"	5 1/3"
1	2 5/8"	2 3/4"	3"	3 1/8"	3 1/8"	3 1/4"	2"	2 11/16"	3 3/16"	4"	5 5/16"
2	5 1/4"	5 1/2"	6"	6 1/4"	6 1/4"	6 1/2"	4"	5 5/16"	6 3/8"	8"	10 11/16"
3	7 7/8"	8 1/4"	9"	9 3/8"	9 3/8"	9 3/4"	6"	8"	9 5/8"	1'-0"	1'-4"
4	10 1/2"	11"	1'-0"	1'-0 1/2"	1'-0 1/2"	1'-1"	8"	10 11/16"	1'-0 13/16"	1'-4"	1'-9 5/16"
5	1'-1 1/8"	1'-1 3/4"	1'-3"	1'-3 5/8"	1'-3 5/8"	1'-4 1/4"	10"	1'-1 5/16"	1'-4"	1'-8"	2'-2 11/16"
6	1'-3 3/4"	1'-4 1/2"	1'-6"	1'-6 3/4"	1'-6 3/4"	1'-7 1/2"	1'-0"	1'-4"	1'-7 3/16"	2'-0"	2'-8"
7	1'-6 3/8"	1'-7 1/4"	1'-9"	1'-9 7/8"	1'-9 7/8"	1'-10 3/4"	1'-2"	1'-6 11/16"	1'-10 3/8"	2'-4"	3'-1 5/16"
8	1'-9"	1'-10"	2'-0"	2'-1"	2'-1"	2'-2"	1'-4"	1'-9 5/16"	2'-1 5/8"	2'-8"	3'-6 11/16"
9	1'-11 5/8"	2'-0 3/4"	2'-3"	2'-4 1/8"	2'-4 1/8"	2'-5 1/4"	1'-6"	2'-0"	2'-4 13/16"	3'-0"	4'-0"
10	2'-2 1/4"	2'-3 1/2"	2'-6"	2'-7 1/4"	2'-7 1/4"	2'-8 1/2"	1'-8"	2'-2 11/16"	2'-8"	3'-4"	4'-5 5/16"
11	2'-4 7/8"	2'-6 1/4"	2'-9"	2'-10 3/8"	2'-10 3/8"	2'-11 3/4"	1'-10"	2'-5 5/16"	2'-11 3/16"	3'-8"	4'-10 11/16"
12	2'-7 1/2"	2'-9"	3'-0"	3'-1 1/2"	3'-1 1/2"	3'-3"	2'-0"	2'-8"	3'-2 3/8"	4'-0"	5'-4"
13	2'-10 1/8"	2'-11 3/4"	3'-3"	3'-4 5/8"	3'-4 5/8"	3'-6 1/4"	2'-2"	2'-10 11/16"	3'-5 5/8"	4'-4"	5'-9 5/16"
14	3'-0 3/4"	3'-2 1/2"	3'-6"	3'-7 3/4"	3'-7 3/4"	3'-9 1/2"	2'-4"	3'-1 5/16"	3'-8 13/16"	4'-8"	6'-2 11/16"
15	3'-3 3/8"	3'-5 1/4"	3'-9"	3'-10 7/8"	3'-10 7/8"	4'-0 3/4"	2'-6"	3'-4"	4'-0"	5'-0"	6'-8"
16	3'-6"	3'-8"	4'-0"	4'-2"	4'-2"	4'-4"	2'-8"	3'-6 11/16"	4'-4 3/16"	5'-4"	7'-1 5/16"
17	3'-8 5/8"	3'-10 3/4"	4'-3"	4'-5 1/8"	4'-5 1/8"	4'-7 1/4"	2'-10"	3'-9 5/16"	4'-6 3/8"	5'-8"	7'-6 11/16"
18	3'-11 1/4"	4'-1 1/2"	4'-6"	4'-8 1/4"	4'-8 1/4"	4'-10 1/2"	3'-0"	4'-0"	4'-9 5/8"	6'-0"	8'-0"
19	4'-1 7/8"	4'-4 1/4"	4'-9"	4'-11 3/8"	4'-11 3/8"	5'-1 3/4"	3'-2"	4'-2 11/16"	5'-0 13/16"	6'-4"	8'-5 5/16"
20	4'-4 1/2"	4'-7"	5'-0"	5'-2 1/2"	5'-2 1/2"	5'-5"	3'-4"	4'-5 5/16"	5'-4"	6'-8"	8'-10 11/16"
21	4'-7 1/8"	4'-9 3/4"	5'-3"	5'-5 5/8"	5'-5 5/8"	5'-8 1/4"	3'-6"	4'-8"	5'-7 3/16"	7'-0"	9'-4"
22	4'-9 3/4"	5'-0 1/2"	5'-6"	5'-8 3/4"	5'-8 3/4"	5'-11 1/2"	3'-8"	4'-10 11/16"	5'-10 3/8"	7'-4"	9'-9 5/16"
23	5'-0 3/8"	5'-3 1/4"	5'-9"	5'-11 7/8"	5'-11 7/8"	6'-2 3/4"	3'-10"	5'-1 5/16"	6'-1 5/8"	7'-8"	10'-2 11/16"
24	5'-3"	5'-6"	6'-0"	6'-3"	6'-3"	6'-6"	4'-0"	5'-4"	6'-4 13/16"	8'-0"	10'-8"

CONCRETE BLOCK TYPES & SIZES

NOMINAL DIMENSIONS W × L × H (ACTUAL DIMENSIONS ARE 3/8" LESS)

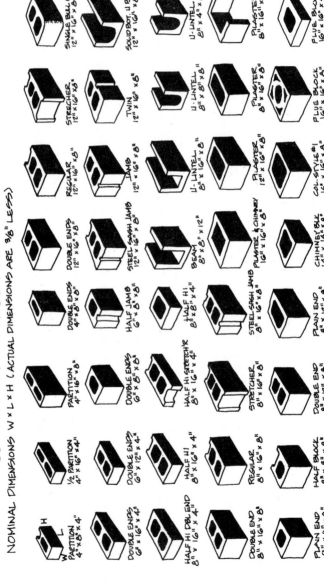

SINGLE BULL NOSE 12" × 16" × 8"

SOLID BOT. U BLOCK 12" × 16" × 8"

U-LINTEL 8" × 4" × 8"

PILASTER 8" × 16" × 8"

FLUE BLOCK 16" × 16" × 4"

STRETCHER 12" × 16" × 8"

TWIN 12" × 16" × 8"

U-LINTEL 8" × 8" × 8"

PILASTER 8" × 8" × 8"

FLUE BLOCK 16" × 16" × 8"

REGULAR 12" × 16" × 8"

JAMB 12" × 16" × 8"

U-LINTEL 8" × 16" × 8"

PILASTER 8" × 16" × 8"

COL. STYLE #1 16" × 16" × 8"

DOUBLE ENDS 12" × 16" × 8"

STEEL SASH JAMB 12" × 16" × 8"

BEAM 8" × 8" × 12"

PILASTER & CHIMNEY 16" × 16" × 8"

CHIMNEY BLK 14" × 14" × 8"

DOUBLE ENDS 4" × 8" × 8"

HALF JAMB 6" × 8" × 8"

HALF HI 8" × 8" × 4"

STEEL SASH JAMB 8" × 16" × 8"

PLAIN END 8" × 12" × 8"

PARTITION 4" × 16" × 8"

DOUBLE ENDS 6" × 8" × 8"

HALF HI STRETCHR 8" × 16" × 4"

STRETCHER 8" × 16" × 8"

DOUBLE END 8" × 12" × 8"

1/2 PARTITION 4" × 16" × 4"

DOUBLE ENDS 6" × 12" × 4"

HALF HI 8" × 16" × 4"

REGULAR 8" × 16" × 8"

HALF BLOCK 8" × 8" × 8"

PARTITION 4" × 8" × 4"

DOUBLE ENDS 6" × 16" × 4"

HALF HI DBL END 8" × 16" × 4"

DOUBLE END 8" × 16" × 8"

PLAIN END 8" × 8" × 8"

178

CONCRETE BLOCK COURSING

CSC	4" HIGH BLK.	8" HIGH BLK.	CSC	4" HIGH BLK.	8" HIGH BLK.
1	4"	8"	38	12'-8"	25'-4"
2	8"	1'-4"	39	13'-0"	26'-0"
3	1'-0"	2'-0"	40	13'-4"	26'-8"
4	1'-4"	2'-8"	41	13'-8"	27'-4"
5	1'-8"	3'-4"	42	14'-0"	28'-0"
6	2'-0"	4'-0"	43	14'-4"	28'-8"
7	2'-4"	4'-8"	44	14'-8"	29'-4"
8	2'-8"	5'-4"	45	15'-0"	30'-0"
9	3'-0"	6'-0"	46	15'-4"	30'-8"
10	3'-4"	6'-8"	47	15'-8"	31'-4"
11	3'-8"	7'-4"	48	16'-0"	32'-0"
12	4'-0"	8'-0"	49	16'-4"	32'-8"
13	4'-4"	8'-8"	50	16'-8"	33'-4"
14	4'-8"	9'-4"	51	17'-0"	34'-0"
15	5'-0"	10'-0"	52	17'-4"	34'-8"
16	5'-4"	10'-8"	53	17'-8"	35'-4"
17	5'-8"	11'-4"	54	18'-0"	36'-0"
18	6'-0"	12'-0"	55	18'-4"	36'-8"
19	6'-4"	12'-8"	56	18'-8"	37'-4"
20	6'-8"	13'-4"	57	19'-0"	38'-0"
21	7'-0"	14'-0"	58	19'-4"	38'-8"
22	7'-4"	14'-8"	59	19'-8"	39'-4"
23	7'-8"	15'-4"	60	20'-0"	40'-0"
24	8'-0"	16'-0"	61	20'-4"	40'-8"
25	8'-4"	16'-8"	62	20'-8"	41'-4"
26	8'-8"	17'-4"	63	21'-0"	42'-0"
27	9'-0"	18'-0"	64	21'-4"	42'-8"
28	9'-4"	18'-8"	65	21'-8"	43'-4"
29	9'-8"	19'-4"	66	22'-0"	44'-0"
30	10'-0"	20'-0"	67	22'-4"	44'-8"
31	10'-4"	20'-8"	68	22'-8"	45'-4"
32	10'-8"	21'-4"	69	23'-0"	46'-0"
33	11'-0"	22'-0"	70	23'-4"	46'-8"
34	11'-4"	22'-8"	71	23'-8"	47'-4"
35	11'-8"	23'-4"	72	24'-0"	48'-0"
36	12'-0"	24'-0"	73	24'-4"	48'-8"
37	12'-4"	24'-8"	74	24'-8"	49'-4"

___ 8. Stone
     ___ *a.* Type unit
          ___ (1) *Ashlar:* Best, for strength and stability, is square-cut units on level beds. Joints of ½″ to ¾″.
          ___ (2) *Squared stone* (coursed rubble): Next best for strength and stability; is fitted less carefully than ashlar, but more carefully than rubble.
          ___ (3) *Rubble:* Built with a minimum of dressing, with joints unevenly coursed, or in a completely irregular pattern. Stones are lapped for bond and many stones extend through wall (when full-width wall) to bond it transversely. If built carefully, with all interstices completely filled with good cement mortar, has ample durability for ordinary structures.
     ___ *b.* Typical materials
          ___ (1) Limestone
          ___ (2) Sandstone
          ___ (3) Quartzite
          ___ (4) Granite
     ___ *c.* Wall types
          ___ (1) Full width
          ___ (2) Solid veneer (metal ties to structural wall)
          ___ (3) Thin veneer (set against mortar bed against structural wall)
     ___ *d.* Pattern type (see p. 185)

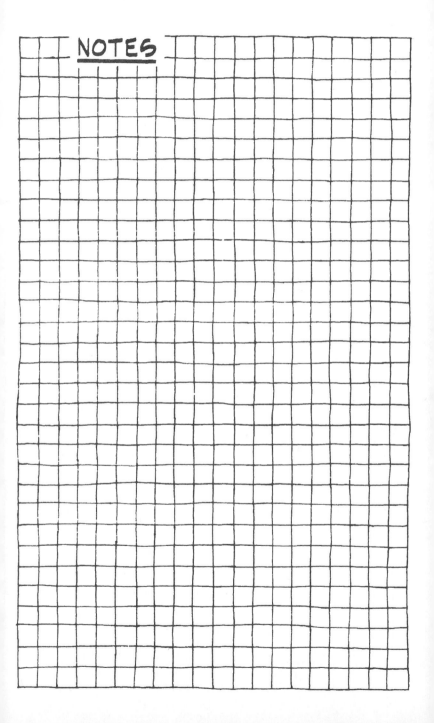

NOTES

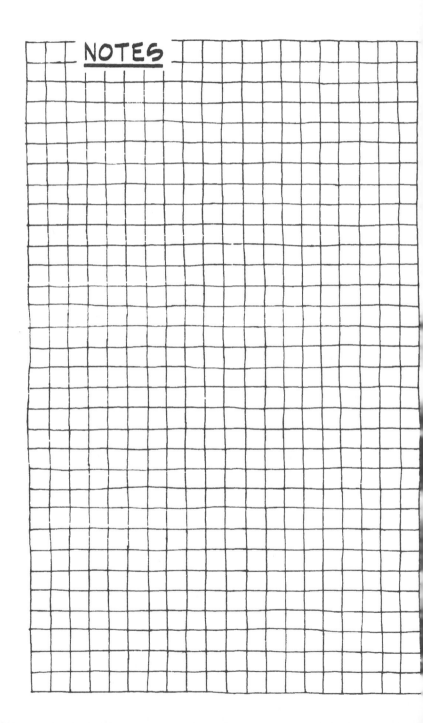

NOTES

___ B. MASONRY MEMBERS (SIZES AND COSTS)

See p. 96 for span-to-depth ratios.

___ 1. Concrete Block (CMU)
    ___ *a.* CMU columns
        See p. 96 for general rule of thumb. Max. ht. to thickness ratio = *20.* Min. size = 12″ × 12″.
    ___ *b.* CMU walls
        ___ (1) Nominal min. thickness: 6″
        ___ (2) Ratio of unsupported length or ht. to thickness: *25 to 35*
            For convenience, use 24. Then the length or height in feet can be divided in half for thickness in inches.

Costs: CMU (Reg. wt., gray, running bond, typ. reinf'g. and grout)

4″ walls:	$4.75/SF	(Typical 25 to 30%M and 75 to
6″ walls:	$5.30/SF	70%L)
8″ walls:	$6.40/SF	(Variations for special block, such as
12″ walls:	$8.55/SF	glazed, decorative, screen, etc. + 15% to 150%)

Deduct 30 to 40% for residential work.

___ 2. Brick Masonry
    ___ *a.* Columns
        ___ (1) See p. 96 for general rule of thumb.
        ___ (2) Usual min. dimension of 12″ (sometimes 8″).
        ___ (3) Maximum height = 20 × least dimensions.
        ___ (4) If unreinforced = 10 × least dimensions.

Costs: 12′ × 12″, standard brick: $27.50/VLF (20%M and 80%L).

    ___ *b.* Pilasters
        ___ (1) Usually considered when wall is 20′ high or more.

      ___ (2) Distance along wall: should not exceed 25×
wall thickness.

      ___ (3) Depth of pilaster: $\frac{1}{2}$ of wall height.

___ *c.* Brick walls

      ___ (1) Maximum ratio of
unbraced length or
height (whichever
least) is 25. For con-
venience use 24.
Then the length or
height in feet can be
divided in half for
thickness in inches.

      ___ (2) Reinforced bearing walls: Nominal mini-
mum thickness: 6″. Maximum ratio of unsupported length or height to thickness = *25.*

      ___ (3) Unreinforced bearing wall:
1 story: 8″ thick
2 stories: 12″ thick
+ 35′: 12″ upper 35′ and + 4″ added to each
35′ below

      ___ (4) Reinforced panel or curtain walls: Nominal
minimum thickness = 4″. Maximum ratio of
unsupported height to thickness = *30.* Maximum ratio of unbraced length to thickness
= *60.*

      ___ (5) Cavity walls: Typical nominal minimum
dimensions of 10″ (including 2″ air space).

Costs: **Standard brick, running bond, (25%M & 75%L) (Variations
of +5%, –20%):**

4″, single wythe, veneer:	**$7.10 to 11.30/SF**
8″, double wythe, cavity-filled:	**$15.30 to 24.50/SF**
12″, triple wythe, cavity-filled:	**$23.55 to 37.40/SF**

For other bonds, add 15% to 30%

    ___ *d.* Brick arches

      ___ (1) Minor arches:

          ___ (*a*) Span: Less than 6′

          ___ (*b*) Configuration: All

          ___ (*c*) Load: Less than 1000 PLF

          ___ (*d*) Span-to-depth: *0.15 max.*

      ___ (2) Major arches:

          ___ (*a*) Span: Over 6′

          ___ (*b*) Configuration: Semicircular & par-
abolic

___ (*c*) Load: Over 1000 PLF
___ (*d*) Span-to-depth: greater than *0.15*

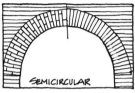

SEMICIRCULAR

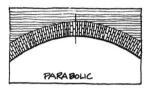

PARABOLIC

JACK

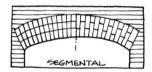

SEGMENTAL

___ 3. Stone Masonry
　　___ *a.* Bearing walls
　　　　___ (1) Nominal minimum thickness = 16″.
　　　　___ (2) Maximum ratio of unsupported length or height to thickness = 14.
　　___ *b.* Nonbearing walls
　　　　___ (1) Nominal minimum thickness = 4″.
　　　　___ (2) Maximum ratio of unsupported length or height to thickness = 18.

Costs: **4″ veneer (most common): $14.15/SF　(40%M　and　60%L)**
**　　　　　　　　　　　　　(Variation: + 50%)**
18″ rough stone wall (dry): $29/CF (40% and 60%L)

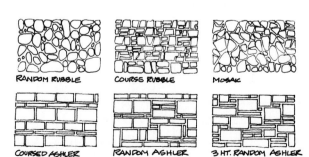

RANDOM RUBBLE　　　COURSE RUBBLE　　　MOSAIC

COURSED ASHLER　　　RANDOM ASHLER　　　3 HT. RANDOM ASHLER

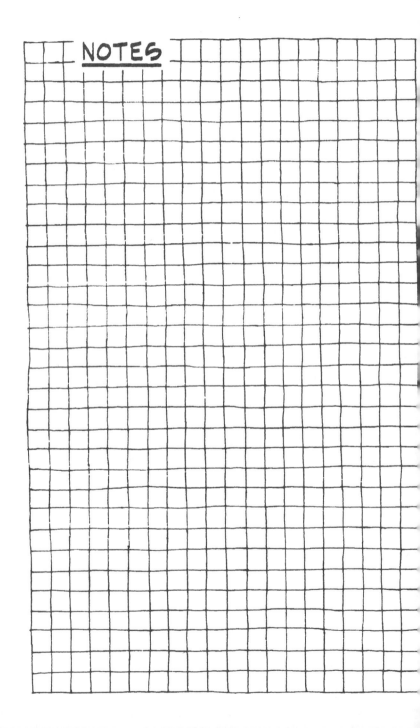

NOTES

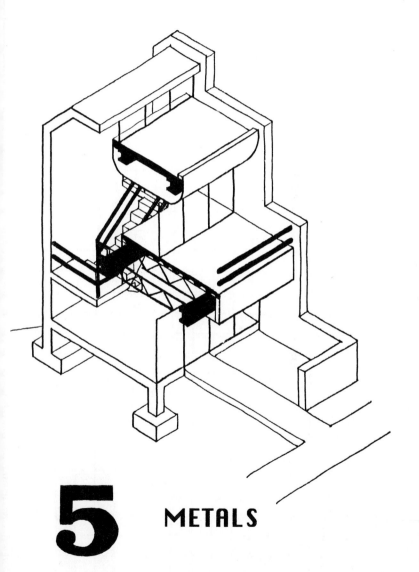

5 METALS

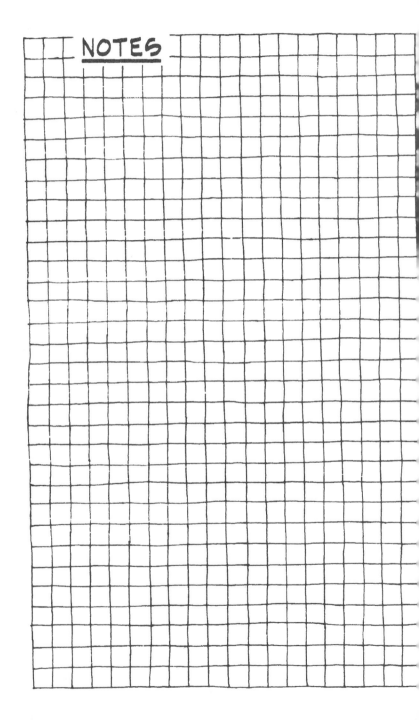

NOTES

___ A. METAL MATERIALS

(4) (19) (32) (38) (45)

___ 1. General
    ___ *a.* Ferrous metals (contains iron)
        ___ (1) Iron: Soft, easily worked, oxidizes rapidly, susceptible to acid.
        ___ (2) Cast iron: Brittle, corrosion-resistant, high-compressive strength. Used for gratings, stairs, etc.
        ___ (3) Malleable iron: Same as above, but better workability.
        ___ (4) Wrought iron: Soft, corrosion and fatigue resistant, machinable. Used for railings, grilles, screws, and ornamental items.
        ___ (5) Steel: Iron with carbon. Strongest metal. Used for structural purposes. See p. 190.
        ___ (6) Stainless steel: An alloy for max. corrosion-resistance. Used for flashing, handrails, hardware, connections, and equipment.
    ___ *b.* Nonferrous metals (not containing iron)
        ___ (1) Aluminum: Soft, ductile, high-corrosion resistance, low strength.
        ___ (2) Lead: Dense, workable, toxic, corrosion-resistant. Improved with alloys for hardness and strength. Used as waterproofing, sound isolation, and radiation shielding.
        ___ (3) Zinc: Corrosion-resistant, brittle, low-strength. Used in "galvanizing" of other metals for corrosion resistance for roofing, flashing, hardware, connections, etc.
        ___ (4) Chromium and nickel: Used as alloy for corrosion resistant bright "Plating".
        ___ (5) Monel: High-corrosion resistance for fasteners and anchors.
        ___ (6) Copper: Resistant to corrosion, impact, and fatigue. Ductile. Used for wiring, roofing, flashing, and piping.
        ___ (7) Bronze: An alloy for "plating."
        ___ (8) Brass: Copper with zinc for hardware, handrails, grilles, etc.
___ 2. Corrosion to Metals
    ___ *a.* Galvanic action, or corrosion, occurs between dissimilar metals or metals and other metals when sufficient moisture is present to carry an electric

current. The farther apart two metals are on the following list, the greater the corrosion of the more susceptible one:

> Anodic (+): Most susceptible to corrosion
> Magnesium
> Zinc
> Aluminum
> Cadmium
> Iron/steel
> Stainless steel (active)
> Soft solders
> Tin
> Lead
> Nickel
> Brass
> Bronzes
> Nickel-copper alloys
> Copper
> Stainless steel (passive)
> Silver solder
> Cathodic (−): Least susceptible to corrosion

___ *b.* Metals deteriorate also when in contact with chemically active materials, particularly when water is present. Aluminum in contact with concrete or mortar. Steel in contact with treated wood.

___ 3. Gauges: See Page 191.

___ 4. Structural Steel

    ___ *a.* General: The most commonly used strength grade of steel is 36,000 yield strength (A-36). For heavily loaded members such as columns, girders, or trusses—where buckling, lateral stability, deflection, or vibration does not control member selection—higher-yield strength steels may be economically used. A 50,000 psi yield strength is most frequently used among high-strength, low-alloy steels.

        High-strength, low-alloy steels are available in several grades and some possess superior corrosion resistance to such a degree that they are classified as "weathering steel."

        Concrete and masonry reinforcing steel (rebar) are 40,000 psi and 60,000 psi. Wire mesh is 60 to 70 ksi.

METAL GAUGES

GAUGE NO.	GRAPHIC SIZES	U.S. STD. REVISED		GRAPHIC SIZES
		DECIMAL	FRACTION	
000	■	.3750"	3/8"	●
00	■	.3437"	11/32"	●
0	■	.3125"	5/16"	●
1.	■	.2812"	9/32"	●
2.	■	.2656"	17/64"	●
3.	■	.2391"	15/64"	●
4.	■	.2242"	7/32°	●
5.	■	.2092"	13/64"	●
6.	■	.1943"	3/18"	●

7	■	.1793"	11/64" +	●
8	■	.1644"	11/64" −	●
9	■	.1495"	6/32" −	●
10	■	.1345"	9/64" −	●
11	■	.1196"	1/8" −	●
12	■	.1046"	7/64" −	●
13	■	.0897"	3/32" −	●
14	■	.0747"	5/64" −	●
15	■	.0673"	1/16" +	●
16	■	.0598"	1/16" −	●
17	■	.0538"	3/64" +	●
18	■	.0478"	3/64" +	●
19	■	.0418"	3/64" −	●
20	■	.0359"	1/32" +	●
21	■	.0329"	1/32" +	●
22	■	.0299"	1/32" −	●
23	■	.0269"	1/32" −	●
24	■	.0239"	1/32" −	●
25	●	.0209"	1/64" +	●
26	●	.0179"	1/64" +	●
27	●	.0164"	1/64" +	●
28	●	.0149"	1/64" −	●
29	●	.0135"	1/64" −	●
30	●	.0120"	1/64" −	●

AVERAGE PHYSICAL PROPERTIES

MATERIAL	ELASTIC LIMIT (psi)		ULTIMATE STRENGTH (psi)			ALLOW. WORKING UNIT STRESS (psi)				MODULUS OF ELASTICITY (psi)	WT. (#/C.F.)
	TEN-SION	COM-PRESSION	TEN-SION	COM-PRESSION	SHEAR	TEN-SION	COM-PRESSION	SHEAR	EXTREME FIBER BENDING		
CAST IRON			25000	75000	20000		9000			12 000 000	450
WROUGHT IRON	25000	25000	48000	48000	40000	12000	12000	8000	12000	28000000	485
STEEL A-36	36000	36000	70000	70000	55000	22000	20000	14500	24000	29000000	490
ALUM. ALLOY 6061-T6	35000		38000		30000	15000			12000	10 000 200	170

___ *b.* Economy: The weight of structural steel per SF of floor area increases with bay size, as does the depth of the structure. Cost of steel may not rise as rapidly as weight, if savings can be realized by reducing the number of pieces to be fabricated and erected. Improved space utilization afforded by larger bay sizes is offset by increases in wall area and building volume resulting from increased structure depth.

Steel frame economy can be improved by incorporating as many of these cost-reducing factors into the structure layout and design as architectural requirements permit.

___ (1) Keep columns in line in both directions and avoid offsets or omission of columns.

___ (2) Design for maximum repetition of member sizes within each level and from floor to floor.

___ (3) Reduce the number of beams and girders per level to reduce fabrication and erection time and cost.

___ (4) Maximize the use of simple beam connections by bracing the structure at a limited number of moment-resisting bents or by the most efficient method, cross-bracing.

___ (5) Utilize high-strength steels for columns and floor members where studies indicate that cost can be reduced while meeting other design parameters.

___ (6) Use composite design, but consider effect of in-slab electric raceways or other discontinuities.

___ (7) Consider open-web steel joists, especially for large roofs of one-story structures, and for floor framing in many applications.

The weight of steel for roofs or lightly loaded floors is generally least when long beams and short girders are used. For heavier loadings, long girders and short filler beams should result in less steel weight. The most economical framing type (composite; noncomposite, continuous simple spans, etc.) and arrangement must be determined for each structure, considering such factors as structure depth, building volume, wall area, mechanical system requirements, deflection or vibration limitations, wind or seismic load interaction between floor system, and columns or shear walls.

___ c. *Composite Construction* combines two different materials or two different grades of a material to form a structural member that utilizes the most desirable properties of each materials.

    ___ (1) Composite systems currently used in building construction include:

        ___ (a) Concrete-topped composite steel decks

        ___ (b) Steel beams acting compositely with concrete slabs

        ___ (c) Steel columns encased by or filled with concrete

        ___ (d) Open-web joists of wood and steel or joists with plywood webs and wood chords

        ___ (e) Trusses combining wood and steel

        ___ (f) Hybrid girders utilizing steel of different strengths

        ___ (g) Cast-in-place concrete slab on precast conc. joists or beams

    ___ (2) To make two different materials act compositely as one unit, they must be joined at their interface by one or a combination of these means:

        ___ (a) Chemical bonding (concrete)

        ___ (b) Gluing (plywood, glulam)

        ___ (c) Welding (steel, aluminum)

        ___ (d) Screws (sheet metal, wood)

        ___ (e) Bolts (steel, wood)

        ___ (f) Shear studs (steel to concrete)

___ (*g*) Keys or embossments (steel deck to concrete, concrete to concrete)
___ (*h*) Dowels (concrete to concrete)
___ (*i*) Friction (positive clamping force must be present)

Individual elements of the composite unit must be securely fastened to prevent slippage with respect to one another.

___ *d.* Shapes and designations

| WIDE FLANGE | I BEAM | CHANNELS | ANGLES | ZEE | TUBE | PIPE |
| W | S | C | L | Z | | |

BEAM
W 36 × 300 ← 300#/LF
  ↑   ↑ DEPTH IN INCHES
      WIDE FLANGE

___ *e.* Open web steel joists
    ___ (1) Types

TYPE	DES-IGNATION	DEPTHS	SPANS	BEARINGS		
				MASONRY	CONC.	STEEL
ECONOMY	K SERIES	8" TO 30"	8'-60'	4-6"	4"	2½"
LONG SPAN	LH SERIES	18" TO 48"	25'-96'	6-12"	6-9"	4"
DEEP LONG SPAN	DLH SERIES	52" TO 72"	89'-144'			

___ (2) Joist designation

25 LH 10 ← CHORD
 ↑ ↑   TYPE OF STEEL
 │ │   LONG SPAN
 │   NOMINAL DEPTH

___ (3) For K Series, span should not exceed depth × 24.

   ___ (4) For long span series, span should not exceed depth × 24 for roof (or × 20 for floor).

   ___ (5) Horizontal or diagonal bridging is required to prevent lateral movement of top and bottom chords, usually from 10 to 15 oc.

   ___ (6) Overhangs can be created by extending top chords (up to 5'6").

___ *f.* Steel decking

   ___ (1) Thickness

Total w/conc.	Deck	Span
2½" to 5"	1½"	2' to 6'
4" to 6"	1½"	6' to 12'
5½" to 7½"	3"	9' to 16'

   ___ (2) Gauges: 16, 18, 20, 22

   ___ (3) For less spans, usually 4', plain deck with rigid insul. on top, is often used. For this type:

      ___ (*a*) Small openings up to 6" sq. may be cut without reinf'g. Larger openings require steel fram'g.

      ___ (*b*) Roof-mounted equipment cannot be placed directly on deck, but must be supported on structure below.

___ *g.* Structural connections

   ___ (1) Rivets (hardly used anymore)

   ___ (2) Bolts

   ___ (3) Welds

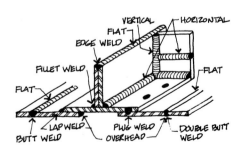

BASIC WELD SYMBOLS									
BEAD	FILLET	PLUG OR SLOT	SQUARE	V	BEVEL	U	J	FLARE V	FLARE BEVEL
⌒	△	⬳	‖	∨	↗	∪	∫	⋎	⫯

SUPPLEMENTARY WELD SYMBOLS					
		WELD ALL AROUND	FIELD WELD	CONTOUR	
				FLUSH	CONVEX
		○	●	—	⌒

STANDARD LOCATION OF ELEMENTS OF WELD SYMBOL

FINISH SYMBOL

CONTOUR SYMBOL

ROOT OPENING, DEPTH OF FILLING FOR PLUG AND SLOT WELDS

SIZE IN INCHES

REFERENCE LINE

SPECIFICATION, PROCESS OR OTHER REFERENCE

TAIL (MAY BE OMITTED WHEN REFERENCE NOT USED)

BASIC WELD SYMBOL OR DETAIL REFERENCE

GROOVE ANGLE OR INCLUDED ANGLE OF COUNTERSINK FOR PLUG WELDS

LENGTH OF WELD IN INCHES

PITCH (C. TO C. SPACING OF WELDS IN INCHES)

WELD ALL AROUND SYMBOL

FIELD WELD SYMBOL

ARROW CONNECTING REFERENCE LINE TO ARROW SIDE OF JOINT (ALSO POINTS TO GROOVED MEMBER IN BEVEL & J GROOVED JOINTS)

___ 5. Light Metal Framing

    ___ *a.* Joists

        ___ (1) Forms an economical floor system for light loading and spans up to 32′

        ___ (2) Depths: 6″, 8″, 9″, 10″, 12″

        ___ (3) Spacings: 16″, 24″, 48″ oc

        ___ (4) Gauges: 12 through 18

        ___ (5) Bridging, usually 5′ to 8′ oc

    ___ *b.* Studs

        ___ (1) Sizes

            ___ (*a*) Widths: ¾″, 1″, 1⅜″, 1⅝″, 2″

            ___ (*b*) Depths: 2½″, 3⅝″, 4″, 6″, 8″

___ (2) Gauges: 14, 15, 16, 18, 20
___ (3) Spacings: 12″, 16″, 24″ oc
___ 6. Miscellaneous Metals
___ *a.* Nails
___ (1) Size: Penny designated as d. A two-penny nail is 1″ long. Each additional "penny" adds ¼″ length, to:

12-penny = 3¼″ long
16-penny = 3½″
20-penny = 4″
30-penny = 4½″
40-penny = 5″
50-penny = 5½″
60-penny = 6″

Rule of thumb: Use nail with length 3× thickness of board being secured.
___ (2) Types

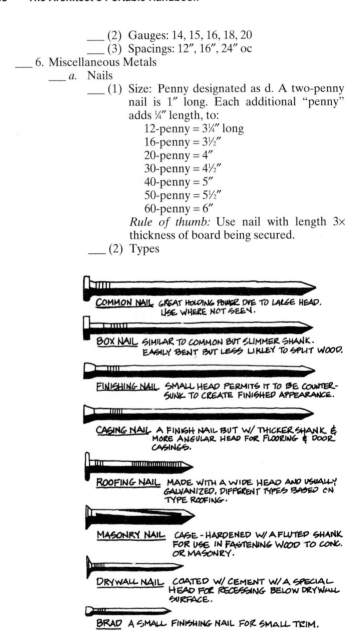

COMMON NAIL GREAT HOLDING POWER DUE TO LARGE HEAD. USE WHERE NOT SEEN.

BOX NAIL SIMILAR TO COMMON BUT SLIMMER SHANK. EASILY BENT BUT LESS LIKLEY TO SPLIT WOOD.

FINISHING NAIL SMALL HEAD PERMITS IT TO BE COUNTER-SUNK TO CREATE FINISHED APPEARANCE.

CASING NAIL A FINISH NAIL BUT W/ THICKER SHANK & MORE ANGULAR HEAD FOR FLOORING & DOOR CASINGS.

ROOFING NAIL MADE WITH A WIDE HEAD AND USUALLY GALVANIZED, DIFFERENT TYPES BASED ON TYPE ROOFING.

MASONRY NAIL CASE-HARDENED W/ A FLUTED SHANK FOR USE IN FASTENING WOOD TO CONC. OR MASONRY.

DRYWALL NAIL COATED W/ CEMENT W/ A SPECIAL HEAD FOR RECESSING BELOW DRYWALL SURFACE.

BRAD A SMALL FINISHING NAIL FOR SMALL TRIM.

___ *b.*   Screws and bolts

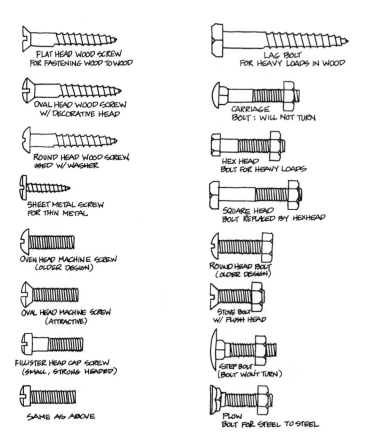

FLAT HEAD WOOD SCREW
FOR FASTENING WOOD TO WOOD

OVAL HEAD WOOD SCREW
W/ DECORATIVE HEAD

ROUND HEAD WOOD SCREW,
USED W/ WASHER

SHEET METAL SCREW
FOR THIN METAL

OVEN HEAD MACHINE SCREW
(OLDER DESIGN)

OVAL HEAD MACHINE SCREW
(ATTRACTIVE)

FILLISTER HEAD CAP SCREW
(SMALL, STRONG HEADED)

SAME AS ABOVE

LAG BOLT
FOR HEAVY LOADS IN WOOD

CARRIAGE
BOLT : WILL NOT TURN

HEX HEAD
BOLT FOR HEAVY LOADS

SQUARE HEAD
BOLT REPLACED BY HEXHEAD

ROUND HEAD BOLT
(OLDER DESIGN)

STOVE BOLT
W/ FLUSH HEAD

STEP BOLT
(BOLT WON'T TURN)

PLOW
BOLT FOR STEEL TO STEEL

___ *c.* Timber connectors (see p. 214 for **costs**)

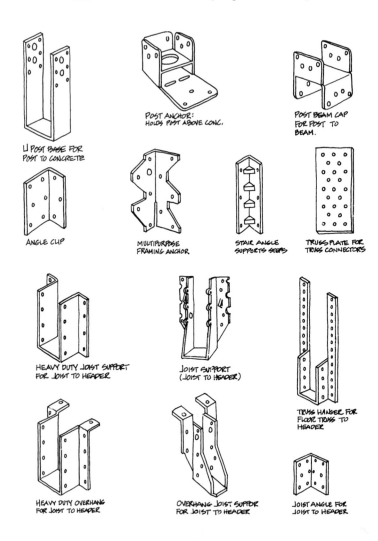

U POST BASE FOR
POST TO CONCRETE

POST ANCHOR:
HOLDS POST ABOVE CONC.

POST BEAM CAP
FOR POST TO
BEAM.

ANGLE CLIP

MULTIPURPOSE
FRAMING ANCHOR

STAIR ANGLE
SUPPORTS STEPS

TRUSS PLATE FOR
TRUSS CONNECTORS

HEAVY DUTY JOIST SUPPORT
FOR JOIST TO HEADER

JOIST SUPPORT
(JOIST TO HEADER)

TRUSS HANGER FOR
FLOOR TRUSS TO
HEADER

HEAVY DUTY OVERHANG
FOR JOIST TO HEADER

OVERHANG JOIST SUPPORT
FOR JOIST TO HEADER

JOIST ANGLE FOR
JOIST TO HEADER

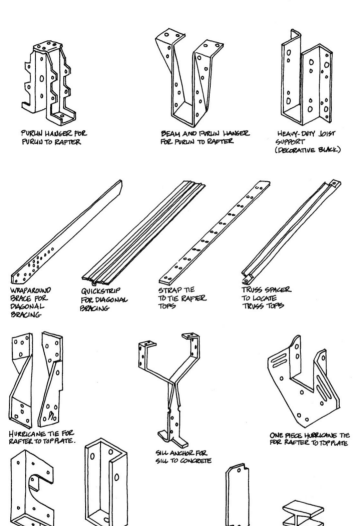

PURLIN HANGER FOR
PURLIN TO RAFTER

BEAM AND PURLIN HANGER
FOR PURLIN TO RAFTER

HEAVY-DUTY JOIST
SUPPORT
(DECORATIVE BLACK)

WRAPAROUND
BRACE FOR
DIAGONAL
BRACING

QUICKSTRIP
FOR DIAGONAL
BRACING

STRAP TIE
TO TIE RAFTER
TOPS

TRUSS SPACER
TO LOCATE
TRUSS TOPS

HURRICANE TIE FOR
RAFTER TO TOP PLATE.

SILL ANCHOR FOR
SILL TO CONCRETE

ONE PIECE HURRICANE TIE
FOR RAFTER TO TOP PLATE

STUD SHOE :
REINFORCES PIPE CUT

FENCE BRACKET
FOR RAIL TO POST

PROTECTION
PLATE FOR WIRING

PLYWOOD CLIP
FOR SHEATHING

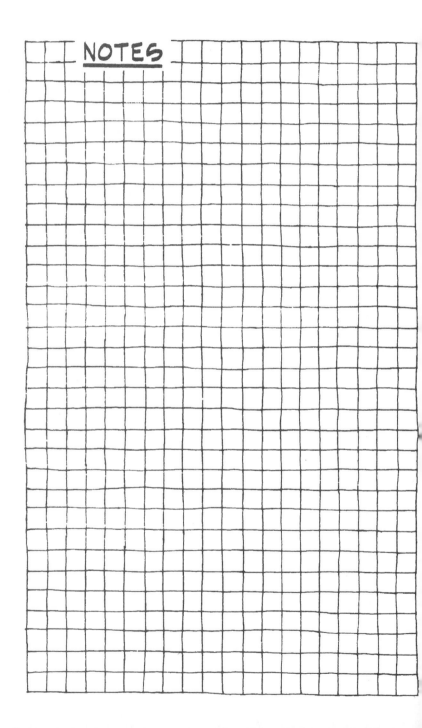

NOTES

__ B. STEEL MEMBERS (SIZE AND COSTS)

(1) (10) (23) (26)

See p. 96 for span-to-depth ratios.

___ 1. *General Costs:* **Steel framing for one-story building:**
20′ × 20′ bays: $7.00/SF
For each added 10′ of bay, up to 40′: +30%
For two- to six-story: +$1.00/SF

___ 2. Light Steel Construction
    ___ *a.* Stud walls
        ___ (1) Widths of 1⅝″, 2½″, 3⅝″, 4″, and 6″.
        ___ (2) Maximum height range from 9′ to 16′. Unbraced length is unlimited if partition is supported both at floor and ceiling. Unbraced length is limited to 14′ if not supported at ceiling.
        ___ (3) Come in load-bearing (LB), 14 GA to 20 GA, and nonload-bearing (NLB), 26 GA to 14 GA.
        ___ (4) *Costs:*
            3⅝″ studs, LB, 16″ oc: $2/SF wall area (20%M)
            Deduct or add 10% for ea. increment of size.

For 24″ oc:	**−30%**
For 12″ oc:	**+70%**
For NLB (25 GA):	**−30%**

    ___ *b.* Joists
        ___ (1) Span 15′ to 30′.
        ___ (2) See p. 96 for rule of thumb on span-to-depth ratio.
        ___ (3) *Costs:*
            8″ deep, 16″ oc, 40 PSF, 15′ span: $2.10/SF floor
            Add 15% for ea. added 5′ span up to 25′.
            For 30′ span, add 75%.
            24″ oc, about same cost.

    ___ *c.* Steel pipe and tube columns
        ___ (1) Minimum pipe diameter: 3½″. Minimum tube size: 3″ SQ.

_____ (2) In general, assuming normal load conditions, the minimum diameter in inches can be estimated by multiplying the height in feet by *0.33*.

_____ (3) *Costs:*
3″ to 6″ dia., or 2″ to 8″ SQ: $25/LF (75%M and 25%L)
4″ to 12″ dia., or 4″ to 12″ SQ: $35/LF
6″ to 12″ dia., or 8″ to 16″ SQ: $60/LF

_____ 3. Heavy Steel Construction
    _____ *a.* Steel decking
        _____ (1) For roofs, depths range from 1″ to 3″, for spans of 6′ to 18′.
        _____ (2) For floors, depths range from 1½″ to 3″ for spans of 7′ to 12′.
        _____ (3) For cellular steel floors:
            Thickness: 4″ to 7½″
            Spans: 8′ to 16′
            Span-to-depth ratio: *50*

        _____ (4) *Costs:*
            1½″, 22 GA: $2/SF (60%M & 40%L) For 16 GA: +$.50/SF; for galvanizing: +12½%
            7½″, 18 GA, long span: $4.70/SF
            4″ concrete on 1½″, 22 GA deck, 6′ span, 125 psf: $2.90/SF.

    _____ *b.* Open web joists
        _____ (1) Span range: 8′ to 48′, up to 100′ for long-span joist.
        _____ (2) Spacings: 4′ to 8′ at floors, 8′ at roofs.
        _____ (3) Manufactured in 2″ increments from 8″ to 30″ deep and 18″ to 72″ for long-span type.
        _____ (4) Range of span-to-depth ratios: *20* maximum for floors and *24* maximum for roofs.
        _____ (5) Designations: Economy K Series, long-span LH Series, and deep, long-span DLH Series.

        _____ (6) *Costs:*
            K Series: $9.50 to $12.50/LF (50%M and 50%L)
            LH & LJ Series: $26.30 to 34.35/LF
            DLH & DLJ Series: $24.45 to 31/LF

___ c. Steel beams
   ___ (1) Usual spans of 10′ to 60′.
   ___ (2) Typical bay sizes of 30′ to 40′.
   ___ (3) Approximate span-to-depth
        ratio: *20.*
   ___ (4) For roof beams, depth of beam
        in inches can be estimated at *0.5* times the
        span in feet.
   ___ (5) For floor beams, depth of beam in inches
        can be estimated at *0.6* times the span in
        feet.
   ___ (6) Steel plate girders: Spans range from 60′ to
        100′ with approximate ratio of span to
        depth: *14.*
   ___ (7) ***Typical steel beam costs:***
        ***$1500* to *$1800* per ton (50% M & 50% L)**
          For small projects use larger costs. For
          larger projects (over 4 stories) use
          smaller costs.
        Use the following table to help estimate
        weight from depth estimated in item *c,*
        above.

Bm. depth (″)	Roof (lb/LF)	Floor (lb/LF)
8	24	31
10	30	39
12	35	45
14	43	53
16	50	60
18	60	76
21	68	83
24	76	84
27	84	94

Table based on minimum roof live load of 20 PSF.
Add 15–25% more weight for snow, etc.

___ d. Steel columns
   ___ (1) See p. 96 for span-to-depth
        ratio.
   ___ (2) In general, the 6 and 8 W
        columns carry most lightweight,
        low-rise construction. The 10,
        12, and 14 W columns have

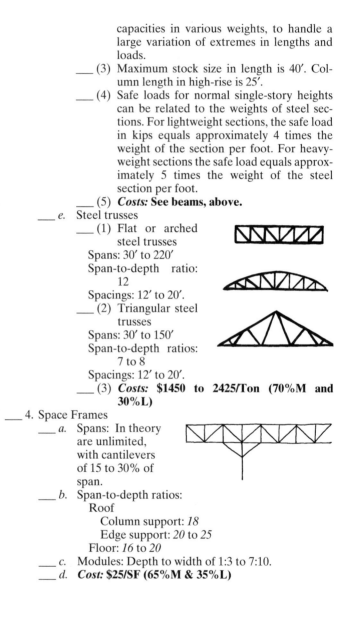

capacities in various weights, to handle a large variation of extremes in lengths and loads.

___ (3) Maximum stock size in length is 40′. Column length in high-rise is 25′.

___ (4) Safe loads for normal single-story heights can be related to the weights of steel sections. For lightweight sections, the safe load in kips equals approximately 4 times the weight of the section per foot. For heavyweight sections the safe load equals approximately 5 times the weight of the steel section per foot.

___ (5) *Costs:* **See beams, above.**

___ *e.* Steel trusses

___ (1) Flat or arched steel trusses
Spans: 30′ to 220′
Span-to-depth ratio: 12
Spacings: 12′ to 20′.

___ (2) Triangular steel trusses
Spans: 30′ to 150′
Span-to-depth ratios: 7 to 8
Spacings: 12′ to 20′.

___ (3) *Costs:* **$1450 to 2425/Ton (70%M and 30%L)**

___ 4. Space Frames

___ *a.* Spans: In theory are unlimited, with cantilevers of 15 to 30% of span.

___ *b.* Span-to-depth ratios:
Roof
Column support: *18*
Edge support: *20* to *25*
Floor: *16* to *20*

___ *c.* Modules: Depth to width of 1:3 to 7:10.

___ *d.* *Cost:* **$25/SF (65%M & 35%L)**

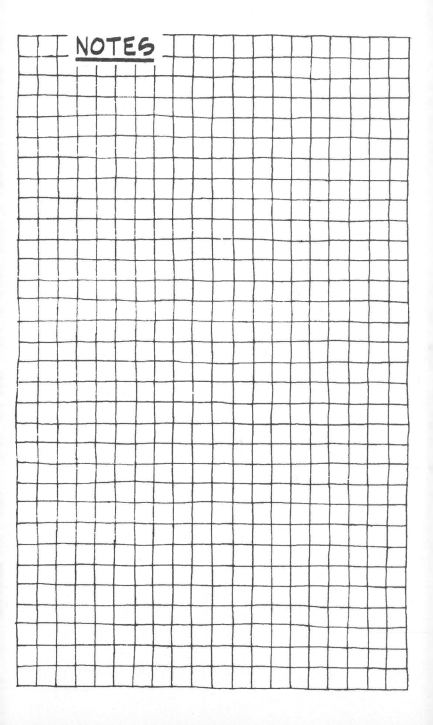

NOTES

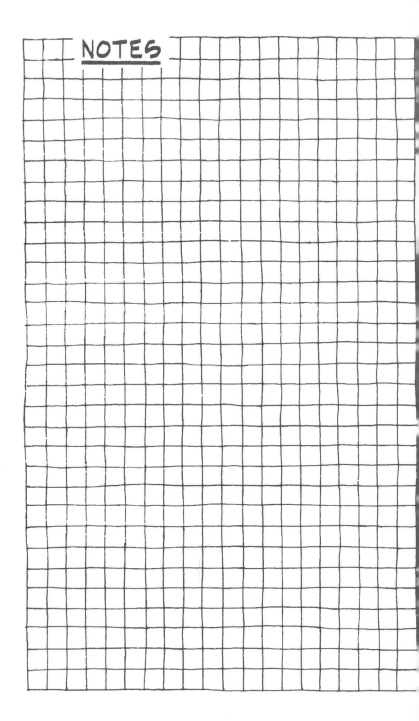

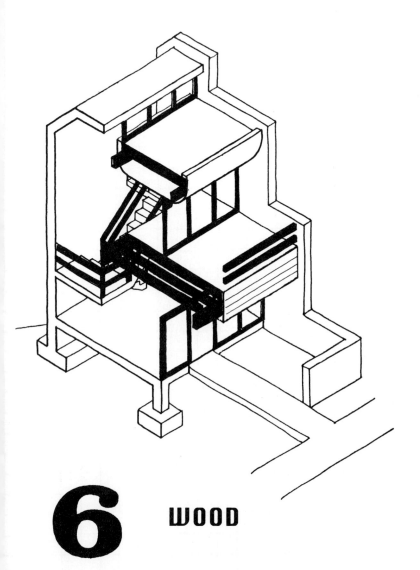

6 WOOD

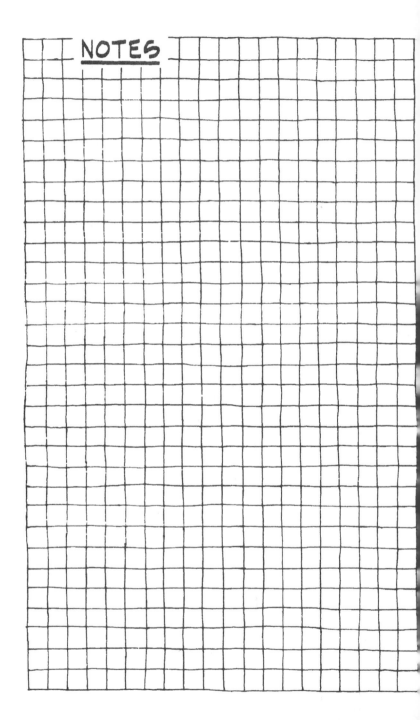

NOTES

__ A. WOOD MATERIALS

$\textcircled{4}$ $\textcircled{11}$ $\textcircled{12}$ $\textcircled{19}$ $\textcircled{31}$ $\textcircled{38}$ $\textcircled{43}$ $\textcircled{45}$

___ 1. General (*Note:* See p. 220 for species table.)

   ___ *a.* *Two general types of wood* and their uses in buildings

      ___ (1) Softwood (from evergreen trees) for general construction

      ___ (2) Hardwood (from deciduous trees) for furnishings and finishes

   ___ *b.* *Moisture and shrinkage:* The amount of water in wood is expressed as a percentage of its oven-dry (dry as possible) weight. As wood dries, it first looses moisture from within the cells without shrinking, after reaching the fiber saturation point (dry cell), further drying results in shrinkage. Eventually wood comes to dynamic equilibrium with the relative humidity of the surrounding air. Interior wood typically shrinks in winter and swells in summer. Average equilibrium moisture content ranges from 6 to 11%, but wood is considered dry enough for use at 12 to 15%. The loss of moisture during seasoning causes wood to be harder, stronger, stiffer, and lighter in weight. Wood is most decay-resistant when under 20%.

___ 2. Lumber

   ___ *a.* *Sizes*

      ___ (1) Sectional

Nominal sizes	To get actual sizes
2×'s up to 8×'s	deduct ½″
8×'s and larger	deduct ¾″

      ___ (2) Lengths

         ___ (*a*) Softwoods: cut to lengths of 6′ to 24′, in 2′ increments

         ___ (*b*) Hardwoods: cut to 1′-long increments

   ___ *b.* *Economy:* best achieved when layouts are within a 2′- or 4′-module, with subdivisions of 4″, 16″, 24″, and 48″

   ___ *c.* *Defects*

DEFECT	END VIEW	LONG VIEW
BOW		

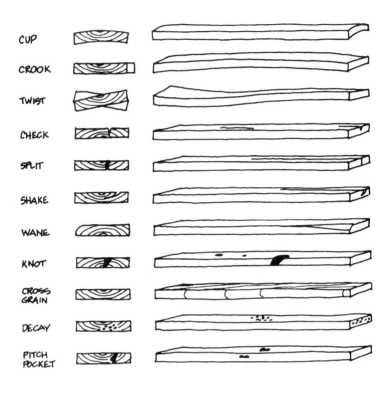

CUP

CROOK

TWIST

CHECK

SPLIT

SHAKE

WANE

KNOT

CROSS GRAIN

DECAY

PITCH POCKET

___ d. *Grades*
    ___ (1) *Factory or shop-type lumber:* used primarily for remanufacturing purposes (doors, windows, millwork, etc.).
    ___ (2) *Yard type lumber*
        ___ (*a*) Boards:
            ___ 1″ to 1½″ thick, 2″ and wider
            ___ graded for appearance only
            ___ used as siding, subflooring, trim
        ___ (*b*) Dimensioned lumber:
            ___ 2″ to 4″ thick, 2″ and wider
            ___ graded for strength (stress gr.)
            ___ used for general construction
            ___ Light framing: 2″ to 4″ wide

___ Joists and planks: 6″ and wider
___ Decking: 4″ and wider (*select and commercial*).
___ (*c*) Timbers:
___ 5′ × 5″ and larger
___ graded for strength and serviceability
___ may be classified as "structural."
___ (3) *Structural grades* (in descending order, according to stress grade):
___ (*a*) Light framing: *Construction, Standard,* and *Utility*
___ (*b*) Structural light framing (joists, planks): *Select Structural, No. 1, 2, or 3* (some species may also be appearance-graded for exposed work).
___ (*c*) Timber: *Select Structural No. 1.*
Note: Working stress values can be assigned to each of the grades according to the species of wood.
___ (4) *Appearance grades*
___ (*a*) For natural finishes: *select A or B.*
___ (*b*) For paint finishes: *select C or D.*
___ (*c*) For gen. const. and utility: *Common, Nos. 1 thru 5.*
___ *e.* *Pressure-treated wood:* Softwood lumber treated by a process that forces preservative chemicals into the cells of the wood. The result is a material that is immune to decay. This should not be used for interiors. Where required:
___ (1) In direct contact with earth
___ (2) Floor joists less than 18″ (or girders less than 12″) from the ground
___ (3) Plates, sills, sleepers in contact with concrete or masonry
___ (4) Posts exposed to weather or in basements
___ (5) Ends of beams entering concrete or masonry, without ½″ air space
___ (6) Wood located less than 6″ from earth
___ (7) Wood structural members supporting moisture-permeable floors or roofs, exposed to weather, unless separated by an impervious moisture barrier

___ (8) Wood-retaining or crib walls
___ (9) In geographic areas where experience has demonstrated the need for exterior construction such as stairs and railings

___ f. *Framing-estimating rules of thumb:* For 16-inch oc stud partitions, estimate one stud for every LF of wall, then add for top and bottom plates. For any type of framing, the quantity of basic framing members (in LF) can be determined based on spacing and surface area (SF):

12 inches oc	1.2 LF/SF
16 inches oc	1.0 LF/SF
24 inches oc	0.8 LF/SF

(Doubled-up members, bands, plates, framed openings, etc., must be added.) Framing accessories, nails, joist hangers, connectors, etc., may be roughly estimated by adding *0.5 to 1.5%* of the cost of lumber. Estimating lumber can be done in *board feet* where one BF is the amount of lumber in a rough-sawed board one foot long, one foot wide, and one inch thick (144 cubic inches) or the equivalent volume in any other shape. As an example, one hundred one-inch by 12-inch dressed boards, 16 feet long, contain:

$$100 \times 1 \times 12 \times 16/12 = 1600 \text{ BF}$$

Use the following table to help estimate board feet:

BF per SF of surface

	12-inch oc	16-inch oc	24-inch oc
2 × 4s	0.8	0.67	0.54
2 × 6s	1.2	1.0	0.8
2 × 8s	1.6	1.33	1.06
2 × 10s	2.0	1.67	1.34
2 × 12s	2.4	2.0	1.6

___ 3. Details

WINDOW ROUGH OPENING

INSIDE WALL TO OUTSIDE WALL.

INSIDE WALL TO OUTSIDE WALL

WALL TO CL'G.

WALL TO CL'G.

OUTSIDE CORNER

OUTSIDE CORNER

OUTSIDE CORNER

___ 4. Laminated Lumber

___ *a.* *Laminated Timber* (Glu-Lam Beams): For large structural members, these are preferable to solid timber in terms of finished dressed appearance, weather resistance, controlled moisture content, and size availability. See p. 224.

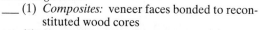

___ *b.* *Sheathing Panels*

___ (1) *Composites:* veneer faces bonded to reconstituted wood cores

___ (2) *Nonveneered panels:*

___ (*a*) Oriented Strand Board (OSB).

___ (*b*) Particle Board

_____ (3) Plywood
    _____ (*a*) Two main types
        _____ *Exterior grade*
        __ Made with waterproof adhes.
        __ C-grade face or better
        __ For permanent exterior use
        _____ *Interior grade*
        __ Made with water-resistant
          adhesives
        __ D-grade face or better
    _____ (*b*) Grading according to face veneers
        _____ N All heartwood or all sap-
          wood (for nat. fin.)
        _____ A Smooth paint grade
        _____ B Solid smooth surface
        _____ C Sheathing grade (lowest
          grade for ext.)
        _____ D Lowest grade of interior
          plywood
    _____ (*c*) Engineered grades:
        _____ *Structural I and II, Standard,*
          and *C-C Exterior*
        _____ Span identification index

THICKNESS
ODD NUMBER OF PLIES.
GRAIN DIRECTION SAME.
FOR FACE & BACK
PLIES (LONGITUDINAL).

32/16 — LEFT HAND NUMBER FOR ROOF SUPPORTS
— RIGHT HAND NUMBER FOR FLOOR SUPPORTS

    _____ (*d*) Thickness: 3 ply = ¼, ⅜
                     5 ply = ½, ⅝, ¾
                     7 ply = ⅞, 1, 1⅛, and
                     1¼ inch
    _____ (*e*) Size sheets: 4′ (or 5′) × 8′ (or 12′)
_____ 5. Structural Wood
    _____ *a.* Strengths

AVERAGE PHYSICAL PROPERTIES

MATERIAL	ELASTIC LIMIT (PSI)		ULTIMATE STRENGTH (PSI)			ALLOWABLE WORKING UNIT STRESS (PSI)				MODULUS OF ELAST. (PSI)	WT. (LB/ C.F.)
	TEN-SION	COM-PRESS.	TEN-SION	COM-PRESS.	SHEAR	TEN-SION	COM-PRESS.	SHEAR	EXTR. FIBER BENDG.		
TIMBER PARALLEL TO GRAIN	3000	3000	10000	8000	500	1200	1000	100	1200	1200000	40
PERPENDICULAR TO GRAIN					3000		300	400			

___ *b.* Wood shrinks across grain much more than parallel to grain. Avoid locking nonshrinking materials to wood.

___ *c.* Wood is much weaker across grain than parallel to grain in both tension and compression. A cross-grain angle greater than 1 in 10 seriously weakens the wood in bending.

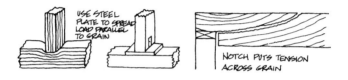

___ *d.* Wood beams deflect or sag more under long-term loads than they do at the beginning. Long-term sag is about 1½ to twice beginning sag.

___ *e.* Wood beams may be weak in resistance to horizontal shear. Since this shear is closest to beam supports, *holes through wood* beams should be avoided near supports. Notches on the ends of joists should not exceed ¼ the depth. Holes bored in joists should not be within *2″* of top or bottom and their diameter should not be greater than *⅓ depth*. Notches at top and bottom should not exceed *⅙ depth* and should not be in middle *⅓ of span*. Holes bored in studs should not be greater than *40%* (60% if studs doubled) and should not be closer to the edge than ⅝″.

___ 6. Finish Wood (Interior Hardwood Plywoods)

    ___ *a.* *Sizes*

        ___ (1) Thicknesses: ⅛″ to 1″ in ¹⁄₁₆″ and ⅛″ increments

        ___ (2) Widths: 18, 24, 32, 36, 48 inches

        ___ (3) Lengths: 4, 5, 6, 7, 8, 10 feet

    ___ *b.* *Types*

        ___ (1) Technical: fully waterproof bond

        ___ (2) Type I (exterior): fully waterproof bond/weather- and fungus-resistant

___ (3) Type II (interior): water-resistant bond
___ (4) Type III (interior): moisture-resistant bond
___ *c.* *Grades*
      ___ (1) Premium 1: very slight imperfections
      ___ (2) Good 1: suitable for natural finishes
      ___ (3) Sound 2: suitable for painted finishes
      ___ (4) Utility 3: may have open defects
      ___ (5) Backing 4: may have many flaws
___ *d.* *Grains and patterns*

ROTARY   FLAT SLICING   QUARTER SLICING   HALF ROUND   RIFT CUT   BACK
WOOD GRAIN FIGURES

BOOK   SLIP   "V"   HERRINGBONE   CENTER   BALANCE

DIAMOND   REVERSE DIAMOND   BOX   REVERSE BOX   VERTICAL BUTT HORIZONTAL BOOK   RANDOM

VENEER MATCHING PATTERNS

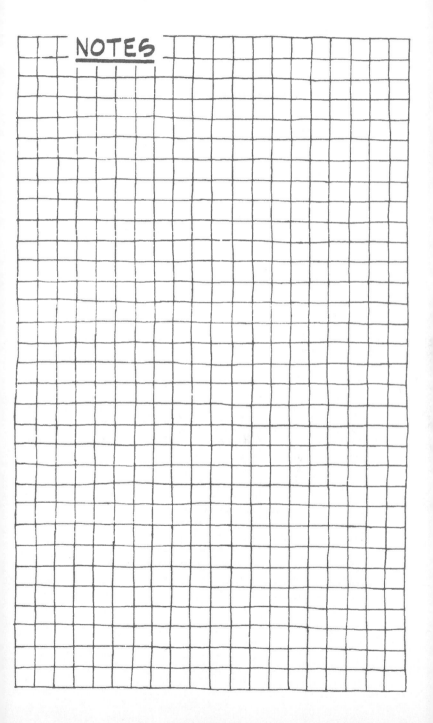

NOTES

7. SPECIES

Legend:
- ● DENOTES COMMON USES AND PROPERTIES
- O POSSIBLE OR LIMITED USAGE
- □ TREATED WOOD ONLY
- ✳ FLAME SPREAD RATING
- SCALE OF 1 TO 10 WHERE 1 IS LOWEST & 10 HIGHEST

| | | TYP. FORMS | | | | USES — BLD'G. | | | | USES — PART'N | |
	SPECIES / COLOR	VENEERS	BOARDS/PLANKS	DIMENSION	STRIPS/BLOCKS	POSTS	FRAMING	SHEATHING	SIDING	FRAMING	PANELING
	SOFTWOODS										
1	CEDAR, WESTERN RED — RED BROWN TO WHITE SAPWOOD	O	●	●		●	●	●	●	●	●
2	CYPRESS, BALD — YELLOWISH BROWN					●	●	●	●	●	●
3	FIR, DOUGLAS (COAST) — REDDISH TAN		●	●	●	●	●	●	●	●	O
4	HEMLOCK, WESTERN — PALE BROWN		●	●		●	●	●	●	●	
5	LARCH, WESTERN — BROWN					●	●	●	●	●	
6	PINE - LEDGEPOLE		●	●		O	●	O	O	O	
7	– PONDEROSA — WHITE TO PALE YELLOW		●	●		O	●	O	●	●	●
8	– RED — LIGHT BROWN		●	●		O	●	O	●	●	●
9	– SOUTHERN — WHITE TO PALE YELLOW		●	●	●	O	●	●	●	●	●
10	– SUGAR — CREAMY WHITE		●	●		●	●	●	●	●	●
11	REDWOOD - OLD GROWTH — DEEP RED TO DARK BROWN	O	●	●		●	O	O	●	O	●
12	SPRUCE - BLACK					O	O	O	O	O	
13	– ENGELMAN — CREAMY WHITE		●	●		O	O	O	O	O	
14	– RED					O	●	O	O	O	
15	–SITKA — LIGHT YELLOWISH TAN		●	●		O	●	O	O	O	
	HARDWOODS										
1	ASH, WHITE — CREAMY WHITE TO LIGHT BROWN	●			O						O
2	BEECH — WHITE TO REDDISH BROWN	●			●						●
3	BIRCH, YELLOW — LIGHT BROWN	●			●						●
4	CHERRY — REDDISH BROWN	●			●						●
5	ELM, AMERICAN — BROWN	●									●
6	LOCUST, BLACK — GOLDEN BROWN					O					O
7	MAHOGANY — REDDISH BROWN	●			●						●
8	MAPLE (HARD) SUGAR — WHITE TO REDDISH BROWN	●			●						●
9	OAK, RED — REDDISH TAN TO BROWN	●			●						●
10	POPLAR, YELLOW — WHT. TO BROWN W/GREEN CAST	●							O		●
11	ROSEWOOD — MIXED REDS, BROWNS & BLACKS	●									●
12	TEAK — TAWNY YELLOW TO DARK BRN.	●			●						●
13	WALNUT, BLACK — DARK BROWN	●	O								●

USES													PROPERTIES									NOTES	
FLOORS			ROOFS		FOUNDATION/OUTDOOR						EQUIP.												
JOISTS	ROUGH	FINISH	RAFTERS	DECKING	PILES	WD. FOUND.	RET. WALLS	POSTS	DECKS	FURNITURE	CABINETS	FURNITURE	SHRINKAGE	BENDG. STRENG.	COMPRESSION ∥	COMPRESSION ⊥	HARDNESS, SIDE	IMPACT, BENDING	RESIST. TO DECAY	WEATHERING	PAINTABILITY		
																						SOFTWOODS	
○			●	●				●	●	●	○	○	2	4	5	4	3	4	8	7	7	*70	1
○			●	●					●	●	○	○	5	6	6	6	6	6	8	7	7	*145-150	2
●	●	●	●	●	■	■	■	■	■				7	7	7	6	7	6	6	5	4	*70-100	3
●			●	●		■	■	■	■				7	6	6	5	6	7	5	5	5	*60-70	4
●			●	●	□				●				8	3	7	6	7	6	6	5	4		5
○			●						■				5	4	5	4	4	5	5	5	5	*93	6
○			●	●		■	■		■		○	○	4	3	4	5	4	5	5	5	6	*105-200	7
○			●	●	■				●		○	○	5	5	5	5	5	6	5	5	4	*142	8
○	●	●	●	●	■	■	■	■	■				7	7	7	6	7	6	5	5	5	*130-190	9
○			●	●					■		○	○	3	3	4	3	3	4	5	5	6		10
○			○	●				●	■	●	○	○	2	5	6	5	5	4	8	7	7	*70	11
○			○	○					□				5	4	5	3	5	5	5	5	5		12
○			○	○					□				5	3	3	3	3	4	5	5	5		13
○			○	○					□				6	5	5	5	5	4	5	5	5		14
○			●	●					□				6	5	5	5	5	5	5	5	5		15
																						HARDWOODS	
		○										●	5	6	6	6	6	6	4	5	5		1
											●	●	8	5	5	5	5	5	5	5	6		2
		○									●	●	7	5	4	4	5	6	5	5	6	*105-110	3
		○									●	●	3	4	5	3	4	3	6	5	5		4
												●	6	3	3	8	4	4	5	5	5		5
					○	○	○						2	8	8	8	8	5	8	5	5		6
		●									○	○											7
		●									○	●	6	6	6	6	6	5	5	5	6	*104	8
		●									○	○	7	3	3	5	5	3	5	5	5	*100	9
											○	○	4	3	3	2	3	3	5	5	7	*170-185	10
											●	●											11
	○		○						○		●	●											12
		○									●	●	4	6	6	4	6	4	7	6	5	*130-140	13

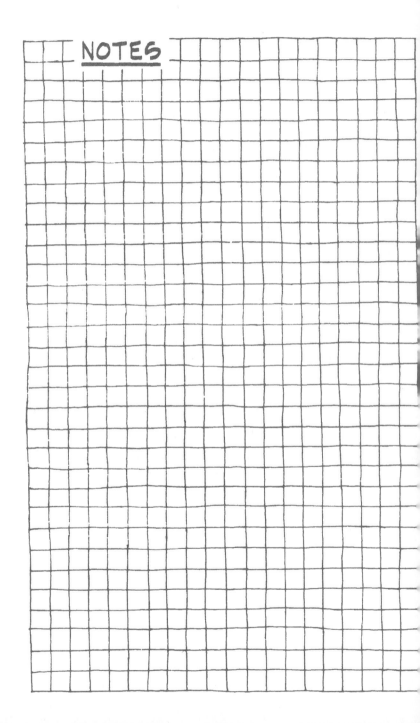

NOTES

__ B. WOOD MEMBERS (SIZE AND COSTS)

(1) (10) (23)

___ 1. General: See p. 96 for span-to-depth ratios.
   Rough lumber costs by board feet:

Studs	**$0.50/BF**
Posts	**0.60/BF**
Joists	**0.55/BF**
Beams (Doug. Fir)	**0.80/BF**

Note: The above are material costs only. Total in-place cost may be estimated by *doubling* the above numbers.

___ 2. Light-Frame Construction
   ___ *a.* Stud walls: Usually 2 × 4s or 2 × 6s at 16″ oc or 24″ oc with one bottom and two 2× top plates.

Approximate cost of stud walls ranges from $.70/SF to $.80/SF (50% M and 50% L).

   ___ *b.* Roof joists and rafters:
   Rule of thumb for roof joists, rafters, and ceiling joists:
   Quick estimates of joist depths in inches can be made by multiplying span in feet by:
      0.4 for rafters with light roofing
      0.45 for ceiling joists
      0.5 for roof joists
   Usual spacing: 24″ oc.

   For more precise sizing, see p. 227.

Approximate costs of between *$.85/SF* to *$1.25/SF* for roof framing (50% M and 50% L). Ceiling joists: *$.60* to *$1.35/SF*.

   ___ *c.* Floor joists
      ___ (1) See p. 96 for general rule span-to-depth ratio.
      ___ (2) Usual span range: 8′ to 24′.
      ___ (3) Usual spacing: 16″ oc.
      ___ (4) Usual span-to-depth ratio Doug. fir: *20.*
      ___ (5) For more precise sizing, see p. 227.

Approximate cost *$1.00*/*SF* to *$3.50*/*SF* (50% M and 50% L)

___ 3. Heavy Timber Construction
    ___ *a.* Wood beams
        ___ (1) See p. 96 for general rule of
             thumb.
        ___ (2) Solid wood beams
            ___ (*a*) Thickness range: 2″ to
                 14″
            ___ (*b*) Spacing range: 4′ to 20′.
            ___ (*c*) Approximate span-to-
                 depth ratios: *16 to 20.*
        ___ (3) Solid wood girders: Commonly used span-
             to-depth ratio for girders with concentrated
             load is *12.* Width will be *3/4* to *1/2* of depth.
             To estimate depth in inches, multiply span
             in feet by *1.*

Approximate cost range from $7.00/LF for 6 × 8 to $13.50/LF for 8 × 16, both 20 LF (smaller sizes: 50% M and 50% L; larger members: 75% M and 25% L).

    ___ *b.* Glu-lam beams
        ___ (1) Usual span range: 16′ to 50′.
        ___ (2) Spacing: 8′ to 30′.
        ___ (3) Thickness range from 3⅛″ to
             10¾″.
        ___ (4) Approximate span-to-depth
             ratio: *24.*
        ___ (5) Ratio of depth to width is
             about 2 to 1 for light beams
             and 3 to 1 for large members.
        ___ (6) Depth varies in 1½″ increments.

Approximate costs: Doug. fir, Industrial Grade:

    3⅛″ × 6″: $10.90/LF (45%M & 55%L). Add $2 for each 3″ depth to 18″.
    3½″ × 6″: $10.70/LF (45%M & 55%L). Add $2.35 for each 3″ depth to 21″.
    5⅛″ × 6″: $12.60/LF (50%M & 50%L) Add $3.20 for each 3″ depth to 24″.
    6¾″ × 12″: $23.90/LF (75%M & 25%L) Add $4.25 for each 3″ depth to 24″.

For Architectural Grade, add 20%.
For prestain, add 10%.

___ *c.* Columns and posts: The ratios of unbraced length to least thickness of most types range from 10 to 30 with *20* a good average.

Approximate costs of *$8.00/LF* for 6 × 6 to *$13.60/LF* for 12 × 12 (same M and L ratios as beams).

___ *d.* Wood decking
   ___ (1) Thickness: 2″ to 4″
   ___ (2) Span-to-depth ratio: *48*
   ___ (3) Spans: 4′ to 22′

Approximate costs of $2.40/SF for 3″ fir to $6.00/SF for 4″ cedar (70% to 90% M, 30% to 10% L).

___ 4. Trusses
   ___ *a.* Light frame trusses
      ___ (1) Usually 2′ oc
      ___ (2) Span to depth ratio: *15*
      ___ (3) Usual spans 30′ to 60′

Approximate cost range: Fink truss, 2 × 45, 3 to 12 slope, 24′ span: $61.30/ea. (55% M and 45% L)

King post, 2 × 45, 4 to 12 slope, 42′ span: $115.70/ea. (75% M and 25% L)

___ *b.* Heavy wood trusses
   ___ (1) Flat trusses
      ___ (*a*) Typical range of spans: 40′ to 160′
      ___ (*b*) Spacing 12′ to 20′
      ___ (*c*) Usual ratio of truss depth to span ranges from *1 to 8* to *1 to 10*.
   ___ (2) Bowstring trusses
      ___ (*a*) Typical range of spans: 40′ to 200′
      ___ (*b*) Spacing: 12 to 20
      ___ (*c*) Usual span to depth ratio of *6 to 8*

___ (3) Triangular trusses
    ___ (*a*) Typical range of spans:
        40′ to 100′
    ___ (*b*) Spacing 12′ to 20′
    ___ (*c*) Usual span-to-
        depth ratio:
        1 to 6

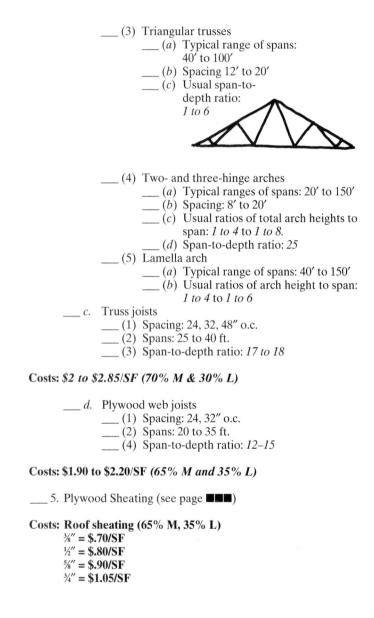

___ (4) Two- and three-hinge arches
    ___ (*a*) Typical ranges of spans: 20′ to 150′
    ___ (*b*) Spacing: 8′ to 20′
    ___ (*c*) Usual ratios of total arch heights to
        span: *1 to 4* to *1 to 8.*
    ___ (*d*) Span-to-depth ratio: *25*
___ (5) Lamella arch
    ___ (*a*) Typical range of spans: 40′ to 150′
    ___ (*b*) Usual ratios of arch height to span:
        1 to 4 to *1 to 6*

___ *c.* Truss joists
    ___ (1) Spacing: 24, 32, 48″ o.c.
    ___ (2) Spans: 25 to 40 ft.
    ___ (3) Span-to-depth ratio: *17 to 18*

Costs: *$2 to $2.85/SF (70% M & 30% L)*

___ *d.* Plywood web joists
    ___ (1) Spacing: 24, 32″ o.c.
    ___ (2) Spans: 20 to 35 ft.
    ___ (4) Span-to-depth ratio: *12–15*

Costs: $1.90 to $2.20/SF *(65% M and 35% L)*

___ 5. Plywood Sheating (see page ■■■)

Costs: Roof sheating (65% M, 35% L)
    ⅜″ = $.70/SF
    ½″ = $.80/SF
    ⅝″ = $.90/SF
    ¾″ = $1.05/SF

TABLE FOR ALLOWABLE SPANS FOR WOOD FLOOR JOISTS & ROOF RAFTERS

MEMBER SIZE →	2 × 6			2 × 8			2 × 10			2 × 12		
ON CENTER SPACING IN INCHES → / ALLOWABLE MAX. SPAN IN FT. & IN. → / CONDITIONS & LOADS ↓	12"	16"	24"	12"	16"	24"	12"	16"	24"	12"	16"	24"
FLOOR JOISTS, 40#/SF LIVE LOAD	10-11	9-11	8-8	14-5	13-1	11-5	18-5	16-9	14-7	22-5	20-4	17-9
CEILING JOISTS, 10#/SF (DRYWALL)	19-1	17-4	15-2	25-2	22-10	19-11	32-1	29-2	25-5			
ROOF RAFTERS												
DRYWALL CEILING, HIGH OR LOW SLOPE 20#/SF	14-2	12-4	10-0	18-9	16-3	13-3	23-11	20-8	16-11	29-1	25-2	20-6
30#/SF	12-6	10-10	8-10	16-6	14-4	11-8	21-1	18-3	14-11	25-7	22-2	18-1
NO CEILING, LOW SLOPE (3 IN 12 OR LESS) 20#/SF	15-4	13-3	10-10	20-3	17-6	14-4	25-10	22-4	18-3	31-4	27-2	22-2
30#/SF	13-3	11-6	9-5	17-6	15-2	12-5	22-4	19-4	15-10	27-2	23-6	19-3
HEAVY ROOF, HIGH SLOPE (3 IN 12 OR MORE) (15#/SF DEAD LOAD) 20#/SF	14-2	12-4	10-0	18-9	16-3	13-3	23-11	20-8	16-11			
30#/SF	12-6	10-10	8-10	16-6	14-4	11-8	21-1	18-3	14-11			
LIGHT ROOF, HIGH SLOPE (3 IN 12 OR MORE) (7#/SF DEAD LOAD) 20#/SF	16-2	14-0	11-5	21-4	18-5	15-1	27-2	23-7	19-3			
30#/SF	13-6	12-0	9-9	18-2	15-9	12-10	23-3	20-1	16-5			

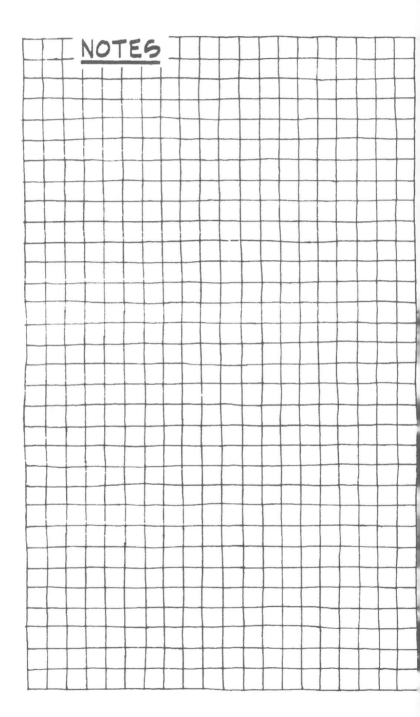

NOTES

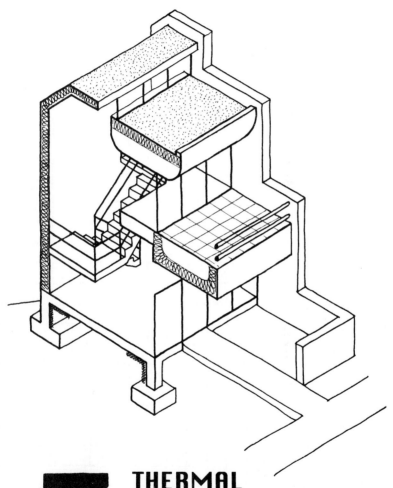

7

THERMAL
AND MOISTURE
PROTECTION

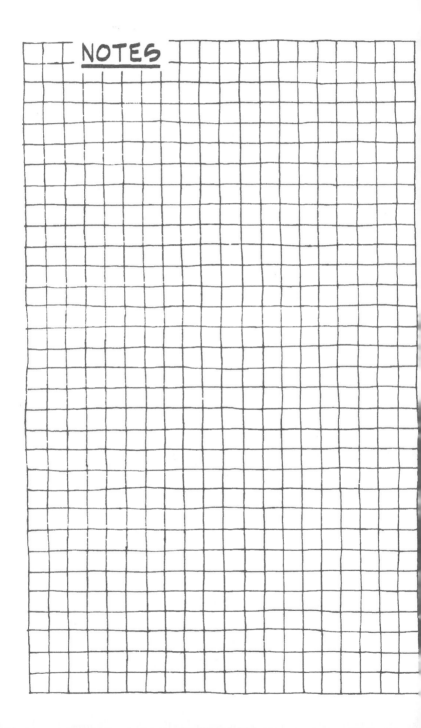

NOTES

___ A. ATTIC VENTILATION

___ 1. When there is attic space under roof, *venting of attic will:*
   ___ a. Reduce heat buildup.
   ___ b. Provide escape route for moisture.
   ___ c. In cold climates, help prevent ice dams from forming.

___ 2. Even when there is *no attic,* the venting effect can still be achieved with at least a *1″* air space above the insulation.

___ 3. In some cases, the argument can be made for having *no venting* at all. This can be done in dry climates and building types where vapor is less of a problem or if the "wet" side of the roof is sealed against vapor migration. Since the codes require venting, but often not enforced, this needs to be checked with building officials.

___ 4. Venting can be done by:
   ___ a. Cross-ventilation
   ___ b. Stack effect
   ___ c. Fans

___ 5. The UBC requires that where climatic conditions warrant, attics or enclosed rafters should have net-free ventilating area of at least $\frac{1}{150}$ of the plan area. This can be reduced to $\frac{1}{300}$ if *50%* of the vent area is at upper portion, at least *3′* above eave, or if a vapor barrier is on warm side of attic insulation.

___ 6. Area Required to Provide 1 SF Vent:

¼″ Screen	1 SF
¼″ Screen w/louvers	2 SF
⅛″ Screen	1.25 SF
⅛″ Screen w/louvers	2.25 SF
1⁄16″ Screen	2 SF
1⁄16″ Screen w/louvers	3 SF

HIP ROOF

GABLE ROOF W/ RIDGE VENT

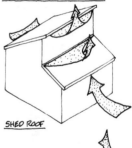

SHED ROOF

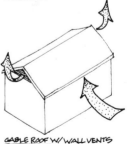

GABLE ROOF W/ WALL VENTS

Costs: Louvers with screens: $25 to $30/SF (35% M and 65% L)
       Bird screen/vents: $26/SF

___ B. WATER AND DAMPPROOFING

___ 1. *Waterproofing* is the prevention of water flow (usually under hydrostatic pressure such as saturated soil) into the building. This is usually basement walls or decks. This can be by:

    ___ *a.* Membranes: Layers of asphalt with plies of saturated felt or woven fabric

    ___ *b.* Hydrolithic: Coatings of asphalt or plastics (elasomeric)

    ___ *c.* Admixtures: To concrete

Typical Costs:
Elastomeric, ¹⁄₃₂″ neoprene: \$1.70/SF (50% M and 50% L)
Bit. membrane, 2-ply felt: \$0.95/SF (35% M and 65% L)

___ 2. *Dampproofing* is the stopping of dampness (from earth or surface water without hydrostatic pressure) into the building. This can be:

    ___ *a.* Below grade: 2 coats asphalt paint, dense cement plaster, silicons, and plastics.

    ___ *b.* Above grade: See paints and coatings, p. 290.

Typical Cost:
Asphalt paint, per coat: \$0.45/SF (50% M and 50% L)

___ C. VAPOR BARRIERS

___ 1. General
     ___ *a.* Vapor can penetrate walls and roof by:
         ___ (1) Diffusion—vapor passes through materials due to:
             ___ (*a*) Difference in vapor pressure between inside and outside.
             ___ (*b*) Permeability of construction materials.
         ___ (2) Air leakage by:
             ___ (*a*) Stack effect
             ___ (*b*) Wind pressure
             ___ (*c*) Building pressure
     ___ *b.* Vapor is not a problem until it reaches its *dew point* and condenses into moisture and deteriorates the building materials of wall, roof, and floor assemblies.
___ 2. Vapor Barriers: Should be placed on the warm or humid side of the assembly. For *cold* climates this will be toward the inside. For warm, humid climates, this will be toward the outside. Barriers are also often put under slabs-on-grade to protect flooring from ground moisture.

     Vapor barriers are measured by *perms* (grains/SF/hr/inch mercury vapor pressure difference). One grain equals about one drop of water. For a material to qualify as a vapor barrier, its perm rate must be *1.0* or less. A good perm rate for foil laminates, polyethylene sheets, etc. equals *0.1* or less (avoid aluminum foil against mortar). See p. 237 for perms of various materials. Care must be taken against puncture of the barrier.

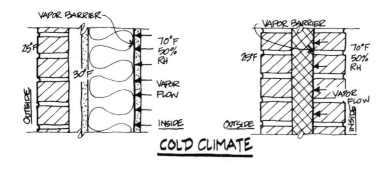

COLD CLIMATE

233

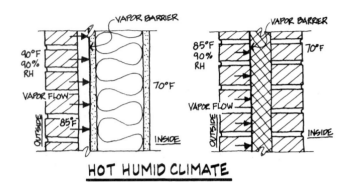

HOT HUMID CLIMATE

Other methods are elastomeric coatings on interior wall board in cold climates and at exterior masonry or stucco walls in hot, wet climates. See p. 290 for coatings. Care must be taken to caulk all joints and cracks (see p. 251).

___ 3. Roof Vapor Retarders

    ___ *a.* As a general guide, should be considered for use when:

        ___ (1) The outside, mean, average January temp. is below 40°F.

        ___ (2) The expected winter, interior, RH is 45% or greater.

    ___ *b.* When vapor is a concern in top of deck insulation, moisture relief vents (preferably one-way) at a min. of one per 1000 SF, should be considered. Vapor retarders generally fall into two classes:

        ___ (1) Bituminous membranes: A typ. 2-ply installation using 3 moppings of steep asphalt rates at less than .005 perms.

        ___ (2) Sheet systems, with sealed laps, such as PVC films, kraft paper, or alum. foil, with perm ratings ranging from 0.10 to 0.50.

___ 4. Asphalt Saturated Felts: See p. 244.

Typical costs: Polyethylene sheets, 2–10 mill. $.10 to $.15/SF

__ D. RADIANT BARRIERS (4)

__ 1. *Reflects* long-wave (invisible) radiation, as a result of sun heating the exterior skin of the building.

__ 2. Use for *hot climates or summer* conditions, only. Effective for exterior summer heat going into building, not the other way, in winter.

ROOF RADIANT BARRIER

AIR SPACE

STRUCTURE

__ 3. Most critical *locations:*
    __ *a.* The roof is most critical since it faces the sun.
    __ *b.* Use at walls can be effective when:
       __ (1) On east and west sides.
       __ (2) Climate is less than 2000 HDD and greater than 2500 CDD. See p. 439.
       __ (3) On south walls when greater than 3500 CDD.
      Note: For HDD and CDD, see App. B, items L and M.

__ 4. Radiation is blocked by a *reflective surface* next to an air space. The barrier can be on either side of the air space, or on both sides.

__ 5. The reflective surface can be *foil-faced batts, refl. alum. foil sheets,* or *reflective paint.*

__ 6. The effectiveness is a measure of *emissivity* (the lower the better):
    __ *a.* Min. for foils should be e = 0.06.
    __ *b.* Min. for paints should be e = 0.23

__ 7. *Added R* value can be approx'd. for summer at e = 0.05:
    __ *a.* Horiz. air space: Reflectance up, R = 5.3
      Reflectance both sides, R = 6.0
    __ *b.* Vert. air space: Reflectance out, R = 3.6
      Reflectance both sides, R = 4.6

__ 8. Must guard against dust-reducing effectiveness.

__ 9. **Costs: Alum. foil barrier: $.25/SF (70% M and 30% L)**

___ E. INSULATION ⑦

___ 1. Insulation is the entrapment of air within modern light-weight materials, to resist heat flow.

___ 2. For minimum total resistance (ΣR) for building elements, find Insulation Zone from App. B, item U., then refer to below:

Zone	Min. insulation, R		
	Cl'g.	Wall	Floor
1	19	11	11
2	26	13	11
3	26	19	13
4	30	19	19
5	33	19	22
6	38	19	22

___ 3. In the design of a building, design the different elements (roof, wall, floor) to be at the minimum ΣR. Each piece of construction has some resistance with lightweight insulations doing the bulk of the resistance of heat flow.

$$\Sigma R = R1 + R2 + R3 + R4 + R5, \text{ etc.} \qquad \text{*(air films)}$$

See p. 237 for resistance (r) of elements to be added.

Another common term is U Value, the coefficient of heat transmission.

$$U = \text{Btuh/ft}^2/°F = \frac{1}{\Sigma R}$$

___ 4. Other factors in control of heat flow

___ a. The *mass* of building elements (such as walls) will delay and store heat. Time lag in hours is related to thermal conductivity, heat capacity, and thickness. This increases as weight of construction goes up with about ½% *per lb/CF*. Desirable time lags in temperate climates are: Roof—12 hrs; north and east walls—0 hrs; west and south walls—8 hrs. This effect can also be used to increase R values, at the approximate rate of *+0.4%* for every added lb/CF of weight.

___ b. Light *colors* will reflect and dark colors will absorb the sun's heat. Cold climates will favor dark surfaces, and the opposite for hot climates. For summer roofs, the overall effect can be 20% between light and dark.

___ c. See page 235 for radiant barriers.

___ 5. Typical Batts:

    R = 11   3½″ thick
    R = 19   6″
    R = 22   6½″
    R = 26   8¼″
    R = 30   9″

___ 6. **Typical Costs:**

    C.L. 'G. batt, 6″ R = 19: $.68/SF (60% M and 40% L)
                9″ R = 30: $.94/SF
    Wall batt,   4″ R = 11: $.46/SF (50% M and 50% L)
                6″ R = 19: $.51/SF
    Add $.15/SF for foil backs.
    Rigid: $.40/SF, ¾″, R = 2.8 to $.95/SF, 2¼″, R = 8.3.

___ 7. Insulating Properties of Building Materials

Material	Wt. #/CF	r value (per in)	Perm
Water	60		
Earth dry	75 to 95	.33	
saturated		.05	
Sand/gravel dry	100–120		
wet			
Concrete req.	150	.11	
lt. wt.	120	.59	
Masonry			
Mortar	130	.2	
Brick, common	120	.2	1 (4″)
8″ CMU, reg. wt.	85	1.11	.4
lt. wt.	55	2	
Stone	±170	.08	
Metals			
Aluminum	165	.0007	0 (1 mil)
Steel	490	.0032	
Copper	555	.0004	
Wood			
Plywood	36	1.25	½″ = .4 to 1
Hardwood	40	.91	
Softwood	30	1.25	2.9 (¾″)
Waterproofing			.05
Vapor barrier			.05

Material	Wt. #/CF	r value (per in)	Perm
Insulations			
Min. wool batt	4	±3.2	>50
Fill		3.7	>50
Perlite	11	2.78	
Board polystyrene		4	1–6
fiber		2.94	
glass fiber		4.17	
urethane		8.5	
Air			
Betwn. nonrefl.		1.34	
One side refl.		4.64	
Two sides refl.			
Inside film		.77 (ave)	
Outside film			
winter		.17	
summer		.25	
Roofing (see p. 244)			
Doors			
Metal			
Fiber core	1.69		
Urethane core	5.56		
Wood, solid 1¾″	3.13		
HC 1⅜″	2.22		
Glass, single	160	(see Page 276)	
Plaster (stucco)	110	.2	
Gypsum	48	.6	
CT	145		
Terrazzo			
Acoustical CLGs			
Resilient flooring		.05	
Carpet and pad		2.08	
Paint			.3 to 1 (see Page 290)

__ F. ROOFING   45

__ 1. General
     __ *a.* Shape: (see p. 231)
         __ (1) Flat
         __ (2) Hip
         __ (3) Gable
         __ (4) Shed
     __ *b.* Pitch: See p. 37 for slopes. Use the following as a guide for roofing selection:

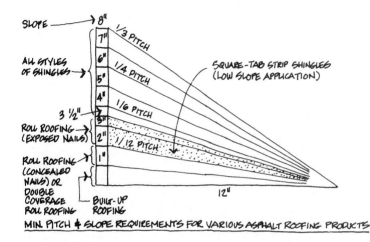

MIN. PITCH & SLOPE REQUIREMENTS FOR VARIOUS ASPHALT ROOFING PRODUCTS

     __ *c.* Drainage: See p. 363
     __ *d.* Fire Resistance: Per the UBC (see page 243), roofing is designated as either nonrated or rated. When rated, roofing must be not readily flammable, provide a degree of fire protection to the deck, not slip from position, and not produce flying brands during a fire. Rated roofs are broken down as follows:
         __ (1) Class A: Resists severe fires, flames on top do not spread more than 6', and no burn thru roof.
         __ (2) Class B: Resists moderate fires, flames on top do not spread more than 8', and no burn thru roof.
         __ (3) Class C: Resists light fires, flames on top do not spread more than 13', and some burn thru roof.

___ 2. Basic Roofing Types
    ___ *a.* Shingles and tiles
        ___ (1) Normally have felt underlayment.
        ___ (2) Laid on pitched roofs of greater than 3 in 12 (or 2 in 12 with special underlayment).
        ___ (3) At high-wind locations, shingles have tendency to blow off roof edges, unless special attachment.
    ___ *b.* Single ply
        ___ (1) Modified bitumen
            ___ (*a*) APP: rubber-like sheets, can be dead level, often with underlayment.
            ___ (*b*) SBS: same as above, but more flexible sheets.
        ___ (2) Single ply (without underlaym't), can be dead level.
            ___ (*a*) EPDM: single rubberized sheets, sealed at seams, unattached or adheared to substrate. Can be rock ballasted. Normally black.
            ___ (*b*) CSPE ("Hypalon"): Like above, but using a synthetic rubber that is normally white.
            ___ (*c*) PVC: Like above, but using plastic-like sheets that are normally white.
    ___ *c.* Coal tar pitch
        ___ (1) Like a built-up roof, of asphaltic products, except coal tar has a lower melt point and is better at self-sealing punctures.
        ___ (2) **Normally is 50% more expensive than BU roofing.**
        ___ (3) Use on very low slopes (1 to 2%).
        ___ (4) Coal tar can be hazardous to work with.
    ___ *d.* Other
        ___ (1) Metal roofing
        ___ (2) Urethane
            ___ (*a*) Sprayed on insulation with sprayed-on waterproof coating
            ___ (*b*) Very good for irregular-shaped roofs
            ___ (*c*) Weak point is delicate coating on top which is susceptible to puncture

___ *e.* Built-up: Plys of asphalt impregnated sheets (often fiberglass) that are adhered together with hot asphalt moppings. (See Design Checklist which follows.)

DESIGN CHECKLIST

___ 1. Roof leaks are often associated with edges and penetrations. Therefore, these require the greatest amount of care.

___ 2. "Flat" roofs should never be dead level. Design substrate or structure for min. of 2% (¼″ per ft) to 4% (½″ per ft) slope for drainage.

___ 3. Place drains at midspans where deflection of structure is greatest.

___ 4. When drains must be placed at columns or bearing walls, add another ½% (approx. $\frac{1}{240}$ the span) to allow for deck or structure deflection.

___ 5. Where camber is designed into structural members, this must also be calculated into the required slope.

___ 6. Provide drainage "crickets" ("saddles") to allow water flow around equip. platforms or against parapets.

___ 7. To prevent ponding, roof drains are best recessed. Drains should be cast iron.

___ 8. For roof drains, scuppers, gutters, downspouts, etc., see p. 363.

___ 9. The drainage system should be laid out to accommodate any req'd. building expansion joints. See p. 248.

___ 10. Roof expansion joints should be provided at: struct. joints; where steel frame or deck changes direction; where separate wings of "L", "U", or "T" shapes; where different type of deck materials meet; where additions are added to exist'g. buildings; where unheated areas meet heated areas; and where movement between vert. walls and roof may occur.

___ 11. Where expansion joints are not used, provide area dividers at *150* to *200* ft, laid out in square or rectangular areas, not restricting the flow of water.

___ 12. All horizontal to vertical intersections, such as walls and equip. platforms should have 45° cants, crickets, flashing, and counter-flashing. Curbs should be 8″ to 14″ high so that there is at least 8″ between top of curb and roof. Premanuf. metal curbs should be 16 GA (or 18 GA with bracing).

___ 13. Roof penetrations of pipes and conduits should be grouped and housed. Keep min. of 18″ between curbs, pipes, and edges of roof. If pitch pockets must be used, reduce size so that no more than 2″ separate edge of metal and edge of penetration.

___ 14. If substrate is preformed rigid insulation, two layers (with offset joints) are best, with top layer installed with long dim. of boards perpendicular to drainage and end joints staggered. Surface must be prepared prior to roofing.

___ 15. Use vapor retarder, when needed. See p. 233.

___ 16. Substrate Decks

    ___ *a. Plywood* should be interior type with exterior glue, graded C-D, or better. Joints should be staggered and blocked or ply clipped. Base ply should be mech. fastened.

    ___ *b. Wood planks* should be min. nominal 1″, T&G, with cracks or knot holes larger than ½″ covered with sheet metal. Edge joints should be staggered. Use separator sheet, mech. fastened as base ply.

    ___ *c. Steel decks* should be 22 GA or heavier. Rigid insulation should be parallel to fluts, which are perpendicular to slope.

    ___ *d. Cast-in-place concrete* should be dry, then primed, unless rigid insulation used; then use vapor retarder or vent insulation.

    ___ *e. Precast concrete* should have rigid insulation. Do not apply first ply to planks.

    ___ *f. Lightweight concrete or Gypsum concrete* must be dry and then have a coated-base ply or vented-base ply mech. attached.

TABLE NO. 32-A—MINIMUM ROOF CLASSES

OCCUPANCY	I	II			III		IV	V	
	F.R.	F.R.	1-HR	N	1-HR	N	H.T.	1-HR	N
A-1	B	B	—	—	—	—	—	—	—
A)2-2.1	B	B	B	—	B	—	B	B	—
A-3	B	B	B	B	B³	C⁴	B³	B³	C⁴
A-4	B	B	B	B	B	B	B	B	B³
B)1-2	B	B	B	B	B³	C⁴	B³	B³	C⁴
B)3-4	B	B	B	B	B	B	B	B	B³
E	B	B	B	B	B	B	B	B	B³
H-1	A	A	A	A	—	A	—	—	A
H)2-3-4-5-6-7	A	B	B	B	B	B	B	B	B
I)1-1.1-2-2	A	B	B	—	B	—	B	B	—
I-3	A	B	B	—	B¹	—	—	B²	—
M	B	B	B	B	NR⁵	NR⁵	NR⁵	NR⁴·⁵	NR⁴·⁵
R-1	B	B	B	B	B²·³	C²·⁴	B²·³	B²·³	C²·⁴
R-3	B	B	B	B	NR	NR	NR	NR	NR

Column group heading: **TYPES OF CONSTRUCTION**

[1] See Section 1002 (b).

[2] Nonrated roof coverings may be used on buildings which are not more than two stories in height and have not more than 3,000 square feet of projected roof area and there is a minimum of 10 feet from the extremity of the roof to the property line on all sides except for street fronts.

[3] Buildings which are not more than two stories in height and have not more than 6,000 square feet of projected roof area and there is a minimum of 10 feet from the extremity of the roof to the property line or assumed property line on all sides except for street fronts may have Class C roof coverings which comply with U.B.C. Standard No. 32-7 and roofs of cedar or redwood shakes and No. 1 shingles constructed in accordance with Section 3204 (e). Special-purpose Roofs.

[4] Buildings which are not more than two stories in height and have not more than 6,000 square feet of projected roof area and where there is a minimum of 10 feet from the extremity of the roof to the property line or assumed property line on all sides, except for street fronts, may have roofs of No. 1 cedar or redwood shakes and No. 1 shingles constructed in accordance with Section 3204 (e).

[5] Unless otherwise required because of location as specified in Parts IV and V of this code, Group M, Division 1 roof coverings shall consist of not less than one layer of cap sheet, or built-up roofing consisting of two layers of felt and a surfacing material as specified in Section 3204 (d) 1.

A—Class A roofing   C—Class C roof covering   N—No requirements for fire resistance   H.T.—Heavy timber
B—Class B roofing   NR—Nonrated roof coverings   F.R.—Fire resistive

ROOFING COMPARISON (DATA AND COSTS)

TYPE		SLOPE IN./FT. MIN. MAX.	UNDER-LAYMENT	FASTEN-ERS	WT. #/SQ.	P PER IN.	FIRE CL.	LIFE YRS	TYPICAL COSTS
UNDERLAYMENT/ ROLL ROOFING	FELT		N/A		15 30	.06			$.009/SQ (10%M $ 90%L) $.0095/SQ.
SHINGLES	ASPHALT	4 / 12	15# FELT	GALV. ST. OR ALUM. ROOF NAILS	300	.44	C / A		$90/SQ. (55%M $ 45%L)
	FIBERGLASS	2	30#		250	.87		25 TO 40	
	WOOD SHAKES	3	30# FELT OR ON WD. STRIPERS	CORR. RESIST. NAILS	150 300		B*	25 50	$195/SQ. (60%M $ 40%L) $200/SQ. *ADD $100/SQ. FOR FIRE RETARDING
TILE	SLATE	4 TO 6	30# FELT	COPPER WIRE & NAILS	700 TO 4000	.05	A	100	$530/SQ. (70%M $ 30%L)
	"SPANISH" CLAY	4	30# FELT	NON-COR. COPPER NAILS / 10d COR. RESIST. GALV.COR PER, OR S.S. BOX NAILS	800 TO 1450	.01	A	100	$475 TO $690/SQ. (65%M $ 35%L)
	CONC.				950		A		$230/SQ.

244

ROOFING COMPARISON (DATA AND COSTS)

TYPE	SLOPE IN./FT. MIN.	MAX.	UNDER-LAYMENT	FASTENERS	WT. #/SQ	J PER IN.	FIRE CL.	LIFE YRS	TYPICAL COSTS
METAL — STANDING SEAM, 22 TO 26 GA. PAINTED	3		30# FELT	ANCHOR CLIPS, GALV NAILS OR SCREWS	130			30 TO 50	$500/SQ (80% H + 20% L)
"FLAT" — BUILT-UP	1/4		N/A	N/A	550		A TO C	20	$80-100/SQ (30% H 70% L).
W/ GRAVEL		3							ADD $35/SQ FOR GRAVEL.
W/ CAP SHEET		6							ADD $35/SQ FOR CAP SHT.
SINGLE PLY			40# FIBERGLASS		40				$175-230/SQ
URETHANE W/ ELAST. COATING					2.5 #/CF	7.2	A TO C		$230-320/SQ (2" THK.)

245

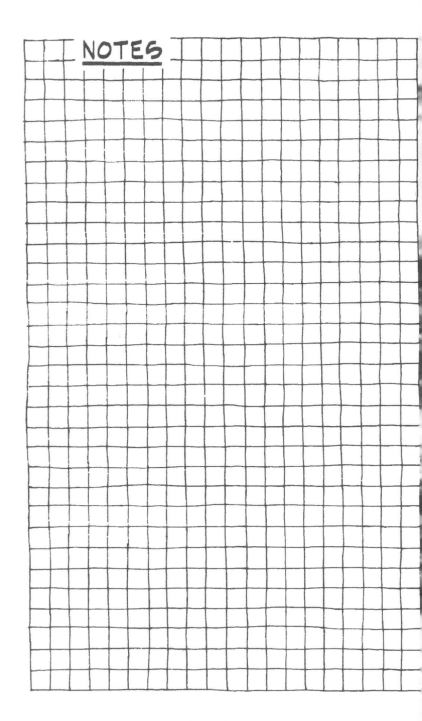

NOTES

__ G. FLASHING (4)

__ 1. Purpose: To stop water penetration at joints and intersections of building elements by use of pliable, long-lasting materials.
__ 2. Materials
    __ *a.* Stainless steel: *best*
    __ *b.* Copper
    __ *c.* Aluminum
    __ *d.* Galvanized metal (must be painted)
    __ *e.* Flexible (PVC, EPDM, etc.)
    __ *f.* Felt: *worst*
__ 3. Locations
    __ *a.* At *roof*
        __ (1) Edges
        __ (2) Where roof meets vertical elements, such as walls
        __ (3) Penetrations
    __ *b.* At *walls*
        __ (1) Copings at top
        __ (2) Foundation sills
        __ (3) Openings (heads/sills)
__ 4. **Costs**
    Complete roof to parapet assembly: ≈ $16/LF
    Complete edge of roof assembly: ≈ $11.50/LF
    Alum. flashing: $2.5 to $4/SF (10% M and 90% L)
    Copper flashing: $5 to $9/SF (45% M and 55% L)
__ 5. Typical Details

FLASHING FOR NON-WALL SUPPORTED DECK

SINGLE PLY   BUILT-UP

- 3" LAP W/ SEALANT
- METAL REGLET
- FASTENERS @ ≈ 24" O.C.
- FLEX. TUBING – 1½ × JT. WIDTH FOR MIN. DIA.
- MEMBRANE FLASH'G. ADHERED TO MEMBRANE W/ ADHESIVE
- SEAL EDGES OF FLASHING
- EPDM MEMBRANE FASTEN TO WD. NAILER

- METAL LAP AT JT.
- REMOVABLE COUNTER FLASH'G.
- 2" WIDE CLIP, ≈ 30" O.C.
- FLEX. VAPOR RETARDER
- BASE FLASH'G.
- WOOD CANT STRIP, NAIL TOP & BOTTOM @ ≈ 16" O.C.

__ H. JOINTS

__ 1. General

    __ *a.* Joints need to be planned because buildings and construction materials move small amounts over time.

        The two greatest reasons of joint failure are not precleaning the joint and not tooling the sealant.

UNTOOLED   TOOLED

    __ *b.* Types

        __ (1) *Expansion joints:* allow for movement. These will often go completely through the building structure with columns on each side of joint. See p. 89 for seismic joints.

        __ (2) *Control joints:* allow for control of cracking of finish materials by providing an indention to induce the crack in a straight line. See p. 160 for conc. slabs. See p. 175 for masonry. See p. 241 for roofing. See p. 281 for plaster.

        __ (3) *Weather seals:* to reduce infiltration through building from outside (or vice versa).

    __ *c.* Locations

        __ (1) New building adjoining existing

        __ (2) Long, low building abutting higher building

        __ (3) Wings adjoining main structure

        __ (4) Long buildings (125′ for masonry, and 200′ for steel or conc. buildings)

        __ (5) Long, low connecting wings between buildings

        __ (6) Intersections at wings of L-, T-, or U-shaped buildings

        __ (7) Control joints along walls and at openings

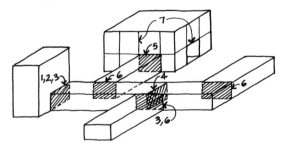

___ *d.* Components
    ___ (1) Sealant
    ___ (2) Joint filler
___ *e.* Widths = thermal expansion + moisture + tolerance.
    ___ (1) Thermal expansion = $Ec \times \Delta t \times L$
        ___ (*a*) Ec, coefficient of thermal expansion of material, as follows:

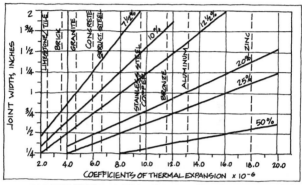

JOINT WIDTHS FOR SEALANTS WITH VARIOUS MOVEMENT CAPABILITIES
FOR 10 FOOT PANELS AT Δt OF 130°F

        ___ (*b*) Δt = max. probable temp. difference the material will experience over time. For ambient conditions, take the difference between items P and Q in App. B. Since materials absorb and/or retain heat, the result should be increased for the type of material (can easily double).
        ___ (*c*) L = Length in inches.
    ___ (2) *Moisture* can add to expansion or to shrinkage depending on the material. See p. 175.
    ___ (3) *Construction tolerance:* depends on material. For PC concrete panels, use: ⅛″ for 10′ lengths and ¼″ for 30′ lengths.

EXAMPLE: ASSUME CONC. WALL PANELS, 5′ WIDE. EXPECT CONC.
Δt OF 120°F & A TOLERANCE OF ⅛″. USE A SEALANT
W/ 20% MOVEMENT CAPABILITIES.
FROM CHART ABOVE: ½″ ($\frac{120°F}{130°F}$) + ⅛″ = $^{19}/_{32}$″ OR ⅝″
SINCE PANEL IS 5′ WIDE: ⅝″ ÷ 2 = $^{5}/_{16}$″ OR ⅜″

___ *f.* Depths:

| | Depth of sealant | |
Joint width	Conc., masonry, stone	Metal, glass, and other nonporous materials
Min. ¼″	¼″	¼″
¼″ to ½″	Same as width	¼″
½″ to 1″	One-half width	One-half width
1″ to 2″	Max. ½″	Max. ½″

___ 2. Sealants

COMPARATIVE PROPERTIES OF SEALANTS

LEGEND: 1 = POOR 2 = FAIR 3 = GOOD 4 = VERY GOOD 5 = EXCELLENT	BUTYL	ACRYLIC, WATER BASE	ACRYLIC, SOLVENT BASE	POLYSULFIDE, ONE PART	POLYSULFIDE, TWO PART	POLYURETHANE, ONE PART	POLYURETHANE, TWO PART	SILICONE	NOTES
RECOMMENDED MAX. JOINT MOVEMENT, % ±	7.5	7.5	12.5	25	25	15	25	25	(1)
LIFE EXPECTANCY IN YEARS	10+	10	15-20	20	20	20+	20+	20+	
MAX. JOINT WIDTH (INCHES)	3/4	3/8	3/4	3/4	1	3/4	1-2	3/4	(2)
ADHESION TO: WOOD	●	●	●	●	●	●	●	●	(3)
METAL	●	●	●	●	◐	●	●	●	(3)
MASONRY/CONC.	◐	●	●	●	●	◐	●	●	(3)
GLASS	●	●	●	●	◐	●	◐	●	(3)
PLASTIC	◐	●	●					●	
CURING TIME (DAYS)	120	5	14	14+	7	7+	3-5	2-5	(4,5)
SHORE A HARDNESS	20-40	30-35	20-40	25-35	25-50	25-45	25-45	30-40	
SELF LEVELING AVAILABLE	N/A		●	●	●		●	●	
NON-SAG AVAILAB.	N/A	●	●	●	◐	●	●	●	
RESISTANCE TO: (SEE LEGEND) ULTRAVIOLET	2-3	1-3	3-4	2	2-3	3	3	5	
CUT/TEAR	2	1-2	1	3	3	4-5	4-5	1-2	
ABRASION	2	1-2	1-2	1	1	3	3	1	
WEATHERING	2	1-3	3-4	3	3	3-4	3-4	4-5	
OIL/GREASE	1-2	2	3	3	3	3	3	2	
COMPRESSION	2-3	1-2	1	3	3	4	4	4.5	
EXTENSION	1	1-2	1	2-3	2.3	4-5	4-5	4-5	

(1) SOME HIGH PERFORMANCE URETHANES & SILICONES HAVE MOVEMENT CAPABILITIES UP TO 50%.

(2) FIGURES GIVEN ARE CONSERVATIVE. VERIFY W/ MANUFACTURER.

(3) PRIMER MAY BE REQUIRED.

(4) CURE TIME FOR LOW TO MED. MODULES SILICONES IS ABOUT 2 HOURS

(5) SILICONE CAN BE APPLIED OVER A WIDE TEMP. RANGE.

___ 3. Checklist of Infiltration Control
    ___ *a.* Tighten seals around windows and doors, and weather stripping around all openings to the outside or to unconditioned rooms.
    ___ *b.* Caulk around all windows and doors before drywall is hung. Seal all penetrations (plumbing, electrical, etc.).
    ___ *c.* Insulate behind wall outlets and/or plumbing lines in exterior walls.
    ___ *d.* Caulk under headers and sills.
    ___ *e.* Fill spaces between rough openings and millwork with insulation (best application with foam).
    ___ *f.* Install dampers and/or glass doors on fireplaces, combined with outside combustion air intake.
    ___ *g.* Install backdraft dampers on all exhaust fan openings.
    ___ *h.* Close core voids in tops of block foundation walls.
    ___ *i.* Control concrete and masonry cracking.
    ___ *j.* Use airtight drywall methods.

___ 4. **Costs**
Exterior joint, ⅜″ × ½″ $1.80/LF (20% M and 80% L)
Interior $1.60/LF
For joint fillers and gaskets: Add 50 to 100%

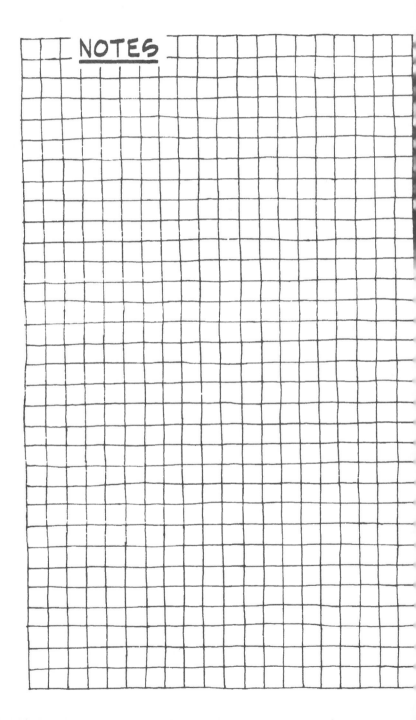

NOTES

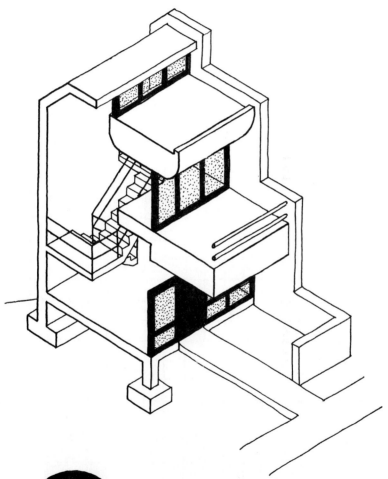

8 DOORS, WINDOWS, AND GLASS

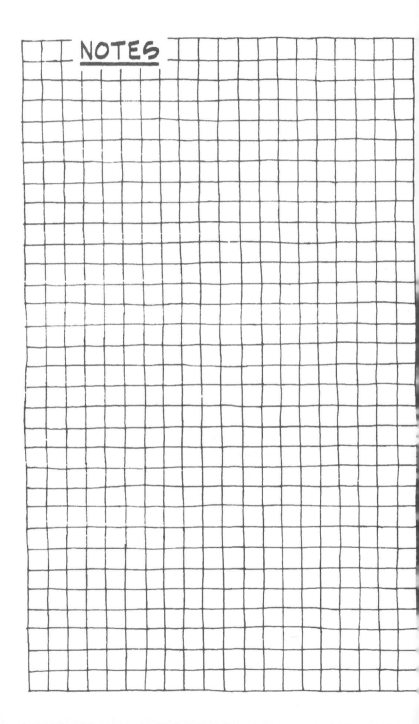

NOTES

__ A. DOORS

__ 1. *Accessible Door Approach* (ADA) (20)

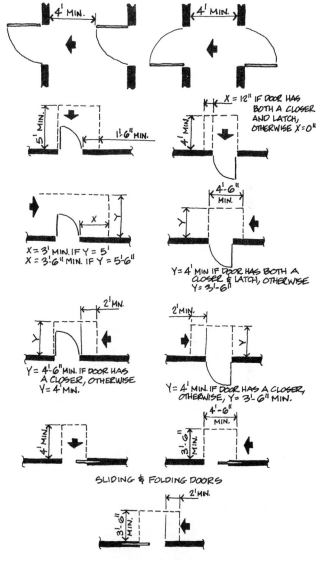

SLIDING & FOLDING DOORS

NOTE: ALL DOORS IN <u>ALCOVES</u> SHALL COMPLY W/ FRONT APPROACHES.

___ 2. *General*   (7)   (12)

   ___ *a.* Types by operation
      ___ (1) Swinging
      ___ (2) Bypass sliding
      ___ (3) Surface sliding
      ___ (4) Pocket sliding
      ___ (5) Folding
   ___ *b.* Physical types

(1) Flush   (2) Panelled   (3) French   (4) Glass

(5) Sash   (6) Jalousie   (7) Louver

(8) Shutter   (9) Screen   (10) Dutch

   ___ *c.* Rough openings (door dimensions +)

	Width	Height
In wood stud walls (r.o.)	+3½″	+3½″
In masonry walls (m.o)	+4″	+2″ to 4″

   ___ *d.* Fire door classifications

Fire door rating (in hours)	Opening class	Use of wall	Rating of wall (in hours)
3	A	Fire walls	3 or 4
		Fire separations	
1½	B	Vertical shafts	2
		Exit stairs	
		Fire separations	

Fire door rating (in hours)	Opening class	Use of wall	Rating of wall (in hours)
1	B	Vertical shafts Exit stairs Fire separations	1
¾	C	Fire-resistive partitions Corridors Hazardous areas	1
½		Limited applic. corridors	1 or less
⅓		Corridors	
20 Min.		Smoke barriers	
1½	D	Severe exterior exposure	2 or more
¾	E	Exterior exposure	1 or less

___ *e.* Energy conservation: Specify doors not to exceed:
   ___ (1) Residential: 0.5 CFM/SF infiltration
   ___ (2) Nonresidential: 11.0 CFM/LF crack infiltration

___ 3. *Hollow Metal Doors and Frames*

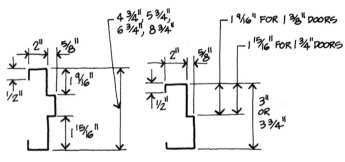

DOUBLE RABBET   SINGLE RABBET

___ *a.* Material (for gauges, see p. 191). Typical gauges of doors (16, 18, 20) and frames (12, 14, 16, 18)

Use	Frame	Door face
Heavy (entries, stairs public toilets, mech. rms.)	12, 14	16
Medium to low (rooms, closets, etc.)	14, 16, 20	18

___ *b.* Doors (total door construction of 16 to 22 GA)

Thickness	1¾″ and 1⅜″
Widths	2′ to 4′ in 2″ increments
Heights	6′8″, 7′, 7′2″, 7′10″, 8′, 10′

Costs:

Frames: 3′ × 7′, 18 GA $4.35/SF (of opening) or 16 GA at 5.00/SF (60% M and 40% L), can vary ±40%.

Doors: 3′ × 7′, 18 GA, 1¾″: $10.90/SF (85% M and 3′ × 6′8″, 20 GA, 1⅜″: $8.60/SF 15% L).

Add: lead lining: $550/ea., 8″ × 8″ glass, $98/ea. Sound: $25, 3 hr: $45, ¾ hr.: $10.

___ 4. *Wood Doors*

    ___ *a.* Types

        ___ (1) Flush

        ___ (2) Hollow core

        ___ (3) Solid core

        ___ (4) Panel (rail and stile)

DRYWALL
CASING
SHIM
FRAME
DOOR

    ___ *b.* Sizes

        Thickness: 1¾″ (SC), 1⅜″ (HC)

        Widths: 1′6″ to 3′6″ in 2″ increments

        Heights: 6′, 6′6″, 6′8″, 6′10″, 7′

    ___ *c.* Materials (birch, lavan, tempered hard bd.)

Flush	Panel
Hardwood veneer	#1: hardwood or pine for transp. finish
Premium: for transp. finish	#2: Doug fir plywood for paint
Good #3: For paint.	
Sound: (for paint only)	

    ___ *d.* Fire doors (with mineral composition cores) B and C labels available, see p. 256.

Typical costs:

        Wood frame: interior, pine: $3.00/SF (of opening)

                      exterior, pine: $5.00/SF

        (triple costs for hardwoods)

        Door: H.C. 1⅜″, hard bd. $6.00/SF

             S.C. 1¾″, hard bd. $8.00/SF (75% M and 25% L.)

             Hardwood veneers about same costs.

        For carved solid exterior doors, multiply costs by 4 to 6.

        Bifold or bypass closet doors with frame and trim: ±$5.25/SF

___ 5. *Other Doors*
    ___ *a.* Sliding glass doors

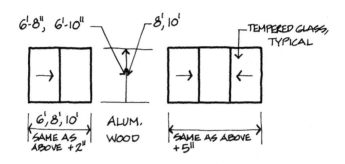

Typical Cost (aluminum with ¼″ temp. glass):
    6′ wide: $340 to $680/ea. (85% M and 15% L)
    12′ wide: $1200/ea.
    Add 10% for insulated glass.

        ___ *b.* Aluminum "Store Front" (7′ ht. typ.)

Typical cost with glass: $25/SF (85% M and 15% L)

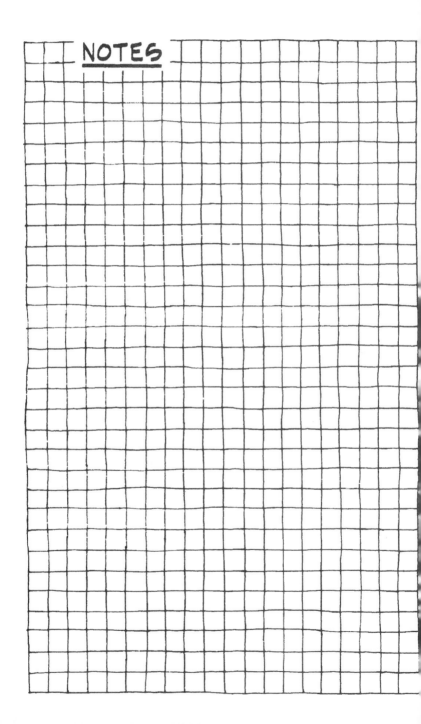

NOTES

__ B. WINDOWS ④ ⑫ ㉜ ㊺

__ 1. General

    __ *a.* In common with walls, windows are expected to keep out:

- winter wind
- rain in all seasons
- noise
- winter cold
- winter snow
- bugs and other flying objects
- summer heat

They are expected, at the same time, to let in:

- outside views
- ventilating air
- natural light
- winter solar gain

    __ *b.* For types by operation, see p. 264.

    __ *c.* For aid to selection of type, see p. 262.

    __ *d.* Windows come in aluminum, steel and wood. See pp. 266 and 267 for typical sizes.

    __ *e.* Energy conservation: Specify windows to not exceed 0.34 CFM per LF of operable sash crack for infiltration.

    __ *f.* **For typical costs, see p. 264.**

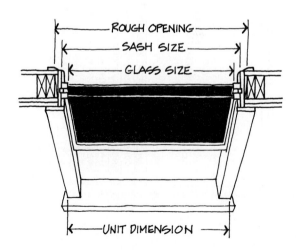

WINDOW TYPES

• INDICATES CHARACTERISTICS

DISADVANTAGES	DOUBLE HUNG	DOUBLE HUNG, REVERSED	CASEMENT, OUT	CASEMENT, IN	AWNING, CANOPY	PIVOTED, VERTICAL	PIVOTED, HORIZONTAL	TOP HINGED, OUT	BOTTOM HINGED, IN	FIXED SASH	JALOUSIE	MONITOR, CONTINUOUS	PROJECTED	HORIZONTAL SLIDING
ONLY 50% OF AREA OPENABLE	•	•												•
DOESN'T PROTECT FROM RAIN, WHEN OPEN	•	•	•			•								•
INCONVENIENT OPER. IF OVER OBSTRUCTION	•	•					•	•						•
HAZ'D. IF LOW VENT NEXT TO WALK			•		•	•	•	•				•	•	
REQUIRES WEATHER STRIPPING	•	•	•	•		•	•	•	•					•
HORZ. MEMBERS OBSTRUCT VIEW	•	•			•		•				•	•	•	
VERT. MEMBERS OBSTRUCT VIEW			•	•										•
WILL SAG IF NOT STRUCTURALLY STRONG			•	•										
GLASS QUICKLY SOILS WHEN VENT OPEN														
INFLOWING AIR CANNOT BE DIVERTED DOWN														•
EXCESSIVE AIR LEAKAGE	•	•	•		•	•	•	•	•		•	•	•	
HARD TO WASH				•	•			•	•		•			
INTERFERES WITH FURNITURE, DRAPES, ETC.						•	•				•			•
SCREENS-STORM SASH DIFFICULT TO PROVIDE						•	•		•		•			•
SASH HAS TO BE REMOVED FOR WASHING	•							•		•		•		

WINDOW TYPES

● INDICATES CHARACTERISTICS

ADVANTAGES	DOUBLE HUNG	DOUBLE HUNG REVERSED	CASEMENT, OUT	CASEMENT, IN	AWNING, CANOPY	PIVOTED, VERTICAL	PIVOTED, HORIZONTAL	TOP HINGED, OUT	BOTTOM HINGED, IN	FIXED SASH	JALOUSE	MONITOR, CONTINUOUS	PROJECTED	HORIZONTAL SLIDING
NOT APT TO SAG	●	●			●	●	●	●	●	●		●		●
SCREEN & STORM SASH EASY TO INSTALL	●	●		●	●			●						●
PROVIDES 100% VENT OPENING			●	●	●	●	●	●	●		●	●		
EASY TO WASH W/ PROPER HARDWARE		●		●		●	●		●					
WILL DEFLECT DRAFTS			●	●	●	●	●		●		●	●		
OFFERS RAIN PROTECTION, PARTLY OPEN					●		●	●	●		●	●	●	
DIVERTS INFLOWING AIR UPWARD					●		●		●		●	●	●	
ODD SIZES ECONOMICALLY AVAILABLE										●	●			●
LARGE SIZES PRACTICAL														●

263

WINDOW TYPES BY OPERATION AND MATERIAL & COSTS

NOTE: GLASS EXCLUDED IN COSTS   * (90%M $10%L)

TYPE	VENT	ALUMINUM	STEEL	WOOD
FIXED	0%	$11/SF AVE. (70%M $30%L)		$23.50/SF AVE. * VARIATION -10% +20% PICTURE WINDOW
CASEMENT	100%		$15/SF AVE (85%M $15%L)	$31.30/SF AVE * VARIATION ±15%
PROJECTED — AWNING / HOPPER	50 TO 100%	$22.50/SF AVE. (75%M $25%L)	$16/SF AVE. *	$37/SF AVE. (85%M $15%L) VARIATION ±25%
SLIDING	50 TO 100%	$15/SF AVE. (80%M $20%L)		$30/SF AVE (LARGE WINDOWS -40%)

DOUBLE-HUNG	50%	$16/SF AVE. *	$23.50/SF AVE. *	$28/SF AVE. (85%M $15%L)
JALOUSIE	100%	$15/SF AVE. (80% M $ 20% L)		
PIVOTING	100%		$14/SF AVE. (85%M $15%L)	

TYPICAL WOOD WINDOW SASH SIZES

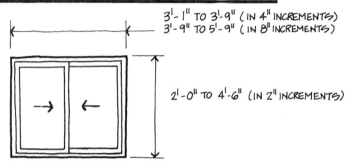

3'-1" TO 3'-9" (IN 4" INCREMENTS)
3'-9" TO 5'-9" (IN 8" INCREMENTS)

2'-0" TO 4'-6" (IN 2" INCREMENTS)

HORIZONTAL SLIDING WINDOWS

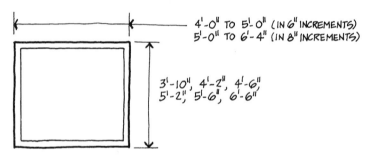

4'-0" TO 5'-0" (IN 6" INCREMENTS)
5'-0" TO 6'-4" (IN 8" INCREMENTS)

3'-10", 4'-2", 4'-6",
5'-2", 5'-6", 6'-6"

PICTURE WINDOWS

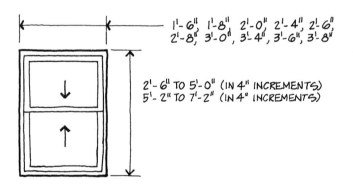

1'-6", 1'-8", 2'-0", 2'-4", 2'-6",
2'-8", 3'-0", 3'-4", 3'-6", 3'-8"

2'-6" TO 5'-0" (IN 4" INCREMENTS)
5'-2" TO 7'-2" (IN 4" INCREMENTS)

DOUBLE HUNG WINDOWS

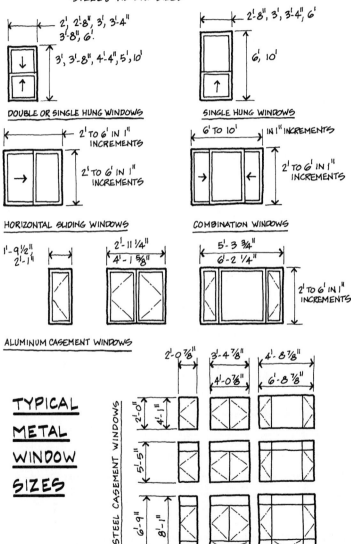

ALUM. : RESIDENTIAL SIZES
STEEL : NO STD SIZES

2', 2'-8", 3', 3'-4"
3'-8", 6'.

3', 3'-8", 4'-4", 5', 10'

DOUBLE OR SINGLE HUNG WINDOWS

2'-8", 3', 3'-4", 6'

6', 10'

SINGLE HUNG WINDOWS

2' TO 6' IN 1" INCREMENTS

2' TO 6' IN 1" INCREMENTS

HORIZONTAL SLIDING WINDOWS

6' TO 10'   IN 1" INCREMENTS

2' TO 6' IN 1" INCREMENTS

COMBINATION WINDOWS

1'-9½"
2'-1"

2'-11 ¼"
4'-1 ⅝"

ALUMINUM CASEMENT WINDOWS

5'-3 ¾"
6'-2 ¼"

2' TO 6' IN 1" INCREMENTS

TYPICAL
METAL
WINDOW
SIZES

STEEL CASEMENT WINDOWS

2'-0 ⅞"

3'-4 ⅞"   4'-8 ⅞"

4'-0 ⅞"   6'-8 ⅞"

2'-0"
4'-1"

5'-5"

6'-9"
8'-1"

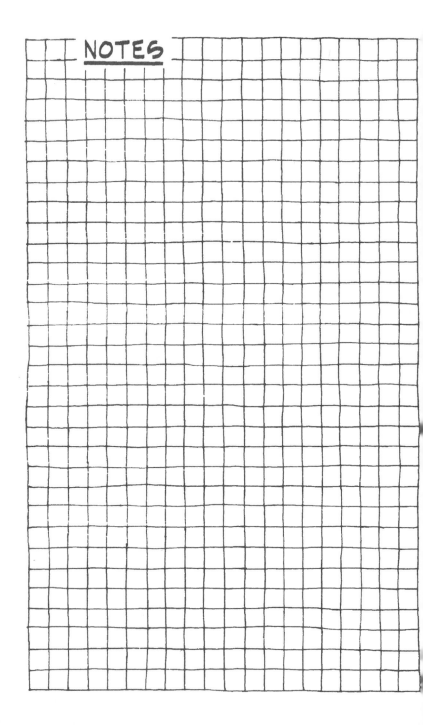

NOTES

___ C. HARDWARE ⑫ ⑳

___ 1. General Considerations: How to . . .
    ___ a. Hang the door
    ___ b. Lock the door
    ___ c. Close the door
    ___ d. Protect the door
    ___ e. Stop the door
    ___ f. Seal the door
    ___ g. Misc. the door
    ___ h. Electrify the door
___ 2. Recommended Locations   ___ 3. Door Hand Conventions

LEFT HAND   RIGHT HAND

LEFT HAND REVERSE   RIGHT HAND REVERSE

⬆ DIRECTION OF TRAVEL ASSUMED TO BE FROM OUTSIDE IN OR FROM KEYED SIDE FOR INTERIOR DOORS.

    ⅊ HINGE
    ⅊ STRIKE FOR DEADLOCKS
    ⅊ PUSH/PULL LATCHES & PLATES
    ⅊ DR PULL OR PUSH BAR
    ⅊ STRIKE FOR LOCKSETS
    40" 42" 45" 48" MAX. (A.D.A.)

___ 4. Specific Considerations
    ___ a. Function and ease of operation
    ___ b. Durability in terms of:
        ___ (1) Frequency of use
            ___ (a) Heavy
            ___ (b) Medium
            ___ (c) Light
        ___ (2) Exposure to weather and climate (Alum. and SS good for humid or coastal conditions)
    ___ c. Material, form, surface texture, finish, and color.
___ 5. Typical Hardware
    ___ a. Locksets (locks, latches, bolts)
    ___ b. Hinges
    ___ c. Closers
    ___ d. Panic hardware
    ___ e. Push/pull bars and plates

___ *f.* Kick plates
___ *g.* Stops and holders
___ *h.* Thresholds
___ *i.* Weatherstripping
___ *j.* Door tracks and hangers
___ 6. Materials
    ___ *a.* Aluminum
    ___ *b.* Brass
    ___ *c.* Bronze
    ___ *d.* Iron
    ___ *e.* Steel
    ___ *f.* Stainless steel
___ 7. Finishes

BHMA #	US #	Finish
___ 600	US P	Primed for painting
___ 605	US 3	Bright brass, clear coated
___ 606	US 4	Satin brass, clear coated
___ 612	US 10	Satin bronze, clear coated
___ 613	US 10B	Oxidized satin bronze, oil rubbed
___ 618	US 14	Bright nickel plated, clear coated
___ 619	US 15	Satin nickel plated, clear coated
___ 622	US 19	Flat black coated
___ 623	US 20	Light oxidized bright bronze clear C
___ 624	US 20D	Dark oxidized statuary bronze CC
___ 625	US 26	Bright chromium plated
___ 626	US 26D	Satin chromium plated
___ 628	US 28	Satin aluminum, clear anodized
___ 629	US 32	Bright stainless steel
___ 630	US 32D	Satin stainless steel

___ 8. ADA-Accessible Hardware

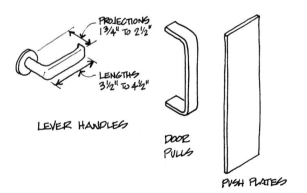

PROJECTIONS
1¾" TO 2½"

LENGTHS
3½" TO 4½"

LEVER HANDLES

DOOR PULLS

PUSH PLATES

___ 9. **Costs**
  Residential: $90/Dr. (80% M and 20% L)
                                    Variation −30%, +120%
  Commercial:
    Office:
      Interior: $180/Dr. (75% M and 25% L)
      Exterior: $350/Dr. (add ≈ $425 for exit devices)
    Note: **Special doors, such as for hospitals, can go up to $570/Dr.**

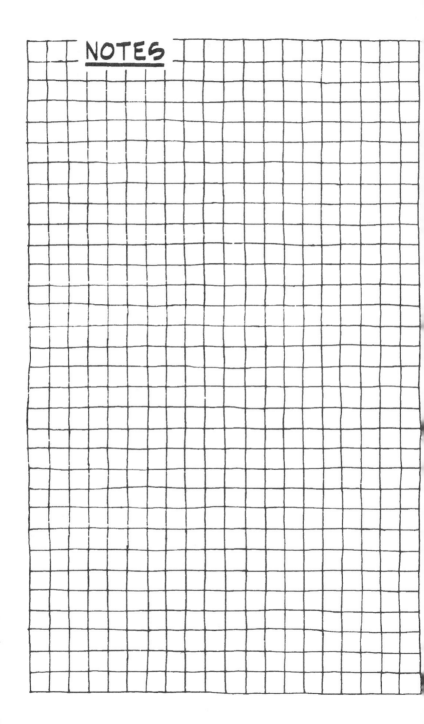

NOTES

___ D. GLASS

___ 1. General: Glass is one of the great modern building materials because it allows the inside of buildings to have a *visual relationship* with the outside. However, there are a number of *problems to be overcome:*

___ 2. Energy: Since more *heat flows through glass than any other building material,* it must be sized and located carefully. See p. 101.

    ___ *a.* Solar: When *heating is needed,* glass can be used on south sides to help. See p. 102. When *heating is to be avoided,* it is best to place glass on north or south sides, avoiding the east and west. The *Shading Coefficient* is the ratio of the total solar heat gain to that of ⅛″ clear glass. 1.0 is no shade, so the lower the better.

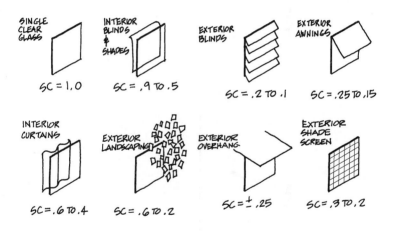

SINGLE CLEAR GLASS   SC = 1.0

INTERIOR BLINDS & SHADES   SC = .9 TO .5

EXTERIOR BLINDS   SC = .2 TO .1

EXTERIOR AWNINGS   SC = .25 TO .15

INTERIOR CURTAINS   SC = .6 TO .4

EXTERIOR LANDSCAPING   SC = .6 TO .2

EXTERIOR OVERHANG   SC = ± .25

EXTERIOR SHADE SCREEN   SC = .3 TO .2

    ___ *b.* Conduction/Convection Heat Flow: Also transfers heat, since glass is a poor insulator. See p. 236.

___ 3. Condensation: As room air comes in contact with cold glass, it drops in temperature, depositing excess water vapor on the surface as liquid condensate. Use the following graph to select glazing to avoid this:

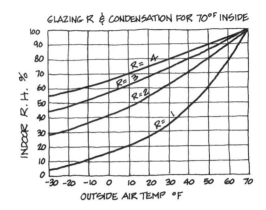

GLAZING R & CONDENSATION FOR 70°F INSIDE

___ 4. Legal Requirements: The UBC requires *safety glazing* at locations hazardous to human impact. Safety glazing is *tempered glass, wired glass,* and *laminated glass.* Hazardous locations are:
    ___ *a.* Ingress and egress doors
    ___ *b.* Sliding glass doors
    ___ *c.* Storm doors
    ___ *d.* Swinging doors
    ___ *e.* Shower and bathtub doors and enclosures
    ___ *f.* Glass in railings
    ___ *g.* Overhead or angled glass and skylights (must be plastic, wired glass, or laminated glass)
    ___ *h.* Glass adjacent to doors and other glass areas, per below:

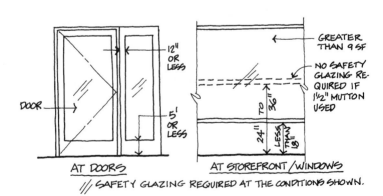

/// SAFETY GLAZING REQUIRED AT THE CONDITIONS SHOWN.

___ 5. Sizing of Glass

   ___ *a.* Determine wind speeds at site by consulting App. B, item S. Convert to pressure:

Wind pressure at 33′ height

Wind (MPH)	70	80	90	100	110	120	130
Pressure (PSF)	12.6	16.4	20.8	25.6	31.0	36.9	43.3

   ___ *b.* Multiply results by the following factors:
      ___ (1) For low, normal, open sites: 1.5
      ___ (2) For high, windy, or gusty sites: 3.0
   ___ *c.* Size: Select glass from below:

MAXIMUM GLAZING AREA VS. PRESSURE

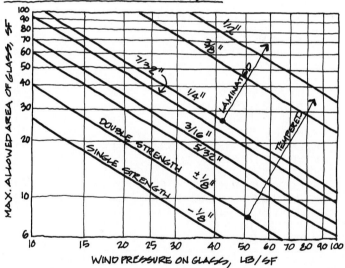

___ 6. **Costs**
   ¼″ Clear float glass: $7.50 to $8.50/SF (45% M and 55% L)
   Modifiers:
      Thickness:
         ⅛″ Glass   −40%
         ⅜″ Glass   +50%
         ½″ Glass   +150%
      Structural:
         Tempered +20%
         Laminated +45%

Thermal:
Tinted or reflective   **+20%**
Double glazed and/or low E **+100%**

___ 7. Typical Glazing Characteristics

Glazing type	R value	Shade coef.	Vis. trans. (%)	Perf. index
___ SINGLE-GLAZED, CLEAR	0.90	1.00	90	0.90
___ SG GRAY-TINTED	"	0.69	43	0.62
___ SG BRONZE-TINT	"	0.71	52	0.73
___ SG GREEN TINTED	"	0.71	75	1.09
___ SG REFLECTIVE	"	0.51	27	0.53
___ SG LOW E, CLEAR	1.40	0.74	84	1.14
___ SG LOW E, GRAY	"	0.50	41	1.82
___ SG LOW E, BRONZE	"	0.52	49	0.94
___ SG LOW E, GREEN	"	0.56	71	1.27
___ DOUBLE-GLAZED, CLEAR	2.00	0.84	80	0.95
___ DG GRAY-TINTED	"	0.85	39	0.69
___ DG BRONZE-TINTED	"	0.59	47	0.80
___ DG GREEN-TINTED	"	0.60	68	1.13
___ DG REFLECTIVE	"	0.42	26	0.62
___ DG LOW E, CLEAR	3.12	0.67	76	1.13
___ DG LOW E, GRAY	"	0.42	37	0.88
___ DG LOW E, BRONZE	"	0.44	44	1.00
___ DG LOW E, GREEN	"	0.47	64	1.36
___ DG POLY FILM, CLEAR	4.5	0.42	53	1.26
___ DG POLY FILM, GRAY	"	0.27	26	0.96
___ DG P FILM, BRONZE	"	0.29	32	1.10
___ DG P FILM, GREEN	"	0.29	45	1.55

Note: Performance Index ("Coolness Index") = Visual Transmission/Shading Coefficient. The higher the number, the better.

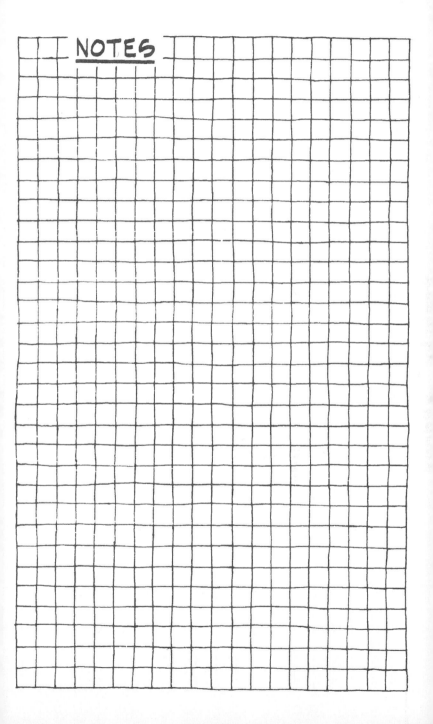

NOTES

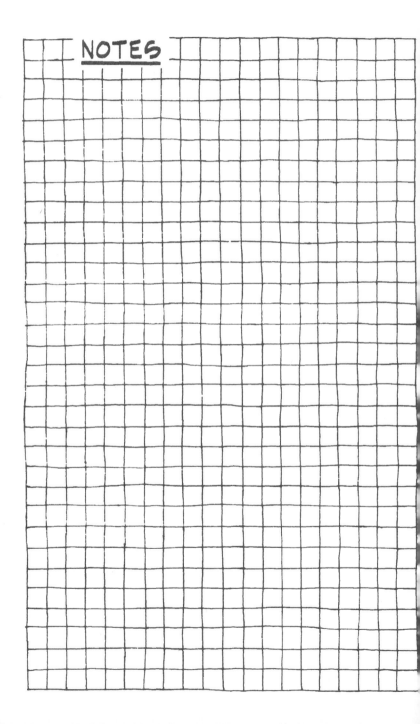

NOTES

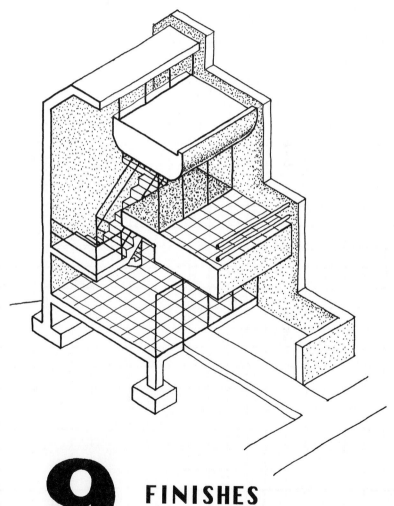

9 FINISHES

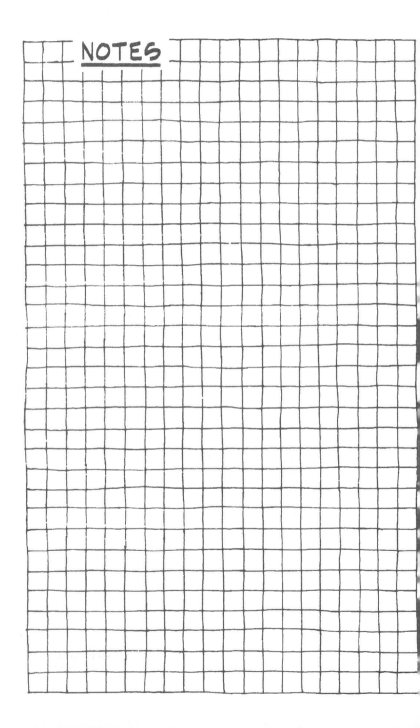

NOTES

__ A. PLASTER

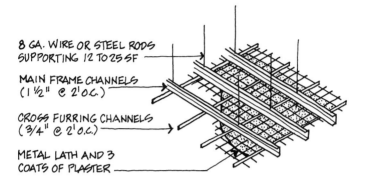

8 GA. WIRE OR STEEL RODS
SUPPORTING 12 TO 25 SF

MAIN FRAME CHANNELS
(1 ½" @ 2' O.C.)

CROSS FURRING CHANNELS
(3/4" @ 2' O.C.)

METAL LATH AND 3
COATS OF PLASTER

TYPICAL
CEILING

___ 1. Exterior (stucco) of cement plaster.
___ 2. Interior of gypsum plaster.
___ 3. Wall supports usually studs at between 12″ and 24″ oc. If wood, use 16″ oc min.
___ 4. Full plaster—3 coats (scratch brown, and finish) but walls of masonry can have 1 or 2 coats.
___ 5. Joints: Interior ceilings: 30′ oc max.
       Exterior walls/soffits: 10′ to 20′ oc.
___ 6. Provide vents at dead air spaces ($\frac{1}{2}$″/SF).

Costs:

ceilings with paint, plaster, and lath	**$2.00 to $5.00/SF (25% M and 75% L) can vary up to +60% for plaster**
walls of stucco with paper-backed wire lath	**$1.00/SF for stucco + $.70/SF for lath (50% M and 50% L)**

B. GYPSUM WALLBOARD (DRY WALL)

(4) (12)

___ 1. Usually in 4′ to 8′ (or 12′)
sheets from ¼″ to 1″ thick
in about ⅛″ increments.

___ 2. Attach (nail or screw)
against wood or metal
framing—usually at 16″
(fire rating) to 24″ oc.

___ 3. Type "X", ⅝″ will give 1
hr. fire rating. Roughly
each additional ½″ layer
will give 1 hr. rating up
to 4 hours, depending on
backing and application.

___ 4. Water-resistant (green)
available for wet areas or
exterior.

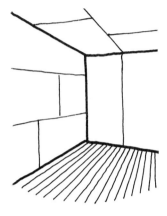

For exterior soffit venting, see p. 231.

Costs:

½″ gyp. bd.	$.55/SF ceilings
on wood	$.85/SF columns and beams
frame	$.50/SF walls
(Approx. 50% M and 50% L)	

Increase 5% for metal frame. Varies about 15% in cost for ⅛′ ea. thickness. Add $.06/SF for fire resistance. Add $.10/SF for water resistance. Add $.20/SF for joint work and finish.

___ C. TILE ④ ⑫

___ 1. Settings
    ___ *a.* Thick set (¾″ to 1¼″ mortar bed) for slopes.
    ___ *b.* Thin set (⅛″ mortar or adhesive) for faster and less expensive application.

___ 2. Joints: ⅛″ to ¼″ (can be epoxy grouted for QT floors).

___ 3. Types
    ___ *a.* Ceramic glazed & unglazed for walls & floors of about ¼″ thick & 4–6″ SQ. Many trim shapes available.
    ___ *b.* Ceramic mosaic for walls & floors of about ¼″ thick & 1″ to 2″ SQ.
    ___ *c.* Quarry tile of earth tones for strong and resistant flooring. Usually ½″ to ¾″ thick by 4″ to 9″ SQ.

Costs: can vary greatly with special imports of great expense. Typical costs:

    Glazed wall tile: $4.30/SF (50% M and 50% L) variation of −25%, +190%

    Unglazed floor mosaic: $6.40/SF (65% M and 35% L) variation of ±5%

    Unglazed wall tile: $4.00/SF (40% M and 60% L) variation of ±10%

    Quarry tile: $7.10/SF (same as above) variation of ±10%

    Bases: $6.20/LF (same as above) variation of ±10%

    Additions: color variations: +10 to 20%
                   abrasive surface: +25 to 50%

__ D. TERRAZZO ④ ⑫

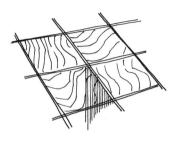

__ 1. A poured material (usu-
ally ½″ thick) of stone
chips in a cement
matrix, usually with a
polished surface.

__ 2. Base of sand and con-
crete.

__ 3. To prevent cracking,
exposed metal dividers
are set approx. 3′ to 6′
oc each way.

__ 4. Newer, high-strength terrazzo (with chemical binders) is
thin set with jointing far less. Can also come in tile pavers of
about 1″ thick × 9″ SQ to 2′ SQ.

Costs:
    $6.00/SF to $12.50/SF (45% M and 55% L)
    Tiles: $12.50 to $20.50/SF

__ E. ACOUSTICAL TREATMENT ④ ⑫

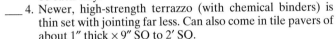

__ 1. Acoustical Ceilings:
Can consist of small
(¾″ thick × 1′ SQ) min-
eral fiber tiles attached
to wallboard or con-
crete (usually glued).
Also, acoustical min-
eral fibers with a
binder can be shot on gypsum board or concrete.

Costs: Small tiles $.85/SF (40% M to 60% L)

__ 2. Suspended Acoustical Tile Ceilings: Can be used to create
a plenum space to conceal mech. and elect. functions. Typical applications are 2′ SQ or 2′ × 4′ tiles in exposed or con-
cealed metal grids that are wire susp. as in plaster ceilings.
The finish of tiles can vary widely.

Costs:
    Acoust. panels $.75 to $1.00/SF (70% M and 30% L)
    Susp. system $1.45 to $1.65/SF (80% M and 20% L)

__ F. WOOD FLOORING   ④ ⑫

___ 1. See p. 225 for structural decking.
___ 2. Finished flooring can be of hardwoods or softwoods, of which oak, southern pine, and Douglas fir are the most commonly used.
___ 3. All heartwood grade of redwood is best for porch and exterior flooring.
___ 4. If substrate is concrete, often flooring is placed on small wood strips (sleepers); otherwise flooring is often nailed to wood substrates (plywood or wood decking).
___ 5. Since wood is very susceptible to moisture, allowance must be made for movement and ventilation. Allow expansion at perimeters. Vapor barriers below concrete slabs are important.
___ 6. Use treated material in hot, humid climates.
___ 7. Three types of wood flooring:
    ___ *a.* Strip
    ___ *b.* Plank
    ___ *c.* Block (such as parque)

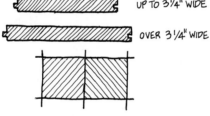

UP TO 3 1/4" WIDE

OVER 3 1/4" WIDE

Typical Costs:
  Wood strip fir $2.75/SF (70% M and 30% L)
    Oak +45% +10% finish
    Maple +45%

__ G. MASONRY FLOORING   ④ ⑫

See Part 4 on materials.

Typical Cost:
  3/4″ × 8″ brick: $6.80/SF (65% M and 35% L)
  Add 15% for special patterns.

___ H. RESILIENT FLOORING

___ 1. Consists of sheets or
   tiles of vinyl, cork,
   rubber, linoleum, or
   asphalt with *vinyl* the
   most commonly used.
___ 2. Is approx. ⅟₁₆″ to ⅛″
   thick with tiles being
   9″ SQ to 12″ SQ.

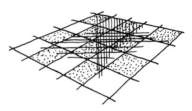

___ 3. Applied to substrate with mastic. Substrate may be plywood
   flooring, plywood or particle board over wood deck, or concrete slabs.
___ 4. Vapor barriers often required under slabs.
___ 5. Vinyl base is often applied at walls for this and other floor
   systems.

A wide range of colors and patterns are available for flooring.

Typical Costs:

Solid vinyl tile	**$2.40/SF (75% M and 25% L) can go up**
⅛ × 12 × 12	**20% for various patterns and colors; dou-**
	ble for 'conductive' type
Sheet vinyl	**$2.75/SF (90% M and 10% L) variation of**
	−20% and +75% due to various patterns
	and colors
Vinyl wall base	**$1.40/LF (40% M and 60% L) can vary**
	+15%

___ I. CARPET ④ ㊺

___ 1. Most wall-to-wall carpeting is produced by looping yarns through a coarse-fiber backing, binding the backs of the loops with latex, then applying a second backing for strength and dimensional stability. Finally the loops may be left uncut for a rough, nubby surface or cut for a soft, plush surface.

___ 2. The quality of carpeting is often determined by its *face weight* (ounces of yarn (pile) per square yard), not its total weight. Weights run:

    ___ *a.* Low traffic: 20–24 oz/SY
    ___ *b.* Medium traffic: 24–32 oz/SY
    ___ *c.* High-end carpet: 26–70 oz/SY

___ 3. A better measure of comparison:

$$weight\ density\ factor = \frac{face\ weight \times 36}{pile\ height} = 02/CY$$

Ideally, this should be as follows:

    ___ *a.* Residential: 3000 to 3600 oz/CY
    ___ *b.* Commercial: 4200 to 7000 oz/CY

___ 4. There are two basic carpet installation methods:

    ___ *a.* *Padded and stitched* carpeting: Stretched over a separate pad and mechanically fastened at joints and the perimeter. Soft foam pads are inexpensive and give the carpet a soft, luxurious feel. The more expensive jute and felt pads give better support and dimensional stability. Padding adds to foot comfort, helps dampen noise, and some say, adds to the life of the carpet.

    ___ *b.* *Glued-down* carpets: Usually used in commercial areas subject to heavily loaded wheel traffic. They are usually glued down with carpet adhesive with a pad. This minimizes destructive flexing of the backing and prevents rippling.

___ 5. Maintenance Factors

    ___ *a.* Color: Carpets in the midvalue range show less soil than very dark or very light colors. Consider the typical regional soil color. Specify patterned or multi-colored carpets for heavy traffic areas in hotels, hospitals, theaters, and restaurants.

    ___ *b.* Traffic: The heavier the traffic, the heavier the density of carpet construction. If rolling traffic is a factor, carpet may be of max. density for min. resistance to rollers. Select only level-loop or dense, low-cut pile.

___ 6. Carpet Materials:

Fiber	Advantages	Disadvantages
Acrylic (rarely used)	Resembles wool	Not very tough; attracts oily dirt
Nylon (most used)	Very tough; resists dirt, resembles wool; low-static buildup	None
Polyester deep pilings	Soft and luxurious	Less resilient; attracts oily dirt
Polypropylene indoor-outdoor	Waterproof; resists fading & stains; easy to clean	Crushes easily
Wool	Durable; easy to clean; feels good; easily dyed	Most expensive

___ 7. **Costs: (90% M and 10% L) (Variation ±100%)**
Repair/level fls: $3.90/SY (45% M and 55% L) Variation −70% +20%
Padding
  Sponge: $4.80/SY (70% M and 30% L) Variation ±10%
  Jute: −10%
  Urethane: −25%
Carpet
  Acrylic, 24 oz, med. wear: $17.95/SY
        28 oz, med./heavy: $22.35/SY
Residential
  Nylon, 15 oz, light traffic: $13.35/SY
        28 oz, med. traffic: $15.70/SY
Commercial
  Nylon, 28 oz, med. traffic: $16.65/SY
        35 oz, heavy: $19.60/SY
  Wool, 30 oz, med. traffic: $26.20/SY
        42 oz, heavy: $29.95/SY
Carpet tile: $11 to $35/SY

CARPET TYPES

TYPE OF WEAVE	CHARACTERISTICS AND BEST USES

 **LEVEL LOOP :** EVEN HEIGHT, TIGHTLY SPACED UN-CUT LOOPS. TEXTURE IS HARD AND PEBBLY. HARD WEARING AND EASY TO CLEAN. IDEAL FOR OFFICES AND HIGH TRAFFIC AREAS.

 **MULTI-LEVEL LOOP :** UNEVEN HEIGHT IN PATTERNS, TIGHTLY SPACED UNCUT LOOPS. TEXTURE IS HARD & PEBBLY. HARD-WEARING & EASY TO CLEAN. IDEAL FOR OFFICES AND HIGH TRAFFIC AREAS.

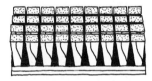 **PLUSH 'CUT' PILE :** EVENLY CUT YARNS WITH MINIMAL TWIST. EXTREMELY SOFT, VELVETY TEXTURE. VACUUMING AND FOOTPRINTS APPEAR AS DIFFERENT COLORS, DEPENDING ON LIGHT CONDITIONS. IDEAL FOR FORMAL ROOMS W/ LIGHT TRAFFIC.

FREIZE 'CUT' PILE : EVENLY CUT YARNS WITH TIGHT TWIST. EXTREMELY SOFT, VELVETY TEXTURE. VACUUMING AND FOOTPRINTS AP-PEAR AS DIFFERENT COLORS, DEPENDING ON LIGHT CONDITIONS. IDEAL FOR FORMAL RM'S WITH LIGHT TRAFFIC.

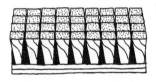 **CUT AND LOOP :** COMBINATION OF BOTH PLUSH AND LEVEL-LOOP, HIDES DIRT FAIRLY WELL. IDEAL FOR RESIDENTIAL APPLICATIONS.

 **INDOOR-OUTDOOR :** CUT, TIGHTLY TWISTED YARNS THAT TWIST UPON THEMSELVES. TEXT-URE IS ROUGH. HIDES DIRT EXTREMELY WELL AND IS NEARLY AS TOUGH AS LEVEL-LOOP. IDEAL FOR RESIDENTIAL APPLICATIONS.

___ J. PAINT AND COATINGS ⑫ ㊺

___ 1. General
    ___ *a.* Paints and coatings: are liquids ("vehicle") with pigments in suspension, to protect and decorate building surfaces.
    ___ *b.* Applications: brushed, rolled, sprayed
    ___ *c.* Failures: 90% due to either moisture problems or inadequate preparation of surface.
    ___ *d.* Surface Preparation:
        ___ (1) Wood: Sand if required; paint immediately.
        ___ (2) Drywall: Let dry (0 to 1 week). If textured surface req'd., primer prior to texture.
        ___ (3) Masonry and stucco: Wait for cure (28 days).
    ___ *e.* Qualities:
        ___ (1) Thickness
            ___ (*a*) Primers (and "undercoats"): ½ to 1 dry mills/coat.
            ___ (*b*) Finish coats: 1 to 1½ dry mills/coat.
        ___ (2) Breathability: Allowing vapor passage to avoid deterioration of substrate and coating. Required at:
            ___ (*a*) Masonry and stucco: 25 perms
            ___ (*b*) Wood: 15 perms
            ___ (*c*) Metals: 0 perms
    ___ *f.* Paint Surfaces:
        ___ (1) Flat: Softens and distributes illumination evenly. Reduces appearance of substrate defects. Not easily cleaned. Usually used on ceilings.
        ___ (2) Eggshell: Provides most of the advantages of gloss without glare.
        ___ (3) Semigloss
        ___ (4) Gloss: Reflects and can cause glare, but also provides smooth, easily cleanble, nonabsorbtive surface. Increases appearance of substrate defects.
    ___ *g.* Legal Restrictions:
        ___ (1) Check state regulations on paints for use of volatile organic compounds (VOC), use of solvents, and hazardous waste problems.
        ___ (2) Check fire department restrictions on spraying interiors, after occupancy or during remodelling.

___ 2. Material Types

    ___ *a.* Water-repellent preservatives: For wood.

    ___ *b.* Stains: Solid (opaque), semitransparent, or clear.

    ___ *c.* Wood Coatings: Varnish, shellac, lacquers.

    ___ *d.* Wood primer-sealer: Designed to prevent bleeding through of wood resin contained in knots and pitch pockets, and to seal surface for other coatings. Usually apply 2 coats to knots. Since material is white, cannot be used on clear finishes.

    ___ *e.* Latex primer: Best first coat over wall board, plaster, and concrete. Adheres well to any surface except untreated wood.

    ___ *f.* Alkyd primer: Used on raw wood. Latex "undercoats" can also be used.

    ___ *g.* CMU filler: A special latex primer to reduce voids and smooth surface on masonry. Does not waterproof.

    ___ *h.* Latex paint: A synthetic, water-based coating, the most popular because it complies with most environmental requirements, is breathable, and cleans up with water. Use for almost all surfaces including primed (or undercoated) wood. Adheres to latex and flat oils. Avoid gloss oils and alkyds other than primers. Subdivided, as follows:

        ___ (1) Polyvinyl acetate (PVA): Most commonly used. Provides 25+ perms.

        ___ (2) Acrylic: Smoother, more elastic, more durable, often used as a primer. Provides less than 5 perms.

    ___ *i.* Alkyd paint: A synthetic semisolvent-based coating, replacing the old oils. This seems to be going out of use due to environmental laws. Used for exterior metal surfaces. Not breathable.

___ 3. Paint Systems and **Costs (30% M and 70% L):**

Material	Finish	Prime	Top coats	Costs
Preparation (sanding, etc., if required) (*or latex undercoat)				**$0.10/SF up to $5/SF**
Exterior				
Wood				
General	gloss	alkyd *	ext. alkyd enamel	**$0.45/SF**
	flat	(same)	ext. alkyd or latex	
	stain		semitrans. or solid	
Floors				
Clear	gloss		alkyd enamel or latex acrylic	
Redw'd.	stain		semitrans. alkyd	
Doors				**$0.45/SF**
Windows				**$0.70/SF**
Masonry, concrete, and stucco				
	clear	prime sealer or CMU filler	water-repellent	**$0.45/SF**
	flat	(same)	exterior latex	
Metals	gloss	galv. iron: zinc oxide steel: zinc chromate	ext. alkyd enamel	**$0.25/SF**
	flat	(same)	ext. latex acrylic	**(same)**
Interiors				
Wood				
General	gloss	enamel undercoat	alkyd enamel or latex enamel	**$0.25 to $0.60/SF**
	flat	(same)	(same)	
Floors	gloss	stain, if req'd.	alkyd floor enamel	**(same)**
	clear	(same)	alkyd base varnish	**(same)**
Plaster/drywall				
	gloss	latex	latex	
	flat	latex	latex	
Brick		latex	latex	**(same)**
CMU		CMU filler	latex	**(same)**
Metals	gloss	see exterior	epoxy or alkyd enamel	**(same)**
	flat		alkyd or latex	

*or latex "undercoat"

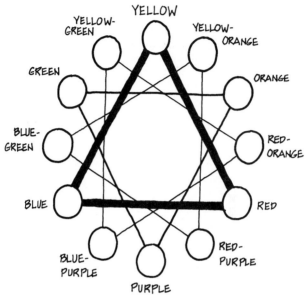

YELLOW

YELLOW-GREEN   YELLOW-ORANGE

GREEN   ORANGE

BLUE-GREEN   RED-ORANGE

BLUE   RED

BLUE-PURPLE   RED-PURPLE

PURPLE

—— PRIMARY COLORS
—— SECONDARY COLORS
—— TERTIARY COLORS

THE COLOR WHEEL
(FOR PIGMENTS)

TINTS

VALUE

SHADES

CHROMA

THINK OF COLOR IN THREE DIMENSIONS

1. HUE ("COLOR")
2. VALUE (LIGHT TO DARK)
3. CHROMA (SATURATION-INTENSITY)

293

___ 1. Basic Color Schemes

   ___ *a. Triadic schemes.*
       Made from any three
       hues that are equidis-
       tant on the color
       wheel.

   ___ *b. Analogous or
       related schemes.*
       Consist of hues that
       are side by side.

   ___ *c. Monochromatic
       schemes.* Use only
       one color (hue) in a
       range of values and
       intensities, coupled
       with neutral blacks
       or whites.

   ___ *d. Complementary
       schemes.* Use con-
       trast by drawing
       from exact opposites
       on the color wheel.
       Usually, one of the
       colors is dominant
       while the other is
       used as an accent.
       Usually vary the
       amount and bright-
       ness of contrasting
       colors.

___ *e.* *Split complementary schemes.* Consist of one hue and the two hues on each side of its compliment.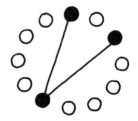

___ *f.* *Double complementary schemes.* Composed of two adjacent hues and their respective hues, directly opposite on the color wheel.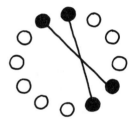

___ *g.* *Many-hued schemes.* Those with more than three hues. These usually need a strong dose of one color as a base with added colors that are closely matched in value.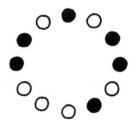

___ 2. Rules of Thumb

     ___ *a.* Your dominant color should cover about ⅔ of the room's area. Equal areas of color are usually less pleasing. Typical areas to be covered by the main color are the walls, ceiling, and part of the floor.

     ___ *b.* The next most important color usually is in the floor covering, the furniture, or the draperies.

     ___ *c.* The accent colors act as the "spice" for the scheme.

     ___ *d.* Study the proposed colors in the lighting conditions of where they will be used (natural light, type of artificial light).

     ___ *e.* The larger the area, the brighter a color will seem. Usually duller tones are used for large areas.

___ *f.* Contrast is greater from light to dark than it is from hue to hue or dull to bright saturation.

___ *g.* Colors that seem identical but are slightly different will seem more divergent when placed together.

___ *h.* Bold, warm (red/orange) and dark colors will "advance." These can be used to bring in end walls, to lower ceilings, or to create a feeling of closeness in a room.

___ *i.* Cool (blue/green), dull and light colors "recede." These can be used to heighten ceilings or to widen a room.

___ *j.* Related colors tend to blend into "harmony."

___ *k.* From an economic point of view, dark colors absorb more light (and heat) and will require more lighting. Light colors reflect light, requiring less lighting.

___ *l.* Colors will look darker and more saturated when reflected from a glossy surface than when reflected from a matte surface.

___ *m.* A color on a textured surface will look darker than on a smooth surface.

___ *n.* Bright colors increase in brilliance with area and pale colors fade when increased in area.

___ *o.* Incandescent (warm) lighting normally adds a warming glow to colors. Under this light, consider "cooling" down or greying bright reds, oranges, or yellows.

___ *p.* Low atmospheric lighting tends to grey down colors.

___ *q.* Fluorescent lighting changes the hue of colors in varying ways depending on the type used. In some instances, it will accent the blue tones and make reds look colder. It may make many colors look harsher.

___ *r.* Southern exposures will bring in warm tones of sunlight.

___ *s.* Northern exposures will bring in cool light.

___ 3. Percent Light Reflected from Typical Walls and Ceilings

Class	Surface	Color	% Light reflected
Light	Paint	white	81
		ivory	79
		cream	74
	Stone	cream	69
Medium	Paint	buff	63
		lt. green	63
		lt. grey	58
	Stone	grey	56
Dark	Paint	tan	48
		dk. grey	26
		olive green	17
		lt. oak	32
		mohogany	8
	Cement	natural	25
	Brick	red	13

___ 4. Typical Reflectance %
   ___ *a.* Commercial
      Ceiling   80%
      Walls   50%
      Floors   20%
   ___ *b.* Industrial
      Ceiling   50%
      Walls   50%
      Floor   20%
   ___ *c.* Classrooms
      Ceiling   70–90%
      Walls   40–60%
      Floor   30–50%
      Desk top 35–50%
      Blackboard 20%

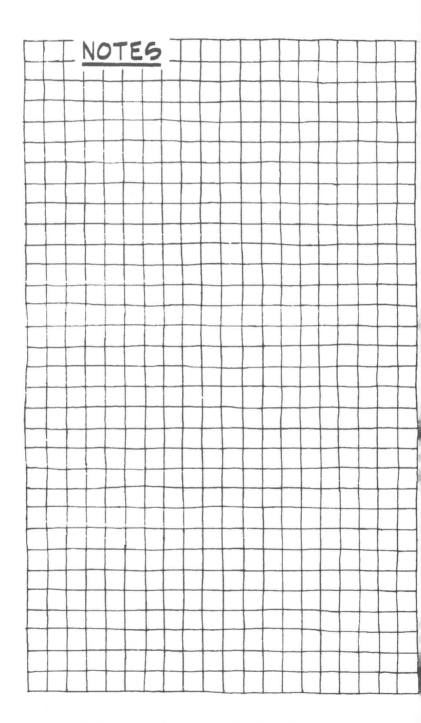

NOTES

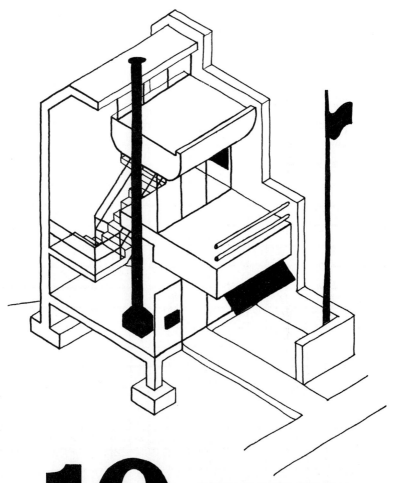

10 SPECIALTIES

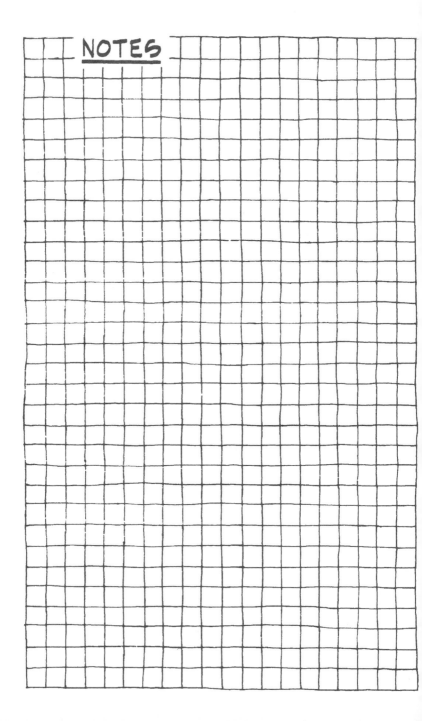

NOTES

__ A. TOILET PARTITIONS

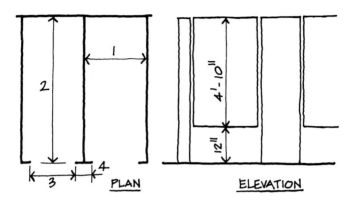

PLAN   ELEVATION

___ 1. Typical widths: 2′6″, 2′8″, 2′10″ (most used), and 3′0″
___ 2. Typical depths:
    ___ *a.* Open front: 2′6″ to 4′0″
    ___ *b.* Closed front: 4′6″ to 4′9″
___ 3. Typical doors: 1′8″, 1′10″, 2′0″, 2′4″, and 2′6″
___ 4. Typical pilasters: 3, 4, 5, 6, 8, or 10 inches
___ 5. For HC accessible, see p. 358–360.

Costs: $370 to $750/each compartment

___ B. FIREPLACES (4)

___ 1. Opening sizes:

W	H	D	S
2'	1.5' to 1.75'	1.33' to 1.5'	
3'	2'	1.67'	6½"
4'	2.12'	1.75'	6"
5'	2.5' to 2.75'	2' to 2.17'	9"
6'	2.75' to 3'	2.17' to 2.33'	9"

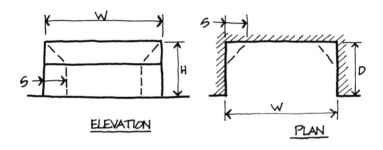

ELEVATION   PLAN

___ 2. For energy conservation, provide:
    ___ *a.* Outside combustion air ducted to firebox
    ___ *b.* Glass doors
    ___ *c.* Blower
___ 3. Per UBC:
    ___ *a.* Hearth extension to front must be 16" (or 20" if opening greater than 6 SF).
    ___ *b.* Hearth extension to side must be 8" (or 12" if opening greater than 6 SF).
    ___ *c.* Thickness of wall of firebox must be 10" brick (or 8" firebrick).
    ___ *d.* Top of chimney must be 2' above any roof element within 10'.
___ 4. **Costs:**
Fabricated metal: $500 to $1500 (75% M and 25% L)

__ C. GRAPHICS (4)

___ 1. General: Visual identification and direction by signage is very important for "wayfinding" to, between, around, in, and through buildings. Signage is enhanced by:

    ___ *a.* Size
    ___ *b.* Contrast
    ___ *c.* Design of letter character and graphics.

___ 2. Road Signage: Can be roughly estimated as follows:

SPEED MPH	VIEWING DISTANCE	ANGLE	SIGN SIZE SF	COPY SIZE INCH HT.
15	220'		8	
30	310'		40	5
40	450'	35°		7
45	660'		90	
50	545'	30°		8½
60	610 – 880'	20°	150	9½

___ 3. Building Signage
    ___ *a.* Site directional/warning signs should be:
        ___ (1) 6' from curb
        ___ (2) 7' from grade to bottom
        ___ (3) 100'–200' from intersections
        ___ (4) 1 to 2.5 FT SQ
    ___ *b.* Effective pedestrian viewing distance 20' to 155'
    ___ *c.* Effective sign size: ≈10'/inch height.
    ___ *d.* Effective letter size: ≈50'/inch height.
    ___ *e.* As a rule, letters should constitute about 40% of sign and should not exceed 30 letters in width.
    ___ *f.* Materials
        ___ (1) Exterior
            ___ (*a*) Building: fabricated aluminum, illuminated plastic face, back-lighted, cast aluminum, applied letter, die-raised, engraved, and hot-stamped.
            ___ (*b*) Plaque and sign: cast bronze or aluminum, plastic/acrylic, stone, masonry, and wood.

___ (2) Interior
    ___ (*a*) Permanent mounting: vinyl tape/ adhesive backing, silastic adhesive, or mechanical attachment.
    ___ (*b*) Semipermanent: vinyl tape square on inserts.
    ___ (*c*) Changeable: dual-lock mating fasteners, magnets, magnetic tape or tracks.

___ *g.* Mounting heights

EXTERIOR SIGNS   INTERIOR SIGNS

___ *h.* Accessibility signage per *ADA* required at:
    ___ (1) Accessible parking, see p. 121.
    ___ (2) Building entries (when accessible, not required when all are).
    ___ (3) Accessible facilities, such as at rest rooms (when accessible, not required when all are).

___ 4. **Costs:**

___ **Freeway, billboard**	**$10,000 to $20,000**
___ **Road/site directional**	**$15 to $30/SF (65% M and 35% L)**
___ **Pylon/monument**	**$12,000 to $18,000 (40% M and 60% L)**
___ **Exterior building, I.D., backlite, with ind. letters**	**$5000 to $7000 (same)**
___ **Plaques, cast alum., or bronze**	**$200 to $300 (85% M)**
___ **Plastic, Bakelite**	**$100/SF (40% M and 60% L)**
___ **Neon, small size**	**$3000 to $3500 (same as above)**
___ **Exit, electrical**	**$70 (45% M and 55% L)**
___ **Metal letters**	**$20 to $40/ea. (60% M and 40% L)**
___ **Plexiglass**	**$65/SF (95% M and 5% L)**
___ **Vinyl**	**$15 to $30/SF (75% M and 25% L)**

__ D. FIREPROOFING (1) (4) (24)

___ 1. See p. 58 for requirements.
___ 2. Thicknesses (in inches) of fire resistance structural materials will give hourly ratings, as follows:

ITEM	NON - COMBUSTIBLE						HEAVY TIMBER	LIGHT WOOD FRAME
	4 HR.	3 HR.	2 HR.	1½ HR.	1 HR.	0 HR.		
STEEL, STRUCTURAL LT. GA. JOISTS STUDS	←	SEE NOTE 3, BELOW				→ SEE NOTE 3c		↑
CONCRETE, COLUMNS WALLS SLABS POST TENSION FLOOR PRE-CAST CONC. COL. BEAMS WALLS SLABS PLANKS TEE BMS	6-8"	14" 6½" 6.2" 6.2" 12" 9½" 6½" 6.2" 8"+2" TOPPG.	12" 6" 5" 5" 10" 7" 6" 5" 8" 3.25"	10" 5" 4.3" 4.25" 8" 7" 5" 4.3" 8" 2.75"	8" 3½" 3½" 3½" 6" 4" 3.5" 3.5" 8" 1.75" ←	TOPPINGS		SEE NOTE 3, BELOW
BRICK, MASONRY. WALLS VAULTS & DOMES (RISE NOT LESS THAN 1/12 SPAN)	6-8"	8" 8"	6" 8"	6" 6"	4" 4"			
C.M.U. MASONRY WALLS	8" SOLID	8"	8"	6"	4"			
WOOD: COLUMNS, FLOOR ROOF BEAMS, FLOOR ROOF TRUSSES, FLOOR ROOF							8×8 6×8 6×10 4×6 8×8 4×6	
WOOD DECK, FLOOR ROOF							3"+1" 1⅛"-2"	↓

___ 3. Applique of fire-resistive materials may be added to members to protect from fire. Use the above table, as well as the following:
  ___ a. Concrete: $1'' \approx 2$ hr. $2''$ to $3'' \approx 4$ hr.
  ___ b. Solid masonry: $2'' \approx 1$ hr., add $1''$/hr to $4'' \approx 4$ hr.
  ___ c. Plaster: $1'' \approx 1$ hr., add $1''$/hr.
  ___ d. Vermiculite (spray-on): $1'' \approx 4$ hr.
  ___ e. Gypsum wallboard: 2 layers ½" type "X" or 1 layer of ⅝" type "X" $\approx$ ¾ to 1 hr.
___ 4. **Costs**
   Spray-on vermiculite: $1.00/SF surface/inch thickness

___ 5. Flame Spread: The UBC requires finish materials to resist the spread of fire as follows:

    ___ *a.* Maximum flame-spread class

Occupancy Group	Enclosed Vertical Exitways	Other Exitways(1)	Rooms or Areas
A	I	II	II (2)
E	I	II	III
I	I	I (6)	II (3)
H	I	II	III (4)
B	I	II	III
R-1	I	II	III
R-3	III	III	III (5)
M	No restrictions		

Notes: (1) Finish classification is not applicable to interior walls and ceilings of exterior exit balconies.

(2) In Group A, Division 3 and 4 Occupancies, Class III may be used.

(3) In rooms in which personal liberties of inmates are forcibly restrained, Class I material only shall be used.

(4) Over two stories shall be Class II.

(5) Flame spread provisions are not applicable to kitchens and bathrooms of Group R, Division 3 Occupancies.

(6) In Group I, Divisions 2 and 3 Occupancies, Class II may be used or Class III when the Division 2 or 3 is sprinklered.

    ___ *b.* Flame spread classification

Class	Flame-spread index
I	0 to 25
II	26 to 75
III	76 to 200

    ___ *c.* Use finishes to meet above requirements

        ___ (1) For woods, see p. 220.

        ___ (2) Aluminum: 5 to 10

        ___ (3) Masonry or Concrete: 0

        ___ (4) Gypsum wallboard: 10 to 25

        ___ (5) Carpet: 10 to 600

        ___ (6) Mineral-fiber sound-absorbing panels: 10 to 25

        ___ (7) Vinyl tile: 10 to 50

        ___ (8) Chemically treated wood fiberboard: 20 to 25

___ 6. Fire Loads: Interior building contents that will start or contribute to a fire. These typically range from 10 (residential) to 50 PSF (office), and can be reduced 80% to 90% by use of metal storage containers for paper.

___ E. OPERABLE PARTITIONS

___ 1. Types

CENTER TRACK   EDGE TRACK   STACKING POCKET   STACKING WITH SWITCHES

___ 2. Data
    ___ (1) Stack widths:
        ___ (a) Accordion: 5″ to 12″
        ___ (b) Panels: 15″ to 17″
    ___ (2) Stack depths: Usually ⅙ to ⅛ of opened width.
    ___ (3) Panels usually 48″ wide.
    ___ (4) Acoustic: STC 43 to 54 available.
    ___ (5) Flame spread: Class I available.
___ 3. **Costs:**
    ___ **Folding, acoust., vinyl, wood-framed: $40 to $70/SF (70% M and 30% L) Variation: −35% to +50%.**
    ___ **Accordion, vinyl-faced: $15 to $30/SF, Variation: ±20%**

___ F. BATHROOM ACCESSORIES

Costs (Given for ave. quality. For better finishes ie., brass, add 75% to 100%):

___ **Mirrors**	**$16.50/SF (80% M and 20% L)**
___ **Misc. small items** (holders, hooks, etc.)	**$15 to $30/EA. (double, if recessed)**
___ **Bars**	
Grab	**$30 to $35/ea.**
Towel	**$15 to $25/ea.**
___ **Medicine cabinets**	**$60–$300/ea.**

___ 1. Types
    ___ *a.* Horizontal (usually best on south side)

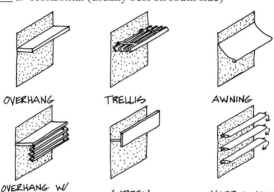

OVERHANG   TRELLIS   AWNING

OVERHANG W/
VERT. TRELLIS   SCREEN   HORZ. LOUVERS

    ___ *b.* Vertical (usually best on east and west sides)

FINS   ANGLED FINS   MOVABLE FINS

    ___ *c.* Egg crates (best for hot climates)

RECTILINEAR   ANGLED VERTICALS   ANGLED HORZ.

___ 2. Costs

___ Canvas awnings	**$25/SF (70% M and 30% L)**
	Variation −30%, +75%
___ Vinyl walkway covers	**≈$15/SF (55% M and 45% L)**
___ Metal carports	**$1650 to $3775/car (75% M and 25% L)**

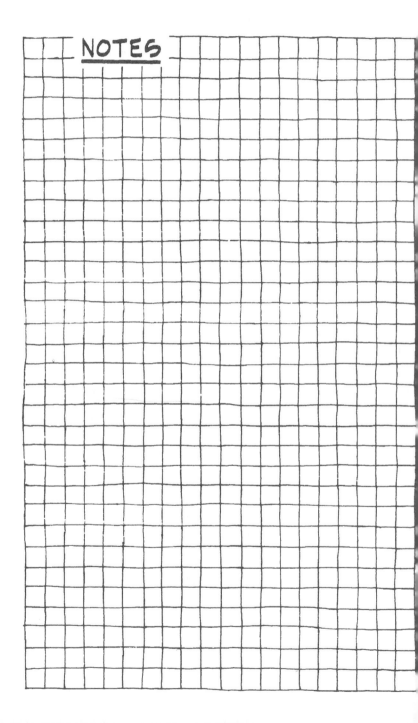

NOTES

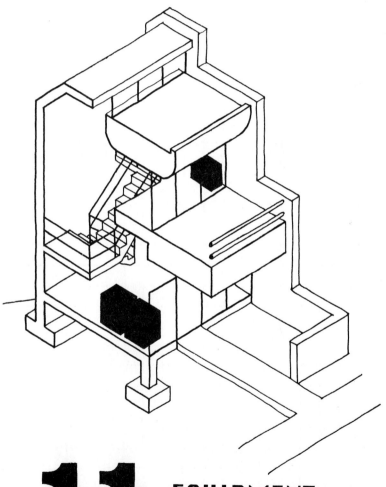

11 EQUIPMENT

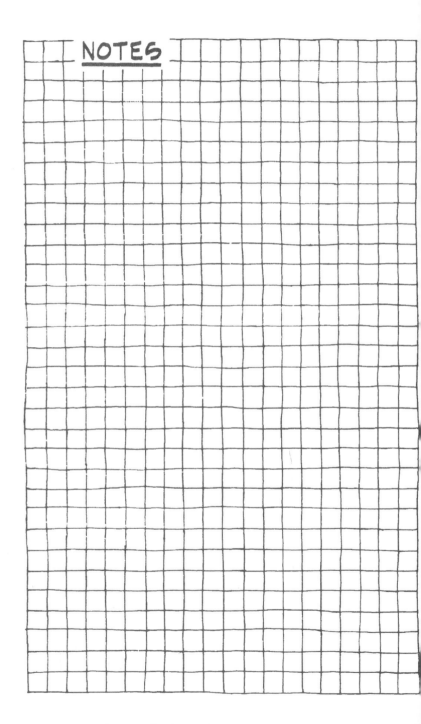

NOTES

(See p. 105, Energy Conservation)

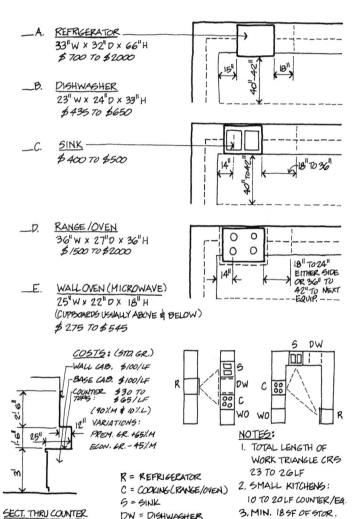

__A. **REFRIGERATOR**
33"W × 32"D × 66"H
$700 TO $2000

__B. **DISHWASHER**
23"W × 24"D × 33"H
$435 TO $650

__C. **SINK**
$400 TO $500

__D. **RANGE/OVEN**
36"W × 27"D × 36"H
$1500 TO $2000

__E. **WALL OVEN (MICROWAVE)**
25"W × 22"D × 18"H
(CUPBOARDS USUALLY ABOVE & BELOW)
$275 TO $545

COSTS: (STD. GR.)
WALL CAB. $100/LF
BASE CAB. $100/LF
COUNTER $30 TO
TOPS: $65/LF
(90%M & 10%L)
VARIATIONS:
PREM. GR. +65%M
ECON. GR. -45%M

SECT. THRU COUNTER

R = REFRIGERATOR
C = COOKING (RANGE/OVEN)
S = SINK
DW = DISHWASHER
WO = WALL OVEN

NOTES:
1. TOTAL LENGTH OF WORK TRIANGLE CRS 23 TO 26 LF
2. SMALL KITCHENS: 10 TO 20 LF COUNTER/EQ.
3. MIN. 18 SF OF STOR. SPACE + 6 SF/PERSON SERVED.

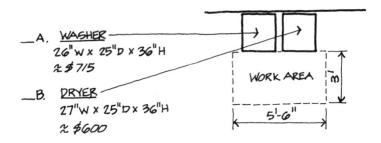

__A. WASHER
26"W x 25"D x 36"H
≈ $715

__B. DRYER
27"W x 25"D x 36"H
≈ $600

WORK AREA

3'

5'-6"

__ C. MISC. COSTS

___ 1. **Vacuum Cleaning Equip: for first 1200 SF = $775 (add $0.15/SF)**

___ 2. **Safes**
   ___ *a.* **Office**
     4 hr., $2.5' \times 2.5' \times 1.5'$ **$3100**
   ___ *b.* **Jeweler's**
     $63'' \times 25'' \times 18''$ **$21,900**

___ 3. **Religious**
   Wood alter   **$1500 to $9000**
   For pews, see p. 320

___ 4. **Library**
   Shelf   **$115/LF (−20%, +10%)**
   Carrels   **$600 to $850/ea.**
   Card catalog   **$65/tray**

___ 5. **Theater**
   Total equip   **$80 to $410/SF stage**
   For seating, see p. 320

___ 6. **Barber**
   Total equip.   **$2400 to $5150/chair**

___ 7. **Cash Register**
   Retail   **$990 to $3850/reg.**
   Restaurant   **$990 to $4950/reg.**

___ 8. **Trash Compactors**   **$650 to $8000/ea.**

___ 9. **Commercial Kitchen Equip.**
    ___ *a.* **By area**
        Office   **$57.50 to $93/SF kit.**
        Restaurant   **$72 to $117/SF kit.**
        Hospital   **$50 to $150/SF kit.**
    ___ *b.* **By item**
        Work tables   **$225 to $290/LF**
        Serving fixtures   **$235 to $300/LF**
        Walk-ins   **$50 to $150/SF (add $1500/ ton for refrigeration machinery)**

___ 10. **Fire Extinguishers**
    Extinguishers   **$125 to $300/ea.**
    Cabinets   **$140 to $200/ea.**
    Hose and cabinets   **$400 to $600/ea.**

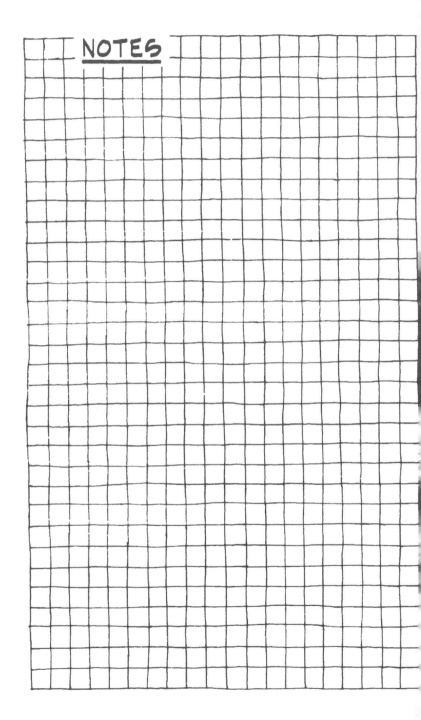

NOTES

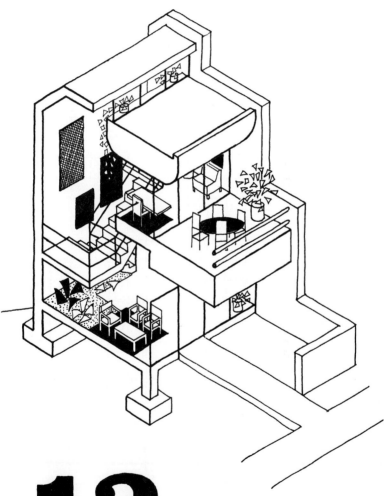

12 INTERIORS

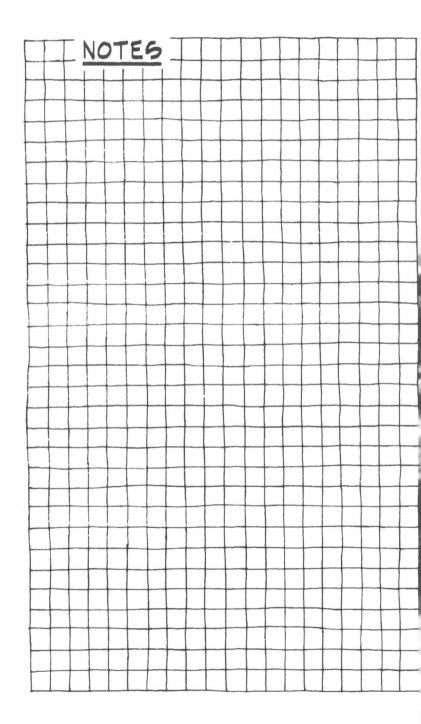

NOTES

A. GENERAL COSTS

Furniture and interior objects costs will vary more than any other item for buildings. These can vary as much as −75% to +500%. Costs given in this part are a reasonable middle value and are "for trade" wholesale. Retail can go up 60% to 175%. Cost location factors given in App. B, line V will not apply as furniture costs are rather uniform across country.

B. MISCELLANEOUS OBJECTS

___ 1. Artwork (photo., reproductions, etc.): **$45 to $250/ea.**
___ 2. Ash urns and trash receptacles: **$90 to $290/ea.**
___ 3. Blinds: **$1.50 to $14.50/SF**
___ 4. Draperies: **$20 to $105/SY**
___ 5. Rugs and mats: **$20 to $100/SY**
___ 6. Interior plants: see p. 151. **For artificial silk plants, double or triple landscape costs.**
___ 7. Fabrics: Association of Contract Textiles (ACT) recommendations. Check for following:

    ___ *a.* Flammability
    Upholstery must pass CAL 117.
    Drapery must pass NFPA 701.
    Wall covering must pass ASTM
    E-84.

    ___ *b.* Abrasion resistance

a	A	Test
15,000 double rubs	30,000 double rubs 40,000	Wyzenbeek Martindale

    ___ *c.* Colorfastness to light
    Must pass Class 4 (40 to 60 hours
    exposure for UV).

    ___ *d.* Colorfastness to wet and dry
    crocking (Pigment colorfastness
    in fabric).

319

___ *e.* Miscellaneous other physical properties
  ___ (1) Brush pill test: measures tendency for ends of a fiber to mat into fuzz balls.
  ___ (2) Yard/seam slippage test: establishes fabric's likeliness to pull apart at seams. Must pass 25 lbs for upholstery and 15 lbs on drapery.
  ___ (3) Breaking/tensile strength test: evaluates fabric's breaking or tearing. Must pass:

Upholstery	50 lbs
Panel fabrics	35 lbs
Drapery over 6 oz	25 lbs
under 6 oz	15 lbs

___ C. FURNITURE

___ 1. Miscellaneous

___ *a.*	Theater	**$115 to $220/seat**
___ *b.*	Church Pews	**$65 to $105/seat**
___ *c.*	Dormitory	**$1900 to $3600/student**
___ *d.*	Hospital Beds	**$700 to $1900/bed**
___ *e.*	Hotel	**$2300 to $7075/room**
___ *f.*	Multiple Seating	
	Classroom	**$65 to $120/seat**
	Lecture Hall	**$110 to $320/seat**
	Auditorium	**$100 to $200/seat**

___ 2. Living/Waiting

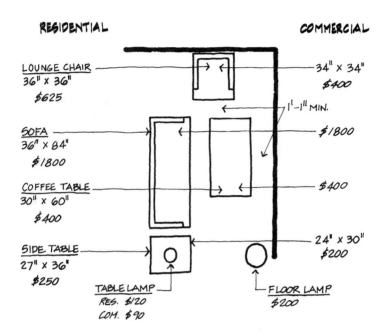

RESIDENTIAL   **COMMERCIAL**

LOUNGE CHAIR — 36" x 36" $625   34" x 34" $400

SOFA — 36" x 84" $1800   1'-1" MIN. $1800

COFFEE TABLE — 30" x 60" $400 $400

SIDE TABLE — 27" x 36" $250   24" x 30" $200

TABLE LAMP — RES. $120 COM. $90   FLOOR LAMP $200

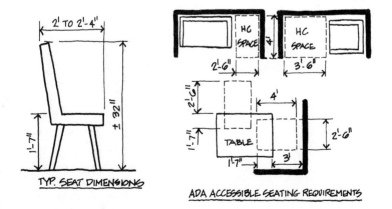

2' TO 2'-4"
± 32"
1'-7"

TYP. SEAT DIMENSIONS

HC SPACE   HC SPACE
2'-6"   3'-6"

2'-6"
1'-7"   4'
TABLE   2'-6"
1'-7"   3'

ADA ACCESSIBLE SEATING REQUIREMENTS

___ 3. Bedroom/Guestroom

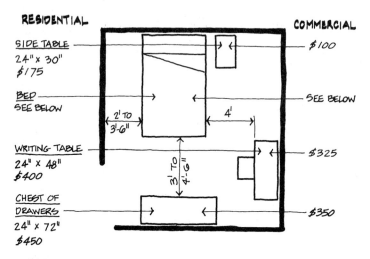

RESIDENTIAL   COMMERCIAL

SIDE TABLE ———— $100
24" x 30"
$175

BED ————   SEE BELOW
SEE BELOW

2' TO
3'-6"   4'

WRITING TABLE ———— $325
24" x 48"
$400

3' TO 4'-6"

CHEST OF
DRAWERS ———— $350
24" x 72"
$450

BED SIZES

	W	L
KING	72	84
QUEEN	60	82
DOUBLE	54	82
SINGLE	39	82
DAY BED	30	75
CRIB	30	53

___ 4. Dining/Conference

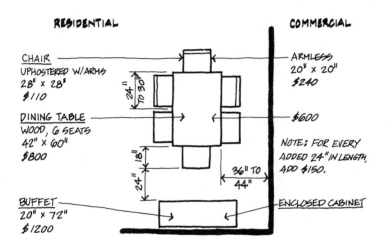

RESIDENTIAL

CHAIR
UPHOSTERED W/ARMS
28" × 28"
$110

DINING TABLE
WOOD, 6 SEATS
42" × 60"
$800

BUFFET
20" × 72"
$1200

24" TO 30"

18"

24"

COMMERCIAL

ARMLESS
20" × 20"
$240

$600

NOTE: FOR EVERY
ADDED 24" IN LENGTH,
ADD $150.

36" TO 44"

ENCLOSED CABINET

___ 5. Restaurant Seating

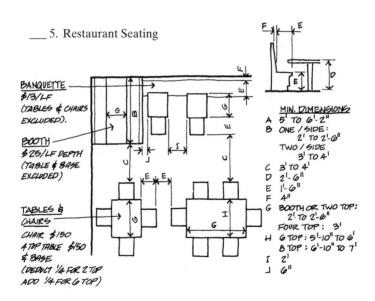

BANQUETTE
$13/LF
(TABLES & CHAIRS
EXCLUDED).

BOOTH
$25/LF DEPTH
(TABLE & BASE
EXCLUDED)

TABLES &
CHAIRS
CHAIR $150
4 TOP TABLE $150
& BASE
(DEDUCT ¼ FOR 2 TOP
ADD ¼ FOR 6 TOP)

MIN. DIMENSIONS
A 5' TO 6'-2"
B ONE / SIDE:
    2' TO 2'-6"
   TWO / SIDE
    3' TO 4'
C 3' TO 4'
D 2'-6"
E 1'-6"
F 4"
G BOOTH OR TWO TOP:
    2' TO 2'-6"
   FOUR TOP: 3'
H 6 TOP: 5'-10" TO 6'
   8 TOP: 6'-10" TO 7'
I 2'
J 6"

___ 6. Office

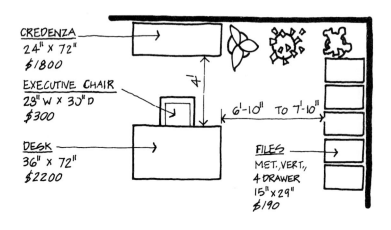

CREDENZA
24" x 72"
$1800

EXECUTIVE CHAIR
23" W x 30" D
$300

DESK
36" x 72"
$2200

7'

6'-10" TO 7'-10"

FILES
MET., VERT.,
4 DRAWER
15" x 29"
$190

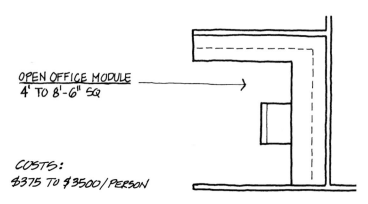

OPEN OFFICE MODULE
4' TO 8'-6" SQ

COSTS:
$375 TO $3500/PERSON

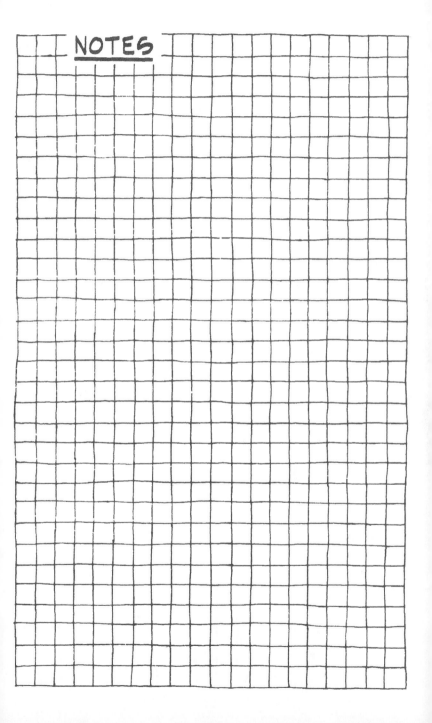

NOTES

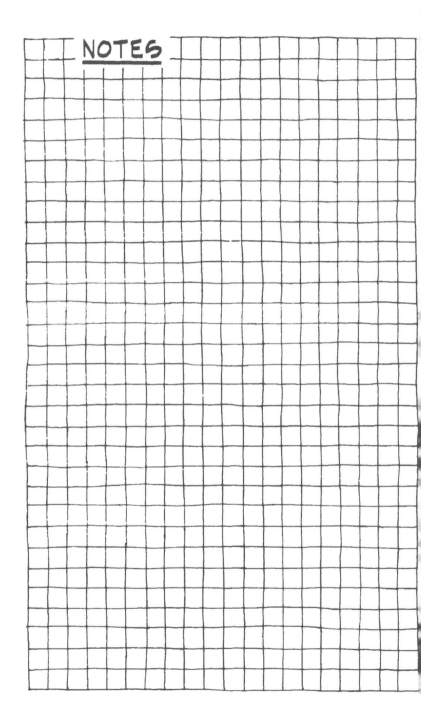

NOTES

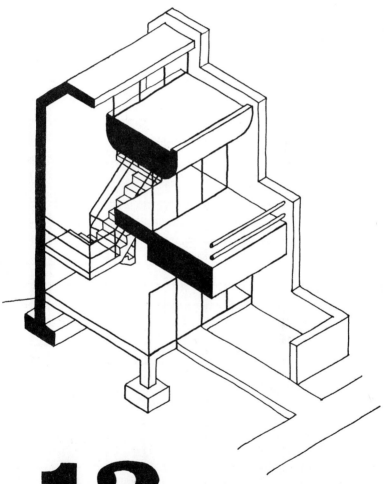

13 ASSEMBLIES

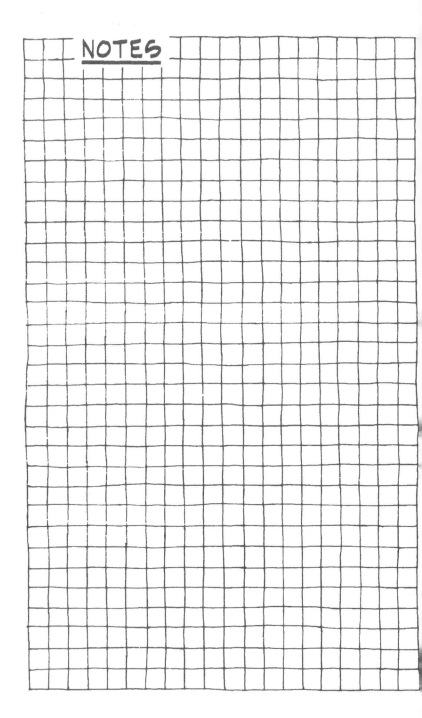

NOTES

__ A. ROOF STRUCTURE ASSEMBLIES

___ 1. Use the table on pp. 330 and 331 to help select a roof structure assembly. See p. 244 for roof coverings. The table shows:
___ 2. *Depth* of assembly in inches
___ 3. *Standard member sizes* in inches
___ 4. *Dead loads* in pounds per square foot
___ 5. Suitable *Live load* range in pounds per square foot
___ 6. Span range in feet
___ 7. *Dimensional stability* affected by:
    D = deflection
    C = creep
___ 8. *Bay size* characteristics by following notes:
    ___ *a.* Maximum beam spacing 8'0"
    ___ *b.* 4' modules
    ___ *c.* 2'8" between trusses
    ___ *d.* Light joists at 16" to 30" oc; heavy joists 4' to 12' oc
    ___ *e.* L ≤ 1.33 W
    ___ *f.* L ≤ 1.33 W, equal column spacing required
    ___ *g.* Up to 8' between subpurlins
___ 9. Suitable for *inclined roofs:*
    Y = yes
    N = no
___ 10. Requires finished *ceiling surface*, by following notes:
    ___ *a.* For visual or fire-protection purposes
___ 11. Service plenum notes
    ___ *a.* Between structural members
    ___ *b.* Under structure
___ 12. *Acoustical:* Comparative resistance to sound transmission:
    Impact
    Airborne
___ 13. *Fire*-resistive ratings per code and Underwriters:
    Unprotected, hours
    Protected, hours
___ 14. *Construction type classification* by code (UBC)
___ 15. Relative *thermal* capacity

ROOF STRUCTURE ASSEMBLIES

	Type	Components	2 DEPTH (IN.)	3 STD. MEMBER SIZE (IN.)	4 DL (PSF)	5 LL (PSF)	6 SPAN (FT.)	7 DIH. STAB.	8 BAY SIZE	9 INCL. ROOF	10 CL'G. SURF.	11 PLENUM	12 IMPACT	12 AIR	13 UNPROT.	13 PROT.	14 CONST. CL.	15 THERMAL	COSTS: ($/SF)
A	WOOD RAFTER	PLYWOOD / JOIST / CEILING	5-13	2x4, 6, 8, 10, & 12	4-8	10-50	10 to 22	D		Y	D	D	P	F		2	III	L	$1.25 TO $2.45
B	WOOD BM. & PLANK	WOOD PLANK / WOOD BEAM	8-22	PLANKS 2, 3, & 4" THICK	5-12	10-50	8-34		D	Y	D	D	P	F		2	IV	M	SEE FLOORS
C	PLYW'D. PANEL	PLYWOOD STRESSED SKIN PANELS	3/8-3/4		3-6	10-50	8-32		C	Y	N	D	P	F		2	III	L	
D	WOOD TRUSSES	PLYWOOD / WOOD TRUSSES / CEILING	12-144		5-15	10-50	30-50	D		Y	D	D	P	F		2	II	L	$1.30 TO $1.60
E	STEEL TRUSS	STEEL DECK / PURLIN / STEEL TRUSS			15-25	10-60	100-200	D	D	Y	D	D	F	F		1-4	I	L	
F	STEEL JOIST	CONCRETE / STEEL DECK / STEEL JOIST / CEILING	11-75	STEEL JOISTS 8-72"	10-28	10-50	76 to 96	D	D	N	D	D	F	F		1-4	I	M	$2.20
G	STEEL JOIST	PLYWOOD DECK / WOOD NAILER / STEEL JOIST / CEILING	10-36	STEEL JOISTS 8-30"	8-20	10-50	76 to 96	D		Y	D	D	P	G		—	I	L	
H	STEEL JOIST	INSULATION / STEEL DECK / STEEL JOIST / CEILING	11-75	STEEL JOISTS 8-72"	6-24	10-50	76 to 96	D		Y	D	D	E	F		2	I	H	$3.60
I	STEEL FRAME	PRECAST CONC. PLANK / STEEL BEAM	4-21+8	CONC. PLANK (6-12")	40-75	30-70	20-60	D U		Y	D	D	F	F		1-4	I	H	$8.70
J	PRECAST CONC.	PRECAST CONC. PLANK / CONCRETE BEAM	4-21+8		40-75	30-70	20-60	D U		Y	N	D	F	G	2-4	3-4	I	H	$11.50
K	ONE-WAY CONC. SLAB	CONCRETE SLAB / CONCRETE BEAM	4-10+8		50-120	>100	10-25+			N	N	D	G	G	4-1	3-4	I	H	$8.50
L	TWO-WAY CONC. SLAB	CONCRETE SLAB / CONCRETE BEAM	4-10+8		50-120	>100	10-30+		C	N	N	D	G	G	1-4	3-4	I	H	$7.65

330

ROOF STRUCTURE ASSEMBLIES

	2 DEPTH (IN.)	3 STD. MEMBER SIZE (IN.)	4 DL (PSF)	5 LL (PSF)	6 SPAN (FT.)	7 DIM. STAB.	8 BAY SIZE	9 INCL. ROOF	10 CLG. SURF.	11 PLENUM	12 IMPACT	12 AIR	13 UNPROT.	13 PROT.	14 CONST. CL.	15 THERMAL	COSTS:
M ONE-WAY RIBBED CONC. SLAB	22-8	20 & 30 W, 6-20 D	40-90	<100	15-50+	C		N	A	A	U	U	1-4	3-4	1	H	$ 8 00
N TWO-WAY RIBBED CONC. SLAB	8-24	19 & 30 30, 6-20 D	75-105	<100	25-60+	C	e	N	Z	D	U	U	1-4	3-4	1	H	$ 8 75
O PRE CAST CONCRETE TEE	16-36	16-36 DEEP	55-85	20-28	80-100	C		Y	A	D	F	U	2-3	3-4	1	H	$ 8 50
P PRECAST DOUBLE TEE	6-16	4,5,6,8, 10 FT WIDE, 6-16" DEEP	35-55	25-60	20-75	C		Y	A	D	F	U	2-3	3-4	1	H	$ 8 50
Q CONCRETE FLAT PLATE	4-14		50-160	<100	35+	C	e	N	Z	D	U	U	1-4	3-4	1	H	$ 6 50
R CONCRETE FLAT SLAB	5-16	4 TO 5 SLAB THICKNESS	50-200	<100	40+	C	f	N	Z	D	U	U	1-4	3-4	1	H	
S GYPSUM DECK	3-6		5-20	>50	<10	D U	g	N	A	D	U	U		2	1	H	

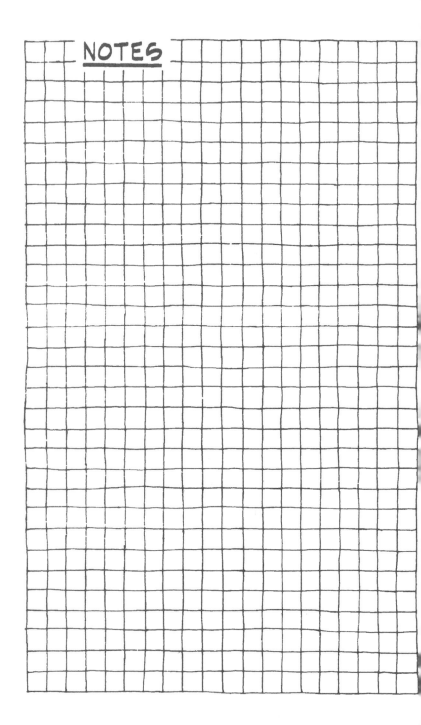

NOTES

__ B. FLOOR STRUCTURE ASSEMBLIES   (4)

___ 1. Use the table on pp. 334 and 335 to help select a *floor structure assembly*. The table shows:
___ 2. *Depth* of assembly in inches
___ 3. *Standard member sizes* in inches
___ 4. *Dead loads* in pound per square foot
___ 5. Suitable *live load* range in pounds per square foot
___ 6. *Span* range in feet
___ 7. *Dimensional stability* affected by:
      D = deflection
      C = creep
___ 8. *Bay size* characteristics, by following notes:
    ___ *a.* Maximum beam spacing 8'0"
    ___ *b.* Light joists at 16" to 30" oc; heavy joists 4' to 12' oc
___ 9. Requires finished *floor surface:*
      Y = yes
      N = no
___ 10. Requires finished *ceiling surface,* by following notes:
    ___ *a.* Yes, visual or fire-protection purposes
    ___ *b.* Yes, visual purposes; differential camber
    ___ N = no
    See p. 341 to help select ceiling assemblies.
___ 11. Service *plenum* notes
    ___ *a.* Between joists, one way.
    ___ *b.* Between trusses or joists, two-way.
    ___ *c.* Under structure, one-way.
    ___ *d.* Between joists—two-way.
    ___ *e.* Under structure.
    ___ *f.* Between ribs—one-way.
___ 12. Acoustical: Comparative resistance to sound transmission:
      Impact
      Airborne
___ 13. *Fire*-resistive ratings per code and Underwriters:
      Unprotected, hours.
      Protected, hours.
___ 14. *Construction type classification* by code (UBC).

FLOOR STRUCTURE ASSEMBLIES

	Assembly	DEPTH (IN.)	STD. MEMBER SIZE (IN.)	DL (PSF)	LL (PSF)	SPAN (FT)	DIM. STAB.	BAY SIZE	FL. SURF.	C'L'G. SURF.	PLENUM	IMPACT	AIR	UNPROT	PROT	CONST. CL.	COSTS ($/SF)
A	WOOD JOIST — PLYWOOD SUBFLOOR / WOOD JOIST	7-13	2 x 6, 8, 10, & 12	5-8	30-40	10 to 18	D		Y	Q	d	P	F			IV	$2 30
B	WD TRUSS OR PLYWD JOIST — PLYWOOD SUBFLOOR / PLYWOOD JOIST OR WOOD TRUSS	13-18	PLY WD JSTS 12, 14, 16, 18, & 20	9-12	30-40	12-30	D		Y	Q	b	P	F			IV	
C	WOOD BEAM & PLANK — WOOD PLANK / WOOD BEAM	10-22	PLANK 2, 3, & 4	6-16	30-40	10-22			O	N	C	P	F			IV	$6 60
D	GLU-LAM BEAM & PLANK — WOOD PLANK / GLU LAM BEAM / WOOD BEAM	8-22	PLANK 2, 3, & 4	6-20	30-40	8-34		d	O	N	C	P	F			IV	$7 40
E	STEEL JOIST — PLYWOOD SUBFLOOR / WOOD NAILER / STEEL JOIST	9-31	STEEL JSTS B-30	8-20	30-40	16-40	D	b	Y	Q	d	P	F			III	$3 60
F	STEEL JOIST — PLYWOOD SUBFLOOR / STEEL DECK / STEEL JOIST	11-75	STEEL JSTS B-72	30-110	30-100	16-90 / 70-120	D	b	N	Q	d	P	F	1-3		II	$4 20 TO $4 85
G	LT. WT. STEEL FRAME — CONCRETE SLAB / LIGHTWEIGHT / STEEL FRAME	21-L		60-90	60-90	10-22			Y	Q	e	P	P			III	$2 85
H	STEEL FRAME — CONCRETE SLAB / STEEL DECK / STEEL BEAM	9-15		35-60	30-100	16-35	D		N	Q	e	P	F	2-4		I-II+NC	$8 70
I	STEEL FRAME — CONCRETE TOPPING / PRECAST CONC. PLANK / STEEL BEAM	8-16	CONC. PLANK 16-48 W 4-12 D	40-75	60-150	35-60	D		O	Q	e	F	F	1-4		I & II FR →	$7 60
J	PRECAST CONC. — CONCRETE TOPPING / PRECAST CONC. / CONCRETE BEAM	9-12	CONC. PLANK 16-48 W 4-12 D	40-75	60-150	35-60			O	N	e	F	C			→	$11 50
K	ONE-WAY CONCRETE SLAB — CONCRETE SLAB / CONCRETE BEAM	4-10		50-120	40-150	10-20			N	N	e	G	G	1-4		→	$8 60
L	TWO-WAY CONCRETE SLAB — CONCRETE SLAB / CONCRETE BEAM	4-10		50-120	40-250	10-30		M 77 1.33	N	N	e	G	G	1-4		→	$7 65

FLOOR STRUCTURE ASSEMBLIES

		DEPTH (IN.)	STD. MEMBER SIZE (IN.)	DL (PSF)	LL (PSF)	SPAN (FT)	DIM. STAB.	BAY SIZE	FL. SURF.	CL'G. SURF.	PLENUM	IMPACT	AIR	UNPROT.	PROT.	CONST. CL.	COSTS ($/SF)
M	ONE-WAY RIBBED CONC. SLAB	8-22	20+30W 6-20 D	40-90	40-150	15-50	C		N	N	4	G	G	1-4		I & II Fire	$8.00
N	TWO-WAY RIBBED CONC. SLAB	8-22	19x19 or 30x30 W 6-20 D	75-105	60-200	25-60	C	L6133 W	N	N	e	G	G	1-4		→	$8.75
O	CONC. FLAT SLAB	6-16	4-5	75-170	60-250	20-40	C	L6137 W	N	N	e	G	G	1-4			$6.85
P	PRECAST DOUBLE TEE	8-18	4,5,6,8, 10 FT. W 6-16 D	50-80	40-150	20-50	C		O	P	4	F	G	2-3		II & I	$8.50
Q	PRE CAST TEE	16-38	16-36 D	50-90	40-150	25-92	C		O	P	4	F	G	2-3		I & II	$8.50
R	COMPOSITE STEEL BEAM / WELDED STUD	4-6		60-200	60-200	70-85	D		N	q	e	G	G				$9.60
S	CONC. FLAT PLATE / COLUMN	5-14		60-125	60-200	18-35	C	L33W	N	N	e	G	G	1-4		→	$6.50

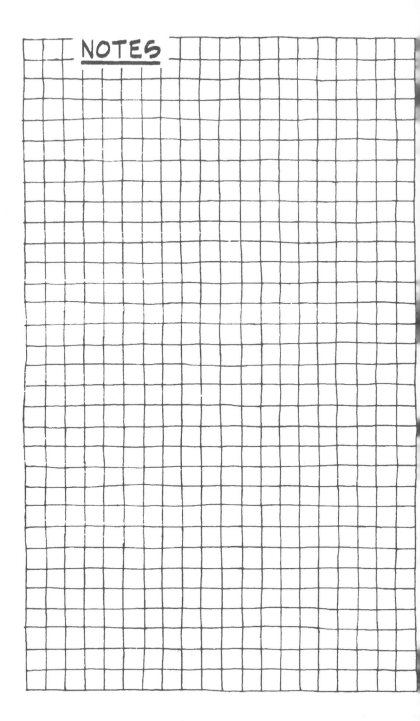

NOTES

___ C. WALLS (4)

___ 1. Use the table on pp. 338 and 339 to help select a wall assembly. See Part 9 for finishes. The table shows:

___ *a.* Overall *thickness* in nominal inches

___ *b.* *Weight* in pounds per square foot

___ *c.* Vertical *span* range for unsupported height in feet

___ *d.* Heat transmission coefficient *U value* in BTU/hr/ SF/°F (see p. 236)

___ *e.* Resistance to airborne *sound* transmission (see p. 112)

___ *f.* *Fire* resistance rating in hours (see p. 55 and 305)

___ *g.* UBC *Construction type* (see p. 55)

___ *h.* **Costs: $/SF of wall surface (one side). Wall finishes (paint, etc.) are *not* included.**

WALL ASSEMBLIES

	THICKNESS (IN.)	WEIGHT (PSF)	VERT SPAN (FT)	U VALUE	ACOUSTICAL	FIRE (HRS)	CONST. TYPE	COST: ($/SF)
A C.M.U. — CMU	8 / 12	55 / 85	UP TO 13 / UP TO 20	0.56 / 0.49	FAIR TO GOOD / FAIR TO GOOD	2-4 / 4	I & II	$4.75 / $8.55
B CMU & INSUL. — CMU, INSULATION, GYPB'D.	8+ / 12+	60 / 90	UP TO 13 / UP TO 20	0.21 / 0.20	EXCELLENT	2-4 / 4	↓	$5.95 / $9.75
C CMU & BRICK — BRICK VENEER, C.M.U., INSULATION, GYPB'D.	4+4 / 4+8	75 / 100	UP TO 13 / UP TO 20	0.19 / 0.18	EXCELLENT	3-4 / 4		$13 TO 17.25 / $16.80 TO 21
D CAVITY — BRICK VENEER, AIR SPACE, INSULATION, C.M.U., GYPB'D.	4+2+4 / 4+2+8	75 / 100	UP TO 9 / UP TO 13	0.12 / 0.11	EXCELLENT	4		$14.30 TO $19 / $18.50 TO $23.30
E CMU & STUCCO — STUCCO, CMU, INSULATION, GYPB'D.	8+	67	UP TO 13	0.16	GOOD	2-4	↓	$6.95
F WOOD STUD — PLYWOOD, WOOD STUDS, INSUL. W/ VAPOR BARRIER, GYPB'D.	4 / 6	12 / 16	UP TO 14 / UP TO 20	0.06 / 0.04	POOR TO FAIR	1	V	$2.80 TO 3.00
G BRICK, WOOD STUD — BRICK VENEER, PLYWOOD, WOOD STUDS, INSULATION, GYPB'D.	4+4	52	UP TO 14	0.07	GOOD TO EXCELLENT	1-2	V	$9.92 TO 15.4.20
H METAL STUD — EXT. WALL FIN., METAL STUDS, INSULATION W/ VAPOR BARRIER, GYPB'D.	4 / 5	14 / 18	UP TO 13 / UP TO 17	0.06 / 0.04	POOR TO FAIR	1-2	II-1	$3.05 TO 3.55 / EXT. FIN. EXCLU.
I BRICK, METAL STUD — BRICK VENEER, PLYWOOD, METAL STUDS, INSUL. W/ VAPOR BARRIER, GYPB'D.	4+4	54	UP TO 15	0.07	GOOD TO EXCELLENT	1-2	II-1	$10.15 TO 14.45

WALL ASSEMBLIES

	THICKNESS (IN)	WEIGHT (PSF)	VERT SPAN (FT)	U VALUE	ACOUSTICAL	FIRE (HRS)	CONST TYPE	COST: ($/SF)
J — INSULATED SANDWICH PANEL (Metal skin / Airspace / Insulated core / Metal skin)	5	6		0.05	POOR TO GOOD		II-N	
K — CONCRETE (Reinf. concrete)	8 / 12	92 / 138	UP TO 17 / UP TO 25	0.68 / 0.55	GOOD	4 / 4	I	$85/SF
L — CONCRETE & INSULATION (Reinf. concrete / Insulation / Gypbd.)	8+	97	UP TO 17	0.13	GOOD	4	III	$86.20
M — BRICK, CONCRETE, INSULATION (Brick veneer / Reinf. concrete / Insulation / Gypbd.)	4+8	112	UP TO 17	0.13	EXCELLENT	4	III	$93.30 TO 97.50
N — PRECAST CONCRETE (Reinf. concrete / Insulation / Gypbd.)	2+ / 4+	23 / 46	UP TO 6 / UP TO 12	0.99 / 0.85	POOR TO FAIR	1-3	III	$80 TO $90
O — PRECAST CONCRETE SANDWICH (Concrete / Insulation)	5	45	UP TO 14	0.14	FAIR	1-3	I & II	$80 TO 90
Q — GLAZED CURTAIN WALL (Alum. frame / Glazing)	5				POOR			SG $30 / DG $40 / MAX $85

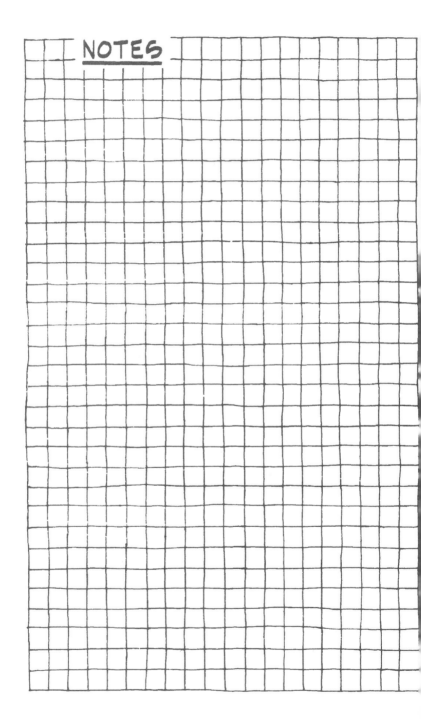

NOTES

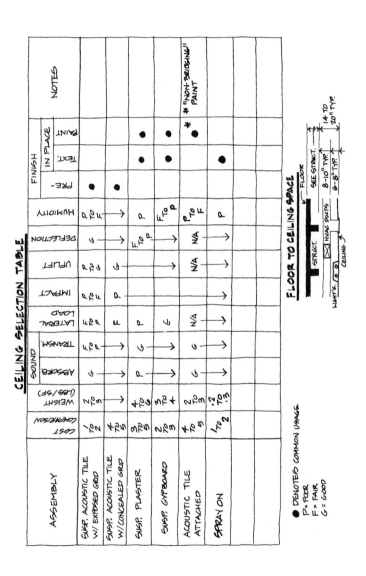

CEILING SELECTION TABLE

ASSEMBLY	COST COMPARISON	WEIGHT (LBS/SF)	SOUND ABSORB.	SOUND TRANSM.	LATERAL LOAD	IMPACT	UPLIFT	DEFLECTION	HUMIDITY	FINISH PRE-	FINISH IN PLACE TEXT.	FINISH IN PLACE PAINT	NOTES
SUSP. ACOUSTIC TILE W/ EXPOSED GRID	1 TO 2	2 TO 3	G →	F TO P	F TO P	P TO F	P TO G	G →	P TO F	●			
SUSP. ACOUSTIC TILE W/CONCEALED GRID	4 TO 5	→	→	→	F	P	G →	→	P	●			
SUSP. PLASTER	3 TO 5	4 TO 6	P →	G →	P		F TO P	F TO P	P		●	●	
SUSP. GYPBOARD	2 TO 3	3 TO 4	→	→	G		G →	→	F TO P		●	●	
ACOUSTIC TILE ATTACHED	4 TO 5	2 TO 3	G →	G →	N/A		N/A →	N/A	P TO F			※ ●	※ "NON-BRIDGING" PAINT
SPRAY ON	1 TO 2	.2 TO .3	→	→	→	→	→	→	P		●		

● DENOTES COMMON USAGE.

P = POOR
F = FAIR
G = GOOD

FLOOR TO CEILING SPACE

14 TO 20" TYP.
8-10" TYP.
6-8" TYP.

SEE STRUCT.
HVAC DUCTS
CEILING J
LIGHTS.
STRUCT.
FLOOR

FLOORING SELECTION TABLE

TYPE	COST COMPARISON	WEIGHT (PSF)	COMFORT	MOISTURE			TRAFFIC — FOOT			TRAFFIC — WHEEL		IMPACT	CLEANING		LOCATION				SUBSTRATE		SLIP RESIST.	CONDUCTIVE	OTHER
				DRY	OCC. WET	FREQ. WET	LOW	MOD	HIGH	RUB.	STEEL		MILD	HEAVY	OUTSIDE	BELOW GR.	ON GRADE	ABOVE GR.	WOOD	CONC.			
STONE	.9 TO 3	15 TO 40	P	●	●	●	○	○	●	○		●	●	○	●	●	●	●		●	○		
BRICK	.4-.9	20 TO 40	P	●	●	●	●	●	●	●		●	●	●	●	●	●	●	●	●	○		
CONCRETE	1.2-2.5	10 TO 75	P	●	●	●	●	●	●	●	○	●	●	●	●	●	●	●		●	●	○	
C.T.	2-4	4-6	P	●	●	●	●	●	●	●			●	●	●	●	●	●	●	●	●	●	
Q.T.	4-5.5	4-6	P	●	●	●	●	●	●	○		●	●	●	●	●	●	●	●	●	●	●	
RESILIENT	.6-2	1-2	G	●	●		●	●	●	○		●	●			●	●	●	●	●	●		
WOOD	3-5	1-10	F	●			●	●	●	●		●	●				●	●	●	●	●	○	
CARPET	1.5-5	.5-1	G	●			●	●	●	●		○	●			●	●	●	●	●	●	○	
EPOXY	3-5	3-7	F	●	●	●	●	●	●	●	●	●	●	●	●	●	●	●	●	●	●	●	

● DENOTES COMMON USAGE OR SUITABILITY

○ DENOTES POSSIBLE OR LIMITED USAGE OR SUITABILITY

* SLIP RESISTANCE

RECOMMENDATIONS FOR STATIC COEFFICIENT OF FRICTION :
NORMAL = 0.5 MIN.   H.C. (ADA) = 0.6 MIN.   RAMP = 0.8 MIN.
0.2 OR LESS IS VERY SLICK. 0.3 TO 0.4 IS SMOOTH. BROOM FINISH CONCRETE IS USUALLY
0.5 TO 0.7. GRIT STRIPES FOR STAIRS OR RAMPS ARE 0.8 OR ABOVE.

THE COEFFICIENT OF FRICTION IS THE RATIO OF HORIZONTAL FORCE TO VERTICAL FORCE.
WAXES SHOULD MEET ASTM D-2047.

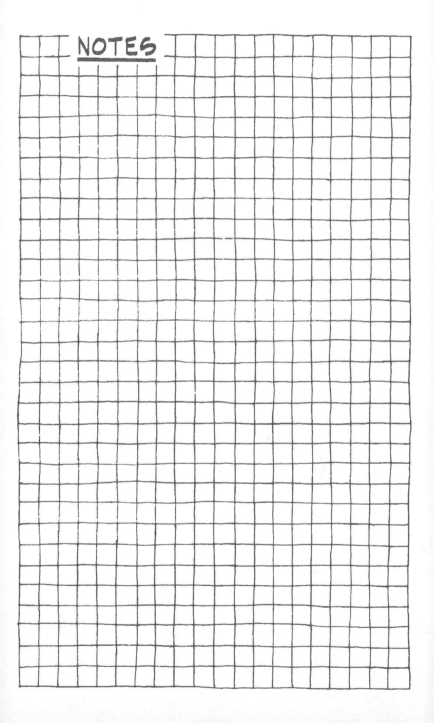

NOTES

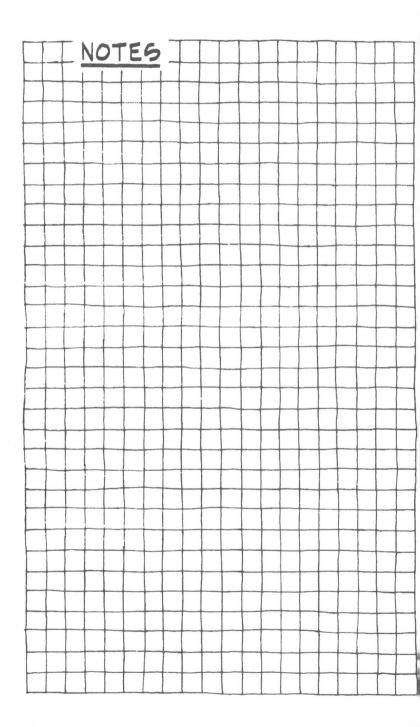

NOTES

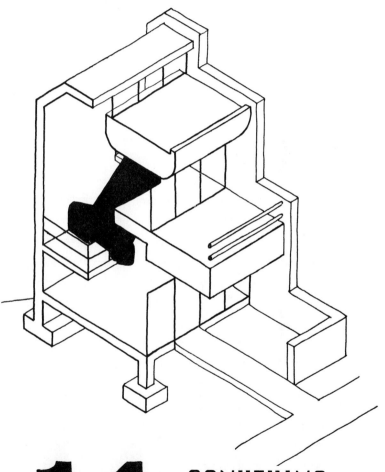

14 CONVEYING SYSTEMS

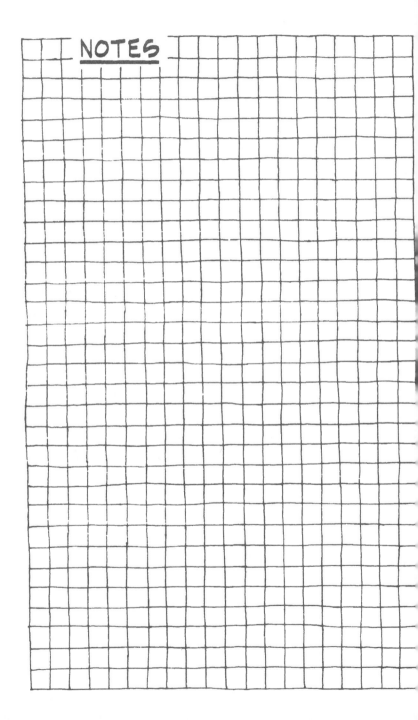

NOTES

__ 1. Hydraulic: The least expensive and slower type. They are moved up and down by a piston. This type is generally used in low-rise buildings (2 to 4 stories) in which it is not necessary to move large numbers of people quickly.

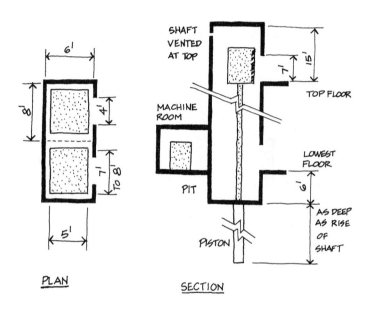

PLAN   SECTION

| Costs for passenger elevators | $25,200 to $58,100/shaft with car and mach.—2 stops. |
| Costs for hydraulic freight elevators | $27,500 to $33,700 + $6000 to $11,200 per stop. |

___ 2. Traction Elevators: Traction elevators hang on a counter-
weighted cable and are driven by a traction machine that
pulls the cable up and down. They operate smoothly at fast
speeds and have no limits.

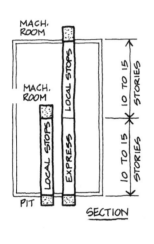

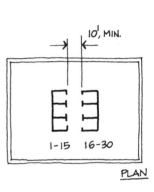

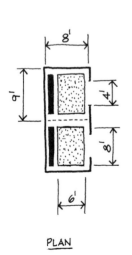

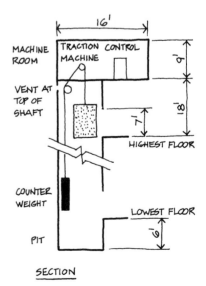

Costs for passenger elevators/shaft	**Range from $62,900 for 2,000 lbs, 200 FPM, 5 stops to $158,000 for 4,000 lbs, 500 FPM, 10 stops.**

(*Note:* For each additional stop add $5000 to $8000. Add for rear door opening $7100 plus $4500 per door. Deduct for multi shafts $2300 to $5000 per additional shaft.)

Costs for Freight Elevators, (2 stops)/shaft	**$38,800 for 2500 lbs to $88,700 for 10,000 lbs (add $4000 to $6000 per additional stop)**

___ 3. Elevator Rules of Thumb
    ___ *a.* Commercial
        ___ (1) One passenger elevator for each 30,000 SF of net floor area.
        ___ (2) One service elevator for each 300,000 SF of net floor area.
        ___ (3) Lobby width of 10′ minimum.
        ___ (4) Banks of elevators should consist of 4 or fewer cars so that people can respond easily to the arrival of an elevator.
        ___ (5) In high buildings, the elevator system is broken down into zones serving groups of floors, typically 10 to 15 floors. Elevators that serve the upper zones express from the lobby to the beginning of the upper zone. The elevators that serve the lower zones terminate with a machine room above the highest floor served.
        ___ (6) Very tall buildings have sky lobbies served by express elevators. People arriving in the lobby take an express elevator to the appropriate sky lobby where they get off the express elevator and wait for the local elevator system.
        ___ (7) Lay out so 200′ maximum walk to an elevator.
        ___ (8) Per *ADA,* accessible elevators *are* required at *shopping centers* and office of *health care* providers. Elevators are *not* required in facilities that are less than 3 stories or less than 3000 SF per floor. But, if elevators are provided, at least one will be accessible (see p. 350).

___ *b.* Residential
      ___ (1) In hotel and large apartment buildings, plan on one elevator for every 70 to 100 units.
      ___ (2) In a 3- to 4-story building, it is possible to walk up if the elevator is broken, so one hydraulic elevator may be acceptable.
      ___ (3) In the 5- to 6-story range, two elevators are necessary. These will be either hydraulic (slow) or traction (better).
      ___ (4) In the 7- to 12-story range, two traction elevators are needed.
      ___ (5) Above 12 stories, two to three traction elevators are needed.
      ___ (6) Very tall buildings will require commercial-type applications.
      ___ (7) Plan adequate space and seating at lobby and hallways.
___ *c.* ADA-accessible elevators (see #8, p. 349):

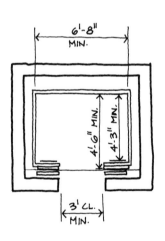
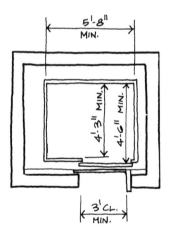

__ B. ESCALATORS

When the building design requires moving large numbers of
people up and down a few floors, escalators are a good choice.

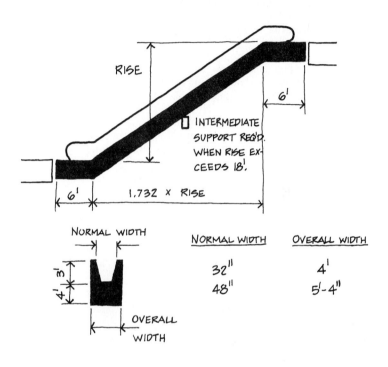

NORMAL WIDTH	OVERALL WIDTH
32"	4'
48"	5'-4"

**Costs range from $81,700 for 10' to 13' rise, 32" width, to
$106,400 for 21' rise, 48" width. Add for glass side enclosure:
$10,000 to $12,000.**

Rules of Thumb

1. All escalators rise at a 30-degree angle.
2. There needs to be a minimum of 10′ clear at top and bottom landings.
3. Provide beams at top and bottom for the escalators internal truss structure to sit on.
4. The escalator will require lighting that does not produce any distorting shadows that could cause safety problems.
5. Escalators need to be laid out with a crowded flow of people in mind. Crossover points where people will run into each other must be avoided.
6. Current trends in the design of retail space use the escalators as a dramatic and dynamic focal feature of open atrium spaces.
7. Because escalators create open holes through building floor assemblies, special smoke and fire protection provisions are necessary.

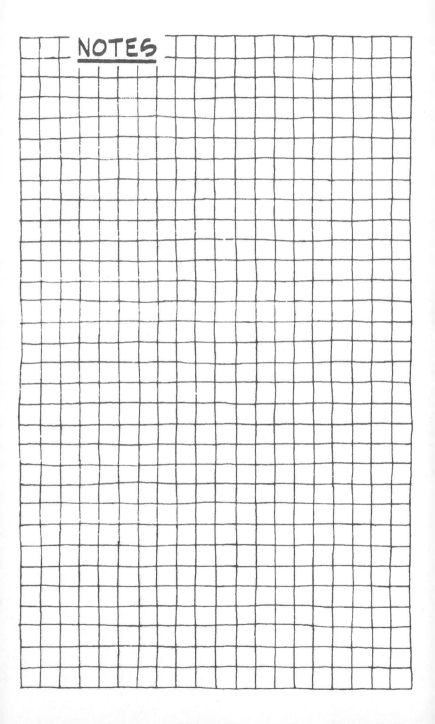

NOTES

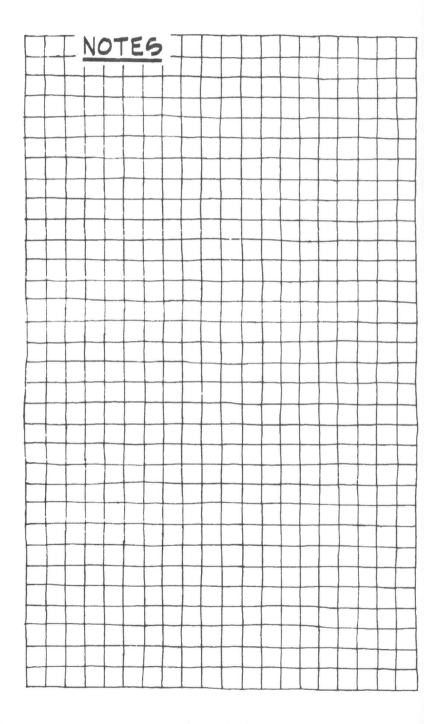

NOTES

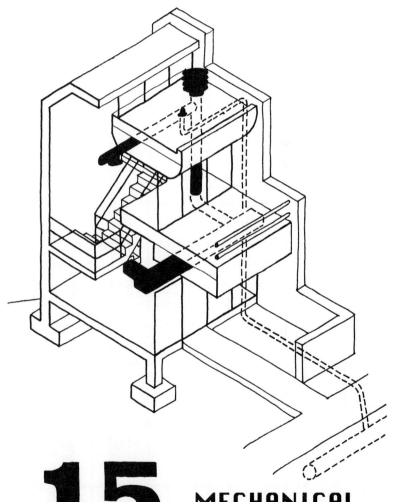

15 MECHANICAL

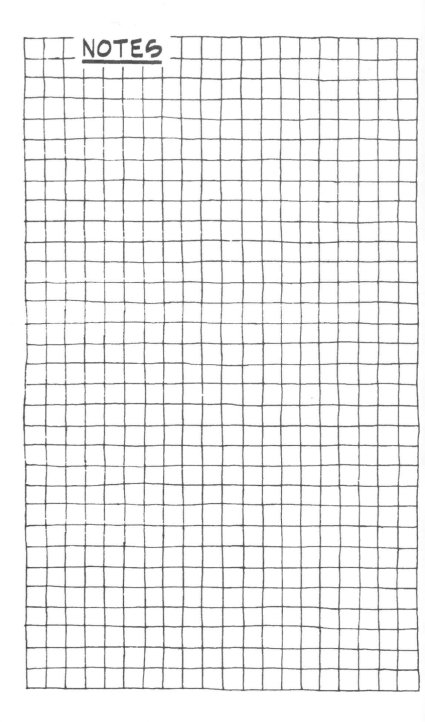

NOTES

__ A. THE PLUMBING SYSTEM

$\textcircled{1}$ $\textcircled{4}$ $\textcircled{7}$ $\textcircled{10}$ $\textcircled{20}$ $\textcircled{24}$ $\textcircled{25}$

See p. 145 for exterior utilities.
See p. 357 thru 360 for toilet rms.
See p. 368 for fixture count (UPC App. C).

The following systems need to be considered:

___ 1. Water supply (p. 361)
___ 2. Plumbing fixtures (p. 362)
___ 3. Sanitary sewer (p. 362)
___ 4. Rain water/storm sewer
    (p. 363)
___ 5. Fire protection (p. 364)
___ 6. Landscape irrigation (p. 366)
___ 7. Gas (p. 366)
___ 8. Other specialties (process, etc.)

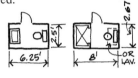

RESIDENTIAL BATHROOMS

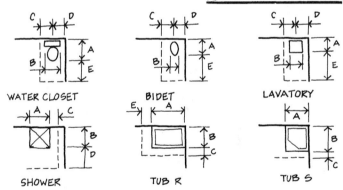

WATER CLOSET   BIDET   LAVATORY

SHOWER   TUB R   TUB S

FIXTURE SIZES AND CLEARANCES (INCHES)

FIXTURE	A		B		C		D		E	
	MIN.	LIB.	MIN.	LIB.	MIN.	LIB.	MIN.	LIB.	MIN.	LIB.
WATER C.	27	31	19	21	12	18	15	22	18	34 - 36
BIDET	25	27	14	14	12	18	15	22	18	34 - 36
LAVATORY	16	21	18	30	2	6	14	22	18	30
SHOWER	32	36	34	36	2	8	18	34		
TUB R	60STD	72	30STD	42	2	8	18 - 20	30 - 34	2	8
TUB S	38		39		2	4				

NOTE: FOR H.C. ACCESSIBILITY, SEE FOLLOWING PAGES.

TOILET ROOMS

SINGLE USER TOILET · · · · · · · · · · · · · · · PUBLIC TOILET

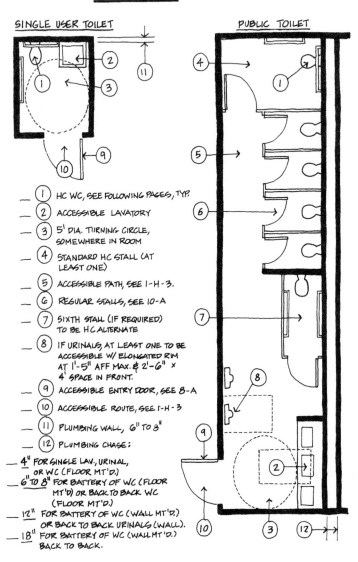

____ (1) HC WC, SEE FOLLOWING PAGES, TYP.

____ (2) ACCESSIBLE LAVATORY

____ (3) 5' DIA. TURNING CIRCLE,
SOMEWHERE IN ROOM

____ (4) STANDARD HC STALL (AT
LEAST ONE)

____ (5) ACCESSIBLE PATH, SEE 1-H-3.

____ (6) REGULAR STALLS, SEE 10-A

____ (7) SIXTH STALL (IF REQUIRED)
TO BE HC ALTERNATE

____ (8) IF URINALS, AT LEAST ONE TO BE
ACCESSIBLE W/ ELONGATED RIM
AT 1'-5" AFF MAX. & 2'-6" x
4' SPACE IN FRONT.

____ (9) ACCESSIBLE ENTRY DOOR, SEE 8-A

____ (10) ACCESSIBLE ROUTE, SEE 1-H-3

____ (11) PLUMBING WALL, 6" TO 8"

____ (12) PLUMBING CHASE:

____ 4" FOR SINGLE LAV., URINAL,
OR WC (FLOOR MT'D.)

____ 6" TO 8" FOR BATTERY OF WC (FLOOR
MT'D) OR BACK TO BACK WC
(FLOOR MT'D.)

____ 12" FOR BATTERY OF WC (WALL MT'D.)
OR BACK TO BACK URINALS (WALL).

____ 18" FOR BATTERY OF WC (WALL MT'D.)
BACK TO BACK.

ACCESSIBLE TOILET STALLS (ADA)

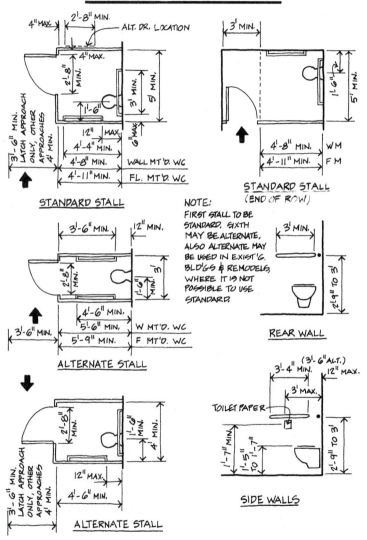

STANDARD STALL

STANDARD STALL
(END OF ROW)

NOTE:

FIRST STALL TO BE STANDARD. SIXTH MAY BE ALTERNATE. ALSO ALTERNATE MAY BE USED IN EXIST'G. BLD'GS & REMODELS, WHERE IT IS NOT POSSIBLE TO USE STANDARD.

ALTERNATE STALL

REAR WALL

ALTERNATE STALL

SIDE WALLS

ACCESSIBLE FIXTURES (ADA)

WATER CLOSETS

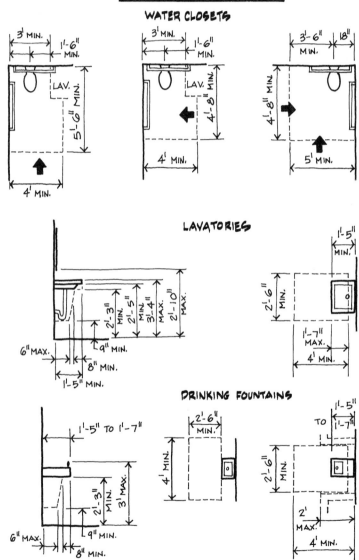

LAVATORIES

DRINKING FOUNTAINS

Costs: **As a rough rule of thumb, estimate $700 to $1000/fixture (50% M and 50% L) for all plumbing within the building. Assume 30% for fixtures and 70% for lines. Also, of the lines, assume 40% for waste and 60% for supply. For more specifics on fixture, only:**

| | **Residential** | | | |
Fixture	**Low**	**Medium**	**High**	**Commercial**
WC	$90	$200	$700	$100 to $200
Lav's	$60	$110	$180	same
Tub/shower	$60	$200	$300	
Urinals				$250
Kit. sinks	$150	$300	$450	

___ 1. *Water Supply*

The water supply is under pressure so there is flexibility in connection of the water main to the building. In warm climates, the *water meter* can be outside but in cold climates it must be in a heated space. For small buildings allow a space of *20″W × 12″D × 10″H*. After entering the building the water divides into a hot- and cold-water distribution system at the hot water heater. For small buildings allow for a *gas heater* a space *20″ dia. × 60″H* and for *electric heaters, 24″ dia. × 53″H*. Where bathrooms are spread far apart, consideration should be given to multiple hot water heaters.

___ If the water is "hard" (heavy concentration of calcium ions), a *water softener* may be needed. Provide *18″ dia. × 42″H* space.

Costs: ≈ **$1000**

___ If water is obtained from a private *well,* a pump is needed. If the well is *deep,* the pump is usually at the bottom of the well. For this case provide space for a pressure tank that is *20″ dia. × 64″H.* If the well is *shallow* (20′ to 25′ deep) the pump may be provided inside the building. Space for pump and tank should be *36″W × 20″D × 64″H.*

Costs: **$10 to $40/LF of well shaft + $4500**

___ Water supply *pipes* are usually copper or plastic and range from ½″ to 2″. Hot & cold pipes are usually laid out parallel. Piping should be kept out of exterior walls in cold climates to prevent winter time freeze-ups.

___ The city water pressure will push water up 2 or 3 stories. Buildings taller than this will need a *surge tank & water pressure pumps.* This equipment takes approximately *100 to 200 S.F.* of space.

***Costs:* $5000 to $20,000**

___ 2. *Plumbing Fixtures*

The men's and women's *restrooms* need to be laid out to determine their size and located in the building. Economical solutions are shared plumbing walls (toilet rooms back to back) and for multistory buildings, stacked layouts.

___ See UPC App. C for *toilet requirements* (WC, lavatories, urinals, and drinking fountains) based on occupancy type. The number of fixtures calculated is the minimum required, not the suggested quantity for good design. A check of the local ordinance should be made to be sure there are not further restrictions. Typical toilet room layouts, including requirements for the handicapped are shown on p. 358.

___ In *cold* climates, chases for plumbing line should not be on exterior walls, or if so, built in from exterior wall insulation.

___ 3. *Sanitary Sewer*

Horizontal runs of drainage piping are difficult to achieve inside the building. The best arrangement is to bring the plumbing straight down (often along a column) and make connections horizontally under the building.

___ The *sanitary drainage system* collects waste water from the plumbing fixtures, which flows by gravity down through the building and out into the city sewer. Because of the slope requirement, long horizontal runs of drainage pipe will run out of ceiling space to fit in. Ideally sanitary drainage pipes should run vertically down through the building collecting short branch lines from stacked bathrooms (called a plumb'g stack). A *4″* stack can serve approx. *50* WCs and accompanying lavatories. A *6″* stack can serve approximately *150* WCs and lavatories. Pipes are typically of cast iron or plastic (ABS). Each fixture is drained through a "P" trap with a water seal. This and venting the system to the roof keep sewer gases from entering the building.

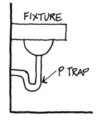

___ The *building drain* runs horizontally under the building collecting waste water from multiple vertical stacks. A *4″ to 6″* pipe requires a min. slope of *1*% and an *8″* pipe requires a minimum slope of ½%. The lowest (or basement) *floor elevation* needs to be set higher than the rim elevation of the next upsteam manhole of the sewer main. If the building drain is below the sewer main, an automatic underground *ejector pump* is needed.

___ At sites where city sewer mains do not exist, a *septic system* will be needed. The size and configuration of private disposal systems vary widely depending on soil conditions, topography, local laws, and the regulated capacity of the system. The most common type includes a *septic tank* (usually 1000 to 1500 gallons) and a *disposal field* of open-joint pipe below the ground. Soil saturation at the wettest time of the year determines final design. As a starting point, allow an area of nearly level ground *40′ × 80′* with short side against building. No part of this area may be closer than *100′* to a well, pond, lake, stream, or river. Also, see p. 141.

Costs: **$2000 to $6000**

___ *Solid waste* is often handled by a *compactor* for larger buildings. A compactor room of *60 SF* is sufficient for a small apartment building; *150 to 200 SF* for a larger building; and much larger for industrial. If a chute is used, plan on *15″ to 30″ dia.* with *24″* a typical dimension.

Costs: **See p. 314.**

___ 4. *Rainwater/Storm Sewer*

The rainwater that falls on the roof and the grounds of a building needs to be collected and channeled into the city storm drain system. If there is none, the site is drained to the street or to retention basins (if required). See page 132.

___ The *roof* slope must be arranged to channel water to drain points, where drainage pipes can carry the water down through the building and out into the storm drainage system (or sheet-drained on to the site).

___ The storm drainage water is kept separate from the sanitary drainage water so the sewage treatment system will not become overloaded in a rain. The following *guidelines* can be used in planning a storm drainage system:

___ *a.* *Flat roofs* need a minimum slope of *2%*.
___ *b.* Except for small roof areas there should be more than one drain point on a roof area.
___ *c.* *Roof drains* are best *located* near exterior walls or interior columns, not at midspans of the structures.

___ *d.* *Backup drains or scuppers* should be provided in case main drains become clogged. These should be *4″* up slope or *2″* above drain. For small buildings, scuppers at exterior walls may be used.

___ *e.* At *sloped roofs,* water may shed off the edge, or to avoid this, roof *gutter and downspouts* may be used. Downspouts typically range from *3″ to 6″* in *1″* increments. Common provision for average rain conditions is *1 sq. in* of cross section for each *150 SF* of roof area.

___ *f.* Horizontal *storm drain* pipes have a min. of *1%* slope. The best strategy is to route them vertically down through the building with a minimum of horizontal lines.

___ *g.* For estimating drain lines and downspouts:

Intensity, inch/hr. (see App. B, item J)	SF roof sq. in, down spout
2	600
3	400
4	300
5	240
6	200
7	175
8	150
9	130
10	120
11	110

Costs: **$500/roof drain (for gutter and downspouts, assume ½ to ⅔ cost)**

___ 5. *Fire Protection*
(See p. 147 for fire hydrants)

___ *a.* A *sprinkler system* is the most effective way to provide fire safety.

___ (1) The UBC requires sprinklers certain occupancies (see p. 58).

___ (2) Sprinkler *spacing* (maximum coverage per sprinkler):

___ Light hazard
200 SF smooth ceiling and beam and girder construction
225 SF if hydraulically calculated for smooth ceiling, as above

130 SF open wood joists
168 SF all other types of const.
___ Ordinary hazard
130 SF all types const, except:
100 SF high pile storage (12′ or more).
___ Extra hazard
90 SF for all types of const.
100 SF if hydraulically calculated.
___ (3) Notes
___ (*a*) Most buildings will be the *225 SF* spacing.
___ (*b*) Max. spacing: Light and Ordinary Hazard = 15′
High pile and Extra Hazard = 12′
___ (*c*) Small rooms of Light Hazard, not exceeding *800 SF,* locate sprinklers max. of *9′* from walls.
___ (*d*) Max. distance from walls to last sprinkler is ½ *spacing* (except at small rooms). Min. is *4″.*
___ (*e*) Cities should be checked to verify that local ordinance is not more stringent than UBC requirements.
___ (*f*) The sprinkler riser for small buildings usually takes about a *2′6″ square space.* Pumps and valves for larger buildings take up to about *100 to 500 SF.*

Costs: **Wet pipe systems: $1.65 to $3.50/SF**
For dry pipe systems, add $.050/SF.

___ *b.* Large buildings often also req'r. a *standpipe* which is a large diameter water pipe extending vertically through the building with fire hose connections at every floor. The system is either wet or dry. The UBC defines three classes (see p. 367).

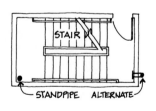

___ (1) *Class I* is dry with 2½″ outlets. There is a connection point on every landing of every required stairway above or below grade, and on both sides of a horizontal exit door. This type of standpipe is for the fire department to connect their large hoses to.

___ (2) *Class II* is wet with 1½″ outlets and a hose. This type is located so that every part of the building is within 30′ of a nozzle attached to 100′ of hose. This type is for use by building occupants or the fire department.

___ (3) *Class III* is wet with 2½″ outlets and 1½″ hose connections. These are located according to the rules for both Class I and II.

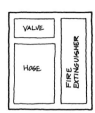

SIAMESE FITTING

Often, two *Siamese* fittings are req'd. in readily accessible locations on the outside of the building to allow the fire dep't. to attach hoses from pumper trucks to the dry standpipe and to the sprinkler riser.

```
┌─────────────────┐
│  ┌───────┐  ┌─┐ │
│  │ VALVE │  │ │ │
│  └───────┘  │F│ │
│           │I│E│ │
│  ┌───────┐ │R│X│ │
│  │ HOSE  │ │E│T│ │
│  │       │ │ │I│ │
│  └───────┘ └─┘ │
└─────────────────┘
```

HOSE CABINET

Also, when required, *fire hose cabinets* will be located in such a way that every point on a floor lies within reach of a *30′* stream from the end of a *100′* hose. A typical recessed wall cabinet for a wet standpipe hose and fire extinguisher is *2′9″W × 9″D × 2′9″H*. See UBC. Table 38-A for standpipe requirements on next page.

___ 6. *Landscape Irrigation*: See p. 153.
___ 7. *Gas:* To allow for the gas meter and piping, provide a space *1′6″W × 1′D × 2′H*.
___ 8. *Solar Hot Water Systems*
    ___ a. In U.S., average person uses *20 gal.* of HW/day.
    ___ b. Mount collectors at tilt equal to about the site latitude.
    ___ c. Typical collectors are 4′ × 8′ and 4′ × 10′.
    ___ d. Typical relationship between collector area and storage volume is *1:3* to *1:7* gal. per SF of collector.
    ___ e. Type of systems
        ___ (1) *Open loop, recirculation:* The most widely used in climates where freezing is of little concern.
        ___ (2) *Open loop, drain down:* Includes valving arrangement from collectors and piping when water temp. approaches freezing.

TABLE NO. 38-A—STANDPIPE REQUIREMENTS

OCCUPANCY	NONSPRINKLERED BUILDING[1]		SPRINKLERED BUILDING[2][3]	
	Standpipe Class	Hose Requirement	Standpipe Class	Hose Requirement
1. Occupancies exceeding 150 ft. in height and more than one story	III	Yes	I	No
2. Occupancies 4 stories or more but less than 150 ft. in height, except Group R, Div. 3	[I and II[4]] (or III)	[5] Yes	I	No
3. Group A Occupancies with occupant load exceeding 1000[6]	II	Yes	No requirement	No
4. Group A, Div. 2.1 Occupancies over 5000 square feet in area used for exhibition	II	Yes	II	Yes
5. Groups I, H, B, Div. 1, 2 or 3 Occupancies less than 4 stories in height but greater than 20,000 square feet per floor	II[4]	Yes	No requirement	No

[1]Except as otherwise specified in Item 4 of this table, Class II standpipes need not be provided in basements having an automatic fire-extinguishing system throughout.

[2]The standpipe system may be combined with the automatic sprinkler system.

[3]Portions of otherwise sprinklered buildings which are not protected by automatic sprinklers shall have Class II standpipes installed as required for the unsprinklered portions.

[4] In open structures where Class II standpipes may be damaged by freezing, the building official may authorize the use of Class I standpipes which are located as required for Class II standpipes.

[5]Hose is required for Class II standpipes only.

[6]Class II standpipes need not be provided in assembly areas used solely for worship.

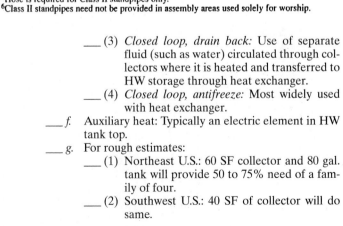

     ___ (3) *Closed loop, drain back:* Use of separate fluid (such as water) circulated through collectors where it is heated and transferred to HW storage through heat exchanger.

     ___ (4) *Closed loop, antifreeze:* Most widely used with heat exchanger.

   ___ *f.* Auxiliary heat: Typically an electric element in HW tank top.

   ___ *g.* For rough estimates:

     ___ (1) Northeast U.S.: 60 SF collector and 80 gal. tank will provide 50 to 75% need of a family of four.

     ___ (2) Southwest U.S.: 40 SF of collector will do same.

Costs: **$3000 to $4000 per system**

APPENDIX C: MINIMUM PLUMBING FACILITIES

Each building shall be provided with sanitary facilities, including provisions for the physically handicapped as prescribed by the Department having jurisdiction. In the absence of such requirements, this Appendix, which provides a guideline for the minimum facilities for the various types of occupancies, (see Section 910, Plumbing Fixtures Required, of the Uniform Plumbing Code) may be used. For requirements for the handicapped ANSI A117.1-1986, Providing Accessibility and Usability for Physically Handicapped People, may be used.

The number of occupants shall be that determined by minimum exiting requirements.

Type of Building or Occupancy[2]	Water Closets (Fixtures per Person)	Urinals[10] (Fixtures per Person)	Lavatories (Fixtures per Person)	Bathtubs or Showers (Fixtures per Person)	Drinking Fountains[3,13] (Fixtures per Person)
Assembly Places – Theatres, Auditoriums, Convention Halls, etc. – for permanent employee use	Male 1: 1-15 2: 16-35 3: 36-55 Female[14] 1: 1-15 3: 16-35 4: 36-55 Over 55, add 1 fixture for each additional 40 persons.	0: 1-9 1: 10-50 Add one fixture for each additional 50 males.	Male 1 per 40 Female 1 per 40		
Assembly Places – Theatres, Auditoriums, Convention Halls, etc. – for public use	Male 1: 1-100 2: 101-200 3: 201-400 Over 400, add one fixture for each additional 500 males and 2 for each 300 females. Female[14] 3: 1-50 4: 51-100 8: 101-200 11: 201-400	1: 1-100 2: 101-200 3: 201-400 4: 401-600 Over 600 add 1 fixture for each additional 500 males.	Male 1: 1-200 2: 201-400 3: 401-750 Over 750, add one fixture for each additional 500 persons. Female 1: 1-200 2: 201-400 3: 401-750		1 per 75[12]
Dormitories[9] School or Labor	Male 1 per 10 Add 1 fixture for each additional 25 males (over 10) and 1 for each additional 20 females (over 8). Female[14] 1 per 8	1 per 25 Over 150, add 1 fixture for each additional 50 males.	Male 1 per 12 Over 12 add one fixture for each additional 20 males and 1 for each 15 additional females. Female 1 per 12	1 per 8 For females, add 1 bathtub per 30. Over 150, add 1 per 20.	1 per 75[12]

Type of Building or Occupancy[2]	Water Closets (Fixtures per Person)		Urinals[10] (Fixtures per Person)	Lavatories (Fixtures per Person)		Bathtubs or Showers (Fixtures per Person)	Drinking Fountains[3,13] (Fixtures per Person)
Dormitories for staff use	Male 1: 1-15 2: 16-35 3: 36-55 Over 55, add 1 fixture for each additional 40 persons.	Female[14] 1: 1-15 3: 16-35 4: 36-55	1 per 50	Male 1 per 40	Female 1 per 40	1 per 8	
Dwellings[4] Single Dwelling Multiple Dwelling or Apartment House	1 per dwelling 1 per dwelling or apartment unit			1 per dwelling 1 per dwelling or apartment unit		1 per dwelling 1 per dwelling or apartment unit	
Hospital Waiting rooms	1 per room			1 per room			1 per 75[12]
Hospital for employee use	Male 1: 1-15 2: 16-35 3: 36-55 Over 55, add 1 fixture for each additional 40 persons.	Female[14] 1: 1-15 3: 16-35 4: 36-55	0: 1-9 1: 10-50 Add one fixture for each additional 50 males.	Male 1 per 40	Female 1 per 40		
Hospitals Individual Room Ward Room	1 per room 1 per 8 patients			1 per room 1 per 10 patients		1 per room 1 per 20 patients	1 per 75[12]
Industrial[6] Warehouses Workshops, Foundries and similar establishments (for employee use)	Male 1: 1-10 2: 11-25 3: 26-50 4: 51-75 5: 76-100 Over 100, add 1 fixture for each additional 30 persons	Female 1: 1-10 2: 11-25 3: 26-50 4: 51-75 5: 76-100		Up to 100, 1 per 10 persons Over 100, 1 per 15 persons[7, 8]		1 shower for each 15 persons exposed to excessive heat or to skin contamination with poisonous, infectious, or irritating material	1 per 75[12]

	Water Closets	Urinals	Lavatories	Bathtubs/ Showers	Drinking Fountains
Institutional – Other than Penal Hospitals or Penal Institutions (on each occupied floor)	Male 1 per 25 Female[14] 1 per 20	0: 1-9 1: 10-50 Add one fixture for each additional 50 males.	Male 1 per 10 Female 1 per 10	1 per 8	1 per 75[12]
Institutional – Other than Penal Hospitals or Penal Institutions (on each occupied floor) For employee use	Male 1: 1-15 2: 16-35 3: 36-55 Over 55, add 1 fixture for each additional 40 persons. Female[14] 1: 1-15 3: 16-35 4: 36-55	0: 1-9 1: 10-50 Add one fixture for each additional 50 males.	Male 1 per 40 Female 1 per 40	1 per 8	1 per 75[12]
Office or Public Buildings	Male 1: 1-100 2: 101-200 3: 201-400 Over 400, add one fixture for each additional 500 males and 2 for each 300 females. Female[14] 3: 1-50 4: 51-100 8: 101-200 11: 201-400	1: 1-100 2: 101-200 3: 201-400 4: 401-600 Over 600 add 1 fixture for each additional 300 males.	Male 1: 1-200 2: 201-400 3: 401-750 Over 750, add one fixture for each additional 500 persons. Female 1: 1-200 2: 201-400 3: 401-750		1 per 75[12]
Office or Public Buildings – For employee use	Male 1: 1-15 2: 16-35 3: 36-55 Over 55, add 1 fixture for each additional 40 persons. Female14 1: 1-15 3:16-35 4: 36-55	0: 1-9 1: 10-50 Add one fixture for each additional 50 males.	Male 1 per 40 Female 1 per 40		
Penal Institutions – For employee use	Male 1: 1-15 2: 16-35 3: 36-55 Over 55, add 1 fixture for each additional 40 persons. Female14 1: 1-15 3:16-35 4: 36-55	0: 1-9 1: 10-50 Add one fixture for each additional 50 males.	Male 1 per 40 Female 1 per 40		1 per 75[12]
Penal Institutions – For prison use Cell Exercise Room	1 per cell 1 per exercise room	1 per exercise room	1 per cell 1 per exercise room		1 per cell block floor 1 per exercise room

Type of Building or Occupancy[2]	Water Closets (Fixtures per Person)		Urinals[10] (Fixtures per Person)	Lavatories (Fixtures per Person)		Drinking Fountains[3,13] (Fixtures per Person)
Restaurants, Pubs and Lounges[11]	Male 1: 1-50 2: 51-150 3: 151-300 Over 300, add 1 fixture for each additional 200 persons	Female 1: 1-50 2: 51-150 4: 151-300	1: 1-150 Over 150, add 1 fixture for each additional 150 males	Male 1: 1-150 2: 151-200 3: 201-400 Over 400, add 1 fixture for each additional 400 persons	Female 1: 1-150 2: 151-200 3: 201-400	1 per 75[12]
Schools – For staff use All schools	Male 1: 1-15 2: 16-35 3: 36-55 Over 55, add 1 fixture for each additional 40 persons	Female 1: 1-15 2: 16-35 3: 36-55	1 per 50	Male 1 per 40	Female 1 per 40	
Schools – For student use Nursery	Male 1: 1-20 2: 21-50 Over 50, add 1 fixture for each additional 50 persons	Female 1: 1-20 2: 21-50		Male 1: 1-25 2: 26-50 Over 50, add 1 fixture for each additional 50 persons	Female 1: 1-25 2: 26-50	1 per 75[12]
Elementary	Male 1 per 30	Female 1 per 25	1 per 75	Male 1 per 35	Female 1 per 35	1 per 75[12]
Secondary	Male 1 per 40	Female 1 per 30	1 per 35	Male 1 per 40	Female 1 per 40	1 per 75[12]
Others (Colleges, Universities, Adult Centers, etc.)	Male 1 per 40	Female 1 per 30	1 per 35	Male 1 per 40	Female 1 per 40	1 per 75[12]
Worship Places Educational and Activities Unit	Male 1 per 125 2: 126-250	Female[14] 1 per 75 2: 76-125 3: 126-250	1 per 125	1 per 2 water closets		1 per 75[12]

Worship Places Principal Assembly Place	Male 1 per 150 2: 151-300	Female 1 per 75 2: 76-150 3: 151-300	1 per 150	1 per 2 water closets	1 per 75[1][2]

Whenever urinals are provided, one (1) water closet less than the number specified may be provided for each urinal installed, except the number of water closets in such cases shall not be reduced to less than two-thirds (2/3) of the minimum specified.

1. The figures shown are based upon one (1) fixture being the minimum required for the number of persons indicated or any fraction thereof.
2. Building categories not shown on this table shall be considered separately by the Administrative Authority.
3. Drinking fountains shall not be installed in toilet rooms.
4. Laundry trays. One (1) laundry tray or one (1) automatic washer standpipe for each dwelling unit or two (2) laundry trays or two (2) automatic washer standpipes, or combination thereof, for each ten (10) apartments. Kitchen sinks, one (1) for each dwelling or apartment unit.
5. Deleted.
6. As required by ANSI Z4.1-1968, Sanitation in Places of Employment.
7. Where there is exposure to skin contamination with poisonous, infectious, or irritating materials, provide one (1) lavatory for each five (5) persons.
8. Twenty-four (24) lineal inches (609.6 mm) of wash sink or eighteen (18) inches (457.2 mm) of a circular basin, when provided with water outlets for such space, shall be considered equivalent to one (1) lavatory.
9. Laundry trays, one (1) for each fifty (50) persons. Slop sinks, one (1) for each hundred (100) persons.
10. General. In applying this schedule of facilities, consideration must be given to the accessibility of the fixtures. Conformity purely on a numerical basis may not result in an installation suited to the need of the individual establishment. For example, schools should be provided with toilet facilities on each floor having classrooms. Temporary workingmen facilities, one (1) water closet and one (1) urinal for each thirty (30) workmen.
   a. Surrounding materials, wall and floor space to a point two (2) feet (0.6 m) in front of urinal lip and four (4) feet (1.2 m) above the floor, and at least two (2) feet (0.6 m) to each side of the urinal shall be lined with non-absorbent materials.
   b. Trough urinals are prohibited.
11. A restaurant is defined as a business which sells food to be consumed on the premises.
   a. The number of occupants for a drive-in restaurant shall be considered as equal to the number of parking stalls.
   b. Employee toilet facilities are not to be included in the above restaurant requirements. Hand washing facilities must be available in the kitchen for employees.
12. Where food is consumed indoors, water stations may be substituted for drinking fountains. Theatres, auditoriums, dormitories, offices, or public buildings for use by more than six (6) persons shall have one (1) drinking fountain for the first seventy-five (75) persons and one (1) additional fountain for each one hundred and fifty (150) persons thereafter.
13. There shall be a minimum of one (1) drinking fountain per occupied floor in schools, theatres, auditoriums, dormitories, offices or public building.
14. The total number of water closets for females shall be at least equal to the total number of water closets and urinals required for males.

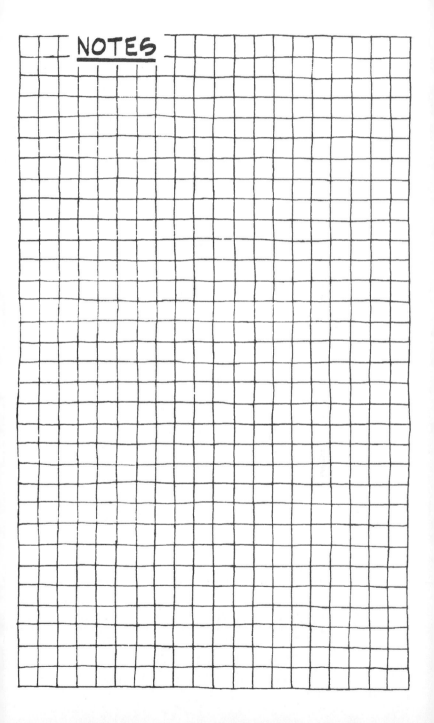

NOTES

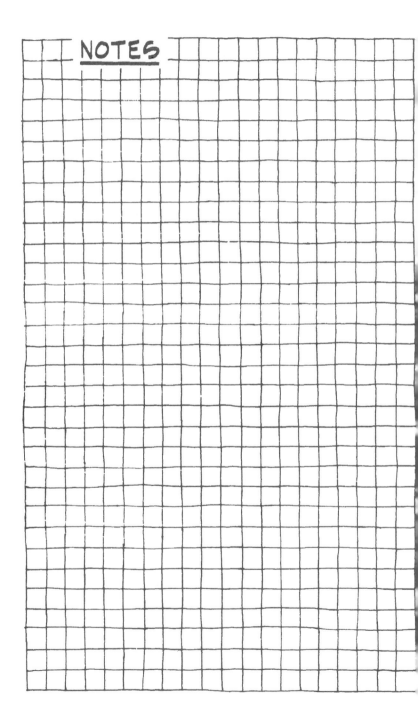

NOTES

___ B. HEATING, VENTILATION, AND AIR CONDITIONING (HVAC) ① ⑩

See p. 376 for selection and **cost** table.

During programming it is useful to do a functional partitioning of the building into major zones for:

___ 1. Similar schedule of use
___ 2. Similar temperature requirements
___ 3. Similar ventilation and air quality
___ 4. Similar internal heat generation
___ 5. Similar HVAC needs

During design, if possible, locate spaces with similar needs together. See App. A, item J for SF/ton estimates by bld'g. type. See page 105 for energy conservation and equipment efficiency.

___ 1. *General*
HVAC systems can be divided into four major parts:
   ___ *a.* The *boiler and chiller* to create heat and cold for the system to use. (In small package systems this is an internal electric coil, gas furnace, or refrigeration compressor).
   ___ *b. Cooling tower* (or air-cooled condenser) located outside to exhaust heat.
   ___ *c. Air handlers* to transfer heat and cold to air (or at least fresh air) to be blown into the building zones. In large buildings this is in a fan room. (In small package systems this is an internal fan).
   ___ *d.* The *delivery system* of ducts, control boxes, and diffusers to deliver conditioned air to the spaces.

___ 2. *Systems for Small Buildings*
   ___ *a. Roof-mounted "package systems"* are AC units that house the first three parts in one piece of equipment that usually ends up on the roof. Used usually in warm or temperate climates. Typical sizes:

Size	Area served	Dimensions	System
2 to 5 tons	600 to 1500 SF	6′L × 4′W × 4′H	Single zone constant
5 to 10 tons	1500 to 4500 SF	10′L × 7′W × 5′H	vol. delivery system; can serve more than
15 to 75 tons	4500 to 22,500 SF	25′L × 9′W × 6′H	one zone with variable air vol. delivery system

Notes:
   1. Units should have *3′ to 4′* of clearance around.
   2. A *ton is 12,000 Btu* of refrigeration.
   3. Each *ton is equal to 400 CFM.*

HVAC SYSTEMS AND COSTS

#	TYPE	HEATING	COOLING	SMALL (BLDG)	LARGE (BLDG)	ELECT.	GAS	OTHER	AIR	PIPES	MIN. OPERATING COST IN COLD CLIMATE	MIN. OPERATING COST IN MODERATE CLIMATE	MAX. CONTROL OF AIR VELOCITY & QUALITY	MAX. INDIVIDUAL CONTROL OF TEMP.	MINIMUM NOISE	MINIMUM VISUAL OBTRUSIVENESS	MIN. SPACE FOR EQUIP.	MIN. MAINTENANCE	MIN. FL. TO FL. HT.	MAX. FLEXIBILITY OF RENTAL SPACE	$ PER SF (50% M & 50% L)	$ TON OFAC (±10%)
1	ROOF MT'D "PACKAGE" UNITS	●	●	●		●	●		●												4	1000
2	CENTRAL FORCED AIR (& "SPLIT" SYSTEMS)	●	●	●		●	●		●		●		●		●	●		●			5	1200
3	FORCED HOT WATER	●		●		●	●						●		●	●		●			5	1200
4	EVAPORATIVE COOLING		●	●		●			●	●	●	●		●	●		●	●			4	1800
5	THROUGH WALL UNITS	●	●	●		●			●								●				1-2	500
6	ELECTRIC BASE BOARD	●	●	●		●			●					●	●		●				1.25	500
7	ELECT. FAN UNIT HEATERS	●		●		●								●			●	●			1	
8	WALL FURNACE	●	●	●		●									●	●	●	●				
9	RADIANT	●		●		●				●			●		●	●	●				2	
10	PASSIVE SOLAR	●		●				●				●					●	●				
11	ACTIVE SOLAR	●		●				●			●	●	●		●		●	●			1.25	
12	STOVES	●		●				●		●	●	●			●						2	
13	SINGLE ZONE CONSTANT VOL.	●	●		●	●	●	●	●							●		●			5	2000
14	MULTI ZONE CONSTANT VOL.	●			●	●		●	●				●		●						7	2200
15	VARIABLE AIR VOLUME	●			●	●		●	●				●	●						●	8	2500
16	DOUBLE DUCT	●	●		●	●		●	●		●		●	●	●	●	●			●	10	3000
17	INDUCTION	●	●		●	●		●				●	●	●	●	●				●	8	2500
18	FAN COIL WITH AIR	●	●	●	●	●		●	●	●			●	●	●	●			●	●	8	2400
19	FAN COIL UNITS	●		●	●	●		●		●	●	●	●	●		●			●	●	7	2200
20	HOT WATER BASE BOARDS	●		●	●	●		●		●	●	●			●		●				4	

Roof Mounted
"Package" Unit

___ b. *Forced-air central heating* heats air with gas, oil
flame, or elect. resistance at a furnace. A fan blows
air through a duct system. The furnace can be up
flow (for basements), side flow,
or down flow (for attic). The
furnace must be vented.
Furnace sizes range
between *2′W × 2.5′D*
× 7′H to *4′W to 7′D ×*
7′H. Main ducts are
typically *1′ × 2′* hori-
zontal and *1′ × .33′*
vertical.

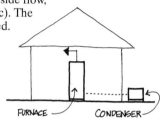

Can add cooling with a "*split system*" by adding
evaporator coils in the duct and an exterior condenser. Typical condensers range from *2′W × 2′D ×*
2′H to *3.5′W × 4′D × 3′H*.

___ c. *Forced hot water*
heating. A flame or
electric resistance
heats water to fin
tube convectors (or
fan coil unit with
blowers). The fueled
boiler must be vented
and provided with com-
bustible air. Boiler sizes
range from *2′W × 2′D × 7′H*
to *3′W × 5′D × 7′H*. Fin tube
convectors are typically *3″D × 8″H*.
Fan coils are *2′W × 2.5′H*. There is *no* cooling.

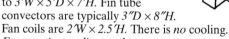

___ d. *Evaporative cooling* works
only in hot, dry climates.
A fan draws exterior
air across wet pads
and into the duct sys-
tem. There is *no* heat-
ing. Cooler size
typically is *3′W × 3′D*
× 3′H. Main duct is typically *1.5′W × 1.5′D*.

___ e. *Through-wall units and package terminal units* are self-contained at an exterior wall and are intended for small spaces. These are usually electric (or *heat pump* in mild climates), which are used for *both* heating and cooling. Interior air is recirculated and outside air is added. Typical sizes:

Package Terminal Units $3.5'W \times 1.5'D \times 1.3'H$
Through-Wall Units $2'W \times 2'D \times 1.5'H$

___ f. *Electric baseboard convectors* beats by electrical resistance in $3''D \times 8''H$ baseboards around the perimeter of the room. There is *no cooling*.

___ g. *Electric fan-forced unit heaters* are much like item *f* above, but are larger because of internal fans recirculating the air. There is *no cooling*. Typical sizes range from $1.5'W \times 8''D \times 8''H$ to $2'W \times 1'D \times 1.8'H$.

___ h. *Radiant heating:* Electrical resistance wires are embedded in floor or ceiling. There is *no cooling*. An alternative is to have recessed radiant panels, typically $2' \times 2'$ or $2' \times 4'$. For alternative cooling and heating use water piping.

___ i. *Wall furnaces* are small furnaces for small spaces. They must be vented. There is *no cooling*. They may be either gas or electric. The typical size is $14''W \times 12''D \times 84''H$.

___ j. Other miscellaneous small systems
    ___ Passive solar heating (see p. 101)
    ___ Active solar heating
    ___ Heating stoves (must be properly vented!)

___ 3. *Custom Systems for Large Buildings*
    These are where the first three parts (see p. 375) must have areas allocated for them in the floor plan. In tall buildings due to distance, mechanical floors are created so that air handlers can move air up and down *10 to 15* floors. Thus mechanical floors are spaced *20 to 30* floors apart.

A decentralized chiller and boiler can be at every other mechanical floor or they can be centralized at the top or base of the building with one or more air handlers at each floor. See page 380 for equipment rooms.

___ *a.* Delivery systems

    ___ (1) *All air delivery systems*

Ducts: Because of their size, are a great concern in the preliminary design of the floor-to-ceiling space. The main supply and return ducts are often run above main hallways because ceilings can be lower and this provides a natural path of easy access to the majority of spaces served.

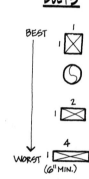

Air rates for buildings vary from *1 CFM/SF to 2 CFM/SF* based on usage and climate. Low velocity ducts require *1 to 2 SF of area per 1000 SF* of building area served. High-velocity ducts require *0.5 to 1.0.* Air returns are required and are about the same size, or slightly larger than the main duct supply.

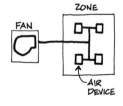

    ___ (*a*) *Single zone constant-volume systems* serve only one zone and are used for large, open-space rooms without diverse exterior exposure. This is a low-velocity system.

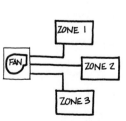

    ___ (*b*) *Multizone constant volume systems* can serve up to eight separate zones. They are used in modest-sized buildings where there is a diversity of exterior exposure and/or diversity of interior loads. This is a low-velocity system.

    ___ (*c*) *Subzone box systems* use boxes that branch off the main supply duct to

LARGE SYSTEMS

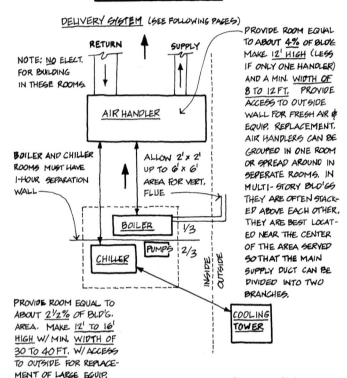

DELIVERY SYSTEM (SEE FOLLOWING PAGES)

RETURN   SUPPLY

NOTE: NO ELECT.
FOR BUILDING
IN THESE ROOMS

AIR HANDLER

BOILER AND CHILLER
ROOMS MUST HAVE
1-HOUR SEPARATION
WALL

ALLOW 2' x 2'
UP TO 6' x 6'
AREA FOR VERT.
FLUE

BOILER   1/3

PUMPS   2/3

CHILLER

INSIDE   OUTSIDE

PROVIDE ROOM EQUAL
TO ABOUT 4% OF BLDG.
MAKE 12' HIGH (LESS
IF ONLY ONE HANDLER)
AND A MIN. WIDTH OF
8 TO 12 FT. PROVIDE
ACCESS TO OUTSIDE
WALL FOR FRESH AIR &
EQUIP. REPLACEMENT.
AIR HANDLERS CAN BE
GROUPED IN ONE ROOM
OR SPREAD AROUND IN
SEPERATE ROOMS. IN
MULTI-STORY BLD'GS
THEY ARE OFTEN STACK-
ED ABOVE EACH OTHER.
THEY ARE BEST LOCAT-
ED NEAR THE CENTER
OF THE AREA SERVED
SO THAT THE MAIN
SUPPLY DUCT CAN BE
DIVIDED INTO TWO
BRANCHES.

COOLING
TOWER

PROVIDE ROOM EQUAL TO
ABOUT 2½% OF BLD'G.
AREA. MAKE 12' TO 16'
HIGH W/ MIN. WIDTH OF
30 TO 40 FT. W/ ACCESS
TO OUTSIDE FOR REPLACE-
MENT OF LARGE EQUIP.
LOCATE AWAY FROM CRIT-
ICAL NOISE AREAS.

REQUIRES ABOUT 1 SF PER 300 SF OF BLD'G.
AREA. LOCATE AWAY FROM PUBLIC AREAS
(100' MIN.) ON GROUND (OR ON ROOF). PRO-
VIDE 4 FT. CLEARANCE BENEATH AND 10 TO
15' ON SIDES.

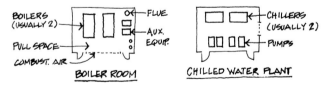

BOILERS
(USUALLY 2)
FLUE
AUX.
EQUIP.
PULL SPACE
COMBUST. AIR

BOILER ROOM

CHILLERS
(USUALLY 2)
PUMPS

CHILLED WATER PLANT

create separate zones. The size of the boxes can be related to the area served:

Box	Area served
4′L × 3′W × 1.5′H	500 to 1500 SF
5′L × 4′W × 1.5′H	1500 to 5000 SF

The main ducts can be high-velocity, but the ducts after the boxes at each zone (as well as the return air) are low-velocity.

___ (*d*) *Variable air-volume* single duct can serve as many subzones as required. It is the dominant choice in many commercial buildings because of its flexibility and energy savings. It is most effectively used for interior zones. At exterior zones hot water or electrical reheat coils are added to the boxes. Each zone's temperature is controlled by the volume of air flowing through its box. Typical above ceiling boxes are:

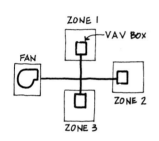

ZONE 1

VAV BOX

FAN

ZONE 2

ZONE 3

8″ to 11″H for up to 1500 SF
served (lengths up to 5′)
up to 18″H for up to 7000 SF

___ (*e*) *Double duct systems* can serve as a good choice where *air quality control* is important. The air handler supplies hot air for one duct and cold air for the other. The mixing box controls the mix of these two air ducts.

___ (*f*) *Variable air-volume dual duct systems.* One duct conveys cool air, one other hot air. This system is most common where dual-duct constant volume system is converted to VAV. The box is generally controlled to provide either heat or cool. Air as required in varying quantities.

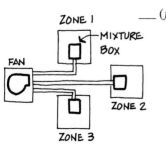

ZONE 1

MIXTURE BOX

FAN

ZONE 2

ZONE 3

___ (2) Air/water delivery systems

Ducts: These types of systems *reduce the duct work* by tempering air near its point of use. Hot and cold water are piped to remote induction or fan coil units. Since the air ducts carry only fresh air, they can be sized at *0.2 to 0.4 SF per 1000 SF* of area served. The main hot and cold water lines will be *2 to 4 inches* diameter, including insulation for medium size buildings.

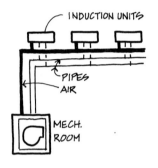

___ (*a*) *Induction* is often used for the *perimeter of high-rise office buildings* and is *expensive*. Air from a central air handler is delivered through high-velocity ducts to each induction unit. Hot and cold lines run to each unit. Each unit is located along the outside wall, at the base of the windows. They are *6 to 12 inches deep* and *1 to 3 feet high*.

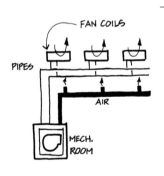

___ (*b*) *Fan coils with supplementary air* are used where there are *many small rooms needing separate control.* Hot and cold water lines are run through the coils. A fan draws room air through the coil for heating and cooling. A separate duct system supplies fresh air from a remote air handler.

The fan coils are *6 to 12 inches deep and 1 to 3 feet high.* They can also be a vertical shape (*2′ × 2′ × 6′ high*) to fit in a closet. They are often stacked vertically in a tall building to reduce piping. Fan coil units can be located in ceiling space.

___ (3) *Water delivery systems* use hot and cold water lines only. No air is delivered to the areas served.

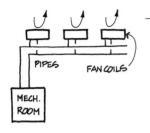

___ (*a*) *Fan coil units* can have hot and/or cold lines with fresh air from operable windows or an outdoor air intake at the unit.

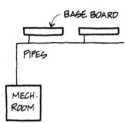

___ (*b*) *Hot water baseboards* supply only heat. Often used in conjunction with a cooling only VAV system for perimeter zones. Baseboards are *6 inches high by 5 inches deep* and as long as necessary.

___ 4. Diffusers, Terminal Devices, and Grilles: Interface the HVAC system with the building interiors for visual impact and thermal comfort. Grilles are side wall devices. Opposite wall should be no greater than about *16′ to 8′* away. Diffusers are down facing and must be coordinated with the lighting as well as uniformly spaced (at a *distance apart of approximately the floor-to-ceiling height*). Returns should be spaced so as to not interfere with air supply.

GRILLE

DIFFUSER

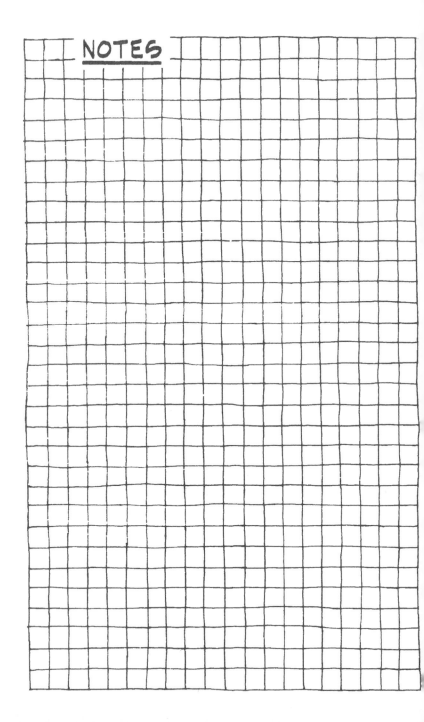

NOTES

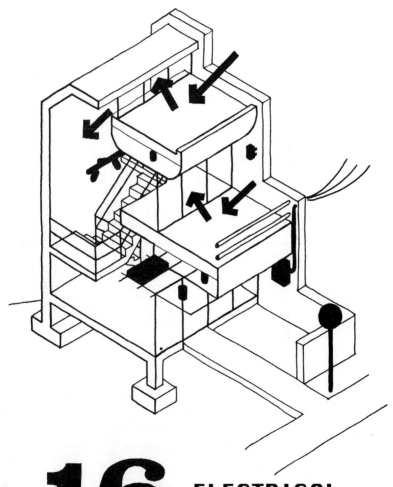

16 ELECTRICAL

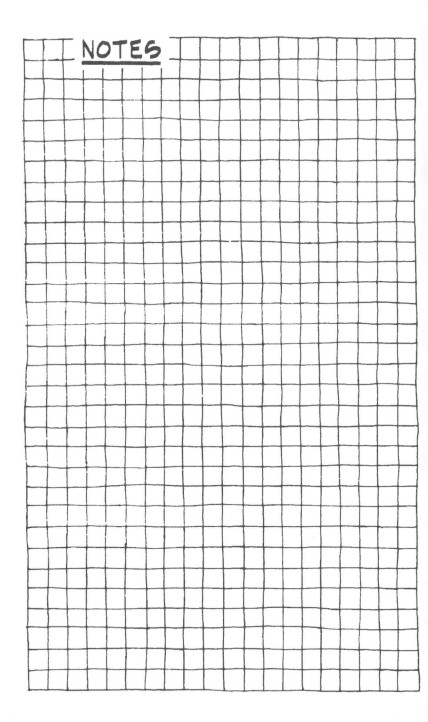

NOTES

__ A. LIGHTING ⑩ ㊶

___ 1. *General*

    ___ *a.* Lighting terms and concepts using the analogy of a sprinkler pipe

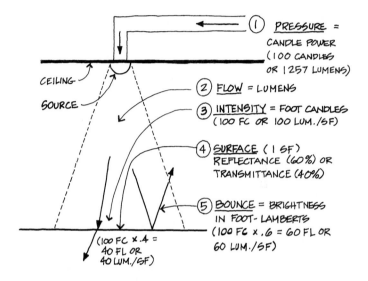

(1) PRESSURE = CANDLE POWER (100 CANDLES OR 1257 LUMENS)

(2) FLOW = LUMENS

(3) INTENSITY = FOOT CANDLES (100 FC OR 100 LUM./SF)

(4) SURFACE (1 SF) REFLECTANCE (60%) OR TRANSMITTANCE (40%)

(5) BOUNCE = BRIGHTNESS IN FOOT-LAMBERTS (100 FC × .6 = 60 FL OR 60 LUM./SF)

CEILING

SOURCE

(100 FC × .4 = 40 FL OR 40 LUM./SF)

    ___ Visible light is measured in lumens.

    ___ One lumen of light flux spread over one square foot of area illuminates the area to one *foot-candle.*

    ___ The ratio of lumens/watts is called *efficacy,* a measure of *energy efficiency.*

    ___ The incident angle of a light beam always equals the reflectance angle on a surface.

    ___ *b.* Considerations in seeing

        ___ (1) *Contrast* between that viewed and surroundings will help vision. Too little will wash out the object. Too much will create a glare. Recommended max. ratios:

___ Task to adjacent area	3 to 1
___ Task to remote dark surface	3 to 1
___ Task to remote light surface	1 to 1
___ Window to adjacent wall	20 to 1
___ Task to general visual field	40 to 1
___ Focal point: up to	100 to 1

___ (2) *Brightness* (How much light?). For recommended lighting levels, see p. 390.

___ (3) *Size* of that viewed. As the viewing task becomes smaller, the brightness needs to increase and vice versa.

___ (4) *Time:* As the view time is decreased, the brightness and contrast needs to increase and vice versa.

___ (5) *Glare:* Not only can too much contrast create glare, but light sources at the wrong angle to the eye can create glare.

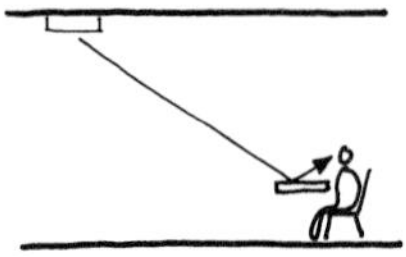

"VEILING REFLECTIONS"

___ (6) *Color:* See p. 293.

___ (7) *Interest*

___ *c.* Types of overall light source

___ *Task lighting* is the brightest level needed for the immediate task, such as a desk lamp. Select from table on p. 390.

___ *General lighting* is the less bright level of surroundings for both general seeing and to reduce contrast between the task and surroundings. It is also for less intense tasks, such as general illumination of a lobby. This type of lighting can be both natural or artificial.

As a *general rule,* general lighting should be about ⅓ that of task lighting down to *20 FC.* Noncritical lighting (halls, etc.) can be reduced to ⅓ of general lighting down to *10 FC.*

For more detail, see p. 390.

___ *d.* *Calculation* of a point source of light on an object can be estimated by:

$$\text{Foot candles} = \frac{\text{Source}}{\text{distance}^2} \times \text{Cosine of incident angle}$$

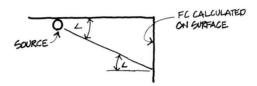

SOURCE CAN BE IN CANDLES, LUMENS, OR FOOT-LAMBERTS

SOURCE

∠

∠

FC CALCULATED ON SURFACE

Light hitting a surface at an angle will illuminate the surface less than light hitting perpendicular to the surface. The cosine of the incident angle is used to make the correction. Doubling the distance from source to surface cuts the illumination of the surface by ¼. Also, see page 410 for other calculations.

DESIGN LIGHTING LEVELS (41)

	TYPE OF ACTIVITY	TYPE OF LIGHTING	FOOTCANDLES X	Y	Z	TYPICAL SPACES
A	PUBLIC SPACES W/DARK SURROUNDINGS	GENERAL AREA LIGHTING THROUGHOUT SPACES	2	3	5	THEATER, STORAGE
B	SIMPLE ORIENTATION FOR SHORT TEMPORARY VISITS		5	7.5	10	DINING, CORRIDORS, CLOSETS, STORAGE
C	WORKING SPACES WHERE VISUAL TASKS ARE ONLY OCCASIONALLY PERFORMED		10	15	20	WAITING, EXHIBITION, LOBBIES, LOCKERS, RESIDENTIAL DINING, STAIRS, TOILETS, ELEVATORS, LOADING DOCKS
D	PERFORMANCE OF VISUAL TASKS OF HIGH CONTRAST OR LARGE SIZE	ILLUMINATION ON TASK	20	30	50	GENERAL OFFICE, EXAM ROOMS, MANUFACTURING, READING ROOMS, DRESSING, DISPLAY
E	PERFORMANCE OF VISUAL TASKS OF MEDIUM CONTRAST OR SMALL SIZE		50	75	100	DRAFTING, LABS, KITCHENS, EXAM ROOM, SEWING, DESKS, FILES, WORK BENCH, READING, MANUFACTURING.
F	PERFORMANCE OF VISUAL TASKS OF LOW CONTRAST OR VERY SMALL AREA		100	150	200	ARTWORK AND DRAFTING, DEMONSTRATION, INSPECTION, SURGERY, LABS, FITTING, RECORDS, CRITICAL AT WORK BENCH, DIFFICULT SEWING, MANUFACTURE ASSEMBLY
G	PERFORMANCE OF VISUAL TASKS OF LOW CONTRAST AND VERY SMALL SIZE OVER A PROLONGED PERIOD.	ILLUMINATION ON TASK BY COMBINATION OF GENERAL AND LOCAL LIGHTING	200	300	500	CRITICAL SURGERY, VERY DIFFICULT MANUFACTURING ASSEMBLY, CLOSE INSPECTION
H	PERFORMANCE OF VERY PROLONGED & EXACTING VISUAL TASK		500	750	1000	
I	PERFORMANCE OF VERY SPECIAL TASKS OF EXTREMELY LOW CONTRAST AND SMALL SIZE		1000	1500	2000	

	AGE	% REFL.	SPEED &/OR ACCURACY
X	<40	>70	NOT IMPORT.
Y	40-55	30-70	IMPORT.
Z	>50	<30	CRITICAL

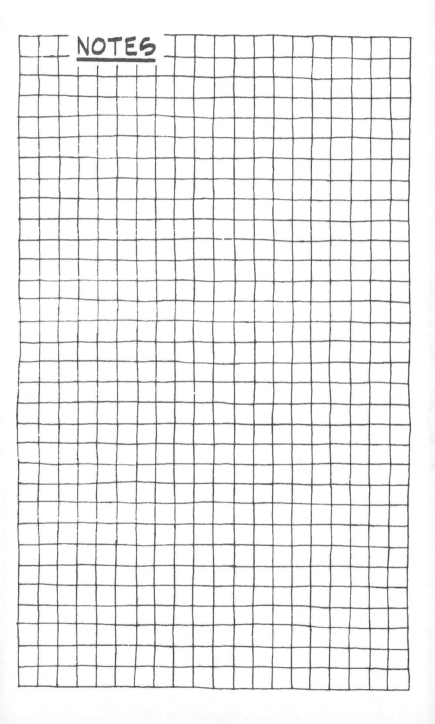

NOTES

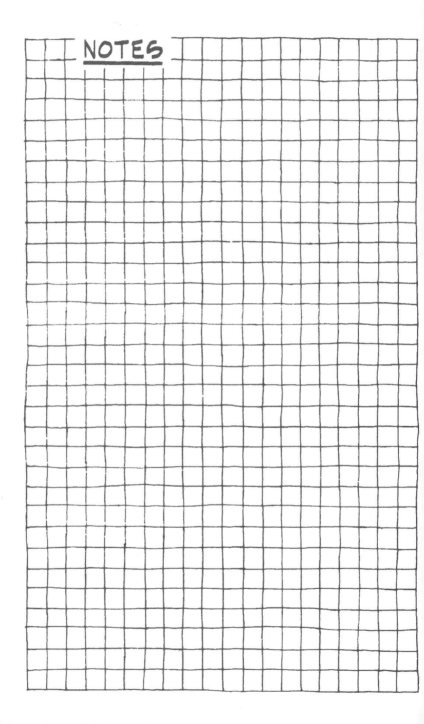

NOTES

___ 2. *Daylighting (Natural Lighting)* (10)
    ___ *a.* General
        ___ (1) Before the design of electric lighting, day-lighting should be considered.

Daylighting is an important connection with the outside world. Even if daylight is not to be used as a primary lighting source, in most buildings there should be some penetration of daylight. The architectural program can be partitioned into spaces where day-lighting can or should be used and spaces where daylight will not be a major factor. The best opportunities for daylight use are in areas where task lighting is not the primary consideration. As the task lighting needs to be more controlled, daylighting becomes more problematic as a lighting solution. Good daylighting opportunity happens where task-lighting needs are not too critical, as in corridors, lobbies, residences. Daylighting is probably not a good idea where task-light constraints are very restrictive, as in a lecture room and hospital operating rooms.

        ___ (2) Daylighting components
            ___ (*a*) Direct sun
            ___ (*b*) Diffuse sky
            ___ (*c*) Indirect sun (sunlight reflected from ground or adjacent structures)

        ___ (3) There are many ways to introduce natural light into buildings, ranging from fairly obvious and common methods to new and emerging technologies:

            ___ (*a*) *Perimeter lighting* involves the size and placement of windows and the use of light shelves.
            ___ (*b*) *Top lighting* includes the use of sky-lights and roof monitors, and even translucent membrane roofs.
            ___ (*c*) *Core lighting* involves the use of atriums and light wells.
            ___ (*d*) *Optical lighting* includes the use of fiber optics, prisms, mirrors, parabolic reflectors, and other means.

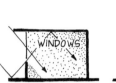

THREE WAYS TO DAYLIGHT

____ *b.* General rules of thumb:

    ____ (1) Daylighting, even more than artificial lighting, needs to be considered early in the design process.

    ____ (2) A useful conceptual approach to conceiving a daylighting scheme is to think in terms of bouncing the daylight off interior surfaces into the area to be lit.

    ____ (3) Direct sunlight is almost always too bright to work under.

    ____ (4) Direct sunlight on critical task areas should be avoided.

    ____ (5) Direct skylight and sunlight should be used sparingly in noncritical areas.

    ____ (6) For the best daylight, consider increasing the number of windows, rather than just increasing the size of one window.

    ____ (7) Daylight should be bounced off surrounding surfaces. In hot climates this should be outside (roofs, ground, walls, etc.) to reduce heat gain.

    ____ (8) Daylight should be brought in high and let down softly.

    ____ (9) Daylight can be filtered through drapes, screens, trees, and plants.

    ____ (10) Daylight from one side of a room can cause a glare problem. Daylight admitted from two or more sides will tend to balance the light in the room.

    ____ (11) Office building window daylighting usually affects the 15′ perimeter of the plan.

    ____ (12) North-facing windows, skylights, or clearstories give the best daylight (may be a bad orientation in cold climates, with northerly winds, for heat loss).

___ (13) Northern orientations will receive only minor direct solar penetration in the early morning and late afternoon in the summer.

___ (14) North light should be used where soft, cool, uniform illumination is needed.

___ (15) South light should be allowed only where intense warm, variable illumination is appropriate.

___ (16) Southern orientations are relatively easy to shield from direct solar penetrations with horizontal louvers or overhangs.

___ (17) Eastern and western orientations are almost impossible to protect from direct solar penetrations (heat and glare) and at the same time see out the window.

___ (18) See p. 104 for solar control of south-, east-, and west-facing glass.

___ (19) Skylights can be a problem, due to heat gain from too much sunlight.

___ (20) Skylights and clearstories can be used to deliver light deep into the interior of a building. Clearstories can be designed to best avoid direct sunlight.

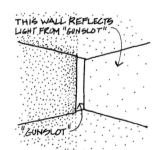

THIS WALL REFLECTS LIGHT FROM "GUNSLOT".

"GUNSLOT"

___ (21) "Gun slots" against wall can provide illumination at minimum heat gain.

___ (22) Often, office daylighting strategies lose their economic effectiveness without *automatic controls* that adjust the level of electric lighting to complement the available natural light during the day. Controls may be Photocell; 2- or 3-step lighting; continuous dimming; or motion detectors.

___ c. Estimating illumination:
Sky brightness values combined with the cosine effect of orientation can be used to estimate surface brightness levels; use the following guidelines:

Overcast skies
will give the most even illumination and are easier to estimate. An overcast sky is 3 times as bright at the zenith as it is around the horizon. The clouds dif-

fuse the solar illumination into a fairly even distribution around the sky. An overcast sky has the following brightness values at noon in an equivalent amount of illumination on a horizontal surface in footcandles:

> Winter 1000 FC
> Spring and fall 1800 FC
> Summer 3000 FC

Clear skies
are very bright around the position of the sun and relatively dark around a point 90° away from the sun—a 10 to 1 variation.

A clear blue northern sky has the following brightness values in foot lamberts, which will produce an equivalent amount of illumination on a horizontal surface in footcandles:

> Winter 500 FC
> Spring and fall 800 FC
> Summer 1000 FC

Direct solar illumination in FC is:

> Winter illumination at noon:
> > On a horizontal surface 3000–6000 FC
> > Perpendicular to sun's rays 6500–9000 FC

> Spring/fall illumination at noon:
> > On a horizontal surface 6000–8000 FC
> > Perpendicular to sun's rays 8000–9000 FC

> Summer illumination at noon:
> > On a horizontal surface 8000–9000 FC
> > Perpendicular to sun's rays 8000–9000 FC

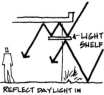

REFLECT DAYLIGHT IN ORDER TO PENETRATE PERIMETER.

THE HEIGHT OF THE WINDOW AND ITS LOCATION INFLUENCE LIGHT DISTRIBUTION.

SILL HEIGHT HAS LITTLE EFFECT ON TASK LIGHTING; HOWEVER, IT PROVIDES FLOOR LIGHTING VARIANCES.

___ *d.* Rules of thumb for *sizing glazing:* Too much day-light can create glare and overheating problems. Daylight can be used to reduce the need for electrical lighting, but too much daylight causes the air conditioning load of the building to rise. The following list provides a useful guide to determining the approximate daylight aperture areas that will balance lighting and AC requirements:

Sidelighting

Window openings	*10*% (*min.*) *to 25*% of floor area; *25*% *to 40*% of wall area
Room depth	*2 to 2½* times window height (usually *15′ to 20′*).

Top lighting

Skylights	*5*% of ceiling (max.).
	Space at *1 to 2* times ceiling to work plane height.
Clearstories	*10*% of wall area.
	Space *1.5* times ceiling to work plane height.
	At a point *15′* from rear wall:
	For overcast sky (1500 FC) climates, provide *15″* of glazing height per *10 FC* on ave. work plane.
	For clear climate (5000 FC), provide *2″.*

SKY BRIGHTNESS VALUES
COMBINED WITH THE COSINE
EFFECT OF ORIENTATION CAN
BE USED TO ESTIMATE SUR-
FACE BRIGHTNESS LEVELS.

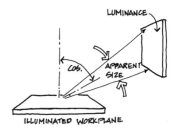

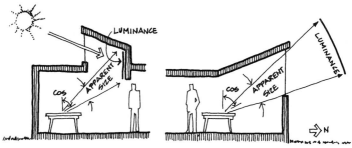

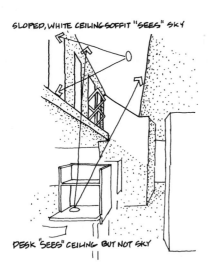

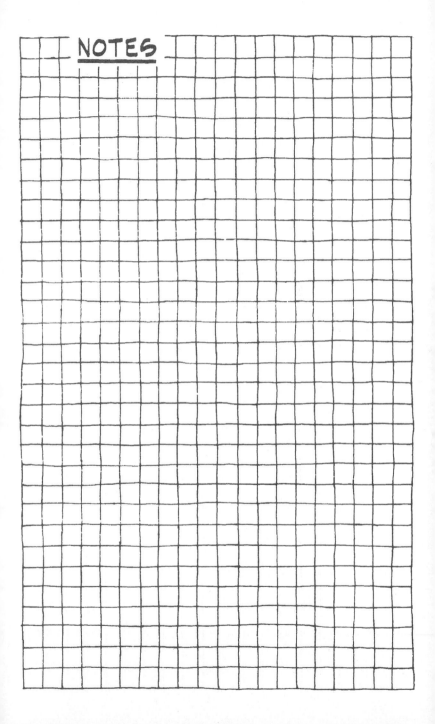

NOTES

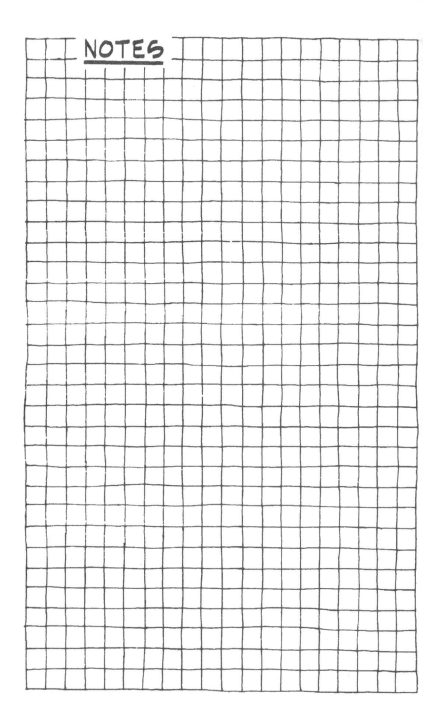

NOTES

___ 3. *Electric (Artificial) Lighting* (for Energy Conservation, see p. 105)

___ *a.* Lamp types

___ (1) *Incandescent* lamps produce a warm light, are inexpensive and easy to use but have limited lumination per watt (*20 to 40*) and a short life. *Normal voltage* lamps produce a point source of light. Most common shapes are A, R, and PAR. *Low voltage* lamps produce a very small point of intense brightness that can be focused into a precise beam of light (for merchandise or art). These are usually PAR shapes or designed to fit into a parabolic reflector. Sizes are designated in ⅛ inch of the widest part of lamp. Tungsten-Halogen (quartz) and low voltage are a special type of incandescent.

___ (2) *Gaseous discharge* lamps produce light by passing electricity through a gas. These lamps require a ballast to get the lamp started and then to control the current.

___ (a) *Fluorescent lamps* produce a wide, linear, diffuse light source that is well-suited to spreading light downward to the working surfaces of desks or displays in a commercial environment with normal ceiling heights (*8′ to 12′*). The deluxe lamps have good color-rendering characteristics and can be chosen to favor the *cool* (*blue*) or the *warm* (*red*) end of the spectrum. *Dimmers for fluorescents are expensive.* Fluorescent lamps produce more light per watt of energy (*50–80 lumens/watt*) than incandescent; thus operating costs are low. The purchase price and length of life of fluorescent lamps are greater than for incandescent and less than for HID. Four-feet lamp lengths utilize 40 watts and are most common. *Designations are F followed by wattage, shape, size, color, and a form factor.*

___ (*b*) *High-intensity discharge* (*HID*) lamps can be focused into a fairly good beam of light. These lamps, matched with an appropriate fixture are well-suited to beaming light down to the working place from a high ceiling (*12′ to 20′*). *Dimming HID lamps is difficult. The lamps are expensive but produce a lot of light and last a long time.* If there is a power interruption, HID lamps will go out and cannot come on again for about *10 minutes* while they cool down. Therefore, *in an installation of HID lamps, a few incandescent or fluorescent lamps are needed to provide backup lighting.*

___ *Mercury vapor* (the *bluish* street lamps). Deluxe version is warmer. *35 to 65* lumens/watt.

___ *Metal halide* are often *ice blue cool* industrial-looking lamps. Deluxe color rendering is almost as good as deluxe fluorescent for a warmer effect. Efficiency is *80 lumens/watt.*

___ *High-pressure sodium* produces a *warm golden yellow* light often used for highways. Deluxe color rendering is almost as cool as deluxe fluorescent for a cooler effect. Efficiency is *100 lumens/ watt.*

___ *Low-pressure sodium* produces a *yellow* color which makes all colors appear in shades of grey. Used for parking lots and roadways. Efficiency is *150 lumens/ watt.*

___ (*c*) *Cold cathode* (neon) has a color
dependent on the gas and the color
of the tube. *Can be most any color.*
Does not give off enough light for
detailed visual tasks, but does give
off enough light for *attracting atten-
tion,* indoors or out.

___ *b.* Lighting systems and fixture types

**Note: Costs include lamps, fixture, & installation
labor, but not general wiring.**

___ (1) *General room lighting*
A large proportion of commercial space
requires even illumination on the work-
place. This can be done a number of ways.
___ (*a*) *Direct lighting* is the most common
form of general room lighting.

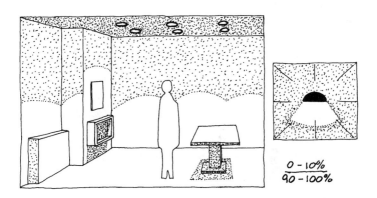

0 – 10%
90 – 100%

All recessed lighting is an example
of a direct lighting system, but a
pendant fixture could be direct if it
emits virtually no light above the
horizontal. Unless extensive wall
washing, or high light levels (as
with fluorescent for general office
lighting) are used, the overall
impression of a direct lighting system should be one of low general
brightness with the possibility of
higher intensity accents.

A guide to determine max. spacing is the *spacing-to-mounting-height ratio.* The mounting height is the height from the working place (*usually 2.5′ above floor*) to the level of the height fixtures.

$$\text{Spacing} = \left(\frac{S}{MH} \right) \times (\text{Mounting Ht.})$$

___ (1) *Wide-beam diffuse lighting* is often fluorescent lights for normal ceiling heights (8′ to 12′). The fixtures will produce a repetitive two-dimensional pattern that becomes the most prominent fixture of the ceiling plane. Typical S/MH = *1.5.*

Typical recessed fluorescent fixture:

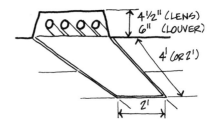

Cost: **2′ × 4′ = \$85 to \$125/ea. (85% M and 15% L) variation of −10%, +20%.**
2′ × 2′ = 25% less

___ (2) *Medium-beam downlighting* is produced with a fixture located in or on the ceiling that creates a beam of light directed downward. In the circulation and lobby areas of a building, *incandescent lamps* are often used. For large areas, *HID lamps* are often selected. In both these cases the light is in the form of a *conical beam,* and *scallops* of light will be produced on wall surfaces.

S/MH is usually about *0.7 to 1.3.*

Typical fixture: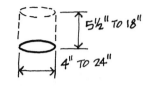

Cost: (per ea. fixture)	Res.	Comm.
Low voltage:	$125	$275 (85% M and 15% L)
Incandescent:	$65	$250 (90% M and 10% L)
Fluorescent:	$125	$275 (85% M and 15% L)
HID:	$125	$450 (80% M and 20% L)

___ (3) *Narrow beam downlights* are often used in the same situation as in (2), but produce more of a spotlight effect at low mounting heights. This form of lighting is used to achieve even illumination where the ceiling height is relatively high. S/MH is usually *0.3 to 0.9.*

Typical fixture: Same as item (2) above

Cost: **Same as item (2) above**

___ (*b*) *Semidirect lighting*

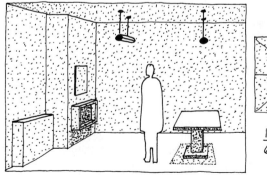

All systems other than direct ones necessarily imply that the lighting fixtures are in the space, whether pendant-mounted, surface-mounted, or portable. A semidirect system will provide good illumination on horizontal surfaces, with moderate general brightness.

Typical fixtures:

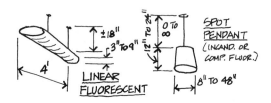

Costs: **Fluor.: $225 to $500 (90% M and 10% L)**
Pendant: $125 to $200 (90% M and 10% L)

___ *(c) General diffuse lighting*

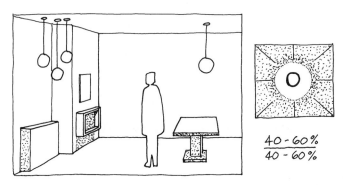

A general diffuse system most typically consists of suspended fixtures, with predominantly translucent surfaces on all sides. Can be incandescent, fluorescent, or HID.

Typical fixture: see sketch above

Cost: **$75 to $550 (90% M and 10% L)**

___ (*d*) *Direct-indirect lighting*

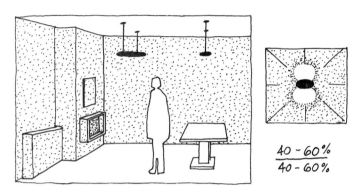

$$\frac{40 - 60\%}{40 - 60\%}$$

A direct-indirect will tend to equally emphasize the upper and lower horizontal planes in a space (i.e. the ceiling and floor).

Typical fixture: same as semidirect

Cost: **Same as Semidirect.**

___ (*e*) *Semi-indirect lighting*

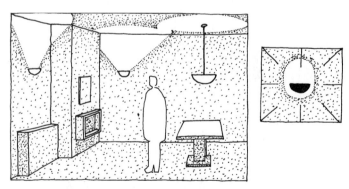

A semi-indirect system will place the emphasis on the ceiling, with some downward or outward-directed light.

Note: ADA requires that, along accessible routes, *wall-mounted* fixtures protrude no more than *4″* when mounted lower than *6′8″* AFF.

Typical fixture:

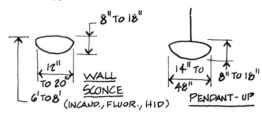

Cost: **Wall sconce: $125 to $550 (90% M and 10% L)**
Pendant: $350 to $2200 (85% M and 15% L)

___ (*f*) *Indirect lighting*

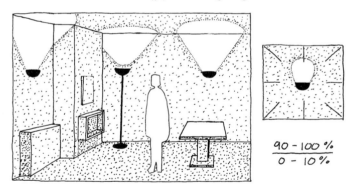

A fully indirect system will bounce all the light off the ceiling, resulting in a low-contrast environment with little shadow.

Typical fixture: Same as Direct-Indirect.

Cost: **Same as Direct-Indirect.**

_____ *(g) Accent or specialty lighting*

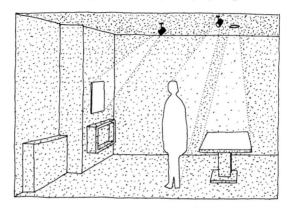

Used for special effects or spot lighting, such as lighting art objects or products on display.

Typical fixtures:

TRACK

RECESSED ACCENT

Costs: **Track $85 to $450 (90% M and 10% L)**
Recessed accent: $100 to $1000 (80% M and 20% L)

___ *c.* Simplified calculations
    ___ (1) For estimating light from one source (such as a painting on a wall lit by a ceiling mounted spot) use the COSINE METHOD shown on Page 389.
    ___ (2) For general room lighting use the ZONAL CAVITY METHOD.

ZONAL CAVITY CALCULATIONS METHOD FOR GENERAL LIGHTING

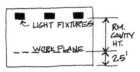

$$\text{ROOM CAVITY RATIO (RCR)} = \frac{(5)\,(H)\,(\text{LENGTH} + \text{WIDTH})}{\text{LENGTH} \times \text{WIDTH}}$$

H = HEIGHT FROM THE WORK PLAN (2.5 FT. ABOVE FLOOR) TO BOTTOM OF LIGHT FIXTURES.

LENGTH & WIDTH = ROOM DIMENSIONS

$$\text{NUMBER OF FIXTURES} = \frac{(\text{FOOTCANDLES}) \times (\text{AREA OF ROOM})}{(\text{LUMENS PER FIXTURE}) \times (CU) \times (\text{MAINT. FACTOR})}$$

FOOTCANDLES = THE DESIRED ILLUMINATION ON THE WORK PLANE. SEE PART 1.

LUMENS PER FIXTURE = (LUMENS PER LAMP) × (NUMBER OF LAMPS IN THE FIXTURE).

CU = COEFFICIENT OF UTILIZATION
    THE COEFFICIENT OF UTILIZATION EXPRESSES THE EFFICIENCY OF THE LIGHT FIXTURE ROOM COMBINATION. IT IS DEPENDENT ON FIXTURE EFFICIENCY, DISTRIBUTION OF LIGHT FROM THE FIXTURE, ROOM SHAPE, AND ROOM SURFACE REFLECTANCES. LIGHT FIXTURE MANUFACTURERS PRINT TABLES LISTING THE CU AS A FUNCTION OF ROOM CAVITY RATIO AND ROOM SURFACE REFLECTANCES FOR EACH INDIVIDUAL LIGHT FIXTURE. SEE NEXT PAGE.

MAINTENANCE FACTOR = VARIES FROM <u>0.85 TO 0.65</u>. THE MAINT. FACTOR ADJUSTS THE CALCULATION FOR THE FACT THAT LAMPS PRODUCE LESS LIGHT AS THEY GET OLDER AND FIXTURES GET DIRTY AND REFLECT LESS LIGHT OUT OF THE FIXTURE.

TYPICAL COEFFICIENTS OF UTILIZATION

INCANDESCENT DOWNLIGHT PATTERN		
ROOM TYPE	HIGH REFL. FIN.	LOW REFL. FIN.
TYP. SMALLER RMS. (MOD. LOW CEILINGS)	0.58 TO 0.68	0.54 TO 0.63
TYP. LARGER ROOMS RELATIVELY HIGH CL'GS	0.60 TO 0.66	0.56 TO 0.63
RELATIVELY LOW CL'G.	0.65 TO 0.70	0.61 TO 0.65

INCANDESCENT PATTERN OF SPHERES		
ROOM TYPE	HIGH REFL. FIN.	LOW REFL. FIN.
TYP. SMALLER RMS. (MOD. LOW CEILINGS)	0.37 TO 0.57	0.25 TO 0.45
TYP. LARGER ROOMS RELATIVELY HIGH CL'G	0.43 TO 0.61	0.30 TO 0.50
RELATIVELY LOW CL'G.	0.57 TO 0.68	0.45 TO 0.61

FLUORESCENT PATTERN OF 2 X 4 FIXTURES		
ROOM TYPE	HIGH REFL. FIN.	LOW REFL. FIN.
TYP. SMALLER RMS. (MOD. LOW CEILINGS)	0.32 TO 0.49	0.22 TO 0.40
TYP. LARGER ROOMS RELATIVELY HIGH CL'G.	0.37 TO 0.52	0.27 TO 0.43
RELATIVELY LOW CL'G.	0.49 TO 0.58	0.40 TO 0.53

FLUORESCENT LUMINOUS CEILING		
ROOM TYPE	HIGH REFL. FIN.	LOW REFL. FIN.
TYP. SMALLER RMS. (MOD. LOW CEILING)	0.23 TO 0.32	0.19 TO 0.29
TYP. LARGER ROOMS RELATIVELY HIGH CL'G.	0.25 TO 0.33	0.21 TO 0.30

FLUORESCENT UPLIGHT		
ROOM TYPE	HIGH REFL. FIN.	LOW REFL. FIN.
NORMALLY NOT USED IN LOW CEILING ROOMS		
TYP. LARGER ROOMS RELATIVELY HIGH CL'G.	0.18 TO 0.33	0.07 TO 0.17
RELATIVELY LOW CL'G.	0.29 TO 0.39	0.14 TO 0.23

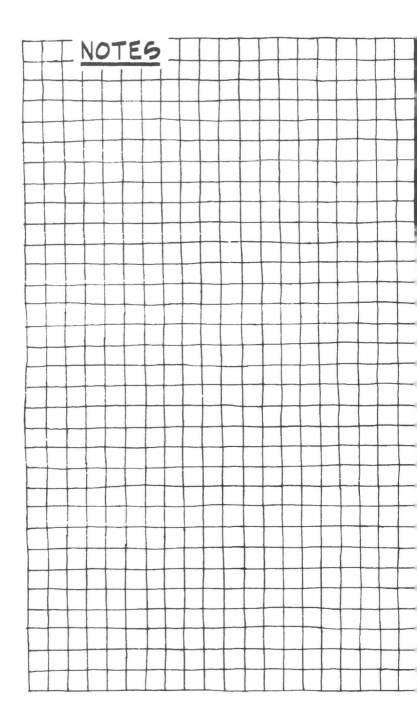

NOTES

For Energy Conservation, see p. 105. For ***Costs,*** see App. A, item K.

___ 1. Electrical Power

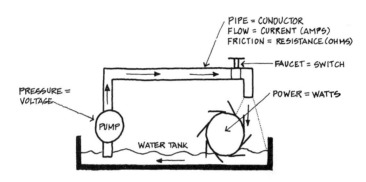

PIPE = CONDUCTOR
FLOW = CURRENT (AMPS)
FRICTION = RESISTANCE (OHMS)
FAUCET = SWITCH
POWER = WATTS
PRESSURE = VOLTAGE
PUMP
WATER TANK

___ *a.* Water analogy (an electrical circuit)
1 volt = Force needed to drive a current of 1 amp through a resistance of 1 ohm.
1 watt = Rate at which electrical energy is consumed in a circuit with a force of 1 volt in a current of 1 amp.

___ *b.* Basic formulas
___ Power formula: Watts = volts × amps
Used to convert wattage ratings of devices to amps. Wires and circuits are rated by amps.
___ Ohm's law:

$$Amps = \frac{volts}{ohms}$$

Devices may draw different amperage even though connected to the same voltage.

___ *c.* *Building power systems* consist of
___ *Transformer* to reduce voltage from utility power grid.
___ *Main switchboard* (sometimes called *service entrance section* or *switchgear*) with main disconnect and distribution through circuit breakers or fused switches.
___ *Subpanels and branch circuits* to distribute power throughout building.

More detailed description based on building size:

___ (1) *Residential and small commercial buildings* typically use *120/240 volt, single-phase* power.

    ___ (*a*) *Transformers* are pole mounted (oil cooled, *18″ dia. × 3′ H*) or for underground system, dry type pad mounted on ground. Both outside building.

    ___ (*b*) *Main switchboard* usually located at power entry to building and typically sized at *20″W × 5″D × 30″H.*

    ___ (*c*) *Branch circuits* should not extend more than *100′* from panel. Panel boards are approx. *20″W × 5″D × 30″ to 60″H.* The max. no. of breakers per panel is *42.*

    ___ (*d*) *Clearance* in front of panels and switch boards is usually *3′ to 6′.*

___ (2) *Medium-sized commercial buildings* typically use *120/208 V, 3-phase* power to operate large motors used for HVAC, etc., as well as to provide 120 V for lights and outlets.

    ___ (*a*) *Transformer* is typically liquid-cooled, pad-mounted outside building and should have *4′* clearance around and be within *30′* of a drive. The size can be approximated by area served:

Area	No. res. units	Pad size
18,000 SF	50	4′ × 4′
60,000 SF	160	4.5′ × 4.5′
180,000 SF		8′ × 8′

    ___ (*b*) *Main switchboard* for lower voltage is approx. *6′W × 2′D × 7′H* (for 2000 amps or less or up to 70,000 SF bld'g.). Provide *3′ to 6′* space in front for access. Higher voltage require access from both sides. *3000 amps* is usually the largest switchboard possible.

___ (*c*) *Branch panels:* For *general* lighting and outlets is same as for residential and small commercial except there are more panels and at least *one per floor.* The panel boards are generally related to the functional groupings of the building.

For *motor* panels, see large buildings.

___ (3) *Large commercial buildings* often use *277/480 V, 3-phase* power. They typically purchase power at higher voltage and step down within the building system.

___ (*a*) *Transformer* is typically owned by the building and located in a vault inside or outside (underground). Vault should be located adjacent to exterior wall, ventilated, fire-rated, and have two exits. Smaller dry transformers located throughout the building will step the 480 V down to 120 V. See below for size.

___ (*b*) *Main switchboard* is approx. *10 to 15′W × 5′D × 7′H* with *4′ to 6′* maintenance space on all sides. Typical sizes of transformer vaults and switchgear rooms:

Commercial building	Residential building	Transformer vault	Switchgear room
100,000 SF	200,000 SF	20′ × 20′ × 11′	30′ × 20′ × 11′
150,000 SF	300,000 SF	(30′ × 30′ × 11′ combination)	
300,000 SF	600,000 SF	20′ × 40′ × 11′	30′ × 40′ × 11′
1,000,000 SF	2,000,000 SF	20′ × 80′ × 11′	30′ × 80′ × 11′

Over *3000 amp,* go to multiple services. XFMR vaults need to be separated from rest of the building by at least *2-hr.* walls.

___ (*c*) *Branch panels*

___ Panels for lighting and outlets will be same as for medium-sized buildings except that they are often located in closets with telephone equip. The area needed is approx. *0.005* × the building area served.

___ Motor controller panel boards for HVAC equip., elev's., and other large equipment are often in (or next to) mechanical room, against a wall. A basic panel module is approx. *1′W × 1.5′D × 7′H.* One module can accommodate 2- to 4-motor control units stacked on top of one another. Smaller motors in isolated locations require individual motor control units approx. *1′W × 6″D × 1.5′H.*

___ (*d*) *Other:* In many bld'gs. an emergency generator is required. Best location is outside near switchgear room. If inside, plan on a room 12′W × 18′ to 22′L. If emergency power is other than for life safety, size requirements can go up greatly. In any case, the generator needs combustion air and possibly cooling.

___ *d.* Miscellaneous items on electrical
___ (1) Circuit symbols on electrical plans

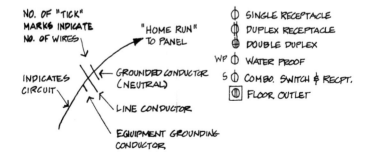

___ (2) Residential
    ___ (*a*) Service drops (overhead lines) must be:
        ___ *10′* above ground or sidewalk
        ___ *15′* above driveways
        ___ *18′* above streets
    ___ (*b*) A min. of *1 wall switch* controlling lighting outlets req'd. in all rooms (but convenience outlets may apply in main rooms).
    ___ (*c*) All rooms require convenience outlet every 12′ along walls, 2′ or longer.
    ___ (*d*) Provide sufficient 15- and 20-amp circuits for min. of *3 watts of power/SF. One* circuit for every *500 to 600 SF.*
    ___ (*e*) A min. of *two* #12 wire (copper), *20-amp* small appliance circuits req'd. pantry, dining, family, extended to kitchen.
    ___ (*f*) A min. of *one* #12 wire, 20-amp circuit req'd. for *laundry* receptacle.
    ___ (*g*) A min. of *one* receptacle per *bathroom* with ground fault circuit interrupter protection (GFCI, required within *6′* of water outlet and at exteriors).
    ___ (*h*) A min. of *one* outlet (GFCI) req'd. in *basement, garage, and patios.*
    ___ (*i*) Provide *smoke detector* in hall outside bedrooms or above stair to upper bedrooms.
    ___ (*j*) Mounting heights:
        Switches, counter receptacles, bath outlets: *4′* AFF
        Laundry: *3′6″* AFF
        Wall convenience outlets: *12″* AFF
___ (3) For outlets and controls req'd. to be *HC accessible,* per *ADA,* place between *18″* and *4′* AFF.
___ (4) Always check room switches against *door swings.*
___ (5) Check flush-mounted wall panels against *wall depth.*

___ (6) Building must always be *grounded* by connecting all metal piping to elect. system, and by connecting elect. system into the ground by either a buried rod or plate outside the building or by a wire in the footing (UFER).

___ (7) Consider *lightning protection* by a system of rods or masts on roof connected to a separate ground and into the building elect. ground system.

___ 2. Building Telephone and Signal Systems

___ a. Small buildings often have a telephone mounting board (TMB) of ¾" plywood with size up to *4′ × 4′*.

___ b. Medium-size buildings often need a telephone closet of *4′ to 6′*.

___ c. Large buildings typically have a *400-SF* telephone terminal room. Secondary distribution points typical throughout building (one per area or floor) usually combined with elect. distribution closets (approx. *0.005 ×* area served).

___ d. *ADA* requires that where public phones are provided, at least *one* must be HC-accessible (1 per floor, 1 per bank of phones). See ADA for special requirements.

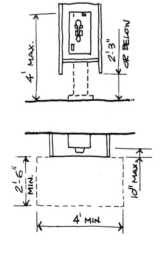

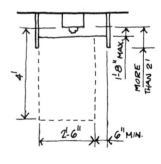

___ 3. Solar Electric (Photovoltaics)

    ___ *a.* Photovoltaics produces electrical energy from *sunlight* via solar electric *panels* facing sunlight (direct or reflected). Although it is most desirable to face these panels into direct sun, they can operate in any sky type of light. *Batteries* store the energy until needed.

    ___ *b.* Because photovoltaics are still *expensive,* they are still presently being used for *remote locations,* such as rural houses away from the power grid.

    ___ *c.* **These type of houses cost about *20 to 30%* above conventional houses. Of the extra cost, about *55 to 60%* is due to photovoltaics and the rest for added energy conservation features to reduce the electric load.**

    ___ *d.* Size collector area at about *10%* of floor area served (*10 watts/SF* of panel). For *retrofits* of less efficient homes, *double or triple* this. If the house is also tied into the *power grid,* then this can all be reduced.

    ___ *e.* Size battery and converter *storage area* at about *1 SF for every 12 SF* of collector area.

    ___ *f.* Collector area is made up of the PV panels, assembled into *modules* and in turn assembled into *arrays.* This should face south *with* a tilt angle within the range of ±15 *deg.* of the site latitude, and be roof- or ground-mounted. A typical PV panel ranges from $13'' \times 4'$ to $4' \times 6'$, but on average is about *6 SF.*

    ___ *g.* Other concerns are no year-around *shadows* on panels; keep collector undersides *cool;* steel-frame mounting for *wind* resistance and, if roof-mounted, prevention of *leaks.*

Costs: **PV presently costs about *$14/watt* (95% M and 5% L). About half is the cost of the electronics and half the cost of structural support. The actual PV system for a house costs about *$10/SF* of the house area. About *10%* of this is for the battery storage, which must be replaced about every *6* years.**

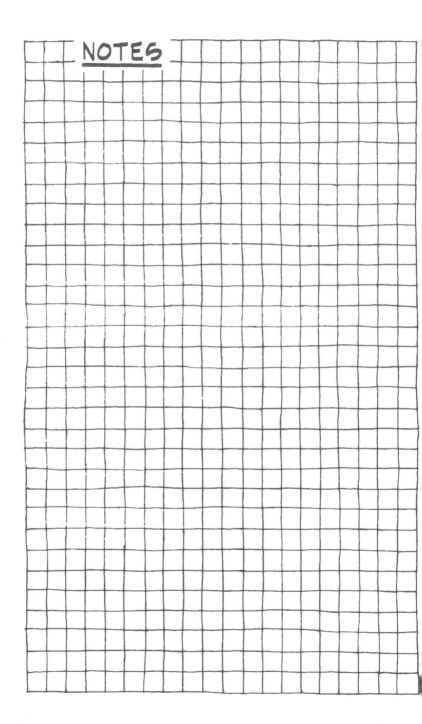

NOTES

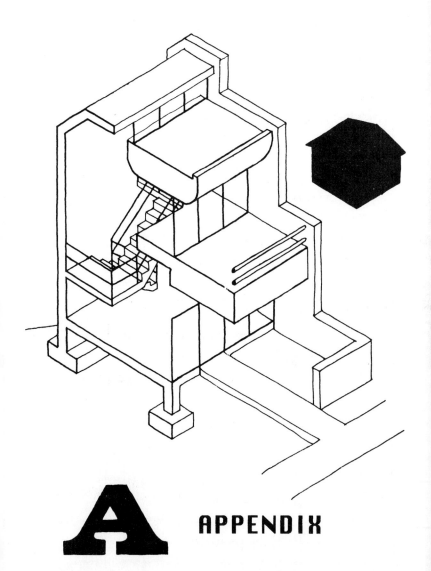

APPENDIX

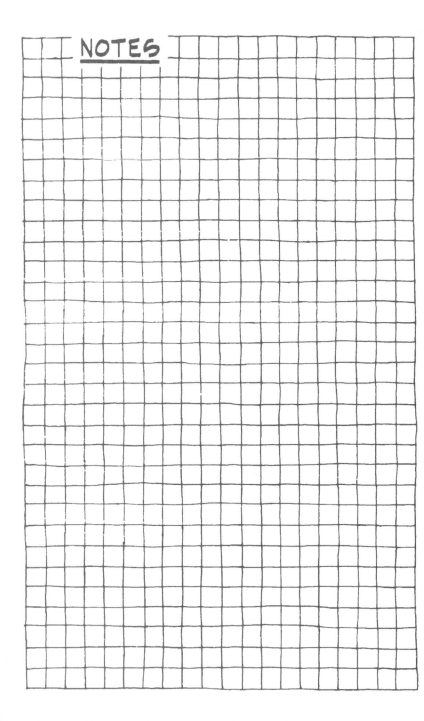

NOTES

___ APPENDIX A BUILDING-TYPE DATA

___ A. *Occupancy type* per UBC. See p. 55. ⟨24⟩

___ B. *Efficiency ratio:* Not published in this edition. See p. 21.

___ C. *Areas* (*SF*): Give typical building areas. ⟨11⟩*

___ D. *Costs* (*$/SF*): Typical SF costs based on areas in item C, above. As a general rule, the projects on the low side do not include any site work or equipment, but projects on the high side may include both. The medium figures do not generally include site work. See p. 25. ⟨11⟩*

___ E. *A/E* (*Architectural/Engineering*) fees (% of item D): Lo equals minimal work, where as high equals comprehensive, detailed services. A highest quality may often go up another 5% from the high shown. In any case, these are rough numbers to begin an estimate of fees. See p. 3. ⟨22⟩

___ F. *FF&E* (*Furniture, Fixture, and Equipment*) *costs* (*$/SF*) are over and above costs given in item D, above, and are for items in buildings, not generally provided by the general contractor. These numbers are for rough beginning planning. See p. 314 and 319.

___ G. *Parking:* Although local zoning ordinances will give exact requirements, these numbers are national standards that can be used for beginning planning. See p. 121.

___ H. *Partition/door density* not published this edition. See p. 256.

___ I. *Fire protection classification* designates what type of sprinklers to use, when required. See p. 364.

___ J. *A/C* (*Air Conditioning*) *loads* are a range, given in SF/Ton. See p. 375. ⟨7⟩

___ K. *Electrical costs* are given in $/SF. See p. 413. ⟨11⟩*

___ L. *Typical power* requirements are given in watts/SF. Typically, lighting takes 20 to 25% of total power. See p. 413.

---

*Data courtesy of BNI Building News. See latest BNI for current data.

APARTMENTS, LOW-RISE (1-3 FL)	Lo	Ave.	High
A. Occupancy Type		R-1	
B. Efficiency Ratio			
C. Area (SF)*	3700	54,000	96,000
D. Costs ($/SF)*	31⁵⁰	49⁰⁵	86¹⁰
E. A/E Fees (% of D)	5	6	8
F. FF&E Costs ($/SF)	3	5	15
G. Parking (CAR/D.U.)	0.3	1	1.5
H. Partition/Door			
I. Fire Prot. Class		LIGHT	
J. A/C (SF/Ton)	400		500
K. Elect. Costs ($/SF)*	2⁴⁰	2⁹⁰	10²⁰
L. Typ. Power (Watts/SF)	20		25
M. Other			

APARTMENTS, MID-RISE (4-7A)	Lo	Ave.	High
A. Occupancy Type			
B. Efficiency Ratio			
C. Area (SF)*	61,000	88,000	105,000
D. Costs ($/SF)*	40⁰⁵	61¹⁰	87¹²
E. A/E Fees (% of D)			
F. FF&E Costs ($/SF)			
G. Parking			
H. Partition/Door			
I. Fire Prot. Class			
J. A/C (SF/Ton)			
K. Elect. Costs ($/SF)*			
L. Typ. Power (Watts/SF)			
M. Other			

APARTMENTS, HIGH-RISE (8-24 FL)	Lo	Ave.	High
A. Occupancy Type			
B. Efficiency Ratio			
C. Area (SF)*	94,000	190,000	370,000
D. Costs ($/SF)*	51⁰⁰	73⁰⁰	99⁴⁰
E. A/E Fees (% of D)			
F. FF&E Costs ($/SF)			
G. Parking			
H. Partition/Door			
I. Fire Prot. Class			
J. A/C (SF/Ton)			
K. Elect. Costs ($/SF)*			
L. Typ. Power (Watts/SF)			
M. Other			

AUDITORIUMS	Lo	Ave.	High
A. Occupancy Type	A-1	7b	A-3
B. Efficiency Ratio			
C. Area (SF)*	9900	29,000	66,700
D. Costs ($/SF)*	120	140	180
E. A/E Fees (% of D)	6	7	9
F. FF&E Costs ($/SF)			
G. Parking			
H. Partition/Door			
I. Fire Prot. Class		LIGHT	
J. A/C (SF/Ton)	150		200
K. Elect. Costs ($/SF)*	10²⁰	15⁴⁰	20¹²
L. Typ. Power (Watts/SF)	20		25
M. Other	ADA REQUIRES CERTAIN NO. SEATS TO BE ACCESS.		

*Data courtesy of BNI Building News. See latest BNI for current data.

AUTO SALES

	Lo	Ave.	High
A. Occupancy Type		B-4	
B. Efficiency Ratio			
C. Area (SF)*	7,700	26,300	53,600
D. Costs ($/SF)*	35⁹⁵	44⁵⁰	60⁵⁰
E. A/E Fees (% of D)			
F. FF&E Costs ($/SF)	1	2⁵⁰	5⁵⁰
G. Parking			
H. Partition/Door			
I. Fire Prot. Class		LIGHT	
J. A/C (SF/Ton)	250		300
K. Elect. Costs ($/SF)*	4⁵⁵	8⁰⁰	9⁵⁰
L. Typ. Power (Watts/SF)	15		25
M. Other			

BANKS

	Lo	Ave.	High
A. Occupancy Type		B-2	
B. Efficiency Ratio		1.4	
C. Area (SF)*	2,900	7,000	95,000
D. Costs ($/SF)*	69⁹⁵	102⁵⁰	180⁰⁰
E. A/E Fees (% of D)	6	10	12
F. FF&E Costs ($/SF)	10	15	20
G. Parking (PER 1000 SF)	2.5	3	3.5
H. Partition/Door			
I. Fire Prot. Class		LIGHT	
J. A/C (SF/Ton)	250		300
K. Elect. Costs ($/SF)*	7²⁰	13⁶⁰	17⁹⁰
L. Typ. Power (Watts/SF)	15		20
M. Other			

CHURCHES

	Lo	Ave.	High
A. Occupancy Type	A-1	TO	A-3
B. Efficiency Ratio			
C. Area (SF)*	4,100	13,400	42,700
D. Costs ($/SF)*	60⁶⁰	87⁸⁰	142⁰⁰
E. A/E Fees (% of D)	5	8.5	12
F. FF&E Costs ($/SF)	see page 320		
G. Parking (PER OCC.)	0.1	0.5	0.6
H. Partition/Door			
I. Fire Prot. Class		LIGHT	
J. A/C (SF/Ton)	150		200
K. Elect. Costs ($/SF)*	4⁸⁰	8¹⁰	12³³
L. Typ. Power (Watts/SF)	20		25
M. Other			

CLUBS, COUNTRY

	Lo	Ave.	High
A. Occupancy Type	A-1	TO	A-3
B. Efficiency Ratio			
C. Area (SF)*			
D. Costs ($/SF)*			
E. A/E Fees (% of D)	4	7	9
F. FF&E Costs ($/SF)	15	20	25
G. Parking (PER 1000 SF)		0.4	
H. Partition/Door			
I. Fire Prot. Class		LIGHT	
J. A/C (SF/Ton)	100		200
K. Elect. Costs ($/SF)*			
L. Typ. Power (Watts/SF)	20		25
M. Other			

*Data courtesy of BNI Building News. See latest BNI for current data.

CLUB, SOCIAL

	Lo	Ave.	High
A. Occupancy Type			
B. Efficiency Ratio			
C. Area (SF)*	9,900	14,000	21,200
D. Costs ($/SF)*	60.09	83.34	107.99
E. A/E Fees (% of D)			
F. FF&E Costs ($/SF)			
G. Parking			
H. Partition/Door			
I. Fire Prot. Class			
J. A/C (SF/Ton)			
K. Elect. Costs ($/SF)*			
L. Typ. Power (Watts/SF)			
M. Other SEE COUNTRY CLUB			

CLUB, HEALTH

	Lo	Ave.	High
A. Occupancy Type			
B. Efficiency Ratio			
C. Area (SF)*	15,900	30,100	66,400
D. Costs ($/SF)*	45.31	61.99	120.09
E. A/E Fees (% of D)			
F. FF&E Costs ($/SF)			
G. Parking			
H. Partition/Door			
I. Fire Prot. Class			
J. A/C (SF/Ton)			
K. Elect. Costs ($/SF)*			
L. Typ. Power (Watts/SF)			
M. Other SEE COUNTRY CLUB			

COLLEGE, CLASSROOMS & ADM.

	Lo	Ave.	High
A. Occupancy Type			
B. Efficiency Ratio			
C. Area (SF)*	35,400	80,100	248,000
D. Costs ($/SF)*	74.58	96.09	160.09
E. A/E Fees (% of D)	4	6.5	9
F. FF&E Costs ($/SF)			
G. Parking (PER STUDENT)		0.45	
H. Partition/Door			
I. Fire Prot. Class		LIGHT	
J. A/C (SF/Ton)	150		200
K. Elect. Costs ($/SF)*	9.75	10.20	15.10
L. Typ. Power (Watts/SF)	15		25
M. Other			

COLLEGE, LABORATORIES

	Lo	Ave.	High
A. Occupancy Type			
B. Efficiency Ratio			
C. Area (SF)*	9,200	42,000	89,300
D. Costs ($/SF)*	150.09	165.09	190.09
E. A/E Fees (% of D)			
F. FF&E Costs ($/SF)			
G. Parking			
H. Partition/Door			
I. Fire Prot. Class			
J. A/C (SF/Ton)			
K. Elect. Costs ($/SF)*			
L. Typ. Power (Watts/SF)	15		20
M. Other			

*Data courtesy of BNI Building News. See latest BNI for current data.

COLLEGE, STUDENT UNION	Lo	Ave.	High
A. Occupancy Type			
B. Efficiency Ratio			
C. Area (SF)*	44,600	90,000	187,000
D. Costs ($/SF)*	78.40	110.00	148.00
E. A/E Fees (% of D)			
F. FF&E Costs ($/SF)			
G. Parking			
H. Partition/Door			
I. Fire Prot. Class			
J. A/C (SF/Ton)			
K. Elect. Costs ($/SF)*			
L. Typ. Power (Watts/SF)	20		25
M. Other			

COMMUNITY CENTER	Lo	Ave.	High
A. Occupancy Type			
B. Efficiency Ratio			
C. Area (SF)*	6000	34,000	206,000
D. Costs ($/SF)*	69.00	98.50	152.00
E. A/E Fees (% of D)	6	8	12
F. FF&E Costs ($/SF)	8	12	18
G. Parking (PER 1000 SF)	3	4	5
H. Partition/Door			
I. Fire Prot. Class		LIGHT	
J. A/C (SF/Ton)	150		200
K. Elect. Costs ($/SF)*	3.10	7.90	12.60
L. Typ. Power (Watts/SF)	20		25
M. Other			

COURT HOUSE	Lo	Ave.	High
A. Occupancy Type			
B. Efficiency Ratio			
C. Area (SF)*	12,300	31,600	332,000
D. Costs ($/SF)*	92.40	112	137.20
E. A/E Fees (% of D)			
F. FF&E Costs ($/SF)			
G. Parking			
H. Partition/Door			
I. Fire Prot. Class		LIGHT	
J. A/C (SF/Ton)	150		200
K. Elect. Costs ($/SF)*	9.90	12.50	14.00
L. Typ. Power (Watts/SF)	20		25
M. Other			

DEPARTMENT STORE / SHOP'G CTR.	Lo	Ave.	High
A. Occupancy Type		B-2	
B. Efficiency Ratio			
C. Area (SF)*	9,700	67,200	620,000
D. Costs ($/SF)*	32.80	47.00	75.40
E. A/E Fees (% of D)*	4	6.5	8
F. FF&E Costs ($/SF)*			
G. Parking (PER 1000 SF)	4	5	5.5
H. Partition/Door			
I. Fire Prot. Class		ORDINARY	
J. A/C (SF/Ton)	200		300
K. Elect. Costs ($/SF)*	3.20	4.10	7.10
L. Typ. Power (Watts/SF)	10		15
M. Other SEE PART 14 ON ADA ELEVATOR REQUIREMENTS			

*Data courtesy of BNI Building News. See latest BNI for current data.

427

DORMITORIES, LOW-RISE (1-3 FL)

	Lo	Ave.	High
A. Occupancy Type		R-1	
B. Efficiency Ratio			
C. Area (SF)*			
D. Costs ($/SF)*			
E. A/E Fees (% of D) SEE PAGE 321	4	6	8
F. FF&E Costs ($/SF)			
G. Parking			
H. Partition/Door			
I. Fire Prot. Class		LIGHT	
J. A/C (SF/Ton)	400		500
K. Elect. Costs ($/SF)*			
L. Typ. Power (Watts/SF)	10		15
M. Other			

DORMITORIES, MID-RISE (4-8 FL)

	Lo	Ave.	High
A. Occupancy Type			
B. Efficiency Ratio			
C. Area (SF)*			
D. Costs ($/SF)*			
E. A/E Fees (% of D)			
F. FF&E Costs ($/SF)			
G. Parking			
H. Partition/Door			
I. Fire Prot. Class			
J. A/C (SF/Ton)			
K. Elect. Costs ($/SF)*			
L. Typ. Power (Watts/SF)			
M. Other			

FACTORIES

	Lo	Ave.	High
A. Occupancy Type	B-2 OR 4		H-3
B. Efficiency Ratio			
C. Area (SF)*	14,300	43,600	186,000
D. Costs ($/SF)*	30.49	51.72	74.50
E. A/E Fees (% of D)	4	8	12
F. FF&E Costs ($/SF)			
G. Parking (PER 1000 SF)	0.75	1.5	2.5
H. Partition/Door			
I. Fire Prot. Class	ORD.-1		EXTRA-2
J. A/C (SF/Ton)	100		150
K. Elect. Costs ($/SF)*	3.60	5.12	14.40
L. Typ. Power (Watts/SF)	25		40
M. Other			

FIRE STATIONS

	Lo	Ave.	High
A. Occupancy Type		B-2	
B. Efficiency Ratio			
C. Area (SF)*	6900	8400	9,600
D. Costs ($/SF)*	98	105	130
E. A/E Fees (% of D)			
F. FF&E Costs ($/SF)			
G. Parking			
H. Partition/Door			
I. Fire Prot. Class			
J. A/C (SF/Ton)	200		300
K. Elect. Costs ($/SF)*	10.12	11.50	14.40
L. Typ. Power (Watts/SF)	10		15
M. Other			

*Data courtesy of BNI Building News. See latest BNI for current data.

FRATERNITY HOUSE

	Lo	Ave	High
A. Occupancy Type		R-1	
B. Efficiency Ratio			
C. Area (SF)*			
D. Costs ($/SF)*			
E. A/E Fees (% of D)	5	15	25
F. FF&E Costs ($/SF)			
G. Parking			
H. Partition/Door			
I. Fire Prot. Class		LIGHT	
J. A/C (SF/Ton)	300		400
K. Elect. Costs ($/SF)*			
L. Typ. Power (Watts/SF)	10		15
M. Other			

GARAGE / COMMERCIAL SERVICE

	Lo	Ave	High
A. Occupancy Type			
B. Efficiency Ratio			
C. Area (SF)*			
D. Costs ($/SF)*			
E. A/E Fees (% of D)	5	5.5	8
F. FF&E Costs ($/SF)			
G. Parking			
H. Partition/Door			
I. Fire Prot. Class		ORD-1	
J. A/C (SF/Ton)			
K. Elect. Costs ($/SF)*			
L. Typ. Power (Watts/SF)			
M. Other			

FUNERAL HOME

	Lo	Ave	High
A. Occupancy Type			
B. Efficiency Ratio			
C. Area (SF)*			
D. Costs ($/SF)*			
E. A/E Fees (% of D)			
F. FF&E Costs ($/SF)			
G. Parking			
H. Partition/Door			
I. Fire Prot. Class			
J. A/C (SF/Ton)	200	300	
K. Elect. Costs ($/SF)*			
L. Typ. Power (Watts/SF)	20	25	
M. Other			

GARAGE / MUNICIPAL REPAIR

	Lo	Ave	High
A. Occupancy Type			
B. Efficiency Ratio			
C. Area (SF)*			
D. Costs ($/SF)*			
E. A/E Fees (% of D)			
F. FF&E Costs ($/SF)			
G. Parking			
H. Partition/Door			
I. Fire Prot. Class			
J. A/C (SF/Ton)			
K. Elect. Costs ($/SF)*			
L. Typ. Power (Watts/SF)			
M. Other			

*Data courtesy of BNI Building News. See latest BNI for current data.

429

GARAGE, PARKING

	Lo	Ave.	High
A. Occupancy Type			
B. Efficiency Ratio			
C. Area (SF)*	66,000	164,000	562,700
D. Costs ($/SF)*	18.12	20.97	32.50
E. A/E Fees (% of D)			
F. FF&E Costs ($/SF)			
G. Parking (PER 1000 SF)			
H. Partition/Door			
I. Fire Prot. Class			
J. A/C (SF/Ton)			
K. Elect. Costs ($/SF)*	.74	.95	1.10
L. Typ. Power (Watts/SF)	3	5	
M. Other			

HOSPITAL

	Lo	Ave.	High
A. Occupancy Type		I-1	
B. Efficiency Ratio			
C. Area (SF)*	22,000	180,000	772,000
D. Costs ($/SF)*	97.12	140.02	192.02
E. A/E Fees (% of D)	4	6.5	9
F. FF&E Costs ($/SF)			
G. Parking (PER BED)	0.75	1.8	3
H. Partition/Door			
I. Fire Prot. Class		LIGHT	
J. A/C (SF/Ton)	150		250
K. Elect. Costs ($/SF)*	12.02	23.02	28.02
L. Typ. Power (Watts/SF)	25		35
M. Other			

GYMNASIUMS

	Lo	Ave.	High
A. Occupancy Type			
B. Efficiency Ratio			
C. Area (SF)*	38,100	160,000	283,000
D. Costs ($/SF)*	70.52	104.02	130.02
E. A/E Fees (% of D)	6	6.5	9
F. FF&E Costs ($/SF)			
G. Parking (PER 1000 SF)		5	
H. Partition/Door			
I. Fire Prot. Class			
J. A/C (SF/Ton)	100		200
K. Elect. Costs ($/SF)*	3.60	7.20	12.02
L. Typ. Power (Watts/SF)	20		25
M. Other			

HOUSING, ELDERLY

	Lo	Ave.	High
A. Occupancy Type	R-1		R-3
B. Efficiency Ratio			
C. Area (SF)*	16,800	64,000	290,000
D. Costs ($/SF)*	72.02	90.02	102.02
E. A/E Fees (% of D)	5	6	8
F. FF&E Costs ($/SF)			
G. Parking (CAR PER DU)	0.3	1.0	1.5
H. Partition/Door			
I. Fire Prot. Class		LIGHT	
J. A/C (SF/Ton)	400		500
K. Elect. Costs ($/SF)*	8.52	10.52	14.02
L. Typ. Power (Watts/SF)	10		15
M. Other			

*Data courtesy of BNI Building News. See latest BNI for current data.

HOUSING, PUBLIC, LOW-RISE

	Lo	Ave.	High
A. Occupancy Type	R-1	R-3	
B. Efficiency Ratio			
C. Area (SF)*	23,700	70,600	105,200
D. Costs ($/SF)*	31.65	49.00	78.00
E. A/E Fees (% of D)	5	6	8
F. FF&E Costs ($/SF)	3	3	5
G. Parking (PER D.U.)	0.3	1.0	1.5
H. Partition/Door			
I. Fire Prot. Class		LIGHT	
J. A/C (SF/Ton)	400		500
K. Elect. Costs ($/SF)*			
L. Typ. Power (Watts/SF)	10		15
M. Other			

ICE-SKATING RINKS

	Lo	Ave.	High
A. Occupancy Type			
B. Efficiency Ratio			
C. Area (SF)*			
D. Costs ($/SF)*			
E. A/E Fees (% of D)	4	7	8
F. FF&E Costs ($/SF)			
G. Parking			
H. Partition/Door			
I. Fire Prot. Class			
J. A/C (SF/Ton)			
K. Elect. Costs ($/SF)*			
L. Typ. Power (Watts/SF)	20		30
M. Other			

JAILS

	Lo	Ave.	High
A. Occupancy Type		I-3	
B. Efficiency Ratio			
C. Area (SF)*	44,600	66,000	360,000
D. Costs ($/SF)*	88.00	102.00	134.00
E. A/E Fees (% of D)			
F. FF&E Costs ($/SF)			
G. Parking			
H. Partition/Door			
I. Fire Prot. Class		LIGHT	
J. A/C (SF/Ton)	250		300
K. Elect. Costs ($/SF)*	12.00	15.00	17.00
L. Typ. Power (Watts/SF)	15		25
M. Other			

LIBRARIES

	Lo	Ave.	High
A. Occupancy Type			
B. Efficiency Ratio			
C. Area (SF)*	6,900	30,100	176,000
D. Costs ($/SF)*	77.00	101.00	140.00
E. A/E Fees (% of D)		SEE PAGE 321	
F. FF&E Costs ($/SF)			
G. Parking			
H. Partition/Door			
I. Fire Prot. Class		LIGHT	
J. A/C (SF/Ton)	250		300
K. Elect. Costs ($/SF)*	7.00	12.50	17.00
L. Typ. Power (Watts/SF)	15		25
M. Other *AT STACKS			

*Data courtesy of BNI Building News. See latest BNI for current data.

MEDICAL CLINICS

	Lo	Ave.	High
A. Occupancy Type			
B. Efficiency Ratio			
C. Area (SF)*			
D. Costs ($/SF)*			
E. A/E Fees (% of D)	6	8	9
F. FF&E Costs ($/SF)	8	12	25
G. Parking (PER 1000 SF)	1.5	3	5
H. Partition/Door			
I. Fire Prot. Class		LIGHT	
J. A/C (SF/Ton)	250		350
K. Elect. Costs ($/SF)*			20
L. Typ. Power (Watts/SF)	15		
M. Other SEE PART 14 ON ADA ELEVATOR REQUIREMENTS			

MEDICAL OFFICE

	Lo	Ave.	High
A. Occupancy Type			
B. Efficiency Ratio			
C. Area (SF)*			
D. Costs ($/SF)*			
E. A/E Fees (% of D)			
F. FF&E Costs ($/SF)			
G. Parking			
H. Partition/Door			
I. Fire Prot. Class			
J. A/C (SF/Ton)			
K. Elect. Costs ($/SF)*			
L. Typ. Power (Watts/SF)			
M. Other SEE MEDICAL CLINICS			

MOTELS

	Lo	Ave.	High
A. Occupancy Type		R-1	
B. Efficiency Ratio			
C. Area (SF)*	57,400	75,900	277,000
D. Costs ($/SF)*	44.32	66.32	76.82
E. A/E Fees (% of D)	3	4	6
F. FF&E Costs ($/SF)	13	17	21
G. Parking (PER P.U.)	0.4	0.8	1.6
H. Partition/Door			
I. Fire Prot. Class		LIGHT	
J. A/C (SF/Ton)	400		500
K. Elect. Costs ($/SF)*	5.40	6.80	7.40
L. Typ. Power (Watts/SF)	15		20
M. Other ALSO, SEE PAGE 321			

NURSING HOMES

	Lo	Ave.	High
A. Occupancy Type	I-1	OR	I-2
B. Efficiency Ratio			
C. Area (SF)*	12,000	32,000	64,000
D. Costs ($/SF)*	92.42	110.02	140.02
E. A/E Fees (% of D)	5	8	11.5
F. FF&E Costs ($/SF)			
G. Parking (PER P.U.)	0.25	0.3	0.35
H. Partition/Door			
I. Fire Prot. Class		LIGHT	
J. A/C (SF/Ton)	200		250
K. Elect. Costs ($/SF)*	15		25
L. Typ. Power (Watts/SF)			
M. Other			

*Data courtesy of BNI Building News. See latest BNI for current data.

OFFICE, LOW-RISE (1-4 FL)	Lo	Ave.	High
A. Occupancy Type		B-2	
B. Efficiency Ratio			
C. Area (SF)*	2,600	11,300	36,500
D. Costs ($/SF)*	44⁹²	63⁵²	105⁵²
E. A/E Fees (% of D)	3	6.5	10
F. FF&E Costs ($/SF)	20	25	35
G. Parking (PER 1000SF)	1.66	2.6	3.5
H. Partition/Door			
I. Fire Prot. Class		LIGHT	
J. A/C (SF/Ton)	250		300
K. Elect. Costs ($/SF)*	3⁵²	6⁹²	10⁴⁰
L. Typ. Power (Watts/SF)	15		20
M. Other			

OFFICE, MID-RISE (5-10 FL)	Lo	Ave.	High
A. Occupancy Type		B-2	
B. Efficiency Ratio			
C. Area (SF)*	36,500	50,400	100,000
D. Costs ($/SF)*	48⁶²	62⁰²	115⁹⁹
E. A/E Fees (% of D)			
F. FF&E Costs ($/SF)			
G. Parking			
H. Partition/Door			
I. Fire Prot. Class			
J. A/C (SF/Ton)			
K. Elect. Costs ($/SF)*	4²²	6¹⁵	11¹²
L. Typ. Power (Watts/SF)			
M. Other SEE OFFICE, LOW RISE			

OFFICE, HIGH-RISE (+10 FL)	Lo	Ave.	High
A. Occupancy Type		B-2	
B. Efficiency Ratio			
C. Area (SF)*	100,000	203,000	733,000
D. Costs ($/SF)*	58⁰²	87⁹²	175⁵²
E. A/E Fees (% of D)			
F. FF&E Costs ($/SF)			
G. Parking			
H. Partition/Door			
I. Fire Prot. Class			
J. A/C (SF/Ton)			
K. Elect. Costs ($/SF)*	5⁹²	7³²	15⁹²
L. Typ. Power (Watts/SF)			
M. Other SEE OFFICE, LOW-RISE			

POLICE STATIONS	Lo	Ave.	High
A. Occupancy Type		B-2	
B. Efficiency Ratio			
C. Area (SF)*			
D. Costs ($/SF)*			
E. A/E Fees (% of D)			
F. FF&E Costs ($/SF)			
G. Parking			
H. Partition/Door			
I. Fire Prot. Class			
J. A/C (SF/Ton)	250		300
K. Elect. Costs ($/SF)*			
L. Typ. Power (Watts/SF)	15		20
M. Other			

*Data courtesy of BNI Building News. See latest BNI for current data.

POST OFFICE	Lo	Ave.	High
A. Occupancy Type			
B. Efficiency Ratio			
C. Area (SF)*	12,300	18,000	23,000
D. Costs ($/SF)*	75.00	92.00	110.00
E. A/E Fees (% of D)			
F. FF&E Costs ($/SF)			
G. Parking			
H. Partition/Door			
I. Fire Prot. Class			
J. A/C (SF/Ton)	200		275
K. Elect. Costs ($/SF)*			
L. Typ. Power (Watts/SF)	15		25
M. Other			

RESEARCH LABORATORIES	Lo	Ave.	High
A. Occupancy Type		H-6	
B. Efficiency Ratio			
C. Area (SF)*	89,000	114,000	140,000
D. Costs ($/SF)*	93.00	120.00	139.00
E. A/E Fees (% of D)			
F. FF&E Costs ($/SF)			
G. Parking			
H. Partition/Door			
I. Fire Prot. Class		LIGHT	
J. A/C (SF/Ton)	100		250
K. Elect. Costs ($/SF)*	7.00	10.00	35.00
L. Typ. Power (Watts/SF)	15		25
M. Other			

RELIGIOUS EDUCATION	Lo	Ave.	High
A. Occupancy Type			
B. Efficiency Ratio			
C. Area (SF)*			
D. Costs ($/SF)*			
E. A/E Fees (% of D)			
F. FF&E Costs ($/SF)			
G. Parking			
H. Partition/Door			
I. Fire Prot. Class		LIGHT	
J. A/C (SF/Ton)	150		200
K. Elect. Costs ($/SF)*			
L. Typ. Power (Watts/SF)	15		20
M. Other			

RESTAURANTS	Lo	Ave.	High
A. Occupancy Type	A-1 or 2		B-2
B. Efficiency Ratio			
C. Area (SF)*	5800	7600	10600
D. Costs ($/SF)*	83.00	110.00	200.00
E. A/E Fees (% of D)	3.5	6	8
F. FF&E Costs ($/SF)	10	15	20
G. Parking (per 100 sf)	10	15	21.5
H. Partition/Door			
I. Fire Prot. Class		LIGHT	
J. A/C (SF/Ton)	150		200
K. Elect. Costs ($/SF)*	9.00	12.00	17.00
L. Typ. Power (Watts/SF)	15		30
M. Other			

*Data courtesy of BNI Building News. See latest BNI for current data.

RETAIL STORE

	Lo	Ave.	High
A. Occupancy Type		B-2 or 4	
B. Efficiency Ratio			
C. Area (SF)*	1,000	30,000	154,000
D. Costs ($/SF)*	39.00	72.00	150.50
E. A/E Fees (% of D)	4	6	9
F. FF&E Costs ($/SF)	10	20	30
G. Parking (per 1000 SF)	3.5	4.5	5.5
H. Partition/Door			
I. Fire Prot. Class		ORD. 2	
J. A/C (SF/Ton)	250	520	300
K. Elect. Costs ($/SF)*	4.00	5.00	15.00
L. Typ. Power (Watts/SF)	10		15
M. Other			

SCHOOLS, ELEMENTARY

	Lo	Ave.	High
A. Occupancy Type	B-2		E-1 or E-2
B. Efficiency Ratio			
C. Area (SF)*	18,000	40,000	91,400
D. Costs ($/SF)*	66.00	71.00	100.00
E. A/E Fees (% of D)	6	7.5	9
F. FF&E Costs ($/SF)			
G. Parking			
H. Partition/Door			
I. Fire Prot. Class		LIGHT	
J. A/C (SF/Ton)	150		250
K. Elect. Costs ($/SF)*	4.00	6.00	11.00
L. Typ. Power (Watts/SF)	15		25
M. Other			

SCHOOLS, JR. HIGH & MIDDLE

	Lo	Ave.	High
A. Occupancy Type		SEE ELEMENTARY	
B. Efficiency Ratio			
C. Area (SF)*	26,000	52,800	123,700
D. Costs ($/SF)*	64.00	89.00	110.00
E. A/E Fees (% of D)			
F. FF&E Costs ($/SF)			
G. Parking			
H. Partition/Door			
I. Fire Prot. Class			
J. A/C (SF/Ton)			
K. Elect. Costs ($/SF)*	6.00	8.00	12.00
L. Typ. Power (Watts/SF)			
M. Other			

SCHOOLS, SR. HIGH

	Lo	Ave.	High
A. Occupancy Type		SEE ELEMENTARY	
B. Efficiency Ratio			
C. Area (SF)*	116,000	184,000	431,700
D. Costs ($/SF)*	57.00	75.00	132,000
E. A/E Fees (% of D)			
F. FF&E Costs ($/SF)			
G. Parking (per student)		0.5	
H. Partition/Door			
I. Fire Prot. Class			
J. A/C (SF/Ton)			
K. Elect. Costs ($/SF)*	7.00	8.00	13.00
L. Typ. Power (Watts/SF)			
M. Other			

*Data courtesy of BNI Building News. See latest BNI for current data.

SCHOOLS, VOCATIONAL

	Lo	Ave.	High
A. Occupancy Type		SEE ELEMENTARY	
B. Efficiency Ratio			
C. Area (SF)*			
D. Costs ($/SF)*			
E. A/E Fees (% of D)			
F. FF&E Costs ($/SF)			
G. Parking (PER STUDENT)		0.5	
H. Partition/Door			
I. Fire Prot. Class			
J. A/C (SF/Ton)			
K. Elect. Costs ($/SF)*			
L. Typ. Power (Watts/SF)			
M. Other			

SPORTS ARENAS

	Lo	Ave.	High
A. Occupancy Type		A-4	
B. Efficiency Ratio			
C. Area (SF)*			
D. Costs ($/SF)*			
E. A/E Fees (% of D)			
F. FF&E Costs ($/SF)			
G. Parking			
H. Partition/Door			
I. Fire Prot. Class		LIGHT	
J. A/C (SF/Ton)	100		200
K. Elect. Costs ($/SF)*			
L. Typ. Power (Watts/SF)	25		30
M. Other			

SUPERMARKETS

	Lo	Ave.	High
A. Occupancy Type		B-4	
B. Efficiency Ratio			
C. Area (SF)*			
D. Costs ($/SF)*			
E. A/E Fees (% of D)	3	7	7.5
F. FF&E Costs ($/SF)			
G. Parking			
H. Partition/Door			
I. Fire Prot. Class		0.20	
J. A/C (SF/Ton)			
K. Elect. Costs ($/SF)*			
L. Typ. Power (Watts/SF)	20		25
M. Other			

SWIMMING POOLS

	Lo	Ave.	High
A. Occupancy Type			
B. Efficiency Ratio			
C. Area (SF)*			
D. Costs ($/SF)*			
E. A/E Fees (% of D)	5	8	9.5
F. FF&E Costs ($/SF)			
G. Parking (PER ACRE)		20	
H. Partition/Door			
I. Fire Prot. Class			
J. A/C (SF/Ton)		100	
K. Elect. Costs ($/SF)*			
L. Typ. Power (Watts/SF)	10		15
M. Other			

*Data courtesy of BNI Building News. See latest BNI for current data.

TELEPHONE EXCHANGES

	Lo	Ave.	High
A. Occupancy Type			
B. Efficiency Ratio			
C. Area (SF)*			
D. Costs ($/SF)*			
E. A/E Fees (% of D)			
F. FF&E Costs ($/SF)			
G. Parking			
H. Partition/Door			
I. Fire Prot. Class			
J. A/C (SF/Ton)	100		150
K. Elect. Costs ($/SF)*			
L. Typ. Power (Watts/SF)	20		25
M. Other			

TERMINALS, BUS

	Lo	Ave.	High
A. Occupancy Type			
B. Efficiency Ratio			
C. Area (SF)*			
D. Costs ($/SF)*			
E. A/E Fees (% of D)			
F. FF&E Costs ($/SF)			
G. Parking			
H. Partition/Door			
I. Fire Prot. Class			
J. A/C (SF/Ton)			
K. Elect. Costs ($/SF)*			
L. Typ. Power (Watts/SF)	15		25
M. Other			

THEATER

	Lo	Ave.	High
A. Occupancy Type		A-1, 2 or 3	
B. Efficiency Ratio			
C. Area (SF)*	18,000	19,000	22,500
D. Costs ($/SF)*	6.19	8.20	9.42
E. A/E Fees (% of D)	6	7	9
F. FF&E Costs ($/SF)	SEE PAGES 315 & 321		
G. Parking (per seat)	0.1	0.25	0.5
H. Partition/Door			
I. Fire Prot. Class		LIGHT	
J. A/C (SF/Ton)	150		200
K. Elect. Costs ($/SF)*			
L. Typ. Power (Watts/SF)	20		25
M. Other			

TOWN HALL

	Lo	Ave.	High
A. Occupancy Type			
B. Efficiency Ratio			
C. Area (SF)*	12,300	46,000	78,000
D. Costs ($/SF)*	90	101	110
E. A/E Fees (% of D)			
F. FF&E Costs ($/SF)			
G. Parking (per 1000 SF)	1.0	3.5	8
H. Partition/Door			
I. Fire Prot. Class		LIGHT	
J. A/C (SF/Ton)	200		300
K. Elect. Costs ($/SF)*	9.20	10.20	14.20
L. Typ. Power (Watts/SF)	15		25
M. Other			

*Data courtesy of BNI Building News. See latest BNI for current data.

*See latest BNI for current data.

WAREHOUSE & STOR. BLD'G	Lo	Ave.	High
A. Occupancy Type	B-2 OR 4		H-3
B. Efficiency Ratio			
C. Area (SF)*	14,000	40,500	400,000
D. Costs ($/SF)*	17.50	31.80	47.25
E. A/E Fees (% of D)	4	5.5	8
F. FF&E Costs ($/SF)			
G. Parking (PER 1000 SF)	1.5	2	2.5
H. Partition/Door			
I. Fire Prot. Class	LIGHT		ORD.-3
J. A/C (SF/Ton)			
K. Elect. Costs ($/SF)*			
L. Typ. Power (Watts/SF)	10		15
M. Other			

WAREHOUSE + OFFICE	Lo	Ave.	High
A. Occupancy Type		SEE WAREHOUSE	
B. Efficiency Ratio			
C. Area (SF)*			
D. Costs ($/SF)*	17.50	31.80	47.25
E. A/E Fees (% of D)			
F. FF&E Costs ($/SF)			
G. Parking			
H. Partition/Door			
I. Fire Prot. Class			
J. A/C (SF/Ton)			
K. Elect. Costs ($/SF)*			
L. Typ. Power (Watts/SF)			
M. Other			

	Lo	Ave.	High
A. Occupancy Type			
B. Efficiency Ratio			
C. Area (SF)*			
D. Costs ($/SF)*			
E. A/E Fees (% of D)			
F. FF&E Costs ($/SF)			
G. Parking			
H. Partition/Door			
I. Fire Prot. Class			
J. A/C (SF/Ton)			
K. Elect. Costs ($/SF)*			
L. Typ. Power (Watts/SF)			
M. Other			

	Lo	Ave.	High
A. Occupancy Type			
B. Efficiency Ratio			
C. Area (SF)*			
D. Costs ($/SF)*			
E. A/E Fees (% of D)			
F. FF&E Costs ($/SF)			
G. Parking			
H. Partition/Door			
I. Fire Prot. Class			
J. A/C (SF/Ton)			
K. Elect. Costs ($/SF)*			
L. Typ. Power (Watts/SF)			
M. Other			

*Data courtesy of BNI Building News. See latest BNI for current data.

__ APPENDIX B: LOCATION DATA

__ A. *Latitude* is given in degrees and minutes. (7)

__ B. *Elevation* is in feet above sea level. See p. 100. (7)

__ C. *Frost line* is inches below top of ground to frost line. (4)

__ D. *Ground temperature* is the constant year-around temp. (deg. F) at about 20 to 30 ft below. See p. 101. (4)

__ E. *Seismic* is UBC earthquake zones. See p. 86. (24)

__ F. *Termite* lists zones of degree of infestation (with 1 being worst). (4)

__ G. *Soils* are the predominant soils for the location. See p. 135. No data available at this publication.

__ H. *Plant zone* is for plant hardiness. See p. 152. (4)

__ I. *Rain, average* in inches per year. See p. 100. (35a)

__ J. *Rain, intensity* is hourly intensity in inches/hour for 5-minute periods to be expected once in 10 years. Some storms have twice as much in some zones. See p. 132 and 364. (4)

__ K. *Percent sun* is yearly average of clear days. See p. 100. (35a)

__ L. *Heating degree days* (*HDD*), base 65 deg. F. See p. 99. (35a)

__ M. *Cooling degree days* (*HDD*), base 65 deg. F. See p. 99. (35a)

__ N. *Percent humidity* (*% RH*) *AM* is yearly average in mornings. See p. 100. (35a)

__ O. *Percent humidity* (*% RH*) *PM* is yearly average in afternoon/evenings. See p. 100. (35a)

__ P. *Winter temperature* is design winter dry-bulb temperature (99%) as recommended by *ASHRAE*. See p. 99. (7)

___ Q. *Summer temperature* is design summer dry-bulb temperature (1%) as recommended by *ASHRAE*. See p. 99.   (7)

___ R. *Wind, average* is yearly average. See p. 100.   (35a)

___ S. *Wind, intensity* is design wind speed per UBC. See p. 85.   (24)

___ T. *Snow* is the ground snow load in LB/SF per UBC. See p. 83.   (24)

___ U. *Insulation* is the recommended zone for min. R value. See p. 236.   (7)

___ V. *Costs* are the city cost indexes to adjust cost given in this book. See p. 25.   (11)*

___ *Other:* (1) Possible radon-producing area. See p. 143.   (45)

---

*Data courtesy of BNI Building News. See latest BNI for current data.

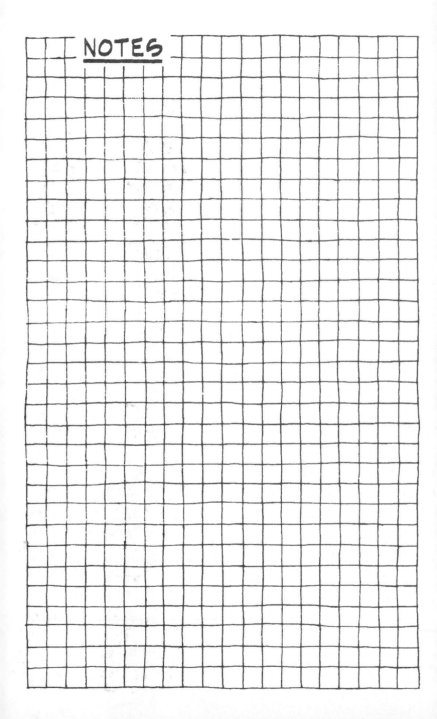

NOTES

LOCATION

Line No.	LOCATION	A LAT.	B ELEV.	C FROST LINE	D GD. TEMP.	E SEISMIC	F TERMITE	G SOILS	H PLANT ZONE	I RAIN AVE.	J RAIN INT.	K % SUN
1	AK ANCHORAGE	61-1	90			4	0		9	15		34
2												
3	AL BIRMINGHAM	33-3	610	3	64	1	1		8	52	7.2	58
4	HUNTSVILLE	34-4	619	3	62	1	1		7	55	6.3	55
5	MOBILE	30-4	211	0	70	0	1		9	65	7.8	60
6	MONTGOMERY	32-2	195	2	67	0	1		8	49	7.5	59
7												
8	AR FT. SMITH	35-2	449	7	64	1	2		7	40	7.4	60
9	LITTLE ROCK	34-4	257	4.5	64	1	2		7	49	7.2	60
10												
11	AZ PHOENIX	33-3	1117	0	72	1	2		8	7	4	81
12	TUCSON	32-1	2584	0	72	1	2		8	11	4	78
13												
14	CA BAKERSFIELD	35-2	495	0	64	4	2		9	6	3.6	75
15	FRESNO	36-5	326	0	64	3	2		9	11	3.6	73
16	LOS ANGELES	34-0	99	0	68	4	2		10	12	3.6	72
17	RIVERSIDE	33-5	1511	0	72	4	2		9		3.6	
18	SACRAMENTO	38-3	17	0	64	3	2		9	17	3.6	73
19	SANTA BARB.			0	64	4	2		10	16	3.6	
20	SAN DIEGO	32-4	19	0	72	4	2		10	9	3.6	72
21	SAN FRANCISCO	37-4	8	0	64	4	2		9	20	3.6	72
22	STOCKTON	37-5	28	0	64	3	2		9	14	3.6	
23												
24	CO COLO. SPRINGS	38-5	6173	10	54	1	3		5	15	4.8	68
25	DENVER	39-5	5283	10	54	1	3		5	15	4.8	67
26												
27	CT BRIDGEPORT	41-1	7	18	52	2A	2		6	42	6.3	56
28	HARTFORD	41-5	15	18	52	2A	2		6	44	6.3	52
29	NEW HAVEN	41-2	6	18	52	2A	2		6		6.3	
30												
31	DE WILMINGTON	39-4	78	6	56	1	2		7	41	6.6	
32												

DATA

L HDD	M CDD	N % RH AM	O % RH PM	P WINT TEMP	Q SUM TEMP	R WIND AVE.	S WIND INT.	T SNOW	U INSUL.	V COST*	OTHER	Line No.
10816	0	73	63	-23	71	7	90		6	130		1
												2
2943	1891	84	57	17	96	7	70	5	3	79		3
3279	1708	85	58	11	95	8	70	10	3	77	(1)	4
1695	2643	86	57	25	95	9	100	0	2	81		5
2277	2274	87	56	22	96	7	80	5	3	75		6
												7
3477	1969	85	56	12	101	8	70		3	74	(1)	8
3152	2045	84	57	15	99	8	70	5	3	78		9
												10
1442	3746	51	23	31	109	6	75	0	3	89	(1)	11
1734	2840	53	25	28	104	8	75	0	3	89		12
												13
2128	2347	65	38	30	104	6	70	0	3	97	(1)	14
2647	1769	78	40	28	102	6	70	0	3	98		15
1595	728	79	64	41	83	8	70	0	1	107	(1)	16
				29	100		70	0	2	97	(1)	17
2772	1198	83	45	30	101	8	70	0	4	100	(1)	18
2487	269	80	59			6	70	0	1	107		19
1284	842	76	62	42	83	7	70	0	1	102		20
3161	115	84	61	35	82	11	70	0	1	112		21
2674	1448	78	44	28	100	8	70	0	4	108	(1)	22
												23
6346	501	63	40	-3	91	10	75		5	92	(1)	24
6014	680	68	40	-5	93	9	75		5	95	(1)	25
												26
5501	746	76	60	6	84	12	85	25	4	103	(1)	27
6174	666			3	91	9	85	25	4	101	(1)	28
				3	88					102	(1)	29
												30
4986	1015	78	55	10	92	9	75	15	4	91		31
												32

*Data courtesy of BNI Building News. See latest BNI for current data.

LOCATION

Line No.	LOCATION	A LAT.	B ELEV.	C FROST LINE	D GD. TEMP.	E SEISMIC	F TERMITE	G SOILS	H PLANT ZONE	I RAIN AVE.	J RAIN INT.	K % SUN
1	DC WASHINGTON	38-5	14	8	58	1	2		7	40	6.6	54
2												
3	FL JACKSONVILLE	30-3	24	0	73	0	1		9	53	7.8+	61
4	MIAMI	25-5	7	0	76	0	1		10	58	7.8+	69
5	ORLANDO	28-3	106	0	74	0	1		9	48	7.8+	65
6	TAMPA	28-0	19	0	76	0	1		10	47	7.8+	67
7												
8	GA ATLANTA	33-4	1005	4	64	2A	1		7	49	7	59
9	COLUMBUS	33-2	242	3	66	1	1		8	51	7.5	59
10	SAVANNAH	32-1	52	0	68	2A	1		9	50	7.5	59
11												
12	HI HONOLULU	21-2	7							23		74
13												
14	IA DES MOINES	41-3	948	30	53	0	2		5	31	7	55
15	DAVENPORT			30	55	0	2		5		6.6	
16	SIOUX CITY	42-2	1095	35	52	1	3		4	25	7	57
17												
18	ID BOISE	43-3	2842	6	55	2B	3		5	12	3	58
19	POCATELLO	43-0	4444	20	53	2B	3		5	11	3.8	56
20												
21	IL CHICAGO	41-5	610	35	54	0	2		4	33	6.3	52
22	PEORIA	40-4	652	25	54	1	2		5		6.3	
23	ROCKFORD	42-1	724	35	54	0	2		5	37	6.3	53
24	SPRINGFIELD	39-5	587	18	56	1	2		5	34	6.3	54
25												
26	IN EVANSVILLE	38-0	381	7	58	1	2		6	42	6.5	55
27	FT. WAYNE	41-0	791	23	55	1	2		5	34	6.2	50
28	INDIANAPOLIS	39-4	793	20	56	1	2		6	39	6.3	51
29	SOUTH BEND	41-4	773	30	54	1	2		5	38	6.3	47
30	TERRE HAUTE	39-3	601	15	56	2A	2		6		6.3	
31												
32												

DATA

L HDD	M CDD	N %RH AM	O %RH PM	P WINT TEMP	Q SUM TEMP	R WIND AVE	S WIND INT	T SNOW	U INSUL	V COST*	OTHER	Line No.
5004	970	83	55	14	93	7	75	20	4	95		1
												2
1402	2520	88	56	29	96	8	95	0	2	80		3
199	4095	84	61	44	91	9	110	0	2	86		4
656	3401	89	55	35	94	9	95	0	2	80		5
739	3324	88	58	36	92	8	100	0	2	82		6
												7
3021	1670	82	56	17	94	9	75	5	3	83	(1)	8
2356	2152	87	54	21	95	7	70	5	3	75	(1)	9
1921	2290	86	53	24	96	8	100	0	2	79		10
												11
0	4389	72	56	62	87	11				125		12
												13
6554	1019	80	60	-10	94	11	80	25	5	89		14
							75	25	5	87		15
6947	940	82	60	-11	95	11	85	35	5	85		16
												17
5802	742	69	43	3	96	9	70		4	92		18
7123	445	72	44	-8	94	10	70		4	88	(1)	19
												20
6455	740	80	60	-5	94	10	75	25	5	103		21
6226	948			-8	91	10	75	20	5	92		22
6952	714	83	61	-9	91	10	75	25	5	92		23
5654	1165	83	61	-3	94	11	75	20	4	89		24
												25
4729	1378	82	59	4	95	11	70	15	4	88	(1)	26
6320	786	82	62	-4	92	10	75		5	88	(1)	27
5650	988	84	62	-2	92	10	75	20	4	95		28
6377	710	82	62	-3	91	10	75	20	4			29
				-2	95		70	20	4	86	(1)	30
												31
												32

*Data courtesy of BNI Building News. See latest BNI for current data.

LOCATION

Line No.	LOCATION	A LAT.	B ELEV.	C FROST LINE	D GD. TEMP.	E SEISMIC	F TERMITE	G SOILS	H PLANT ZONE	I RAIN AVE.	J RAIN INT.	K % SUN
1	KS TOPEKA	39-0	877	15	58	2A	2		6	33	7.3	58
2	WICHITA	37-4	1321	12	60	1	2		6	29	7.3	62
3												
4	KY LEXINGTON	38-0	979	7	59	1	2		6	46	6.4	52
5	LOUISVILLE	38-1	474	6	58	1	2		6	44	6.4	53
6												
7	LA BATON ROUGE	30-3	64	0	70	0	1		9	56	7.8	60
8	LAKE CHARLES	30-1	14	0	72	0	1		9	53	7.8+	58
9	NEW ORLEANS	30-0	3	0	72	0	1		9	60	7.8+	60
10	SHREVEPORT	32-3	252	18	68	1	1		8	44	7.6	59
11												
12	MA BOSTON	42.2	15	30+	52	2A	2		6	44	5.7	55
13	LOWELL	42.3	90	35	48	2A	1		5		5.7	
14	NEW BEDFORD	41-4	70	18	54	2A	2		6		6.2	
15	SPRINGFIELD	42-1	247	25	52	2A	1		5		6.0	
16	WORCESTER	42-2	986	30	52	2A	2		5	48	5.7	54
17												
18	MD BALTIMORE	38-8	14	8	58	1	2		7	42	6.6	59
19												
20	ME LEWISTON	44-0	182	50	50	2A	3		5		5.2	
21	PORTLAND	43-4	61	48	50	2A	3		6	44	5.4	55
22												
23	MI DETROIT	42-2	633	30	50	1	3		5	31	5.8	50
24	FLINT	40-0	760	30	49	1	3		5	29	6.0	47
25	GRAND RAPIDS	42-5	681	20	50	0	3		5	34	6.0	44
26	KALAMAZOO	42-1	930	20	52	1	3		5		6.2	
27	LANSING	42-5	852	25	50	1	3		5	30	6.0	48
28												
29	MN DULUTH	46-5	1426	50	48	0	3		3	30	6.2	49
30	MINNEAPOLIS	44.5	822	50	46	0	3		4	26	6.4	54
31	ROCHESTER	44.0	1297	38	49	0	3		4	28	6.4	50
32												

DATA

L HDD	M CDD	N % RH AM	O % RH PM	P WINT TEMP	Q SUM TEMP	R WIND AVE.	S WIND INT.	T SNOW	U INSUL.	V COST*	OTHER	Line No.
5319	1380	83	59	0	99	10	80	20	4	83		1
4787	1684	80	55	3	101	12	80	15	4	81		2
												3
4814	1170	82	60	3	93	9	70	15	4	85	(1)	4
4525	1342	81	58	5	95	8	70	15	4	89	(1)	5
												6
1673	2605	88	59	25	95	8	90	0	2	84		7
1579	2682	91	63	27	95	9	100	0	2	82		8
1490	2686	88	63	29	93	8	100	0	2	86		9
2269	2444	88	58	20	99	8	70	0	3	78		10
												11
5593	699	72	58	6	91	13	85	30	5	101	(1)	12
				-4	91		80	35	5	94	(1)	13
				5	85		85	20	5	91	(1)	14
				-5	90		80	30	5	94	(1)	15
6950	359	74	57	0	89	10	80	30	5	96	(1)	16
												17
4706	1138	77	54	14	93	9	75	20	4	90		18
												19
				-7	88		80	70	6	87	(1)	20
7501	254	79	59	-6	87	9	85	60	5	89	(1)	21
												22
6563	615	81	60	3	91	10	75	25	5	95	(1)	23
7068	456	81	62	-4	90	10	75	30	5	91	(1)	24
6927	570	83	63	1	91	10	75	30	5	88	(1)	25
				1	92		75	30	5	86	(1)	26
8298	530	85	64	-3	90	10	75	30	5	88	(1)	27
												28
9901	150	81	63	-21	85	11	75		6	93	(1)	29
8007	662	79	60	-16	92	11	75		6	98		30
8277	479	83	65	-17	90	13	80		6	93		31
												32

*Data courtesy of BNI Building News. See latest BNI for current data.

LOCATION

Line No.	LOCATION	A LAT.	B ELEV.	C FROST LINE	D GD. TEMP.	E SEISMIC	F TERMITE	G SOILS	H PLANT ZONE	I RAIN AVE.	J RAIN INT.	K % SUN
1	MO KANSAS CITY	39-1	742	15	58	2A	2		6	35	7.4	60
2	ST. JOSEPH	39-5	809	20	55	2A	2		5		7.4	
3	ST. LOUIS	38-5	535	12	58	2A	2		6	34	6.6	55
4	SPRINGFIELD	37-1		8	59	1	2		6	39	7.4	58
5												
6	MS BILOXI	30-2	25	0	70	0	1		9		7.8	
7	JACKSON	32-2	330	1	67	1	1		8	53	7.5	59
8												
9	MT BILLINGS	45-5	3567	25	50	1	3		5	15	4.2	55
10	GREAT FALLS	47-3	3664	60	50	2B	3		5	15	3.6	51
11												
12	NC CHARLOTTE	35-0	735	5	62	2A	2		7	43	7.4	59
13	RALEIGH	35-5	433	3	62	2A	2		7	42	7.4	59
14	WINSTON-SALEM	36-1	967	4	62	2A	2		7	42	7.4	59
15												
16	ND FARGO	46-5	900	55	46	0	3		3	20	6.4	54
17												
18	NE LINCOLN	40-5	1150	28	54	1	2		5	27	7.2	59
19	OMAHA	41-2	978	30	53	1	2		5	30	7.2	60
20												
21	NH MANCHESTER	43-0	253	45	46	2A	3		5		5.6	
22												
23	NJ NEWARK	40-5	132	15	54	2A	2		6	44	6.3	64
24	TRENTON	40-1	144	12	55	2A	2		6		6.3	
25												
26	NM ALBUQUERQUE	35-0	5310	6	60	2B	2		5	8	4.6	76
27												
28	NV LAS VEGAS	36-1	2162	0	70	2B	2		8	5	3.8	80
29	RENO	39-3	4404	20	58	3	2		5	7	3.2	80
30												
31												
32												

DATA

L	M	N	O	P	Q	R	S	T	U	V		
HDD	CDD	% RH AM	% RH PM	WINT TEMP	SUM TEMP	WIND AVE.	WIND INT.	SNOW	INSUL.	COST*	OTHER	Line No.
5283	1333	81	59	2	99	11	75	20	4	86		1
				-3	96		75	25	4	84		2
4938	1468	83	59	2	97	10	70	20	4	90		3
4660	1374	82	58	3	96	11	70	15	4	84		4
												5
				28	31				2			6
2389	2320	91	58	21	97	7	80	5	3	81		7
												8
7212	553	66	44	-15	94	11	80		5	87		9
7766	391	67	45	-21	91	13			6	87		10
												11
3342	1546	82	54	18	95	7	70	10	3	79	(1)	12
3531	1394	85	54	16	94	8	75	15	3	77	(1)	13
3874	1303	83	55	16	94	8	75	15	3		(1)	14
												15
9343	476	81	62	-22	92	12	85	35	6	90		16
												17
6375	1124	82	58	-5	99	10	80	25	5	85		18
6194	1166	81	59	-8	94	11	80	25	5	87		19
												20
				-8	91		75		5	88		21
												22
4972	1091	73	53	11	92	9	80	20	4	102	(1)	23
				11	91		75	30	4	97	(1)	24
												25
4414	1254	60	29	12	96	9	70	10	4	86	(1)	26
												27
2532	3029	40	21	25	108	9	80	5	3	97		28
6030	357	70	31	5	95	7			3	100		29
												30
												31
												32

*Data courtesy of BNI Building News. See latest BNI for current data.

LOCATION

Line No.	LOCATION	A LAT.	B ELEV.	C FROST LINE	D GD. TEMP.	E SEISMIC	F TERMITE	G SOILS	H PLANT ZONE	I RAIN AVE.	J RAIN INT.	K % SUN
1	NY ALBANY	42-5	277	30+	46	2A	3		5	36	5.7	49
2	BINGHAMTON	42-1	1590	30+	51	1	2		5	37	5.8	42
3	BUFFALO	43-0	705	30+	51	1	3		6	38	5.7	43
4	NEW YORK	40-5	132	15	54	2A	2		6	44	6.3	64
5	ROCHESTER	43-1	543	30+	50	1	3		6	31	5.4	46
6	SYRACUSE	43-1	424	30+	50	1	3		6	39	5.4	44
7												
8	OH AKRON	40-1	1210	15	54	1	2		5	36	6.0	46
9	CINCINNATI	39-1	761	10	58	1	2		6		6.3	
10	CLEVELAND	41-2	777	23	54	1	2		5	35	6.0	45
11	COLUMBUS	40-0	812	10	56	1	2		5	37	6.2	48
12	DAYTON	39-5	997	10	54	1	2		5	35	6.2	49
13	TOLEDO	41-4	676	20	54	1	2		5	32	6.0	50
14	YOUNGSTOWN	41-2	1178	15	53	1	2		5	37	6.0	44
15												
16	OK LAWTON	34-3	1108	8	62	1	2		5/6		7.2	
17	OKLA. CITY	35-2	1280	8	64	2A	2		5/6	31	7.4	64
18	TULSA	36-1	650	8	62	1	2		5/6	39	7.5	63
19												
20	OR EUGENE	44-1	364	13	56	2B	3		7	46	3.4	43
21	PORTLAND	45-4	21	13	54	2B	3		8	37	3.4	39
22												
23	PA ALLENTOWN	40-4	376	15	53	2A	2		6	44	6.3	56
24	ERIE	42-1	732	25	51	1	2		6	39	5.7	44
25	HARRISBURG	40-1	335	18	52	1	2		6	39	6.3	54
26	PHILADELPHIA	39-5	7	12	54	2A	2		7	41	6.4	56
27	PITTSBURGH	40-3	1137	15	54	1	2		6	36	6.2	44
28	SCRANTON	41-2	940	25	51	2A	2		5		6.0	
29												
30	RI PROVIDENCE	41-4	55	18	54	2A	2		6	45	6.2	55
31												
32												

DATA

L	M	N	O	P	Q	R	S	T	U	V	OTHER	Line No.
HDD	CDD	% RH AM	% RH PM	WINT TEMP	SUM TEMP	WIND AVE.	WIND INT.	SNOW	INSUL.	COST*		
6927	494	80	57	-6	91	9	70	30	5	87		1
7344	330	82	63	-2	86	10			5	83		2
6798	476	80	63	2	88	12			5	90	(1)	3
4868	1089	72	56	11	92	9	80	20	4	115	(1)	4
6713	531	81	61	1	91	10	70	40	5	90		5
6768	506	81	61	-3	90	9	70	35	5	87		6
												7
6241	625	80	61	1	89	10	75	15	5		(1)	8
5069	1080			1	92			15	4	83		9
6178	625	79	62	1	91	11			5	91	(1)	10
5686	862	80	59	0	92	8	70	20	4	89		11
5689	947	80	60	-1	91	10	70	20	4			12
6570	622	84	60	-3	90	9		15	5	89	(1)	13
6560	485	82	62	-1	88	10	75	25	5	85	(1)	14
												15
				12	101		80	5	3	77		16
3735	1914	80	54	9	100	12	75	10	3	83		17
3731	2043	81	56	8	101	10	70	10	3	81	(1)	18
												19
4799	261	91	60	17	92	8	80		4	90		20
4691	332	86	60	17	89	8	85		1	95		21
												22
5815	751	80	56	4	92	9	70	30	5	91	(1)	23
6768	402	78	66	4	88	11			5		(1)	24
5335	1006	76	54	7	94	7	70	25	4	85	(1)	25
4947	1075	76	55	10	93	10	75	25	4	98	(1)	26
5950	645	79	57	1	89	9	70	30	4	89		27
				1	90		70		5	87		28
												29
5908	574	75	55	5	89	11	90	20	4	98	(1)	30
												31
												32

*Data courtesy of BNI Building News. See latest BNI for current data.

LOCATION

Line No.	LOCATION	A LAT.	B ELEV.	C FROST LINE	D GD. TEMP.	E SEISMIC	F TERMITE	G SOILS	H PLANT ZONE	I RAIN AVE.	J RAIN INT.	K % SUN
1	SC CHARLESTON	32-5	9	0	67	2A	1		9	52	7.6	58
2	COLUMBIA	34-0	217	3	65	2A	1		8	49	7.4	60
3												
4	SD RAPID CITY	44-0	3165	28	50	1	3		4	16	5.4	62
5	SIOUX FALLS	43-4	1420	38	50	0	3		4	24	6.8	57
6												
7	TN CHATTANOOGA	35-0	670	5	63	2A	2		7	53	6.8	58
8	KNOXVILLE	35-5	980	8	60	2A	2		7	47	6.6	56
9	MEMPHIS	35-0	263	3	63	3	2		7	52	6.8	59
10	NASHVILLE	36-1	577	5	60	1	2		7	48	6.5	57
11												
12	TX ABILENE	32-3	1759	4	68	0	2		7	23	7.2	67
13	AMARILLO	35-1	3607	6	61	1	2		6	19	6.0	72
14	AUSTIN	30-2	597	3	73	0	1		8	32	7.4	63
15	BEAUMONT	30-0	18	0	70	0	1		9		8	
16	CORPUS CHRISTI	27-5	43	0	76	0	1		9	30	8	61
17	DALLAS	32-5	481	4	69	0	1		8	29	7.5	70
18	EL PASO	31-5	3918	2	68	1	2		6	8	4.8	80
19	HOUSTON	29-4	50	0	76	0	1		9	45	8	56
20	LUBBOCK	33-4	3243	5	64	0	2		7	18	6	72
21	SAN ANTONIO	29-3	792	1	76	0	1		9	29	7.8	62
22	WACO	31-4	500	4	71	0	1		8	31	7.6	63
23	WICHITA FALLS	34-0	994	8	66	1	2		7	27	7.2	67
24												
25	UT OGDEN	41-1	4455	18	55	3	3		5		4.5	
26	SALT LAKE	40-5	4220	16	55	3	3		5	15	4.5	62
27												
28	VA NORFOLK	36-5	26	2	60	1	1		8	45	7.2	58
29	ROANOKE	37-2	1174	15	57	1	2		7	39	6.6	59
30	RICHMOND	37-3	162	4	57	1	2		7/8	44	7.0	56
31												
32												

DATA

L HDD	M CDD	N % RH AM	O % RH PM	P WINT TEMP	Q SUM TEMP	R WIND AVE.	S WIND INT.	T SNOW	U INSUL.	V COST*	OTHER	Line No.
2147	2093	86	56	25	94	9	110	0	2	79		1
2629	2033	87	51	20	97	7	75	10	3	81	(1)	2
												3
7301	667	71	50	-11	95	11	80	15	5	81	(1)	4
7885	749	81	60	-15	94	11	80	40	5	83		5
												6
3583	1578	86	56	13	96	6	70	5	3	77	(1)	7
3658	1449	86	59	13	94	7	70	10	3	79	(1)	8
3207	2067	81	57	13	98	9	70	10	3	81		9
3756	1661	84	57	9	97	8	70	10	3	83	(1)	10
												11
2621	2467	74	50	15	101	12	80	5	3			12
4231	1428	73	45	6	98	14	80	15	4			13
1760	2914	84	57	24	100	9	70	5	2	80		14
				27	95		95	0	2			15
970	3574	90	62	31	95	12	100	5	2			16
2407	2809	82	56	18	102	11	70		3	82	(1)	17
2664	2096	57	28	20	100	9	70	5	3			18
1549	2761	90	60	27	96	8	100	0	2	86		19
3516	1676	75	47	10	98	12	80	10	3	78		20
1606	2983	84	55	25	99	9	80	0	2	80		21
2126	2891	84	57	21	101	11	70	5	3			22
3011	2506	82	51	14	103	12	80	5	3			23
												24
				1	93		70		5	85	(1)	25
5802	981	67	43	3	97	9	70		5	87	(1)	26
												27
3446	1458	78	57	20	93	11	90	10	3	83		28
4315	1085	78	53	12	93	8	70	25	4	81		29
3960	1336	78	57	14	95	8	75	15	3	85	(1)	30
												31
												32

*Data courtesy of BNI Building News. See latest BNI for current data.

LOCATION

Line No.	LOCATION	A LAT.	B ELEV.	C FROST LINE	D GD. TEMP.	E SEISMIC	F TERMITE	G SOILS	H PLANT ZONE	I RAIN AVE.	J RAIN INT.	K % SUN
1	VT BURLINGTON	44·3	331	50	46	2A	3		4/5	34	5.0	44
2	RUTLAND	43·3	620	50	46	2A	3		4/5		5.4	
3												
4	WA SPOKANE	47·4	2357	25	50	2B	3		6	17	3.0	47
5	SEATTLE	47·3	386	5	52	3	3		8	39	3.2	38
6												
7	WI GREEN BAY	44·3	683	50	49	0	3		4/5	28	6.0	52
8	MADISON	43·1	858	50	50	0	3		4/5	31	6.3	51
9	MILWAUKEE	43·0	672	50	50	0	3		5	31	6.2	52
10												
11	WV CHARLESTON	38·2	939	15	60	1	2		6	42	6.3	48
12	HUNTINGTON	38·2	565	15	60	1	2		6	41	6.3	44
13												
14	WY CHEYENNE	41·1	6126	24	52	1	3		4/5	13	4.8	64
15												
16												
17												
18												
19												
20												
21												
22												
23												
24												
25												
26												
27												
28												
29												
30												
31												
32												

DATA

L HDD	M CDD	N % RH AM	O % RH PM	P WINT TEMP	Q SUM TEMP	R WIND AVE.	S WIND INT.	T SNOW	U INSUL.	V COST*	OTHER	Line No.
7953	379	77	59	-12	88	9	75		6	94	(1)	1
				-13	87		75		5	87	(1)	2
												3
6882	411	78	52	-6	93	9	75		5	99	(1)	4
5121	184	83	62	21	84	9	80		1	106	(1)	5
												6
8143	381	82	63	-13	88	10	90	40	6	92		7
7642	467	84	61	-11	91	10	80	40	5	90		8
7326	470	80	64	-8	90	12		40	5	97		9
												10
4697	1007	83	56	7	92	6	70		4	87	(1)	11
4676	1121	83	58	5	94	7	70		4	89	(1)	12
												13
7310	309	65	44	-9	89	13	80		5	91		14
												15
												16
												17
												18
												19
												20
												21
												22
												23
												24
												25
												26
												27
												28
												29
												30
												31
												32

*Data courtesy of BNI Building News. See latest BNI for current data.

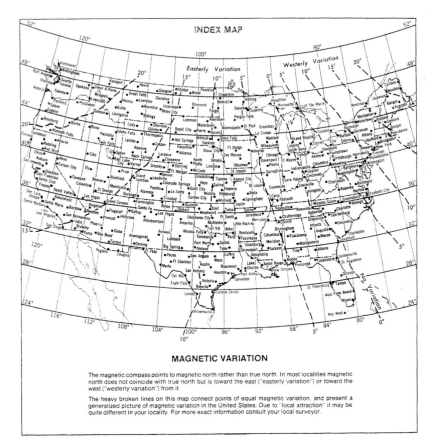

MAGNETIC VARIATION

The magnetic compass points to magnetic north rather than true north. In most localities magnetic north does not coincide with true north but is toward the east ("easterly variation") or toward the west ("westerly variation") from it

The heavy broken lines on this map connect points of equal magnetic variation, and present a generalized picture of magnetic variation in the United States. Due to "local attraction" it may be quite different in your locality. For more exact information consult your local surveyor.

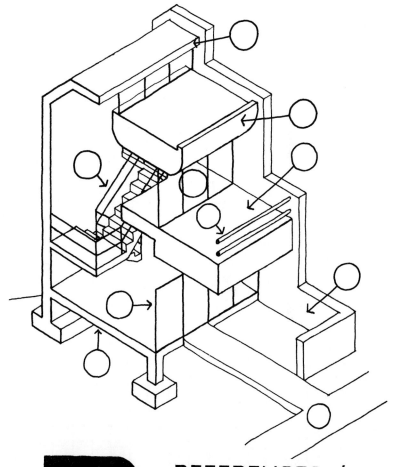

R

REFERENCES /
INDEX

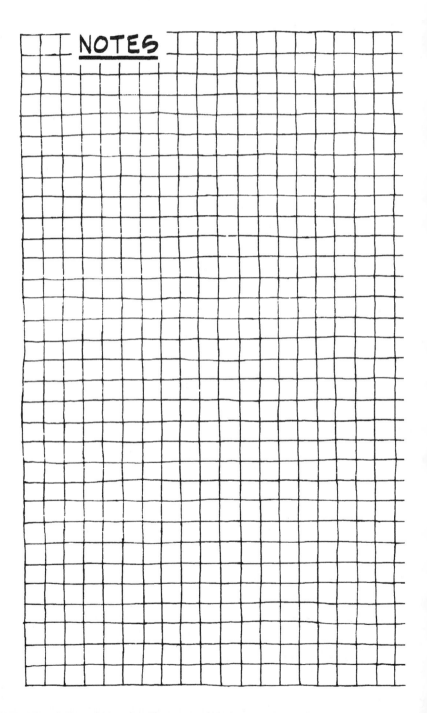

NOTES

___ REFERENCES

This book was put together from a myriad of sources including the help of consultants listed on p. 463. References shown at the front of a section indicate general background information. A reference shown at a specific item indicates a copy from the reference. The major book references are listed as follows, and many are recommended for architects' libraries:

— (1) Allen, Edward, and Iano, Joseph. 1989. *The Architect's Studio Companion, Technical Guidelines for Preliminary Design.* New York: John Wiley & Sons, Inc.

— (2) Ambrose, James, 1981, *Simplified Design of Building Foundations.* New York: John Wiley & Sons, Inc.

— (3) American Institute of Architects, 6th ed., 1970. *Architectural Graphic Standards.* New York: John Wiley & Sons, Inc.

— (4) American Institute of Architects, 8th ed., 1988. *Architectural Graphic Standards.* New York: John Wiley & Sons, Inc.

— (5) American Institute of Architects, 1988, *The Architect's Handbook of Professional Practice,* David Haviland, editor.

— (6) American Institute of Architects, 1981, *Energy in Architecture.*

— (7) Ballast, David Kent. 1988. *Architect's Handbook of Formulas, Tables, & Mathematical Calculations.* New Jersey: Prentice-Hall.

— (8) Ballast, David Kent. 1990. *Architect's Handbook of Construction Detailing.* New Jersey: Prentice-Hall.

— (9) Better Homes and Gardens. 1975, *Decorating Book.*

— (10) Bovill, Carl. 1991, *Architectural Design, Integration of Structural and Environmental Systems.* New York: Van Nostrand Reinhold Co.

— (11) Building News. 1993, *General Construction, 1993 Cost Book.* William D. Mahoney, editor-in-chief.

— (12) Ching, Francis. 1975. *Building Construction Illustrated.* New York: Van Nostrand Reinhold Co.

— (13) Ching, Francis. 1990. *Drawing—A Creative Process.* New York: Van Nostrand Reinhold Co.

— (14) Clayton, George T., 1973, *The SITE PLAN in Architectural Working Drawings.* Chicago: Stipes Publishing Co.

— (15) Construction Specifications Institute. 1988, *Master-format, Master List of Section Titles and Numbers.*

— (16) Craftman Book Co. 1993, *1993 National Construction Estimator.* Edited by Martin D. Kiley and William M. Moselle.

— (17) Craftman Book Co. 1993, *1993 Building Cost Manual.* Edited by Martin D. Kiley and Michael L. Kiley.

— (18) Dept. of the Army, 1969, *FM-34 Engineer Field Data.*

— (19) Elliott, H. M., 1979, *How Structures Work, A Structural Engineering Primer,* unpublished.

— (20) Federal Register, 1991. *Americans with Disabilities Act* (ADA).

— (21) Foote, Rosslynn F., 1978, *Running an Office for Fun and Profit, Business Techniques for Small Design Firms.* Pa.: Dowden, Hutchinson & Ross, Inc.

— (22) Guidelines Publications, 1990. *Design Services Appraiser.*

— (23) Guidelines Publications, 1975. *Architectural Rules of Thumb.*

— (24) International Conference of Building Officials. 1991. *Uniform Building Code.* Tables 33A, 5A. through D, 17A, 23A, 32A, and 38A reproduced from the 1991 edition of the *Uniform Building Code*™, copyright © 1991, with permission of the publisher, the International Conference of Building Officials.

— (25) International Association of Plumbing and Mechanical Officials. 1991. *Uniform Plumbing Code.* App. C is reprinted from the *Uniform Plumbing Code* with permission of the International Association of Plumbing and Mechanical Officials copyright © 1991.

— (26) International Conference of Building Officials. 1991. *Dwelling Construction Under the Uniform Building Code.*

— (27) Libbey-Owens-Ford Co., 1974, *Sun Angle Calculator.*

— (28) Lockard, William K., 1968, *Drawing as a Means to Architecture.* New York: Van Nostrand Reinhold.

— (29) Lockard, William K., 1982, *Design Drawing.* New York: Van Nostrand Reinhold.

— (30) Lynch, Kevin, 1962. *Site Planning.* Mass.: The MIT Press.

— (31) McGraw-Hill Book Co. 1993. *Sweet's Catalog File.*

— (32) McGraw-Hill Book Co. 1966. *Time Saver Standards.* John H. Callender, editor in chief.

— (33) Means, R. S. Co. Inc., 1993. *Means Building Construction Cost Data.*

— (34) Means, R. S. Co. Inc., 1993. *Means Assemblies Cost Data.*

— (35) Munsell, A. H. 1946. *A Color Notation.* Munsell Color Co., Inc.

— (35a) National Oceanic and Atmospheric Administration, 1992, *Comparative Climatic Data for the U.S.*

— (36) National Roofing Contractors Association, 1983. *Handbook of Accepted Roofing Knowledge.*

— (37) National Roofing Contractors Association, 1981. *The NRCA Roofing & Waterproofing Manual.*

— (38) Parker, Harry, and MacGuire, John, 1967, *Simplified Engineering for Architects and Engineers.* New York: John Wiley & Sons.

— (39) Parker, Harry, and MacGuire, John, 1954, *Simplified Site Engineering for Architects and Engineers.* New York: John Wiley & Sons.

— (40) Peña, William, with Parshall and Kelley, 1977. *Problem Seeking.* Washington D.C.: A.I.A. Press.

— (41) Schiler, Marc, 1992, *Simplified Design of Building Lighting.* New York: John Wiley & Sons.

— (42) Stasiowski, Frank A., 1991, *Staying Small Successfully,* New York: John Wiley & Sons, Inc.

— (43) U.S. Navy, 1972, *Basic Construction Techniques for Houses and Small Buildings.* New York: Dover Publications, Inc.

— (44) Watson, Donald, and Labs, Kenneth, 1983, *Climatic Design.* New York: McGraw-Hill Book Co.

— (45) Wing, Charlie. 1990. *The Visual Handbook of Building and Remodeling.* Pa.: Rodale Press.

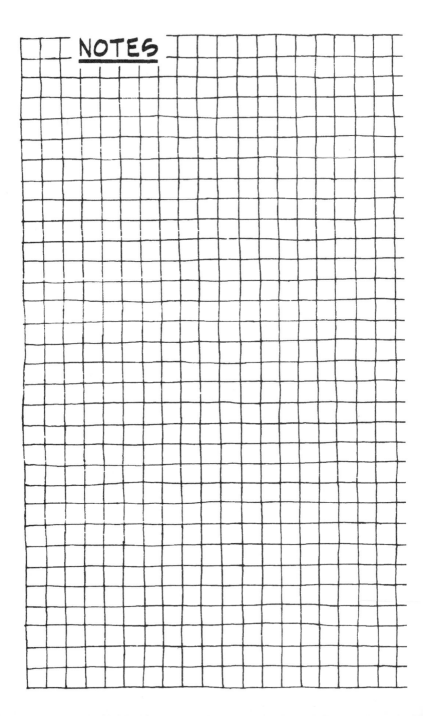

NOTES

Acknowledgments

Thanks to the following people for their professional expertise in helping with this book:

Special thanks to: Ray Beltran, Ed Denham, and Bill Mahoney.

Also, thanks to: Roger Alven, Steve Andros, Bob Ball, Marsha & Ken Caldwell, Doug Collier, Lane Garrett, Rick Goolsby, Peggy Gustave, Zamir Hasan, Glenn Heyes, Doug Hood, Norm Littler, Bill Lundsford, Randy Pace, Bert Rowe, Renee Tinsley, and Craig Walling.

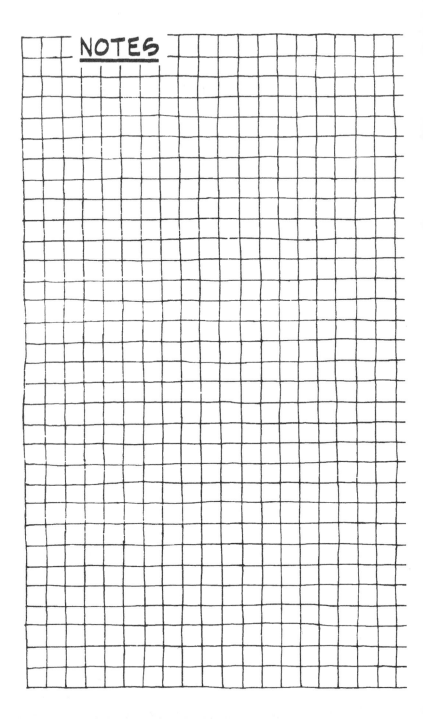

NOTES

Index

A

Abrasive, 319
AC, 127, 146, 423
Accessibility (ADA)
  area of rescue, 63
  controls, 417
  doors, 255
  elevators, 349
  general, 77
  hardware, 270
  lighting, 407
  parking, 121
  ramps, 65
  route, 78
  seating, 321
  signs, 304
  telephones, 418
  toilets, 358–360
Accounting, 4
Acoustical tile, 284
Acoustics, 109
Active, 105
ADA (*see* Accessibility)
Adobe, 173
Aggregate, 157
AIA, 6
Air entrainment, 157
Air film, 236
Aisle, 68

Algebra, 35
Alloy, 189
Aluminum, 189, 259
Amps, 413
Angle, 35
Arch, 95, 184
Architectural concrete, 161
Architectural services/fees, 3
Area, 31, 423
Art, 319
Ashlar, 180, 186
Asphalt (*see* AC)
Assemblies, 327
Attic, 231
Attic ventilation, 231

B

Backfill, 131
Bar joist (*see* Open-web joist)
Baseboard heating, 378, 382
Base coat (*see* Paint)
Basement, 59, 162
Base ply (*see* Roofing)
Base sheet (*see* Roofing)
Bath accessories, 308
Bathrooms, 357, 358
Batt, 237
Battery (*see* Photovoltaic)

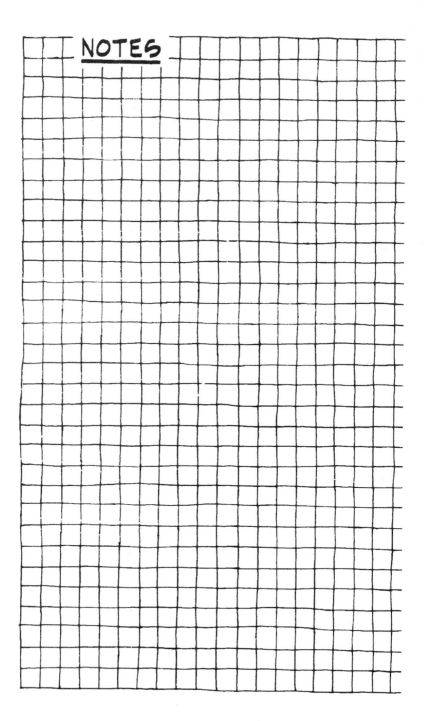

NOTES

ABOUT THE AUTHOR

Pat Guthrie, AIA, is a registered architect in seven states, and founder and principal of John Pat Guthrie Architects, Inc., based in Phoenix, Arizona. He previously worked as a project architect with Peter A. Lendrum & Associates in Phoenix and with Frankfurt Short Emery and McKinley in New York City. He also served as a design engineer with the U.S. Army Corps of Engineers.

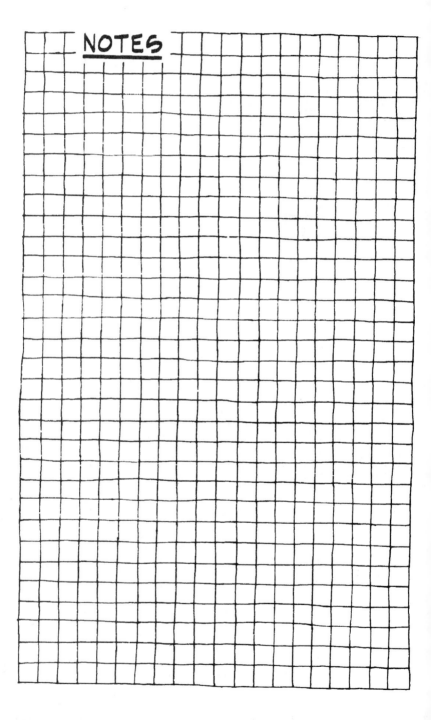

NOTES

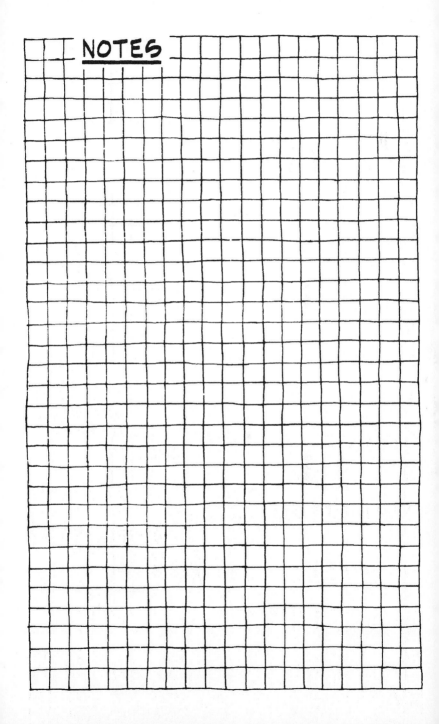

NOTES

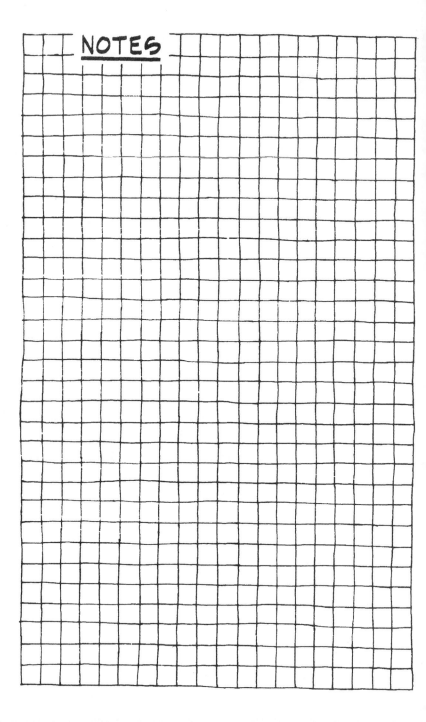

NOTES